D1260889

Praise for *Tonight We Die As Men*

"A product of original research and an important contribution to the literature… An amazingly detailed glimpse into the tragic experiences of this heroic parachute battalion."
Mark Bando, author of *101st Airborne: The Screaming Eagles at Normandy*

"It will be hard to find a better book about a single airborne battalion in World War II… The two British authors take the reader back to Toccoa, Georgia, and the initial training received (some would say endure) by the men of the 506th PIR, commanded by Col. Robert F. Sink, then on to airborne training at Fort Benning and Camp Mackall. They also flesh out the personalities mentioned in the book so that by the time the regiment is in England and preparing for its baptism of fire in Normandy, the reader has developed a fondness for each trooper."
Mason Webb, *World War II History*

"Ian Gardner and Roger Day have set out to tell the story of the 3rd Battalion of the famed 101st Airborne Division 506th Parachute Infantry Regiment. The objective of the battalion was to capture and secure the two wooden bridges built by the Germans over the Douve River east of Carentan, as access to what became known as Utah Beach. Despite the successful achievement of this important objective by the 3rd Battalion, accomplished with heavy losses, the authors found that little had been written about the battalion. In fact, they call the 3rd a 'forgotten battalion,' as opposed to the 2nd Battalion of 'Band of Brothers' fame."
James C. Roberts, *Washington Times*

"The most comprehensive, factual World War II history I have ever read. The reader is given a vivid account of the day to day life of the combat soldier in Europe. I appreciate the fact that I have met some of these men personally and now I am more aware of what they went through to defend our freedom."
Lamar Davis, Stephens County Historical Society, Toccoa, GA

Praise for *Deliver Us From Darkness*

"A powerful survey indeed."
The Midwest Book Review

"The experiences of the ordinary soldier and civilian are graphically explained and this book is highly recommended, not just for war historians but particularly as a valuable reminder of the sacrifices made almost seventy years ago, so that we can enjoy our current freedoms."
The Historical Association

"That's the beauty of books like this, not just to tell the larger story but to uncover small acts of heroism … for future generations to read."
The Journal

NO VICTORY IN VALHALLA

NO VICTORY IN VALHALLA

The Untold Story of Third Battalion 506 Parachute Infantry Regiment from Bastogne to Berchtesgaden

IAN GARDNER

FOREWORD BY ED SHAMES

First published in Great Britain in 2014 by Osprey Publishing,
PO Box 883, Oxford, OX1 9PL, UK
PO Box 3985, New York, NY 10185-3985, USA
E-mail: info@ospreypublishing.com

Osprey Publishing is part of the Osprey Group

A CIP catalogue record for this book is available from the British Library

ISBN: 978 1 4728 0133 3
e-book ISBN: 978 1 4728 0922 3
PDF ISBN: 978 1 4728 0923 0

Index by Sharon Redmoyne
Maps by Ian Gardner
Typeset in Bembo and Van Dijck
Originated by PDQ Media, Bungay, UK
Printed in China through Asia Pacific Offset Limited

14 15 16 17 18 10 9 8 7 6 5 4 3 2 1

Front cover: Courtesy of NARA

Osprey Publishing is supporting the Woodland Trust, the UK's leading woodland conservation charity, by funding the dedication of trees.

www.ospreypublishing.com

Contents

Foreword

If you wanted to read a novel about World War II this is not your book. However, if you wish to be informed about the true history of the Battle of the Bulge, you hold in your hands just that. The author who gave us one of the greatest works about the 3rd Battalion, 506th Parachute Infantry Regiment (506 PIR) in Normandy, entitled *Tonight We Die as Men*, and also the sequel *Deliver Us From Darkness* – the day by day account of how millions of Dutch citizens were freed from the yoke of German slavery – has given us a third volume. Here Ian Gardner provides us with an insight into exactly how it was to be minimally equipped for the extreme cold when the 101st Airborne Division was deployed around Bastogne. During that bitter winter of 1944/45, shivering for warmth, our mission was simple – kill or capture the enemy.

As one who served from the beginning in just about every firefight with 3rd Bn (I Co, Bn Operations Sergeant, and HQ Co First Sergeant) to the very end with 2nd Bn, I still find it incredible that Ian, with pure undiluted facts, has been able to guide the reader through practically each and every muddy, miserable freezing step of the way! If you are a history "buff," then I'm sure you will agree that this is a great and informative book about what those of us who survived believe to be the most important battle of World War II. It has been said "had we not prevailed at Bastogne" then the Allies would still be fighting for victory in Europe.

Edward D. Shames
506th Parachute Infantry Regiment, August 1942–September 1945
First Battlefield Commission – 101st Airborne Division Normandy

Preface

To accurately chronicle the actions of any war or battle while holding the reader's interest is a difficult task. Many written historical accounts are typically fact-filled, with strategies and maneuvers that may be accurate but are hopelessly boring to the casual reader. To bring the reader into the story, one must look at the event from the perspective of those who were there. In this book, Ian Gardner has captured the human story and gives the reader the necessary background information as well as the personal interactions that make this account of the 3rd Battalion, 506th Parachute Infantry Regiment a very real and personal recount of a story not yet fully told.

This book takes readers into the minds of the men who served in the European Theater of Operations in the darkest and coldest days during the Battle of the Bulge in Bastogne through to the sometimes desperate and sometimes euphoric days in Germany as the war in Europe waned and the men counted their points to go home. Ian, through the accounts of hundreds of eyewitnesses to history, brings the days at the end of 1944 and beginning of 1945 into sharp focus. Detailed descriptions of the men and women who were in the middle of "The Rendezvous with Destiny" give the reader a sense of how coping with war and its tragedies is something unique to each person who has had to stand against the ravages of battle and even nature.

No Victory in Valhalla also tells the story of the other units that served with distinction but did not garner the attention of historians or media for accolades of their bitter fight against considerably larger German forces. Notable strategic actions, individual courage, bravery, and heavy losses make up the history of 3 Bn, which prevailed against overwhelming enemy artillery and tanks. It is this story of courage and determination, told here with sensitivity and insight, that only the soldier who was actually there can accurately recount.

It is my humble pleasure to have been able to read the story of these brave and largely unrecognized men. For those who did not return and gave the supreme sacrifice, this is a fitting testament to their memory. Ian Gardner has once again done a superb job of honoring and recognizing the service of so many ordinary Americans who served in an extraordinary way to battle tyranny and provide freedom for millions and asked nothing in return.

George E. Koskimaki
101st Airborne Division HQ – World War II
Author and historian

Acknowledgments

No Victory in Valhalla owes a huge debt of gratitude to Jimmy Martin and Ed Shames, who convinced me that this final chapter in their story could and should be recorded for posterity. I could never have imagined when co-writing *Tonight We Die As Men* with Roger Day that it would define my life for the next 13 years and bring me into contact with so many incredible people such as Reg Jans. Without Reg's help, *No Victory* would be a shadow of what it is now. Over the last decade Reg has become one of the foremost battlefield guides operating in the Ardennes and guest expert for many premier World War II tour companies. Reg has probably forgotten more than I will ever know about Bastogne and the Battle of the Bulge and I will be forever grateful for his loyalty, assistance, and continued enthusiasm. Likewise Foy and Recogne locals Joël Robert and Jean-François d'Hoffschmidt have both been incredibly helpful to this project.

The early years were costly, but with much support and understanding from my wife Karen and my folks we made it through. Looking back it all seems like a distant dream but only those who really know me will understand how close I came to losing everything. Partly because of this Ed Shames and Jim Martin have become passionate supporters and their television, radio, and numerous public appearances have helped enormously to raise awareness of my work not just in the USA but also many other places around the world. At this point I would also like to say a few words of thanks to 101st Airborne historian Mark Bando and his brilliant books such as *Vanguard of the Crusade* and *The 101st Airborne at Normandy*. Right from the start, Mark, despite a busy schedule, was always on hand to offer me help and advice.

The huge amount of time invested in *No Victory*, not only by Ed and Jim but also by Lou Vecchi, Harley Dingman, and Manny Barrios, has made this book come to life. With each passing year my list of contributors dwindles a little more. When I started back in 2001 there were around 55 veterans on the "team." Many, like Ralph Bennett, Joe Beyrle, Ray Calandrella, Hank DiCarlo, Teddy Dziepak, Johnny Gibson, Ben Hiner, David Morgan, Bob Rommel, George Rosie, Don Ross, Harold Stedman, and Bob Webb, are speaking from the grave via tapes and notes compiled while they were still with us.

Other personal insights come from interviews provided over 30 years ago to George Koskimaki while he was researching his groundbreaking books on the 101st Airborne Division. George was the radio operator for MajGen Maxwell Taylor during World War II and his work has inspired several generations, myself included – and so the wheel of synergy turns full circle. Jimmy McCann's widow Pat also provided me with a wonderful cassette tape originally recorded for George by Alex Andros, which also featured personal recollections about Bastogne from Harry Begle, Dud Hefner, Clark Heggeness, Gene Johnson, Pete Madden, Frank Malik, Jim McCann, Bob Stroud, and Gordon Yates. Everyone except Andros has since passed away, but the information these H Company men left behind on that October afternoon in 1991 was a true gift from above.

As usual this section has been one of the hardest parts of the book to compile, as I am anxious not to forget any of my many contributors. If anyone's name has been overlooked I hope you will accept my sincere apologies. Individual thanks are extended by country to the following.

United States of America: Kathleen "Tachie" Anderson, Fred Bahlau (HQ Co), Mark Bando, Manny Barrios (I Co), Ralph Bennett (H Co), Joe Beyrle II, Sharon Bunker, Don Burgett (A Co), Ray Calandrella (Co HQ), Denis and Donna Cortese, Dan Cutting, Louis DeNegre, Mario "Hank" DiCarlo (H Co), Harley Dingman (I Co), Carole Dingman, Bob Dunning (81mm Mortar Ptn), Teddy Dziepak (I Co), John Gibson (Medical Detachment), Ben Hiner (Co HQ), Bob Izumi (G Co), Ken Johnson (H Co), John Klein, Gerry and Bobbie Lord, Piet "Pete" Luiten, James Martin (G Co),

Pat McCann, Earl McClung (E Co), Karen McGee, George McMillan (I Co), James Melhus (MG Ptn), Tim Moore, Neil Morgan, Joe Muccia, Ray Nagell (B Battery, 321st GFA Bn), Jennie O'Leary – Sun City Library Arizona, Carolyn Packert, Bonnie Pond, Jake Powers, Rich Riley, Doyle Rigden, Bobbie Rommel (MG Ptn), Ken Ross (502nd PIR), Bob Saxvik, David Schultz, Ed Shames (I Co, 3/506 Co HQ, 506 RHQ, 2/506 and E Co), Ray Skully (G Co), Harold Stedman (I Co), Tom Stedman, John Sushams, Ann Tanzy, Helen Thomas, Kathy Tozzi, Lou Vecchi (H Co), John Vecchi, Bob Webb Jr, Bill Wedeking (MG Ptn).

Belgium: Ivonne Dumont, Jean-François d'Hoffschmidt, Philippe d'Hoffschmidt, Reg Jans, Jean-Marie Koeune, Adjutant Eric "Rony" Lemoine, Maguy Marenne, André Meurisse, Robert Remacle, Joël Robert, Jules and Denise Robert, Philippe Wilkin.

Germany: Florian Beierl, Klaus Ibel.

United Kingdom: Brigitta Culf, Roger Day, Robert Dudley, and Alan Tomkins.

I would like to extend a special thank you to the following people: Doug Barber and Dave Bevis for their belief and invaluable assistance, Donald van den Bogert for the help with the photographs, Greg Gray for his help proof-reading the manuscript, Tim Moore for providing me with the G Co Morning Reports, Bob Smoldt for Robert Harwick's personal letters, Geoff Walden and his wonderful website "The Third Reich in Ruins," Marcus Cowper, Bruce Herke, Emily Holmes, Kate Moore, and the creative team at Osprey, Brian Gottlieb who on my behalf was given unlimited access to the The George E. Koskimaki Collection, the US Army Military History Institute, Carlisle Barracks (Pennsylvania), and Gerhard Roletscheck (President of the Society for the Modern History of Landsberg am Lech) whose help on Chapter 13 was crucial.

Lastly, my parents (Dennis and Joan) always encouraged me to follow my dreams and I would like to dedicate this book to the memory of my dad Dennis Edward Gardner who died on March 6, 2012, after a long battle with heart and kidney disease. Since I started work on *No Victory in Valhalla* the following people have also passed away: Ralph Bennett, Jack Brown, Bob Dunning, George Dwyer, Philippe d'Hoffschmidt, Ken Johnson, Earl McClung, and Ray Skully… RIP gentlemen, it's been one heck of a ride.

Introduction

When *Tonight We Die As Men* was first published in 2009, we remaining soldiers of the 506th Parachute Infantry Regiment became admirers of Ian Gardner's work. None of us could have imagined our experiences would become the subject of such detailed research, scholarly pursuit, and popular fascination.

In recent years and over the course of many conversations, I have come to know Ian well and right from the start could tell that his background as a British paratrooper gave him an additional insight into our experiences. The questions he asked demonstrated to me an in-depth knowledge of what we as a unit went through, which when researching and writing an objective account of a complex historical event is a significant advantage. Ian is associated with many premier World War II researchers, authors, and historians, such as my friends Mark Bando and Reg Jans. I am delighted Ian has written this account of the 3rd Battalion from the Battle of the Bulge to the end of the war because our story forms a natural trilogy.

After fighting in Normandy and Holland we were looking forward to some "down time" in the relative safety and comfort of Mourmelon, France, but on December 16, our hopes in this regard were abruptly ended. With little notice, and with only inadequate weapons, ammunition, proper clothing, and limited other crucial supplies, we were trucked into Belgium to take positions around the city of Bastogne, which straddled a crucial road network. Here we were to make a stand to deny the Germans clear passage to Antwerp. To this day it is difficult to express the misery we endured over the three weeks that followed – frequent enemy assaults (including armor and artillery), freezing temperatures, basic rations, and lack of water. Although nearly 70 years have passed since we lived like animals in foxholes and bunkers, Bastogne has become a permanent part of my consciousness. I am frequently asked, "What got you through?" To be blunt it was the rigorous and unforgiving selection process of our early training when only the fanatically tough and dedicated made the grade. This paid dividends for the 101st Airborne Division in Normandy and Holland but especially during the Battle of the Bulge. Not once during my time on the line at Bastogne did I ever hear any talk of defeat, much less surrender. We always knew we would prevail and accomplish our mission of stopping the German offensive in our area of operations. However, we must not forget that there were over 30 units involved in the battle for Bastogne, including the 10th Armored Division, whose Sherman Tank Destroyers made such a huge contribution to the final American victory.

After Bastogne the 506th PIR were mainly involved with defensive operations in Alsace Lorraine and Germany before heading to Bavaria. As things progressed, we "originals" became increasingly concerned with surviving the war. Many of the replacements began to taunt us about not being as tough as we thought we were. Few of them had seen real combat so the jibes were somewhat understandable. By early May 1945, we were aware of the possibility of moving into Hitler's rumored "Alpine Redoubt" and were convinced we would be facing a determined force. Much to our surprise and relief this was not the case and the next two months turned out to be the best time of "Our War." In addition to normal duties everyone did their best to uphold the age-old tradition of all conquering armies by scavenging everything and anything we could lay our hands on. Our short time at Berchtesgaden and in Austria at Zell am See after VE Day is still remembered fondly to this day.

Those like me who had been through every combat operation since Normandy were classified under a point system, and as a "high point man" with an ASR (Army Service Record) score of 85, I was sent home in September 1945.

Upon my return, I was hoping to go back to my old job as a toolmaker in Ohio and was surprised to learn that there were no vacancies. In 1942 I had left my reserved occupation against the wishes of my employers and volunteered for the 506th PIR. I was shocked that many of my colleagues who had elected not to join the services had earned a small fortune while working on lucrative government contracts. Consequently, I was unemployed much of the time during my first two years after coming home and began to wonder just what I had been fighting for. That being said, military service gave many guys like me a wider perspective on the world as a whole, as prior to the war we were all very provincial in our thinking. Friendships were made with people whom ordinarily I would never have met and many of those associations still remain to this day.

If the Allies had not prevailed the results to our world would have been catastrophic. I can truly speak for everyone by saying our generation really did save the world. It has been gratifying to live long enough to see the recent historical scholarship and interest in "Our War." We who remain hope that the lessons of World War II will not be forgotten.

Jim "Pee Wee" Martin – "Toccoa Original"
G Company / 506th PIR / 101st Airborne Division – World War II
November 2012

1

"Johnny, we hardly knew you"

Camp Châlons, Mourmelon-le-Grand – November 28–December 18, 1944

Mourmelon-le-Grand was a dreary, long-suffering French town some 20 miles from Reims, which through the ages had endured the embrace of soldiers from many nations. Caesar is said to have quartered two divisions of infantry and several squadrons of light horse at Mourmelon during the latter stages of his Gallic campaign. Despite its name, Mourmelon was really no more than one long street dotted with a few shops and cafés and most definitely not to be confused with Mourmelon-le-Petit, which, as its name suggests, is even smaller.

As battalion supply sergeant Ben Hiner from Morgantown, West Virginia, glanced out of his office window at Camp Châlons, he was shocked to see 1st Lt John Williams standing outside 3rd Battalion Headquarters (3rd Bn HQ). Six months earlier, Williams had almost ended Hiner's life after shooting him "accidentally" with a German pistol. Williams had just taken over as executive officer (XO) for Headquarters Company (HQ Co) and was deep in conversation as the 23-year-old staff sergeant rushed outside to confront him. "Don't you walk away," Hiner demanded as Williams, face drained white, turned to leave. "You nearly killed me back in St-Côme ... no letter of apology – you couldn't even be bothered to visit me in the hospital. What were you thinking?" Visibly shaken by the unexpected encounter, the lieutenant kept walking. As Ben followed Williams along the road he called out, "If Colonel Wolverton had been alive to see what you did to me he would've had something to say about it – are you listening to me, Sir?"

LtCol Robert Lee Wolverton had been horrifically slaughtered in Normandy moments after landing on June 6, 1944. The men from 3rd Bn were passionate about their leader as was Col Robert F. Sink, the commander of the 506th Parachute Infantry Regiment (506th PIR) – affectionately known in combat as "The Fox" and in garrison as "Uncle Bob." From the early training days in Georgia at Camp Toccoa, Col Sink had developed a respect and admiration for the "Point"-trained West Virginian ("Point" means a graduate of the prestigious West Point Military Academy). It was obvious that Wolverton's immediate successors following his death – Maj Oliver Horton and LtCol Lloyd Patch – were both highly capable, but to the "originals" they could never be in the same league.

A New Englander from Massachusetts, Lloyd Patch was a short but muscular leader who had been responsible for destroying a gun battery on D-Day for which he was awarded the Distinguished Service Cross. As a captain serving in 1st Bn, Patch was commanding HQ Co on June 6, when he assembled a group of six soldiers from various regiments and led them in a highly successful attack against a 105mm gun site near Ste-Marie-du-Mont. Reversed, the captured guns were then used by the Americans to neutralize enemy machine-gun positions, allowing Patch and his small team to capture the town. Despite Patch's track record, the veterans from 3rd Bn truly believed that Maj Robert Harwick was cut from the same cloth as Wolverton and, therefore, the only true candidate for command. Originally from H Co, Harwick had been 3rd Bn XO in Holland, and temporary commander after Maj Horton was killed at Opheusden, on October 5, 1944. When Lloyd Patch took over on November 21, Bob Harwick was re-assigned to 1st Bn, where he became LtCol James LaPrade's XO.

During the occupation the Germans had used the adequate facilities at Camp Châlons (which included three magnificent cinemas) as a tank depot and airfield. Everyone was horrified by the traditional

French-style latrines, each designed with two footprints set into concrete either side of a shallow drainage hole. Immediately plans were commissioned and 1/Sgt Fred Bahlau (HQ Co) was asked by Col Charlie Chase (regimental XO) to oversee the building of a new set of toilets and washrooms. Accommodation was basic but clean, with all junior ranks sleeping 32 men to a barrack block. The senior NCOs fared better and were quartered three men to a room, each equipped with its own stove and basic amenities.

By the end of November 1944, acting company commanders 1st Lt Joe Doughty (G Co), 1st Lt Jim "Skunk" Walker (H Co), and 1st Lt Fred "Andy" Anderson (I Co) finally received their captain's bars after several years' service and action in Normandy and Holland. Walker, a fiery redhead from Alabama, summoned platoon sergeant Ralph Bennett (3 Ptn) into his office to discuss a suitable punishment for being late returning to Ramsbury in the United Kingdom when the battalion was mobilized for Holland:

> It made me laugh that Walker always looked like someone had asked him a question to which he did not know the answer – and this day was no exception. The captain's antagonistic attitude improved during the interview, when I smugly reminded him about my exemplary conduct in Holland and that I'd won the Silver Star. I figured that there was no way that he could even think about charging me with being "absent without leave" (AWOL). It was a close run thing but in the end the SOB relented and dismissed me with nothing more than a warning followed by a few choice words.

Not all members of 3rd Bn lived up to the unit's meritorious war record. After spending most of the previous six months in the stockade, Pvt Howard "Sunny" Sundquist (H Co) was posted back to 1 Ptn. Capt Walker and platoon sergeant Frank Padisak unanimously blocked the move and Sundquist was "side swiped" to 1st Bn. Sgt Lou Vecchi (H Co 1 Ptn) from Martinez, California remembers, "Not long afterwards

Sundquist went AWOL and vanished without a trace. Months later he was arrested and I appeared as a witness at his court martial, where I am pleased to say the lizard was found guilty of desertion and given a substantial prison sentence."

Back-dated leave passes from Holland slowly began to filter through, and despite the fact that there had been several reports of a sniper taking potshots at Allied troops in Reims, the city was still popular, but ultimately everyone dreamed of Paris. After what the men had been through, the three- or seven-day passes could not come fast enough, and inevitably disappointment and frustration soon set in. Joe Doughty discovered that Camp Châlons was not going to be quite the relaxed three-month posting he had first imagined. Somewhat taller than average, Doughty was a quiet, fair man, who had a relaxed but firm attitude toward discipline and was well respected by the company. However, soldiers like Pvt Macrae Barnson from Los Angeles, California demanded a completely different approach. Although Barnson was an unstoppable combat asset (having been seriously wounded in Normandy and Holland) he was a total nightmare in camp. Earlier on November 22, Macrae had gone AWOL after returning from the 10th Replacement Depot. Finally, on December 10, Barnson's luck ran out when the Military Police brought him back to Mourmelon whereupon he was incarcerated in the regimental guard house to await trial.

Ironically the weather took a turn for the worse and heavy rain reduced the camp to a 6in-deep sea of mud. Gravel was requisitioned and bricks recovered from ruined buildings to construct company streets and sidewalks. In a letter home to his parents, Cpl Bob Webb from the Communications Platoon wrote the following:

> Things are back to normal and it's the same old training all over again. The camp is getting better all the time and the mail has been coming in pretty good and I have already received a couple of Christmas and birthday presents. However, the packages just don't make a Christmas, and the only gift that I want is for the war to be over. Our chaplain

called me the other day and wanted permission to give my name to Anthony Wincensiak's parents as "best friend" and first point of contact. Anthony was killed in Normandy and was my assistant before I got busted. He was a lovely, 18-year-old Polish kid who although new to the outfit was liked by everyone. I wrote his folks last night. I knew it would be hard but when I got into it – boy was it tough!

Five hundred and forty enlisted men and 38 officers under command of Maj Franklin Foster were flown into Mourmelon as replacements for the 506th PIR, who had suffered around 60 percent losses in Holland. During the flight, five aircraft, hampered by poor weather, were forced to return to the United Kingdom. The new soldiers had previously been processed through the Casual Detachment at Denford Farm Base Camp in Berkshire and temporarily attached to Service Co before being assigned. Twenty-year-old Pvt Bob Izumi, a Japanese-American, was one of 40 new men posted to G Co:

My parents had settled on the west coast in the late 1890s. Before the attack on Pearl Harbor my dad was a teacher specializing in Japanese language. Following the declaration of war with Japan, President Franklin D. Roosevelt issued Executive Order 9066, which permitted the military to circumvent the constitutional safeguards of American citizens in the name of national security. The order set in motion the evacuation and mass incarceration of any persons with Japanese ancestry living in the USA. Strangely those of Chinese or Korean origin were not interred like us but instead were permitted to wear armbands stating their particular race.

The Izumi family were sent to Manzanar Internment Camp in California where they grew their own food and lived in tarpaper barracks.

My parents were deeply upset by what was happening but at the time it was all a big adventure to me. Most of us had jobs on campus

> making products for the War Effort such as camouflage netting and earned around $7.00 per month. We went to school and were taught by volunteer teachers who came from all over America. Helen Ely taught me history and it was through her that my younger brother Roy and I gained permission to leave the camp in 1943 and continued our studies in Iowa.
>
> I finished my education and volunteered to join the US Army in June 1944. The military was still segregated at the time so I had no choice but to enlist in the 442nd Regt Combat Team – a Japanese-American unit more commonly known as "The Nisei" whose motto was "Go for Broke." I was only attached to the 442nd until September 1944, when the opportunity arose for me transfer into the 101st Airborne Division and train to be a paratrooper.

Upon arrival at Mourmelon, Izumi was posted to 3 Ptn G Co, which at the time did not officially have a platoon leader or even an assistant. Due to the temporary lack of leadership, mortar sergeant Harvey Jewett managed to persuade Pvt Clyde McCarty, Pvt Harry Barker, and Pfc Stan Davis to go AWOL. The four men were arrested the following evening and returned to G Co where they were immediately confined to quarters. Two days later Capt Doughty reduced Jewett to the rank of private although no formal charges were made against the other three soldiers. Initially Izumi wondered what he had gotten himself into but the situation soon resolved itself after discipline was restored.

The squalid conditions on the line during the last three weeks in Holland saw hundreds hospitalized with non-combat-related injuries such as yellow jaundice and emersion foot, like 26-year-old T/5 Teddy Dziepak from I Co. "I was sent to England for about five weeks recovering from trench foot and returned to 1 Ptn in late January 1945. My stay in hospital gave me the opportunity to write every day to my wife Bette in Perth Amboy, New Jersey, who I was missing terribly."

As the battalion was preparing to leave Holland, 1st Lt Bill Wedeking (OC [Officer Commanding] MG [Machine-Gun] Ptn) was evacuated after being diagnosed with yellow jaundice (probably caused by ingesting contaminated water). Although a form of hepatitis, the acute liver complaint is most visible in the white conjunctiva, when the eyes of the sufferer become bright yellow. "After spending two days in a hospital near Brussels, I was flown back to the UK and sent to a specialized medical facility in Scotland." In Wedeking's absence, Lt Fenton was brought in to command the platoon, ably assisted by T/Sgt George "Doc" Dwyer. Doc took over from S/Sgt Nathan "Nate" Bullock, who graciously stepped back down to section leader, alongside S/Sgt August Saperito (ex G Co).

After escaping from the Germans in France, when Doc had returned to England he was posted to the Parachute School at Chilton Foliat, and much to his regret missed out on Holland. Several other men had also managed to escape and return to England, such as Pfc Jimmy Sheeran and Pvt Bernie Rainwater (I Co), Cpl Martin Clark and Pvt Joe Mielcarek (MG Ptn), and Pfc Ray Calandrella and T/4 Joe Gorenc (Co HQ). The Geneva Convention stated that all escapees who made it back to their parent units were entitled to return home under the ZI (Zone of the Interior) option. After reaching the United Kingdom on September 9, Marty Clark was debriefed by the authorities and was in the process of taking the ZI option when he bumped into Joe Gorenc in London. Like his escape partner "Doc" Dwyer, Joe had refused ZI and rejoined 3rd Bn, although at the time it was probably more for financial reasons than anything else. The week before D-Day, Joe had won $2,000 in a card game. Unable to send his winnings home, Gorenc asked his immediate superior, Ed Shames (who was then battalion S3 operations sergeant) to hide the cash in his private billet above the grocery store at Ramsbury.

Back in London after an emotional reunion and a few drinks, Joe invited Marty to Ramsbury for a "proper goodbye." Marty recalls, "The guys encouraged me to stay even though the machine-gun platoon didn't really need my services anymore. Once we reached Holland, Joe sorted out a position for me at Battalion HQ in the S3, but it wasn't the safe and comfortable job he'd originally promised."

On October 6, outside the battalion command post (CP) at Boelenham Farm near Opheusden, Clark was badly wounded by a mortar burst along with 1st Lt Alex Bobuck (Adjutant) and 1st Lt Lewis Sutfin (81mm Mortar Ptn). Both officers were hit in the legs by shrapnel while another fragment pierced Clark's right lung, almost killing him.

Pfc Don Ross (S3 runner) had also been captured in Normandy. Don's younger brother Ken joined the 101st Airborne at Mourmelon. Ken recalls: "My brother's experience with the 506th inspired me to become a paratrooper. The training I received was tough but nowhere near as tough as his. Those guys who passed selection for the 506th back in Toccoa were forged from steel and we all knew it. Despite that my dream was to fight alongside Don as a member of 3/506 but after he went missing I opted for the 502nd PIR where I was assigned to RHQ [Regimental HQ] Demolition Ptn."

After being wounded Pfc Jim Martin (2 Ptn G Co) was evacuated to the 61st General Hospital at Witney in Oxfordshire before being sent to the 10th Replacement Depot at Lichfield. Jim's experience was altogether different from that of many others, as he recalls: "A prison would have treated its worst inmates more humanely. The colonel in charge of the depot encouraged his staff to be brutal and I witnessed many beatings." Jim was not alone in thinking that the severe conditions were specifically designed for a higher turnover of manpower.

> In early November about a dozen guys from G Co, myself included, were told we were being sent to a regular infantry unit. Of course we all wanted to go back to the 506th but were told that this was not negotiable. The following day, under the watchful eye of the Depot NCOs, we were virtually forced onto the train that was to take us to our new unit. During one of the later stops in France we noticed a parachute drop going on nearby and decided to go "AWOL." Eventually we made it to a makeshift command post (CP) and discovered that the paratroopers were from the 504th PIR. The soldiers manning the CP were surprised to see us and enquired

> where on earth we had come from. We explained our situation, and to cut a long story short, despite interference from the replacement depot, the 504th contacted the 506th who then furnished us with the necessary travel permits for our return to Mourmelon.

Despite the enormous influx of new soldiers the most radical changes to the battalion were experienced among the officers. This was not surprising due to the fact that during the battalion's 72 days in Holland 17 commissioned men from the 506th had been killed. By the end of November 1944, G Co received several new lieutenants, including 1st Lt Lawrence Fitzpatrick and 2nd Lt Sherman Sutherland (formerly A Co and battlefield commission) who subsequently became 1st Lt Frank Rowe's assistant in 2 Ptn. 1st Lt John Weisenberger (previously assistant battalion S1) was re-assigned to G Co as XO, while 1st Lt Blaine Pothier became temporary XO for the battalion.

After recovering from his leg wound, former adjutant Alex Bobuck was promoted to captain and posted to a regular infantry unit as a foreign liaison officer. When 1st Lt Pete Madden rejoined 3/506, he returned to HQ Co, taking up his previous post commanding the 81mm mortar platoon, alongside 2nd Lt Frank Southerland. Lt Southerland seemed to fit in and was well liked by the men, unlike his predecessor Lewis Sutfin. At the same time 23-year-old family man Gil Morton was promoted to platoon sergeant after Roy Burger received his battlefield commission and was posted to HQ 2/506 mortars. Each 81mm squad was made up of seven men, including the squad leader who was usually a corporal. The complete weapon system weighed 136lb and could be broken down into three parts: tripod, tube, and base-plate (which by itself weighed 46lb). As a consequence the majority of the mortar platoon lost anything up to 4in in height during their wartime service!

H Co received its fair share of new officers, including 2nd Lt Harry Begle and lieutenants Lawrence, Wilkinson, and Smith. Harry Begle recalls, "Along with Lt Ed Wilkinson, I was posted to 2 Ptn as assistant to 1st Lt Clark Heggeness, so rather unusually the platoon had three officers on its table of organization." 1st Lt Bob Stroud from 1 Ptn (nicknamed the "Forty Thieves" by Col Wolverton) recalls his new assistant, Lt Smith: "Smith stuck to me like glue and every time I'd turn around he'd be right there like some sort of anxious puppy." 2nd Lt Willie Miller rejoined 3 Ptn after being wounded at Opheusden, and was relieved to learn it was still under the able and efficient command of 1st Lt Alexander Andros from Illinois. 1/Sgt Gordon Bolles was another familiar face. A regular soldier, "Pop" Bolles had been with the outfit since Toccoa. "Pop" had a wonderful sense of humor and was the only "top kick" (slang for "first sergeant") to serve throughout the entire war with the same company.

The old sweats in I Co – first lieutenants Floyd Johnston (1 Ptn) and Don Replogle (3 Ptn) – welcomed 1st Lt Jerome Knight and second lieutenants Denver Albrecht and Roger Tinsley. Knight and Albrecht took over 2 Ptn, while Tinsley joined Johnston. The new intake replaced Mickey Panovich, Ray Eisenhauer, Charles Santarsiero, and Jim Nye. Always unpopular, Nye (2 Ptn) had been posted to F Co in Holland, while Panovich (1 Ptn) and Santarsiero (3 Ptn) were badly wounded. Santarsiero's injuries were so severe that he spent the next three years in hospital. After attending teaching college, Sgt Harley Dingman (3 Ptn) from Carthage, New York, had been called up at the age of 21 in May 1943 and was sent to Camp Wheeler in Macon, Georgia:

> After basic training, I accepted promotion to corporal and stayed on at Wheeler as an instructor. Several months later I opted to join the paratroops. Not long after qualifying for my wings I was shipped to the UK and posted to I Co. At the time it took a little while for the guys who had just come back from Normandy to accept me as a junior NCO but everything worked out OK by the time we jumped into Holland. Later in the campaign up on the island, I was acting as an artillery observer when a small piece of shrapnel lodged in my hand. The wound was minor and I thought nothing more until a week or so later when it started showing signs of infection. Shortly afterwards,

> I was evacuated and spent the next five weeks in a succession of hospitals. By early December, I was ready to return to the battalion but frustratingly got held back by bureaucracy at a replacement depot. One day I thought, "To Heck with the paperwork" and smuggled myself onto a truck bound for Mourmelon. When I got back to the company, Capt Anderson called me into his office. Anderson had a very dry sense of humor and told me that not only was I about to be accused of desertion but also they were billing me for the loss of a Thompson submachine gun! He thought it was highly amusing that I'd "deserted" to come back to the outfit when usually it was the other way around. He had me believing for a while that I was going to be court martialed but then he burst out laughing and asked me if I'd like to take the job of acting 3 Ptn sergeant – which of course I accepted without hesitation. There was a bottle of liquor on the table and Anderson offered up a drink to toast my new "promotion." I was quite GI at the time and figured there was no way an enlisted man like me should be drinking with an officer! So I graciously refused, saluted, and marched out feeling a lot happier than when I went in.

Still recovering from wounds received in Normandy, Pvt Bob Penner, Pfc Lonnie Gavrock, and Sgt Manny Barrios returned to I Co. After being hit by shrapnel Manny had hooked up with Bob Harwick (who was also on the run from the enemy) in St-Côme-du-Mont where they were both liberated on June 8/9, 1944. "I was posted to 3 Ptn and put in charge of the 60mm mortar squad, where the only person I recognized was Harold Stedman," Manny later recalled.

Soon after Gavrock arrived back at Mourmelon complications set in and Lonnie (who still had a bullet lodged dangerously close to his heart) was sent back to the hospital for the duration. Like Gavrock, Sgt Len "Sam" Goodgal (1 Ptn) was wounded at "Bloody Gully" in Normandy on June 13, but was lucky enough to make a full recovery. He recalls: "Some of our replacements, like privates Bob Chovan and Bill Chivvis, had proven themselves in Holland but they were not bonded like the rest of us who had been through basic training at Toccoa. Some of these guys came in, got killed or wounded and we never knew them. I think most of us, who were now veterans of one or more campaigns, felt that they should have got more recognition as they gave everything, including in some cases their lives. I was no great soldier – I was just there like so many others."

Twenty-year-old Chivvis joined 1st Squad on June 20, as a scout. "Len and the boys called me 'Joe,' after the cartoon character from 'Willie & Joe.' Everyone joked that I was the most 'sorry arsed' soldier in I Co, although it is fair to say, Len was a pretty close second!"

A small number of troops from the 506th were selected for temporary duty with the 9th Troop Carrier Command Pathfinder Group to train as Pathfinders. Pvt Irvin Schumacher from H Co joined 1st Lt Shrable Williams (Regt HQ Co) and around a dozen other soldiers to undergo an intensive two-week course at Chalgrove in Oxfordshire. Others like Pfc George McMillan (I Co 2 Ptn) were accepted as Air Dispatchers and also returned to the United Kingdom.

One of McMillan's friends was Pvt Al Cappelli from Wayne, Pennsylvania, who joined 2 Ptn as a wireman in the communications section a few days before the jump into Holland. Cappelli recalls: "I had been hurt during the early stages of the campaign by a blast from a German grenade which damaged my back. Our squad leader at the time, Sgt Joe Madona from Winthrop, Massachusetts, killed the soldier who threw the grenade and saved my life. I spent eight days in hospital and was told that our medic, T/5 Robert Evans' careful treatment kept me from further injury. I can't say enough about Joe Madona, who used to joke that we were the only 'Dagos' in the outfit – so we'd better make it shine!"

On November 29, two days after arriving at Mourmelon, Cappelli's kidneys became so inflamed that he could no longer urinate. Capt Anderson immediately sent Al for treatment to the 99th General Hospital in Reims. "During my two-week stay," Cappelli remembers, "I didn't think anyone really cared, but when Joe Madona came to visit with our platoon sergeant Albert Wall and three other guys, I actually wept with pride." 3rd Bn surgeon Capt Barney Ryan was also at the same hospital working on detached service with 502nd PIR regimental surgeon Maj Douglas Davidson.

Unusually a number of parachute-trained senior NCOs were attached to both the 101st and the 82nd airborne divisions (albeit temporarily) from the 509th Parachute Infantry Bn (originally part of the First Allied Airborne Task Force). One of these men, Sgt Walter Patterson, was assigned to 1 Ptn H Co as a mortar squad leader, as Lou Vecchi recalls: "Patterson had a lot of experience and seemed to fit in right away. Walt took over the 4th Squad from Don Zahn (who had recently received a battlefield commission) and stayed with the platoon until the end of the war."

The superb recreational facilities at Mourmelon meant that those who showed any sporting prowess competed for positions on the regimental football, basketball, or boxing teams. Joe Madona and Cpl Stan Stasica (H Co), rejoined the "Sky Train" football team to begin regular training sessions for "The Champagne Bowl," an important game scheduled against the 502nd PIR in Reims on Christmas Day. John Wiesenberger and Lawrence Fitzpatrick were coaching the team when replacement and ex-high-school-football star Pvt John Kilgore (3 Ptn G Co) was sent on a work detail to deliver football strips. Wiesenberger recognized Kilgore's name and asked if he would be willing to join Sky Train. "Of course I couldn't say no and was pleased to learn that my squad mate, Pvt Albert Gray, had also been selected," Kilgore later recalled.

Pfc Harold Stedman (3 Ptn I Co) began to connect with Pvt Richard Shinn, who had joined the company just before Holland. "Richie came from San Francisco where he lived with his parents who were both Korean. It turned out that Shinn, a gifted prewar boxer, had previously trained at the same gym as my cousin and competed against him in several competitions. Shinn knew I was keen on amateur boxing and taught me enough to qualify for a place on the team that was still in the process of being re-formed. Richie always told me, 'Stay in shape and maybe you won't get killed' – and of course, as I later came to realize, he was right."

Sgt Hank DiCarlo (1 Ptn H Co) had a large sum of money at his disposal. "I hadn't been paid properly since May and having just received all my back salary, I was loaded." Shortly afterwards Hank was approached by 1st Lt Derwood Cann (battalion S2), who had just been given an unexpected three-day pass to Paris. Cann wanted to borrow $500 and Hank trusted him enough to pay it back over the next few months in easy installments.

Four years of German occupation had not seemingly changed Paris in any way except for the fact that now it cost a small fortune to purchase anything. Many began their leave at the Café de la Paix or "Caffay De La PX" to meet old friends and decide which places to visit. Parisians straggled by, often clutching scuffed old briefcases containing family heirlooms, which they were hoping to sell to the new occupiers. Barroom rhetoric changed from "women" to "when the war was going to end" as by now most people just wanted to go home. Before the men went on leave a rumor began to circulate that the 506th might be parachuting into Berlin. Bob Webb spent two days in Paris and recalled, "The American troops were constantly getting rooked on the money exchange! Twelve months earlier, I had made a $20 bet with a colleague that the war would be over by February 15, 1945 – which still seemed possible if the Russians achieved their aims in the east. However, we had a saying in the 506th that 'Things would always get better before they got worse!'" Sgt Ken Johnson (2 Ptn H Co) adds, "In places like Mourmelon a bar of soap could buy you almost anything – liquor, laundry, even a woman if you tried hard enough."

Pvt Bob Dunning from the 81mm mortar platoon had been wounded in Holland. "I discharged myself from hospital and returned to the outfit in early December. Because my hip was still causing problems, I was put on limited duty and worked as an orderly for HQ Co. Despite my temporary position it was still good to be back with the guys and I went on leave to Paris with Jack Manley and Herb Spence, where we met up with three USO girls, one of whom I knew from Atlanta."

The United Services Organization (USO) was a non-profit entertainment company. The overseas operation was also known as the "Foxhole" circuit. Although the big stars were not paid for their appearances, many of the regular performers worked full time in concert and other associated units.

"Most people who were lucky enough to get a furlough were only allowed into Mourmelon or Reims but I wanted Paris so badly that I just couldn't wait any longer," recalls Cpl Bob Rommel (MG Ptn). He continues:

> After losing 75 percent of our platoon in Holland we didn't give a damn about anything and just wanted to have fun. One of our guys "borrowed" a car from the airfield and five of us piled into the tiny vehicle (still wearing working dress) and went AWOL to Paris. It was so cramped that one of the boys had to lie across our laps on the back seat. On the way we blew all the tires and had to hitch a lift from a passing truck. We hadn't been in Paris long when we were stopped and arrested by the Military Police (MPs). One of the guys managed to get away but the rest of us were marched to a police station to be processed. While we were dozing in the waiting room, another MP walked in and asked if we were for the American Red Cross Club at Gare de l'Est? I looked up and said, "Yeah that's us" and he replied, "OK boys, you are coming with me." We followed the "Snowdrop" (all MPs wore white helmets) outside before bolting in every direction. Although we were "free" again, the only problem was that none of us had any money and we were still dressed in fatigues. After a few days on the "run" I was so despondent that I gave myself up and was promptly sent back to camp.

Previously Helen Briggs had been the American Red Cross representative for 3/506 in the United Kingdom. For the last few months "Briggsy" had been assigned to the Gare de l'Est railway station:

> There was a hotel at the station with about 20 rooms where we were billeted. Our job was to make donuts for the various organizations and serve the hospital trains. While I was in charge, our kitchen worked three shifts per day and more than two million donuts were produced by hand. In the hotel, which was also our American Red Cross Club, we had seven bathrooms where a soldier could sign in with a serial number and get a hot bath. Our place became very popular with the Military Police, who were constantly on the lookout for AWOLs. When the German offensive began the MPs collected all the guys on leave from the 101st and held them at the club until they could get transportation to Mourmelon via Reims. I managed to procure a bottle of Cognac for the 3rd Bn mail clerk, Pvt Richard "Swede" Stockhouse as a "thank you" for helping me distribute my "Poop Sheet" [a monthly current affairs bulletin] while the outfit was in Holland. I nearly got into serious trouble for allowing the guys to gamble while they were waiting for transportation.

Doc Dwyer had only been in Paris for one day when, like hundreds of others, he was recalled. "Luckily I had time to visit a French friend and his family who helped me and Joe Gorenc after we escaped from a German prison train in the Loire valley during the Normandy campaign."

Earlier that week, Hank DiCarlo had been asleep in the H Co sergeants' mess at Mourmelon when 2nd Lt Don Zahn entered the room around 2am and turned on the lights. Zahn (who had saved DiCarlo's life in Normandy) had been assigned to 1st Bn and came direct from a midnight meeting at Regimental HQ. "We woke to find him rooting around in Bob Martin's barracks bag for a set of binoculars he had loaned him several days before," recalls Hank. "When we asked what the heck he was doing, Zahn replied that the Germans had attacked our troops along the German border in Belgium and the 101st were being sent behind the 82nd Airborne [who were pre-designated as combat reserve] to plug the gaps made by the enemy tanks." It had not gone unnoticed by Hank and his buddies that the nearby airfield had been unusually active for the last 12 hours with scores of P-47 Thunderbolts constantly landing, refueling, and taking off.

1st Lt Burton Duke (Bazooka Ptn) had been posted to 3 Ptn G Co when he returned from hospital. Immediately after the officers' meeting at Regimental HQ, Duke, accompanied by T/5 Russell Kerns, visited a nearby ordnance depot to obtain some much-needed ammunition. Initially the man in charge refused to comply but eventually he agreed to sign a requisition after certain threats were made against his establishment. The following day Duke was transferred back to the "Rocket Launchers" while first lieutenants Perrin Walker and Lawrence Fitzpatrick were posted into G Co to fill the gap.

Shortly after 2200hrs on December 17, the 101st began to mobilize and prepare for movement. All available equipment and supplies were secured and placed on transport provided by the logistical center at Oise near Paris. Nearest to Mourmelon, Oise was one of several enormous support bases belonging to the Southern Command Section – run by BrigGen Charles Thrasher. "The following morning we awoke to discover that the 506th PIR was going back to war," recalls Hank DiCarlo. "The company was due to go on leave in Paris and to say we were disappointed was an understatement."

The divisional advance party, consisting of B/326 Airborne Engineer Bn, 101st Reconnaissance Ptn, and a detachment from Divisional HQ were first to depart. The 506th PIR had less than one day to get organized for the mission and everything had to be done at the double. "Most of our weapons were still being repaired and many were issued a variety of other small arms still covered in Cosmoline packing grease," remembers DiCarlo. "They also gave us small cans of gasoline and cloth with which to clean off the grease. I had absolutely no ammunition for my Thompson submachine gun but at least it was something familiar to fight with." The 801st Airborne Ordnance Co was responsible for the repair of all weapons as 1/Sgt Robert "Bob" Higgins recalls: "Our small workshop had been overwhelmed due to an earlier decision by Division to assess and repair just about everything unless it was in near-perfect condition.

When the order came for mobilization we went into overdrive and took on 15 extra armorers and, during the next 48 hours, overhauled around 5,000 firearms." Those soldiers who went to the front unarmed were told that their personal weapons would follow on within a few hours. When that did not happen, many joked that they had been equipped with nothing more than a hangover and a pair of silk stockings.

Before the battalion left Mourmelon, two soldiers from a quartermaster unit arrived and began distributing the ammunition ordered earlier by Burton Duke. S/Sgt Ralph Bennett recalls, "At most my rifleman had no more than 12 rounds each and 100 rounds per machine gun." The following day, at 1500hrs, un-briefed and still with only a pitiful amount of small-arms cartridges, the regiment (accompanied by the 321st Glider Field Artillery [GFA] Bn) clambered aboard 40, 18-wheeler semi-tractor units parked in front of Divisional Headquarters. Every rear-wheel-drive vehicle was towing an open trailer weighing 10 tons. Each combination was commanded by an officer or senior NCO and had a driver and co-driver. In total 380 trucks were used to transport the division.

The order of departure was as follows: 501st PIR (less I Co – who were held back through "personal" issues) plus 907th GFA Bn and B Battery from 81st Airborne Antiaircraft (AA) Bn, closely followed by the remainder of 81st AA Bn, 101st Divisional HQ plus Signal and Artillery HQ, 506th PIR plus 321st GFA Bn, 326th Airborne Engineer Bn (less B Co), 502nd PIR plus 377th Parachute Field Artillery (PFA) Bn, 327th Glider Infantry Regiment (GIR) plus 401st GIR, and 463rd PFA.

The 326th Airborne Medical Co and, not surprisingly, the 801st Airborne Ordnance Co were the last to depart. The 801st convoy was towing a miscellaneous array of equipment, including two 75mm howitzers and several generator trailers full of spare tires.

"Sitting back to back for warmth, we set off and headed northeast across the battlefields of World War I such as the Marne, Verdun, and Sedan," recalls Hank DiCarlo, "before continuing into Belgium and the freezing hills of the Ardennes." The silhouettes of the men looked somewhat downtrodden as they huddled together in the darkness. As the vehicle lights went on, some people tried to sleep, some talked quietly, while others stared into the night lost in their own thoughts. At one point part of the convoy was stopped and the occupants ordered to de-truck when an Allied night fighter buzzed the vehicles several times before disappearing into the darkness.

Originally heading for Werbomont, 30 miles north of Bastogne, the movement order was changed en route and the 101st Airborne redirected to Bastogne. Lacking any form of "snow chains," the rear-wheel-drive prime movers were not suited to the icy road conditions and the 107-mile journey to Bastogne was fraught with delays. The vehicle carrying the 81mm mortar platoon had to stop due to a crash, as Bob Dunning recalls: "One of the lead trucks skidded off the road in a small town and went through the front of a house blocking the road. Since we couldn't get around the wreck, S/Sgt Morton told us to find shelter as best we could in local houses until the road was reopened." Nineteen-year-old Pfc Ewell Martin, from Mississippi, had joined G Co in late November, and been assigned to 1 Ptn. He recalls: "During the journey, we opened a bottle of champagne that I'd purchased in Reims and passed it around. It wasn't long before I needed to use the latrine (a 5-gallon oil drum), which was full to the brim by the time it got to me." During one stop in an unknown French village the inhabitants came out with food and bottles of wine. "It felt good to have a couple of drinks in my belly," recalls Manny Barrios.

Finally, during the early hours of Tuesday, December 19, the 506th and 321st GFA de-trucked at a crossroad in the village of Champs, 3 miles northwest of Bastogne. Half-jokingly the drivers were told, "We'll be right back so keep the engines running." Attached to the 506th were a team of four specially rigged evacuation jeeps from the 326th Airborne Medical Co, whose job was to transport casualties from the front-line aid stations to the divisional clearing hospital at Herbaimont.

It was an unusual way to begin a large-scale combat operation but this mission would write the most brilliant and courageous chapter in the history of the 506th PIR.

2

"Ghost front"

December 17–19, 1944

Nicknamed "Hitler's Fireman," German Feldmarschall Walter Model's Heeresgruppe B's (Army Group B) unexpected thrust northwest across the German border into the Belgian Ardennes on December 16, 1944 jeopardized the entire American First and Ninth Army front. In December the Allied footprint across this part of Europe was maintained by three main US groups: First Army (LtGen Courtney Hodges), Third Army (LtGen George Patton), and Ninth Army (LtGen William Simpson). Part of the battle group in the central Ardennes was the 4th, 28th (aka the "Keystone Boys"), and 106th infantry divisions plus the 9th Armored Division constituting VIII Corps, led by LtGen Troy Middleton, which along with V Corps and VII Corps collectively formed First Army. The 9th Armored was on its first deployment and had never been in combat, while the 4th and the 28th infantry divisions would be reduced by around 50 percent after two weeks of bitter fighting in the Hurtgen Forest.

It was to be the most serious defeat of US armed forces since Japan invaded the Philippines three years earlier. The breakthrough, supported by 1,000 Stug self-propelled guns (SPGs), Mk III, IV, and V Panther (aka "Panzer") tanks, penetrated over 50 miles in three days.

The idea was to drive a wedge between the British in Holland and Americans in France, and to capture the Belgian seaport of Antwerp. Known as Operation *Watch on the Rhine*, the "Last Hope" offensive was the brainchild of Commander-in-Chief West, Feldmarschall Gerd von Runstedt. The 88-mile front, running due south from Monschau

Bastogne Overview 1944

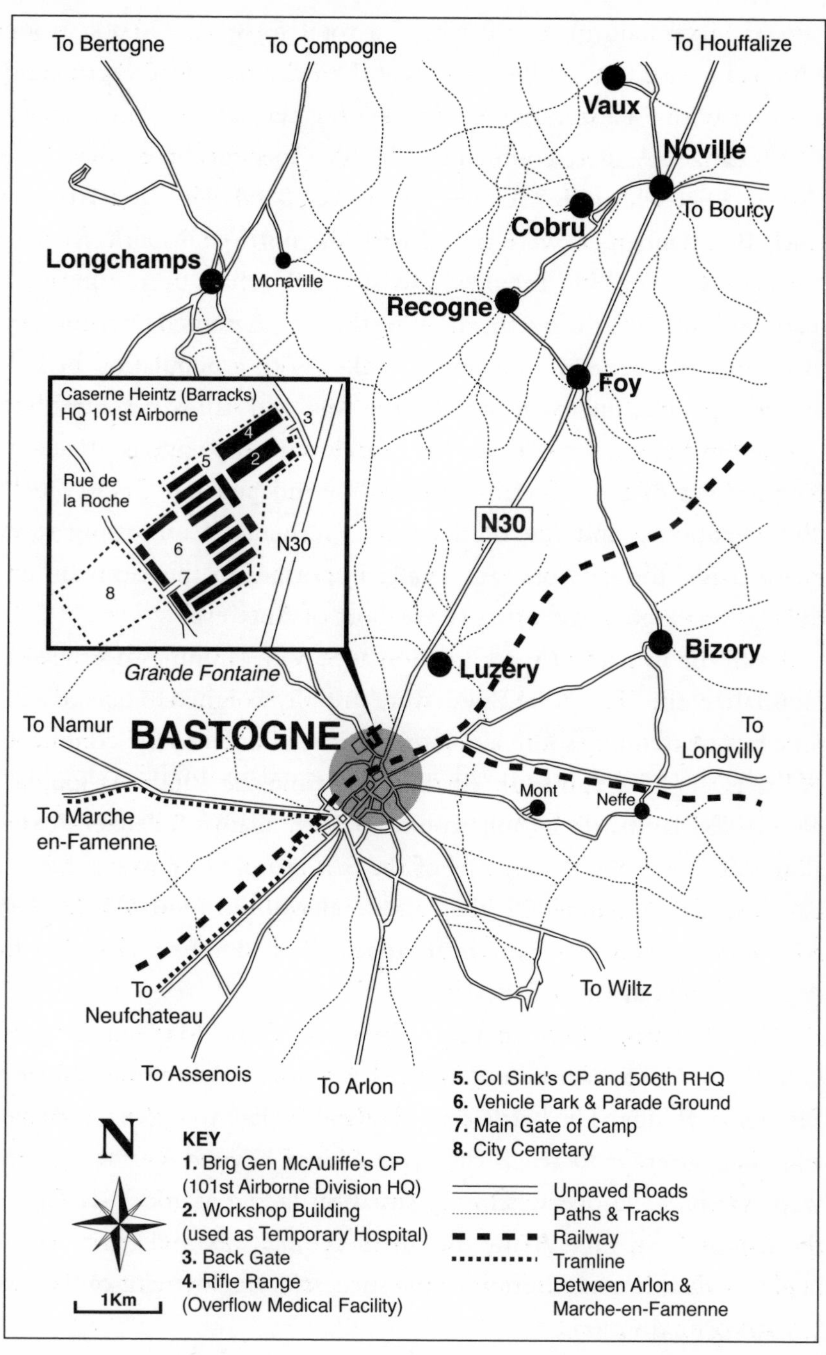
To Bertogne
To Compogne
To Houffalize
Vaux
Noville
To Bourcy
Cobru
Longchamps
Monaville
Recogne
Foy
Caserne Heintz (Barracks)
HQ 101st Airborne
Rue de
la Roche
N30
N30
Bizory
Luzery
Grande Fontaine
To Namur
BASTOGNE
To
Longvilly
Mont
Neffe
To Marche
en-Famenne
To
Neufchateau
To Wiltz
To Assenois
To Arlon
N
1Km
KEY
1. Brig Gen McAuliffe's CP
(101st Airborne Division HQ)
2. Workshop Building
(used as Temporary Hospital)
3. Back Gate
4. Rifle Range
(Overflow Medical Facility)
5. Col Sink's CP and 506th RHQ
6. Vehicle Park & Parade Ground
7. Main Gate of Camp
8. City Cemetary
Unpaved Roads
Paths & Tracks
Railway
Tramline
Between Arlon &
Marche-en-Famenne

(in western Germany) along the Belgian border to Echternach (in eastern Luxembourg), encompassed a total force of 250,000 troops who had over 2,000 artillery pieces at their disposal. Heeresgruppe B, together with 5.Panzer-Armee, formed the central core of the attack. The 6.Panzer-Armee, commanded by SS-Oberstgruppenführer Josef "Sepp" Dietrich, and 7.Armee, led by General der Panzertruppen Erich Brandenberger, were tasked with the north and south. MajGen Norman Cota's 28th Infantry Division (ID) had been fighting a rearguard action to the north, allowing the 10th Armored Division time to occupy Bastogne and deploy its tanks. With a population in 1944 of 4,500 people, the town of Bastogne was, and still is, a central hub. Located in the southeastern corner of Belgium, Bastogne is situated in the province of Luxembourg, close to the independent Grand Duchy of Luxembourg and the border with Germany. Comprising seven major roads, the network was vitally important to the Germans and their ultimate goal to capture the seaport of Antwerp.

From the important road junction at St Vith (18 miles northeast of Houffalize) the "Keystone Boys" were initially assigned to defend a 21-mile front extending south along the German border to the confluence of the rivers Sûre and Our. At the same time the 106th ID fought a bloody six-day battle in and around St Vith against 5.Panzer-Armee alongside the 7th and elements of the 9th armored divisions. Several days later on December 22, the commander of the 106th ID, MajGen Alan Jones, suffered a serious heart attack and had to be replaced by his deputy, BrigGen Herbert Perrin.

The 2nd and 99th infantry divisions from MajGen Leonard Gerow's V Corps carried out another essential blocking maneuver at Elsenborn Ridge. The battle caused serious delays to 6.Panzer-Armee and their attempt to reach the river Meuse beyond Verviers in the west. Despite the overwhelming situation facing V and VIII Corps, the troops from First Army did an incredible job, and their actions made a valuable contribution to the successful deployment of the two US airborne divisions.

Caserne Heintz

At the time, 46-year-old BrigGen Anthony McAuliffe (divisional artillery commander) was in charge of the 101st Airborne, after Gen Maxwell Taylor had been recalled to Washington, DC for an urgent conference with the War Department. It is a little known fact that Taylor and McAuliffe had pet names for each other – "Major Killer" and "Minor Killer." However, when word reached Taylor of the German breakthrough, he immediately made plans to return. Taylor's assistant, BrigGen Gerald Higgins, had just arrived in Belgium from the United Kingdom and sensibly acquiesced to Tony McAuliffe who had a better understanding of what was happening.

The previous morning (the 18th), while on his way to Werbomont, McAuliffe decided to visit Bastogne and get an impromptu situation report from Troy Middleton at his HQ in the Caserne Heintz (Heintz Barracks) on Rue de la Roche. The barracks had previously been in use as a "boot camp" by the Hitler Youth, and when liberated on September 10, the main gate was still decorated with the German national emblem. On the other side of the main entrance, lined by a neatly trimmed row of small conifers, was a tar macadam vehicle park and parade ground. Adjacent to a pair of tall radio antennas (belonging to VIII Corps Signal Co) and facing the square were eight oblong-shaped accommodation blocks. Situated behind the two-storey barracks were several larger buildings, comprising of garage, saddlers, and carpentry workshops plus an indoor rifle range 100 yards long. These barracks would become McAuliffe's HQ for the next two and a half weeks. Opposite the caserne, across Rue de la Roche, was the cemetery. During the ensuing battle this would see much use as a temporary burial ground.

Into the abyss

McAuliffe had left Mourmelon ahead of the divisional advance party with his aide, Lt Ted Starrett, G3 divisional operations officer LtCol Harry Kinnard, and driver Sgt Irwin Brown. During the meeting at

Caserne Heintz, LtGen James Gavin – deputy commander of the 82nd Airborne Division and now, due to the absence of Matthew Ridgeway, temporary commander of XVIII Airborne Corps (part of the First Allied Airborne Army) – appeared with vitally important news. Gavin had just come from Werbomont, where MajGen Gerow and V Corps were clearly in trouble. After some discussion it was decided to assign the 82nd Airborne to V Corps and deploy them around Werbomont.

Intelligence revealed that Heeresgruppe B and 5.Panzer-Armee, led by General der Panzertruppen Hasso von Manteuffel, were now well on their way. After advising Mourmelon of the change in plan, McAuliffe sent LtCol Kinnard to a crossroad, codenamed "X," near Herbaimont, along the N4, 7 miles northwest of Bastogne. Here the road is dissected by the N826 that runs northeast to Bertogne and southwest to Libramont and Libin. Spanned by a pontoon bridge, the river Our was only 3 miles further west. Immediately upon arrival Kinnard instructed the MPs to direct all traffic belonging to the 101st to Bastogne, and not Werbomont as previously planned.

First to arrive, 1/501 were redirected to the village of Neffe, 2 miles east of Bastogne, where a number of German tanks were now massing. Their ultimate goal was the river Meuse and the garrison town of Namur in southern Belgium. The Panzer-Lehr-Division (an inexperienced training division), 26.Volksgrenadier-Division ("People's Army" Division) under command of Generalmajor Heinz Kokott, and 2.Panzer-Division had already been forced towards Bastogne. Collectively these three main enemy assault groups made up the 47.Panzerkorps and would ultimately be tasked to capture the city, while further north 116.Panzer-Division supported by 560. Volksgrenadier-Division were targeting Houffalize.

Several makeshift tank forces had been formed by the 10th Armored Division (from Third Army) to defend the eastern approaches of Bastogne. The 10th Armored (known as the "Tiger Division") was commanded by MajGen William Morris, who had dispatched two groups, codenamed Combat Command A and B, to the battlefront. Each command was made up of around 50 tanks, one battalion of infantry, a company of engineers, and antiaircraft units equipped with "quad fifties" (a truck or half-track mounted with four .50cal machine guns).

Combat Command A went to the river Sûre on the southern flank of the German advance while Combat Command B headed to Bastogne. Led by Col William Roberts, Combat Command B was divided into three forces and initially deployed in a wide arc, facing east, 5 miles from the city. Task Force Desobry, led by Maj William Desobry (CO [Commanding Officer] of the 20th Armored Infantry Bn) was sent north with 15 tanks to Noville. Task Force Cherry, under LtCol Henry Cherry, headed northeast to Longvilly. Meanwhile Task Force O'Hara, commanded by LtCol James O'Hara, moved southeast to Wardin. The three armored groups established roadblocks in an attempt to stem the advance of the 47.Panzerkorps. Many of the personnel who made up the German Volksgrenadier, or "People's Army," units were conscripted and given the most basic of military training. Among the Volksgrenadier infantry were teenage boys, older men, and in some cases even women; others came from across Europe as prisoners of war, press-ganged into service under threats of retribution. It was a desperate attempt to turn the Allied tide, and now the 26.Volksgrenadier-Division, together with the rest of 47.Panzerkorps, would be at the very forefront of the battle.

The presence of Team Cherry at Longvilly actually influenced General Fritz Bayerlein (the CO of Panzer-Division-Lehr) into delaying his attack on Bastogne until the following morning. Bayerlein stopped briefly at Mageret after local intelligence reported a convoy of American tanks were heading his way. Fortunately for the Allies, this decision turned out to be a grave error of judgment, because at that moment, Bastogne was his for the taking. However, the early deployment of 1/501 turned out to be crucial and in fact coincided with the delayed attack at 0730hrs on December 19, from the over-cautious Bayerlein. During the first hour of the battle the Volksgrenadiers suffered 84 casualties and were unable to break the resolve of the 501st

PIR. The arrival of the 101st came as no great surprise to Hitler and his senior commanders, who had been hoping to achieve their aims before the Allied parachute divisions could be fully deployed.

Back at Caserne Heintz, McAuliffe decided to take over VIII Corps CP – located below ground level on the southern side of the camp. For reasons of safety Gen Middleton moved his command center to Neufchâteau (12 miles away to the southwest). The bunker system at the barracks ran underneath the building and was accessed by a single flight of stairs. McAuliffe selected the first chamber on the left at the base of the steps for his work and sleeping area. The 81st AA Bn and 326th Airborne Engineer Bn also established their HQs at the barracks. The 101st Airborne Signal Co called a meeting with all the communication officers to determine on which road or in which direction each regiment was located in order to begin running wire between switchboards. The following evening, Middleton ordered the 705th Tank Destroyer (TD) Bn to proceed north from Neufchâteau and assist the 101st Airborne.

Softly spoken, McAuliffe – who often described himself as "an Old Croc" – felt that the 101st Airborne could realistically hold Bastogne for 48 hours, before needing full back-up from Gen George Patton's Third Army, who at that moment were 100 miles away, fighting through the "West Wall" beyond Saarbrücken.

Patton's staff had trained for such a scenario and when Gen Eisenhower asked him to counterattack from the south, Patton was confident he could deliver. While Third Army was being redirected, Patton mobilized his 4th Armored Division, who were being held in reserve near Fénétrange, 20 miles further south across the border in Alsace Lorraine.

Commanded by MajGen Hugh Gaffey, 4th Armored was desperately short of tanks and crews. Gaffey split the division into three battle groups, codenamed "A," "B," and "R" (Reserve), and issued orders for "A" to spearhead north through Luxembourg while "B" advanced further to the west, with "R" on their far-left flank.

As Middleton was leaving for Neufchâteau he smiled and wished McAuliffe and Kinnard good luck, adding, "Tony – now don't let yourself get surrounded." Although Gen Middleton would be instrumental in organizing Allied tank tactics and roadblocks during the next few weeks, luckily McAuliffe and Kinnard chose to ignore his advice. Rather than create one straight line to the north, McAuliffe decided to gamble on a defensive ring around Bastogne, 14 miles in length, thinking it would be easier to command and maintain. Ultimately Von Manteuffel would need total control of the roads to keep 5.Panzer-Armee freely on course and moving toward Antwerp. McAuliffe ordered every man under his command in the pocket of Bastogne (approximately 11,840 paratroopers and 6,500 other troops, totaling around 18,000) to form and defend the perimeter at all costs. In contrast, the enemy forces directed against the 101st at that time numbered 38,000 (although this was reduced to around 20,000 shortly before Christmas).

As McAuliffe was settling in, Capt Willis McKee from the 326th Airborne Medical Co arrived, seeking permission to relocate the 101st field hospital closer to Bastogne from Herbaimont. Believing the hospital was safer where it was, Tony refused and sent McKee back to his unit, which would turn out to be a disastrous and costly mistake.

Boots on the ground

Just after midnight on December 18, the commander of 3rd Bn HQ Co, 28-year-old Capt Jim Morton from New York, was sent with 1/Sgt Fred Bahlau, Sgt Dennis Wester, and Sgt William Cooley as part of the regimental advance party to the village of Orsinfaing in Belgium. Also with Morton was his runner, Pvt Charles Coppala Jr, who had recently been transferred from G Co. Shortly after dawn, Morton was ordered northeast to Champs where Col Sink had already established a forward CP. After posting guides along the road to Mande-St-Étienne near "Crossroad X," the regimental convoy was re-routed to Champs with the last vehicles passing through at 0600hrs the following morning.

When at 0400hrs 3rd Bn arrived at Champs, nobody seemed to know what was happening. But after unloading, the troops set about digging temporary defensive positions on the northern edge of the village. The ground here was muddy and partially saturated with water. Barely audible in the distance, the men could hear explosions of artillery and tank fire possibly coming from Neffe or Noville.

A few hours later the regiment was formed into a combat team (consisting of 1st Bn, 3rd Bn, Regt HQ Co, and 321st GFA) and marched through Hemroulle along Rue de la Roche to a large field south of the barracks, with 2nd Bn bringing up the rear. Commanded by LtCol Edward Carmichael, most of the 321st GFA were detached and sent northwest to Grande Fontaine and Savy where Carmichael established his CP inside the schoolhouse. The 321st consisted of 12 75mm pack howitzers belonging to A and B batteries who were centrally controlled by their own HQ Battery.

It was vitally important for McAuliffe to be close to his artillery, and the CP at the barracks allowed him quick access to the 321st, who were now only 500 yards away. McAuliffe had around 130 guns at his disposal, including a significant number of M1, 155mm field guns, nicknamed "Long Toms." With a range of up to 14 miles, the 155s were operated by the 333rd Field Artillery Group, whose African-American crews were part of VIII Corps and had recently been incorporated with a battery from another black unit, the 969th Field Artillery Bn. During the first two days, artillery ammunition was in plentiful supply and no doubt helped to keep the German forces pinned down during the early stages of the battle.

B Battery was located on a large farm half a mile south of Savy overlooking Grande Fontaine. At least one gun was attached to 3/506 as gunner Pvt Ray Nagell recalls: "Initially my crew was sent forward in support of 1st and 3rd Bn. Each 75mm pack howitzer had a 12-man team including a sergeant, who acted as the section commander. I operated the elevation and deflection, via the optics, using two sighting stakes placed into the ground in front of the howitzer. Using these stakes

I was able to accurately place the crosshairs from my dial-sight onto pre-recorded targets around Noville. Most of the time our positions were protected by a defensive circle of .50cal MGs from the 81st AA Bn."

Radio operator Pfc Victor Sauerheber (HQ Battery) was re-assigned to Col Sink, in order to coordinate the newly attached artillery support. "Because my boss 1st Lt Bill Nugent (a forward observer) was in hospital back at Mourmelon with pneumonia they posted me to the 506th." Col Sink established a permanent CP in one of the accommodation blocks overlooking the holding area on the northern side of the caserne. Bizarrely, among the abandoned equipment inside the building were silk stockings and passports belonging to a group of Belgian nurses who had been assisting VIII Corps before the attack.*

The previous occupants had departed in such a hurry that the remnants of their supper, along with several half-written letters, were spread across the tables in one of the rooms. Stored in another room were around 30 large sacks of flour previously procured by LtCol Carl Kohls (Div G4 supply officer) from the municipality of Bastogne. Seven tons of flour and 2 tons of tinned biscuits had been stored at the Catholic Seminary in Bastogne for safekeeping. The flour store at the barracks prompted many Americans to think that there was a bakery somewhere on site. The man behind the donation was Acting Mayor Leon Jacqmin, who had been appointed three months earlier by Troy Middleton.

Painted in large letters on the wall of one room were the words "We'll be back – The Yanks" which solicited a response from the paratroopers along the lines of "Hell, when did we ever leave?" "For the most part over the next three days," continues Vic Sauerheber, "I worked at Sink's CP manning the radio. It was an exhausting time and I don't think I slept at all for the first 72 hours."

After reaching the holding area by the barracks and dispersing his squad, Sgt Hank DiCarlo remembers the delay before fresh orders

* It is interesting to note that all citizens of Belgium were and still are required to carry their passports at all times as a means of personal identification.

arrived: "We waited in the bitter cold for almost five hours and the only sound was the stamping of feet as everyone did their utmost to restore some semblance of warmth and circulation. A fortunate few had overcoats but most like me were clad only in basic combat uniform – although I did have a woolen sweater underneath my jacket."

The platoon commanders briefed their men as best they could on the uncertain tactical situation. "Col Patch told me that he couldn't say where the breakthrough was exactly," recalls 1st Lt Clark Heggeness (2 Ptn H Co), "but that we had been ordered to proceed north." Shortly afterwards it was decided to place 2nd Bn in reserve at nearby Luzery. Before the battalion moved out Capt Anderson took Sgt Barrios and seven of his men and designated them as a makeshift recon squad, as Manny recalls: "Part of our job was to act as Forward Observers (FOs) and also a kind of mobile reserve. It turned out from then on we got all the chicken-shit jobs. Over the next few weeks, I taught my boys a heck of a lot about soldiering and I truly believe that they made a valuable contribution to I Co and the battalion." In Manny's absence, Harold Stedman was given command of the 60mm mortar squad until further notice.

3rd Bn and 3 Ptn E Co (Regt Patrols Ptn), led by 2nd Lt Ed Shames and S/Sgt Amos "Buck" Taylor, were ordered to advance 3 miles to Foy, along the main road (designated N30), also known as the Route de Houffalize. 3 Ptn was desperately under strength at the time and consisted of roughly two rifle squads and a 60mm mortar team. Shortly before leaving Mourmelon, Shames was given 2nd Lt Richard Hughes (previously 2 Ptn) as a temporary assistant platoon leader. "I don't really know why they gave me Hughes because he had no experience with the kind of work we were now expected to be doing," recalls Ed, who was well aware of the chaotic situation the Allies now found themselves in.

The city seemed quiet and those civilians brave enough to remain were handing out scalding hot coffee along Rue de la Roche (N834). Leaving the holding area, 3rd Bn made their way to the N30 and began their march into history. Within minutes the men came across elements of the 10th Armored Division, who had by now been fighting their rearguard action in Bastogne for the last eight hours. A few hours before 2nd and 3rd battalions moved out of the city, 1st Bn, commanded by LtCol James LaPrade, was sent ahead to penetrate beyond Foy into Noville in support of Task Force Desobry.

Crisis at Noville

Situated in a geographic bowl, Noville (except for its western approaches) was surrounded by rolling hills making the town difficult to protect from 2.Panzer-Division. It was vital for 1st Bn to help stabilize Noville in order to give 3rd Bn more time to establish and strengthen its defensive positions at Foy. Since 0530hrs, 2.Panzer-Division had been attacking along the Houffalize and Bourcy roads. Subsequently, over 12 enemy tanks had been knocked out by Task Force Desobry between Vaux and Cobru. The heavy shelling and the rhetoric of retreating US infantry prompted Maj William Desobry (the armored task force commander) to ask Col Roberts (Combat Command B CO) for permission to withdraw.

When Desobry discovered that 1/506 were preparing to leave Bastogne he decided to stay and sent a jeep to collect LtCol LaPrade. Thus the two men were able to discuss their critical but limited options. When Desobry learned about LaPrade's lack of ammunition, he immediately ordered two trucks from his own service company to deposit caches at several points along the N30 between Foy and Noville. Later, as 1st Bn came through, the soldiers were able to help themselves to whatever ammo and grenades they could carry. Shortly afterwards, word came back down the line to halt and the men took cover in a nearby woodland while the company commanders were briefed by LaPrade on the forthcoming attack.

Noville was just beyond the next hill as 1st Bn moved out under a protective cover of mortar and artillery fire. With A Co attacking north, B Co was sent west across the Cobru road to consolidate the high ground, as 2nd Lt Hubert Porter recalls: "1st Lt Ed Long and I took 1 Ptn and secured the high ground. While we were digging in the platoon came under heavy attack from three tanks and supporting infantry." C Co moved east beyond the open marshy fields toward the heavily wooded ridgeline where the Germans were also waiting. A skirmish line was rapidly formed along the edge of the woods facing the enemy, who were equipped with seven tanks. Although one Panther was destroyed, C Co took heavy casualties. At 1400hrs the enemy stepped up their attack on the eastern flank of Noville, and after 2 hours of intense fighting both rifle companies were pulled back under cover from C Co's support platoon, leaving the 155mm M-10 Sherman tank destroyers to hold off the Panzers. Knowing the enemy were heading west from nearby Bourcy, LaPrade and Desobry called in smoke from 321st GFA and 420th Armored Field Artillery Bn (part of Task Force Desobry) to help cover the battalion as it withdrew into Noville. A small party of FOs from B Battery had also moved forward with 1st Bn, as Pfc Jay Stone recalls: "My group comprised of 1st Lt Francis Canham, Sgt Bill Plummer, and our jeep driver Pvt Wendell Byrne. The wiremen did an amazing job under the circumstances and kept our communications open to the 'Fire Detection Center' – who relayed the information to the guns. Lt Canham had joined the outfit five months earlier and was a great guy who always mucked in with the team but never shirked his responsibilities."

During the evening Capt Barney Ryan (3rd Bn surgeon) was ordered forward from Foy by BrigGen Higgins along the N30 (which remarkably was still open) to assist 1st Bn at Noville. The medical facility belonging to 1/506 was situated in the first house on the right (owned by the Beaujean family) on the southern edge of town. Ryan took over the 1st Bn aid station to allow their surgeon, Capt Joseph Warren, to go out and collect the wounded who numbered around 50 men.

In the meantime the 1st Bn XO, Maj Robert Harwick, had made his own way to Bastogne, after missing the recall notice while touring the American battlefields from World War I:

> I left Mourmelon on December 19 at 0800hrs, after hitching a ride on an ammunition truck. Across the Belgian border we encountered

> heavy equipment convoys moving to the rear. My driver and I started to wonder what was going on when we began passing small groups of men from the 28th IID – all heading the wrong way. Upon reaching Bastogne, 506th Regimental HQ told me that 1st Bn had already moved to Noville so I set off on foot without a helmet or weapon. The first 3 miles were quiet and I passed a few men stringing communications wire and an ambulance that had crashed into a tree. From here I could see mortar shells bursting on the hill up ahead. I carried on for another mile or so before the mortar fire forced me into a roadside ditch. The church steeple at Noville was clearly visible through the fog and parts of the town seemed to be on fire. As there appeared to be no sign of my battalion, I started back to check on the situation and ran into a patrol from 3/506 who confirmed that my outfit was actually in Noville!

Dashing from cover to cover behind a number of large haystacks, Harwick cautiously made his way into town, careful to avoid several dead bodies that were lying in the road covered by white bed sheets.

Noville is situated astride a crossroad with Bourcy to the east and Cobru to the west. Dominating the eastern side of the junction was a neo-gothic church. Built in 1882, the pointed steeple of l'Église St-Étienne could be seen for miles. Next door was a presbytery and home to 50-year-old Louis Delvaux, the priest of Noville and Bourcy.

The impressive two-storey house was completely surrounded by a 5ft-high stone wall. Directly behind the presbytery was a farmhouse then owned by the Felten family (now Rigaux), which connected to a milking shed and barn. It was here that Maj Harwick found Capt Warren in the process of evacuating a number of wounded. The aid station for 10th Armored and Task Force Desobry had been located in a café immediately south of the church but was badly damaged by shellfire earlier in the day.

Medical officer Capt John "Jack" Prior had been assigned to the 20th Armored Infantry Bn a few days before and was now attached to Task Force Desobry. He recalls: "An ammunition dump was located directly behind the café, which caught the attention of the German artillery spotters. At around 0900hrs the café's large front window was blown out, forcing us to crawl around on the floor in order to treat the wounded. However, we did manage to load four priority patients onto one of our half-track ambulances, but it was then damaged by tank fire and rendered unserviceable."

At that moment the fog surrounding the town lifted, revealing a skirmish line of some 30 enemy tanks between Vaux and Bourcy. "Luckily the four casualties in the half-track were unharmed and we managed to bring them back to the aid station," Prior continues. Despite the fact that Desobry had his CP in a schoolhouse, diagonally opposite the presbytery, LaPrade decided to establish his own HQ slightly further south along the main road at the DeMontigny house. At that moment the colonel believed that the sturdy property would afford him better protection against incoming artillery fire. The window of the "operations room" was immediately boarded up and barricaded for additional security.

After picking up a helmet and an M1A1 carbine, Bob Harwick was directed by Capt Warren to LaPrade's new CP. As the major walked away a mortar shell exploded nearby and Warren was hit in both wrists by shrapnel. "The main road was partially blocked by a huge tree and beyond that two half-tracks were burning. Across the street, I noticed a jeep partially buried under a collapsed wall and several houses in flames. Mortar shells rained down through the smoke, sending rubble flying everywhere." When Harwick reported for duty, Desobry and LaPrade were already in the poorly lit "Ops Room" desperately trying to coordinate B Co, 705th TD Bn and various company commanders, using a single, 1:100,000 scale map!

As Harwick was setting up a message center in an adjoining chamber, the maintenance officer from 10th Armored Division, Capt James Rewell, pulled up outside in his recovery vehicle. Moments after the company commanders had left the building, a shell burst through the window killing LaPrade instantly. The blast also seriously wounded Rewell while Desobry was struck in the head and face by shrapnel. It would appear that Rewell's vehicle might have compromised the CP after being spotted by one of the enemy FOs.

Like it or not, Bob Harwick was now in command, and after a quick consultation with Maj Charles Hustead (who replaced Desobry as armored task force commander) he continued organizing the defense around the town. During the late afternoon, elements of C Co, 705th TD Bn were called forward from Foy to assist. At the time there was little or no communication between Combat Command B and 506th Regimental HQ.

Word soon leaked about Desobry's earlier request for withdrawal and confusion over the order only grew worse after the major was wounded, as Capt Prior recalls: "Since we had no functioning transport or litters [stretchers], I thought about surrendering along with my patients but apart from the café's owners, none of my staff would agree to the idea." Luckily, at that moment a platoon from the 705th TD Bn were outside on the road with their Shermans and Dr Prior grabbed his chance. "Using the doors from the café, we strapped all of our wounded [including Maj Desobry and Capt Rewell – who, after regaining consciousness, discovered he was wearing LaPrade's helmet] to the tanks and headed for Bastogne." Shortly after leaving Noville, the small armored force came under enemy tank fire causing further casualties. After a 3-hour delay the convoy eventually made it to a casualty collection point, possibly the main medical facility located at the Catholic Seminary in Bastogne, where the 501st PIR also had their Regimental HQ.

After discharging his patients, Dr Prior established another aid station to serve the 20th Armored Infantry Bn, in a large commercial garage on Rue de Vivier. Two days later (December 21), due to lack of suitable heating, Prior was forced to relocate to a three-storey house (where a Chinese restaurant now stands) on the southern edge of town along the Route de Neufchâteau.

Back in Noville, Bob Harwick sent a report to Regimental HQ outlining the situation and requested another doctor to replace Warren and Ryan. Harwick recalls: "The casualties were gathered up and I sent for a couple of 2.5-ton trucks and litters which duly arrived accompanied by our regimental dentist, Capt Samuel 'Shifty' Feiler." As it grew dark the enemy shellfire decreased, making the job of loading the casualties much easier. Medic T/5 Owen Miller, who had been working diligently at the aid station, helped to load the wounded from 1st Bn onto the transport. "It was only when they had gone that I realized Captain Warren still had my very expensive Parker 51 fountain pen," recalls Miller.

As he was about to depart, Feiler, who hailed from New York, offered Ryan a lift to Foy – which he graciously accepted. During the short journey, Barney loaned "Shifty" his pristine Walther P38 pistol just in case he got into any trouble. The wounded were taken to the seminary (which later became the divisional hospital) before being evacuated to the 326th Airborne Medical Co Clearing Station near Herbaimont. "After the casualties had gone," recalls Bob Harwick, "we used the lull in enemy activity to lay mines and flares in preparation for the inevitable final attack. However, we had lost all radio communications with the 506th Regimental HQ and were unable to inform them that we were now virtually surrounded."

Beneath the iron sky – Foy and Recogne

Previously, on December 19, as 3rd Bn marched north during the early afternoon along the N30, they had been perplexed to see increasing numbers of troops from the 28th ID and remnants of the 9th Armored Division heading toward them. Many of the beleaguered troops were horrified when they found out the paratroopers were advancing north to close with the enemy. "These people had cold weather clothing and seemed far better prepared for a winter war than we were," recalls Ed Shames. "The only extra garments we had at our disposal were either discarded by the 'Keystone Boys' or liberated later from the Germans!"

Ralph Bennett remembers, "We wouldn't let any of those soldiers pass by without taking every round of ammunition that they had in their possession." Harley Dingman was unarmed except for a .38 Smith

Foy Overview, December 1944

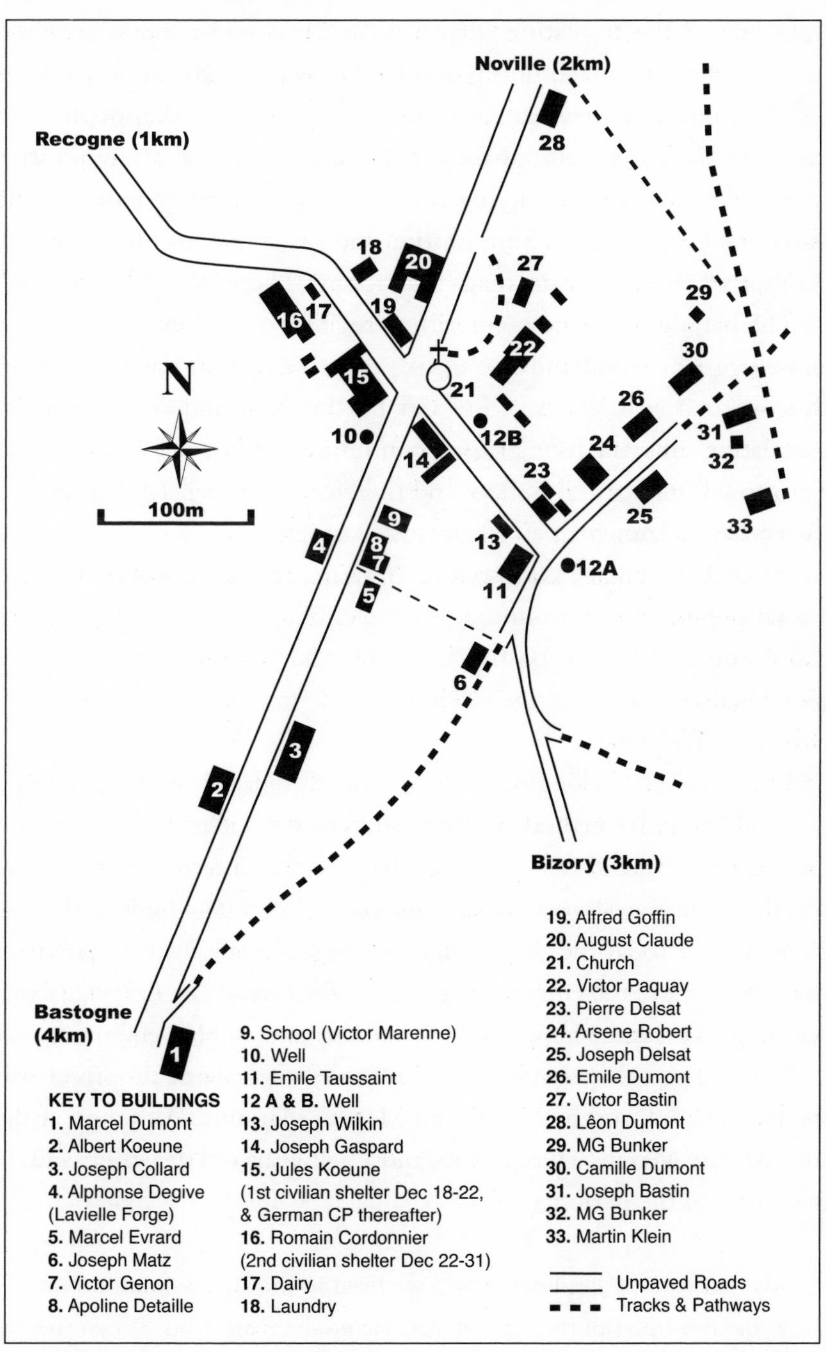
Noville (2km)
Recogne (1km)
Bastogne (4km)
Bizory (3km)
N
100m
1
2
3
4
5
6
7
8
9
10
11
12A
12B
13
14
15
16
17
18
19
20
21
22
23
24
25
26
27
28
29
30
31
32
33
KEY TO BUILDINGS
1. Marcel Dumont
2. Albert Koeune
3. Joseph Collard
4. Alphonse Degive (Lavielle Forge)
5. Marcel Evrard
6. Joseph Matz
7. Victor Genon
8. Apoline Detaille
9. School (Victor Marenne)
10. Well
11. Emile Taussaint
12 A & B. Well
13. Joseph Wilkin
14. Joseph Gaspard
15. Jules Koeune (1st civilian shelter Dec 18-22, & German CP thereafter)
16. Romain Cordonnier (2nd civilian shelter Dec 22-31)
17. Dairy
18. Laundry
19. Alfred Goffin
20. August Claude
21. Church
22. Victor Paquay
23. Pierre Delsat
24. Arsene Robert
25. Joseph Delsat
26. Emile Dumont
27. Victor Bastin
28. Lêon Dumont
29. MG Bunker
30. Camille Dumont
31. Joseph Bastin
32. MG Bunker
33. Martin Klein
Unpaved Roads
Tracks & Pathways

& Wesson revolver and managed to take a Thompson submachine gun from one of the retreating infantrymen. In contrast, other armored troops (belonging to Combat Command B) were handing out whatever spare ammunition they had, as Hank DiCarlo recalls: "Although these guys also looked exhausted they still managed to find a few positive words of encouragement. Lying beside a weapons carrier, in the middle of the road, was a pile of ammunition and I was able to collect enough .45 ACP to charge all nine magazines for my Thompson [270 rounds]."

The battalion was now entering a region covered by dense spruce and evergreen woodland not unlike North Carolina, or the Brecon Beacons in south Wales. Dissected by the N30 and overlooked by undulating hills, the tiny farming community of Foy was built around a crossroad in a natural hollow and therefore a perfect staging area for the enemy to launch an attack against Bastogne.

In 1944 the village consisted of 26 farms and dozens of barns with a total population of around 130 people. The close-knit community was dominated by the Bastin, Dumont, and Koeune families. Some individuals worked for the d'Hoffschmidt family who lived in the château at Recogne.

Except for that belonging to the d'Hoffschmidt family there were no cars and the only method of transportation was either by horse or on foot. At the crossroad central to the village on the eastern side of the N30 was the dour gray stone Chapelle Ste-Barbe, originally built in the late 16th century. Today the chapel's main distinguishing feature is a poignant inscription above the entrance that reads, "*Hic Domus Dei Et Porta Coeli*," meaning "This is the House of God and the Gate to Heaven."

Close to the chapel and located on the same side of the street was the local school, run by Victor and Marthe Marenne. Although at the time Maguy Marenne was just six and a half years old she still has vivid memories of the period:

> My dad was the headmaster and we lived in private accommodation at the front part of the schoolhouse facing the main road. When the

> Germans launched their attack into the Ardennes, most of the men in the village over the age of 17 headed west, attempting to escape from the inevitable forced labor. Along with a nephew and many others my dad went to Recogne – leaving mom behind to look after my brother, two sisters, and me. The idea was to return after the Germans had passed by, but of course that never happened. On December 18, we watched the first American convoys [from Task Force Desobry] moving through the village en route to Noville. In the evening, as the sound of battle began to draw nearer, we went across the street to Jules Koeune's house on the corner, diagonally opposite the church. The Koeunes (who were related to my mother) ran a successful fruit and vegetable business and allowed us to shelter in their substantial cellar.

The large basement was accessed by a small flight of stone steps that led to a sunken doorway. The low, brick, vaulted cellar was divided into four separate areas where the Koeunes kept their market stock. The storage rooms were connected by a long corridor studded at regular intervals by four slit windows that faced east onto the N30 at ground level. The cellar ran the entire length of the impressive two-storey building. At its center was a concrete staircase that allowed access to the house. The basement quickly began to fill up with locals. "When the American paratroopers began to dig in around us there were about 45 people, predominantly women and children, sheltering in the basement," recalls Maguy. "One of the younger girls, Ghislaine Bastin, was heavily pregnant, and despite the extreme circumstances, it didn't stop the older women from socially isolating her because she was unmarried."

Other families such as the Roberts decided to abandon everything before the Americans arrived. As Jules Robert, who was nine years old in 1944, recalls, "On December 19, my parents (Arséne and Victoire) took the entire family, including my grandfather, Henri, to Recogne, where we found temporary shelter in the basement at Café Dominique." The small hostelry owned by the Dominique family was attached to their farm and located along the road leading to Cobru, a short distance from the church.

"After about three days, the fighting became so bad that we decided to leave the Dominiques and move west to my uncle who lived at Longchamps," continues Jules. "As we were approaching Monaville, shells were flying over our heads, mainly from the direction of the Fazone Woods. When we got to Longchamps it was deserted so we headed southwest to Champs, where dad had a friend who he hoped would give us shelter. The heavy money box full of coins that I'd been carrying became a liability so my dad decided to bury it and come back later when things calmed down."

Shortly after the Robert family departed, the Dominiques also decided to leave. According to 21-year-old Roger Dominique, "It became so dangerous that my parents were forced to abandon their animals and escape further northwest to Bertogne."

When the Roberts reached Champs, the Germans had mined the road. Jules remembers:

> The soldiers ushered us through the roadblock and we found ourselves outside of the encirclement, although we didn't realize it at the time. We stayed at Champs for two days before continuing on through enemy lines towards Houmont (southwest of Bastogne), where we found shelter in the basement of Sulbout Farm, which was being used by the Germans as an aid station. The French-speaking medics who occupied the other side of the cellar seemed unconcerned with our presence and even fed us from time to time. The wounded were constantly being brought in and many of them seemed to be teenagers screaming for their mothers.
>
> The Germans utilized any mode of transport they could lay their hands on, including captured American jeeps, motorcycles with sidecars, and even civilian vehicles. The image of the wounded and the blood-soaked floor is something my family will not forget, and never quite knowing what the Germans were going to do with us was a terrible feeling.
>
> Eventually, Sulbout was destroyed by fire and we moved to another farm nearby owned by the Clarence family. We had just made ourselves comfortable in the kitchen when the German medics transferred their

aid station and forced us yet again down into the cellar. One morning I happened to be upstairs in the kitchen with my sister Denise (then aged ten) when we witnessed something quite strange. A German officer was lying on a couch and seemed to be unwell when another soldier came in and made the man a cup of coffee. Moments later the officer collapsed and two other men arrived, wrapped his body in tarpaulin and threw it in the back of a vehicle before driving away toward some nearby woodland. We never did find out what was going on.

A few days later, when the Germans needed more space, we were asked to leave. My dad had no idea what we were going to do as we packed up our meager belongings and set off down the road. We had not gone far when intense rifle fire forced us into a nearby barn. Bullets were bouncing off the steel girders and we were in no doubt that whoever was shooting seemed to be targeting us. Eventually the firing stopped and we continued south to Lavaselle and a big farm owned by Henri Cop, who, along with his family, was in the process of evacuating. Although the house had been burned to the ground the surrounding barns were still habitable. Mr Cop said it would be OK for us to stay in one of the stables with the animals which we knew would provide us with warmth. We couldn't believe our luck when a day or so later (around January 15/16) the Americans arrived and set up a field kitchen. We stayed at the farm for about a month and were fed like kings, unlike many of the troops who had been trapped inside the pocket during the encirclement.

All the king's men – Philippe's story

Overlooking Recogne, about a mile northwest of Foy, is the Château d'Hoffschmidt, known locally as "The Whitehouse." Built in 1842, the beautiful three-storey manor house still belongs to the d'Hoffschmidt family, who own some of the surrounding farmland as well as the dense area of woods along the ridge overlooking Recogne and Foy known as the Bois Champay (Champay Woods). In 1944, two large ornamental ponds adorned the grounds in front of the château, which was also planted with European beech trees to create a luxurious rural idyll for the family – who have played an important role in the community for the last 400 years.

Before the war, Baron François d'Hoffschmidt employed dozens of local people as domestic staff, forestry, and farm workers. At Christmas, Francois would personally wrap and give presents to local children, who were always excited to visit the "big house." At the time around one-third of the properties in Recogne were owned by the family, the front doors of which were painted in a burgundy color with a white diagonal stripe. Located on the southeastern edge of the château grounds was a large tenant farm run by Nestor Degives, from where there was direct road access to the ridge and the Bois Champay. This logging track, known locally as Route Madame, would later become vital to the Americans during their occupation of the woods.

François d'Hoffschmidt's son, Philippe, was 15 years old in 1944 and, despite his privileged upbringing, did not escape unscathed. "My mother Juliette died in 1940 during the early stages of the occupation and my father, who had been wounded in World War I, joined the National Movement of Belgium (NMB)." François gathered intelligence for the resistance in Bastogne and also harbored several "divers" (people hiding from the authorities) in the château and nearby stable. "After the liberation in September 1944, things quickly returned to normal," recalls Philippe. "On Monday, December 18, 1944, I was attending college at Marche-en-Famenne, when we heard about the German attack and the following day asked the principal if I could return to Bastogne. Initially he denied permission but after convincing him that I would go to Namur, I managed to catch the last tram back to Bastogne that halted on the edge of the city around 4pm." The long-distance tram service ran from Arlon on the Luxembourg border to Bastogne's southern railway station (Gare du Sud) before continuing northwest for 30 miles to Marche-en-Famenne. The service was closed in 1951 and today nothing remains to show the tramline ever existed. Philippe continues:

While making my way home, I was stopped along the N30 by troops from the SR (Belgian Secret Army) and sent back to Bastogne. Once out of sight, I headed west through the woods toward Savy in an attempt to reach Recogne. Approaching the château at Rolley, I came under several bursts of machine-gun fire. Not sure what to do, I took cover and began to sing the nursery rhyme "Frere Jacques" in French. The gunfire stopped, and, still singing, I walked forward, until an American soldier [502nd PIR] stood up, motioned to me with his hand and said, "Hello boy, come in." Once inside the castle, I bumped into my eldest sister, Gabrielle, with her two children who told me that my father, three other sisters, a cousin, and some of the domestic staff had already left Rolley and gone northwest to Givry. That night, as American artillery fire intensified, the château began to fill with civilians.

The following morning (December 20) I decided to catch up with my father, and before leaving said goodbye to my sister, not knowing if I would ever see her again. Approaching Champs, the outgoing American artillery fire was so close I could feel the pressure waves against my chest. Not long afterwards I arrived at the Gelis Farm in Givry and began to ask if anyone had seen François d'Hoffschmidt. Initially people were reluctant to say anything until they realized he was my father. I learned that he had joined a larger group who were now heading to Givroulle [not far from Crossroad X where 326th Airborne Medical Co had been attacked and captured the night before].

As I was making my way to Givroulle I met up with my father and the rest of the family who had just been turned back by a German roadblock. Returning to Givry we joined around 25 other people sheltering in the house and stable at Gelis Farm. The next day (December 21) the Germans arrived [from 26.Volksgrenadier-Division] with their horses and carts. I was surprised to see that among them were dozens of soldiers, who couldn't have been more than 16 years old, using pushchairs to carry machine guns and ammunition. These teenage troops were very aggressive and could barely be controlled by their officers and senior NCOs. On Christmas Eve the entire village was occupied and we ended up sharing the kitchen of the farmhouse with the soldiers. That evening to celebrate Christmas we managed to steal a few cups of hot mulled wine from the Germans. Many soldiers were coming back to the farm from the front lines for some rest and dozens of horse-drawn ambulances were also bringing in wounded. As the situation became more desperate the troops were immediately sent back into combat. One of these told me that he had been fighting non-stop for the last 56 hours and was now a physical and nervous wreck.

Around this time all of the able-bodied amongst us were ordered forward into the front line [now at Champs] to dig trenches. I took my father's place on the work detail and spent the next three days digging defensive positions 500 yards away from the American lines. The Germans didn't care if we lived or died and digging in the frozen ground was back-breaking work. By accident, one man broke the handle of a pick and then a shovel. Claiming it was sabotage, the Germans took the poor fellow to one side and shot him in the head.

When we returned to the farm, I told my family and a few other men to hide in a nearby barn amongst the cows, where I knew we would be warm and hopefully safe from further work details. Some new troops arrived and rounded up anyone they could find but luckily failed to check the stalls where we were hiding. This might seem strange but despite being hungry everyone respected the fact that the livestock still belonged to somebody, and therefore very few were ever slaughtered by the refugees or the Germans – besides, after what we had seen everyone felt that the American forces would soon prevail. On the morning of January 12/13, we were liberated by the troops from the 17th Airborne Division and I immediately headed back to Rolley to look for my sister and her two children. It had been nearly three weeks since any of us had changed our clothes so you can imagine how we must have smelt. Before we could all return to Recogne, my father had to get permission from the military authorities in Bastogne, which was denied for several days, because they said our home was designated as unsafe. In the meantime, while waiting for permission, we stayed in Savy with the Mayor of Longchamps, Gustave Stilmant. On January 16, the authorities granted permission for us to return, but despite having all the correct paperwork we were stopped by American forces near Monaville at Belle Fontaine Farm. A couple of days later we made it back to what was left of the château and found the house occupied by the Americans, who allowed us to live in the basement where the kitchen was located. After the war, my father, who had just about lost everything, went to the bank and borrowed enough money to repair the château and rebuild his other properties … which in a way became his legacy to Recogne.

One man – one bullet

When 3rd Bn reached Foy during the late afternoon of December 19, the men were deployed along a 2-mile front stretching from the railway line (that ran southeast through Bastogne to Gouvy) to Recogne in the northwest.

"It was still daylight when we arrived," recalls Jim Martin. "Col Sink personally directed us toward our final locations. To me, the colonel never looked flustered, no matter how bad the situation might have seemed." Sink selected a handful of men from G Co 1 Ptn including Ewell Martin to act as security while he drove into Noville for a meeting with 1st Bn. "I can remember watching for snipers as the colonel surveyed the town which was burning. The stench of the fire was horrible and it is something that I have never forgotten."

Back in Foy, G Co moved west and took up positions facing toward Recogne. At the time nobody imagined that Foy would become so important to the outcome of the campaign. Potentially the road through the two villages afforded safe passage for any enemy troops and vehicles moving northwest toward the high ground overlooking Hemroulle. "That first night," recalls Jim Martin, "1 Ptn were on the left flank aligning with 3/502 [led by LtCol John Stopka – who were holding

3/506 Line of defense, Foy
December 19, 1944

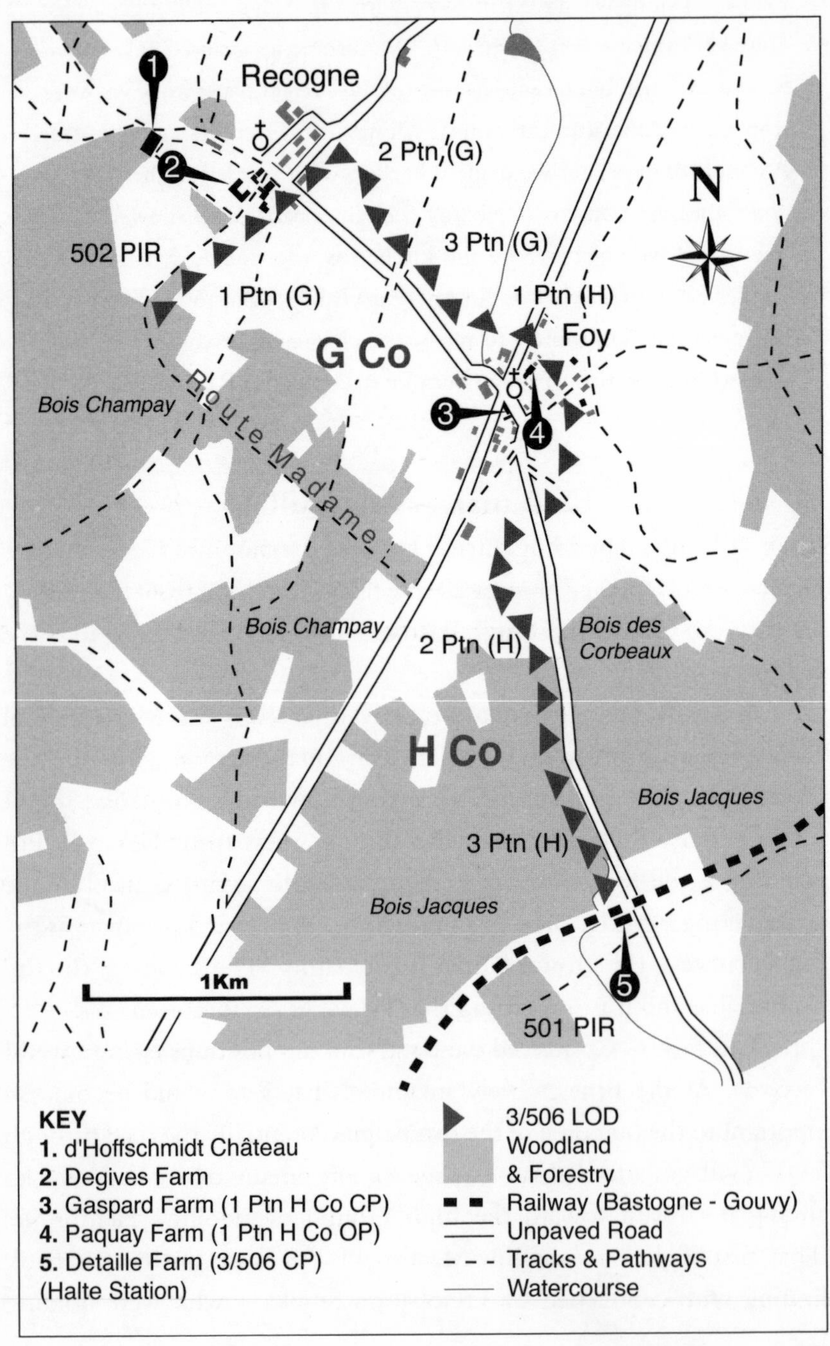

Recogne
2 Ptn (G)
N
3 Ptn (G)
502 PIR
1 Ptn (G)
1 Ptn (H)
Foy
G Co
Bois Champay
Route Madame
Bois Champay
Bois des Corbeaux
2 Ptn (H)
H Co
Bois Jacques
3 Ptn (H)
Bois Jacques
1Km
501 PIR
KEY
1. d'Hoffschmidt Château
2. Degives Farm
3. Gaspard Farm (1 Ptn H Co CP)
4. Paquay Farm (1 Ptn H Co OP)
5. Detaille Farm (3/506 CP)
(Halte Station)
3/506 LOD
Woodland & Forestry
Railway (Bastogne - Gouvy)
Unpaved Road
Tracks & Pathways
Watercourse

the line to Longchamps]. 2 Ptn (my platoon) held the central sector, and 3 Ptn were on our right connecting with H Co [H/506] who for the most part were deployed on the eastern side of the N30." The Line of Defense (LOD) for G Co began in the west on the edge of the Bois Champay and ran down Route Madame past the Degives Farm and Château d'Hoffschmidt along the northeastern edge of Recogne, before turning due south across open ground paralleling the road back into Foy.

Col Patch established his CP at Detaille Farm, located on the extreme right flank of 3rd Bn's LOD. The sizeable two-storey house had only recently been abandoned by the Detaille family and was marked on the map as "Halte Station" because in the 1920s the building had been the rail terminus for Bizory. The sector allocated to H Co followed a secondary road that ran perpendicular to the N30 for about 1,500 yards to the railway embankment at Detaille Farm. Initially 1st Lt Bob Stroud (H Co 1 Ptn) was told to deploy his men across the N30 on the extreme northern edge of Foy.

Stroud placed Sgt Lou Vecchi's 2nd Squad on the left of the main road while Sgt Hank DiCarlo's 1st Squad and Sgt Bob Martin's 3rd Squad occupied the area immediately to the right. Sgt Walter Patterson's 4th Squad remained in reserve. "Bob Martin was always a bit aloof," recalls Lou Vecchi. "Bob's Dad was a police officer and for some reason he thought himself as being better than some of the other guys in the platoon. Back in September, Martin had taken a lot of criticism during the attack on Eindhoven after he withdrew his squad at a critical moment, leaving our right flank with I Co completely exposed."

Along with communications sergeant Gordon Yates and Cpl Nick Snyder, Stroud established his CP in the Gaspard Farm at the crossroads in the center of Foy. A short while later Stroud received orders from Capt Walker to redeploy to the railway line over on the right flank to help bolster the defenses of 3 Ptn. "At first it didn't register quite how far away it was until Sgt Martin came back and told me he was having a hell of a time reaching it." After a brief conversation with Alex Andros, Bob decided to deploy all four of his squads locally in a line because of the wide frontal area the company was now expected to cover. Shortly afterwards a decision was made by Battalion to bring elements of I Co out of reserve (who were desperately short of rifles) and place them into the area between Stroud and Clark Heggeness (2 Ptn). I Co were sent east with what weapons they could muster, toward the railway line, and deployed around the battalion CP. Manny Barrios was part of that group. "I took a couple of guys and set up a forward observation post (OP) close to the railway and began feeding information back to the battalion via radio."

"Foy was so quiet when we arrived it seemed almost like a ghost town," recalls Vecchi, who was 23 years old at the time. "The only sound being made was by us as we dug in. I didn't see any civilians but noticed dozens of animals still in their pens and stalls which were adjoined to some of the houses. As they appeared to be hungry, especially the pigs, we thought it best to release all the livestock we subsequently came across. I deployed my squad on the western side of the road across the open ground with the church behind us over to the right. At one point 3rd Squad were on my left but I don't remember seeing anyone from G Co or the 502nd enter our area."

Lt Stroud gathered the NCOs and told them that the company was going to create a defensive bubble around the village. "As my squad was straddling the main road," recalls Hank DiCarlo, "I established a roadblock facing north controlled by Jack Grace and his machine-gun crew (consisting of Pfc Jimmy Igoe and Pfc Wilber Johnson), while my bazooka team dug a large two-man fire trench several yards further east to protect against incursions from the open fields to our right." Two-man bazooka teams like this proved crucial during the campaign and ultimately accounted for around 40 enemy tanks and SPGs. Leaving his assistant Cpl Luther Myers (York, Pennsylvania) in charge of the squad, Hank set off with Lou Vecchi to look for a decent observation post from which to direct fire. "Along the way we took anything we could carry from the farms and barns to keep us warm," recalls Vecchi. Behind Hank's position, adjacent to the church was a three-storey farmhouse, the upper floors of which afforded 1 Ptn perfect views across the area to the northeast. "After reporting my positions to the company CP, I made the rounds to be sure my guys were all dug in and ready to deal with any eventuality."

The H Co line blended with G Co to create a semi-circular pocket around Foy, which then dog-legged southwest dissecting the Bizory road, before meandering in a northerly direction, through the Bois Jacques (Jacques Woods) to Detaille Farm. Back in Foy, the property Hank and Lou selected for the OP had two improvised concrete grain shafts built into the back wall descending to a storage facility beneath the building. "We took it in turns through the night to 'stag on' in the OP where there was a small window overlooking the northern approaches," remembers Vecchi.

Like many others, the Paquay family who owned the farm had taken refuge in the basement of the Koeune house across the street. At dusk a recon patrol from Volksgrenadier-Regiment 78 appeared through the mist, walking along the N30 into the H Co front line. As one of the enemy scouts cautiously moved forward, he was challenged and mortally wounded at close range. After a brief exchange of gunfire, the enemy patrol slipped away, leaving their colleague lying sprawled in the road. As the German still appeared to be alive, 23-year-old battalion medic T/5 Johnny Gibson was called forward to assist. "The casualty had suffered a massive wound to the chest and his neck was still warm as I pressed my fingers against the jugular but found no pulse," recalls Gibson. "A couple of the H Co guys told me that as the Volksgrenadier approached their positions, he was nonchalantly whistling and had his rifle slung over his shoulder. I have often wondered if perhaps the man actually wanted to be captured." The corpse remained in the road for the next three weeks and was eventually covered by a thick layer of ice and snow.

Later that night as DiCarlo was doing his rounds he stopped to spend a few moments with Pfc Joe Harris. "Carefully shielding a cigarette, Harris, who was my last man on the right, remarked, 'Whatta you think Hank? Is this where the crap finally hits the fan?' Wrapping the ends of a blanket around me, I replied, 'I really don't know, Joe, but from the look of it, somebody is going to catch hell around here and I hope to God it's not going to be us!"

It was getting dark when Clark Heggeness handed a basic sketch map to his assistant, 2nd Lt Harry Begle, who recalls, "I had just ordered six of our men to dig in along the dirt road to the right of 1 Ptn when Clark asked me to locate the railroad and establish contact with the 501st – who were supposed to be holding the ground east of the tracks. We didn't even have a password at that point so I was seriously concerned about getting shot by one of their guys. After walking about 500 yards to the edge of the woods, I couldn't find the railway [which had been covered by a light dusting of snow] and decided to report back to Clark before bedding down for the night in a large haystack directly opposite our position."

While Begle was on patrol, 1st Squad leader Sgt Ken Johnson was making sure his replacements knew exactly what was expected of them. "Private Franklin 'Frank' Kneller was only 19 and by far the most inexperienced, and as like me he also came from New Jersey and went to school in the next town, I kept him by my side." The open ground between the trees now occupied by 2 Ptn had previously been used as a quarry, leaving the area littered with dozens of holes, as Ken recalls: "Kneller and I occupied one of the larger pits that afforded enough space for both of us to share quite comfortably. We were told that I Co was to our left somewhere in the woods, although personally I never actually saw them." At the time the line held by 2 and 3 platoons was supported by a 75mm howitzer from 321st GFA and a .50cal gun mounted on a half-track from Task Force Desobry. "It was a nightmare," recalls Kneller. "The company as a whole didn't even have enough decent shovels to go around and the boots I'd been issued the day before were a couple of sizes too small!"

3 Ptn H Co was supposed to link up at the railway line near the 3rd Bn CP but the 501st were nowhere to be seen. In fact E and F/501 were actually located 1 mile further east at Bizory, with D Co in reserve no

more than 400 yards away in a block of woods behind Detaille Farm. Despite this the 501st were active around the 3rd Bn flank as witnessed by Al Cappelli. "I bumped into a soldier on patrol from E/501 who I knew from Jump School. We chatted for a while and I asked him about my hometown buddy Hank DiSimone who was also serving in the same company."

"3 Ptn took up positions in a wooded area [Bois Jacques]," recalls Alex Andros, who spoke with a slight lisp. "My assistant, 2nd Lt Willie Miller, dug in on our far-right flank. I believed in the buddy system of two men to a foxhole and placed each trench about 100 yards apart. However, the forest was so dense that a single enemy soldier could have marched between any of our positions without ever being seen."

A faint rumble of tanks could now be heard coming from the direction of Noville. Unable to communicate with 1st Bn, Col Sink was anxious to know if the road was still open and called on 2nd Lt Ed Shames for assistance. "As it was getting dark," recalls Ed, "Col Sink drove up in his jeep and asked me to mount a foot patrol from Foy northeast along the main road toward Noville." Sink told Shames that he should go no further than the haystacks on the southern edge of town. During the briefing, Shames was amused to see Maj Clarence Hester (regimental S3) and Capt Bill Leach (regimental S2) both crammed into the back seat of the vehicle alongside LtCol Robert Strayer (CO of 2/506).

By this time, Capt Richard Winters was on the 2nd Bn staff and 1st Lt Norman Dike was the new commander of E Co. Shames continues:

> Among the scouts I selected for the recon were Pvt Earl McClung, Pfc Wayne "Skinny" Sisk, Pvt Don "Cosmetic" Moon, Pvt Ed Stein [who had only just joined the platoon] and mortar man Pfc Rod Strohl. The heavy fog meant that visibility was down to a few yards as we carefully worked our way into the blackness along the road. On the outskirts of Noville, I placed my guys in all round defense before moving forward the last few hundred yards with Strohl.

> Peering into the mist we could just make out the silhouettes of what looked like the haystacks that Col Sink had told me about. Strohl then commented that they were the funniest damn haystacks he'd ever seen. Suddenly we heard engines being started and it was then we realized they were actually Kraut tanks [from 2.Panzer-Division]. I put my lips to Rod's ear and whispered, "Let's get the hell out of here," and carefully retraced our steps back to the boys. Once clear we double-timed back to the northern edge of Foy and reported to Sink, who inquired, "Well, Shames, what did you find?" "We counted 18 tanks sir," I replied. Strayer then asked, "What type?" "Big ones," I spluttered, before continuing, "… I don't know, sir, we didn't hang around long enough to ask!" Strayer was not impressed and tried to order me back to physically identify the enemy armor but luckily Col Sink stepped in and dismissed me.

The colonel then instructed Shames and his platoon to join I Co and wait for further orders.

Earlier, 1st Lt Floyd Johnston from 1 Ptn I Co was told to take a patrol out beyond Recogne, as Len Goodgal recalls: "He couldn't get any volunteers, so finally I agreed and coerced Richie Shinn and Pvt Bob Steele into joining me. We moved out across the fields to a small wooded area at the bottom of the hill from where we could just about see some enemy tanks parked up. After returning to the LOD around midnight we reported our findings, and the following morning the area was bracketed by artillery."

A matter of life and death – disaster at Crossroad X

After stopping off to collect more wounded from the chapel at the Catholic Seminary in Bastogne, "Shifty" Feiler set off at 2130hrs for the 326th Airborne Medical Co Clearing Station at Ste-Ode near Herbaimont. Less than 30 minutes after leaving Bastogne the tiny convoy approached Crossroad X – the same place visited by LtCol Kinnard the previous afternoon.

The hospital was located in an open field behind a sparsely wooded area on the northern side of the N4. It was believed that any German attack would come from the east and therefore the medical facility would be well away from the danger zone. Earlier the convoy from 801st Airborne Ordnance Co had driven up from Bastogne and parked beyond the crossroad, as 1/Sgt Bob Higgins recalls: "Our commander, Capt John 'Pat' Patterson, had been ordered by the divisional supply officer, LtCol Carl Kohls, to proceed to the road junction and wait for further instructions. We could see a tank parked up nearby which gave us some feeling of security although we had our truck mounted with .50cal heavy machine guns, manned and ready for action."

Throughout the day dozens of empty supply vehicles returning to Mourmelon (which had overshot the crossroad) were directed south by the ordnance men along the N826 toward Libin. Later that evening, another convoy carrying gasoline and ammunition came up from Bastogne and parked behind the 801st. "Around 2000hrs we began to hear machine-gun fire in the distance," recalls Bob Higgins, whose jeep and trailer were the last in their convoy and therefore nearest to the crossroad. "Pat came down the line and told me that he had a bad feeling and we should move the vehicles and equipment as soon as possible."

Arriving from Bastogne, Shifty Feiler and his men thought it odd that every light in a nearby farmhouse should be switched on. Feiler had expected to see at least one MP directing traffic, but as his driver approached Crossroad X both vehicles were flagged down by a group of men dressed in civilian clothes. Feiler and his colleagues had unwittingly stumbled into the beginning of an attack against the medical facility by the 116.Panzergruppe. The fanatical spearhead of tanks, half-tracks, and vehicles (some captured previously from the 106th ID) had come from Houffalize via Bertogne and Givroulle, looking for a way around the river Our to Dinant, when they discovered the tents belonging to the hospital.

The enemy, who numbered around 100 men, merged with a large group of refugees before neutralizing the outposts covering the hospital's northern approaches. The Sherman tank that had been guarding the junction was quickly captured and employed by the Germans to destroy another OP further south. Back on the main road, Feiler was growing more and more suspicious when, after a couple of minutes, the first truck was ushered onto a nearby track. A stocky-looking man approached Feiler's vehicle and asked where they were going. Co-driver Sgt Dobbins replied, "326th Medical Hospital; we've got wounded men in the back – is there a problem?" After checking the rear of the lorry, the man politely asked Feiler's driver, "Pracky," to pull forward and park up behind the other vehicle. No sooner had he finished speaking when another small convoy arrived behind them. It was then that Feiler, who was Jewish and spoke German, realized his worst fears as the man barked an order in his native tongue and enemy soldiers appeared on the road from all directions.

As instructed, Dobbins climbed out of the cab along with Feiler (who was now clutching the pistol given to him earlier by Barney Ryan) and began guiding Pracky toward the other vehicle. "As the Krauts moved toward the convoy of trucks, I heard Captain Feiler call out to me, 'Dobbins, bring the vehicles back – quick!' As we reversed out onto the road, the Germans were focusing their attention on the other convoy and took the first three drivers prisoner. Things got a little confused for a few minutes, and thank heavens they did because Pracky and the other driver were able to reverse both of our vehicles onto the road and proceed toward the junction. At that point we were standing behind Pracky's vehicle when all hell broke loose." The attack started when a group of German half-tracks entered the field behind the N4 and began spraying the tents with machine-gun fire.

Further up the line Bob Higgins got the shock of his life. "As we were getting ready to move, our convoy came under enemy cannon fire," he recalls. "Fortunately for us the 20mm shells were set to explode at a much greater range. However, a few hit one of the ammunition trucks parked behind me." A driver in the other convoy opened fire with a

.50cal machine gun, and the Germans blasted away with everything they had, devastating the cab before doing the same thing to the others. Feiler and his team threw themselves into a ditch as the vehicles burst into flames, including their own, which still contained the wounded who never uttered a sound as the fuel erupted around them.

While the firefight was raging, Feiler's group ran over to the house (still ablaze with light) and hid behind a pile of sugar beet. A few seconds later the 20mm cannon began to target the building. The paratroopers rushed to the rear of the property and made their way behind an embankment to a nearby field where they stopped for a moment and listened to the escalating commotion. The 801st were now returning fire into the woods opposite with their .50cal machine guns as they began to pull out along the N4 toward Marche. Several men from the black American 333rd Field Artillery Group (who by coincidence happened to be nearby) and some hospital staff came through the woods and jumped onto Bob Higgins' trailer.

Back at the crossroad, in a panic, thinking he was going to be captured, Feiler threw his pistol (the P38 given to him earlier by Barney Ryan) into a ditch and headed toward the escaping convoy. Dobbins recalls, "I could see the blackout lights on one of the last vehicles and sprinted after it." Luckily Feiler and the others managed to climb aboard another vehicle belonging to the 801st and make good their escape.

Around midnight, the gunfire finally stopped when the enemy troops entered the hospital. Some of the more critically injured patients, who were awaiting transfer to the 107th Evacuation Hospital at Libin, were brutally murdered in their beds, while officers like William Desobry were spared. The divisional surgeon, LtCol David Gold, surrendered the company and was given 30 minutes to gather his staff, wounded, and equipment for transportation. After being anesthetized for an emergency operation, Desobry regained consciousness in the back of an ambulance, completely unaware of the events that had just taken place around him.

The situation facing the 801st was one of complete chaos, as Bob Higgins reveals:

It was pouring with rain as we drove away, causing my driver to crash into the vehicle in front. At the same time we were rear-ended by another truck loaded with hand grenades, seriously injuring the two guys from the 333rd Artillery Group who were riding on our trailer. Worse still, one of the medics [possibly Pvt Henry Sullivan] on another trailer was crushed and died the following morning.

My jeep was completely wrecked, but luckily two of our guys had abandoned another when their trailer overturned. I managed to uncouple the twisted tow cart and pile all of our equipment in the back of the second vehicle. Further down the road two more of our trucks (carrying vitally important spares) broke down and we told the drivers that a recovery vehicle would be sent out as soon as possible. A short while later we caught up with the rear echelon of our convoy who had stopped at the pontoon bridge over the Our.

I moved forward on foot to see what was happening and walked into a heated argument between a major and a tanker, who, it transpired, was guarding the bridge and flatly refusing to blow it up. The technical sergeant, who was commanding a Sherman, told the officer (whose vehicle was blocking the traffic) to get out of the way and that he would blow the bridge when he decided. The officer acquiesced and we trundled on and eventually caught up with the rest of our outfit who had been redirected south along a gravel road toward St Hubert. Capt Patterson wanted to stay here for the night. But when we found out the engineers who were occupying the village didn't have any explosives to demolish a nearby bridge and absolutely no heavy weapons, we decided to continue on. Luckily a local farmer and his very attractive wife acted as our guides and we spent the rest of the night working our way via St Hubert to Neufchâteau. En route we came across a Canadian Army logging detachment blocking the road seemingly unconcerned with the urgency until we informed them that the Germans were coming! After informing VIII Corps HQ (who knew nothing of the attack), Capt Patterson reported to Bastogne and had only just returned to Neufchâteau when the enemy cut the road.

Although this disaster caused the virtual collapse of the 101st Airborne's second echelon medical facilities, it could have been much worse. About half an hour before 116.Panzergruppe arrived, the commander of the 326th, Maj William Barfield, had led the first evacuation to Libin, taking with him five ambulances and a number of medical staff. Luckily, during the 20-mile trip back to Herbaimont, Barfield's convoy and several others following were forced to return to Libin after the bridge at Sprimont was found to have been destroyed. This small stroke of good fortune meant that over 100 medics were still available for duty and could be reabsorbed back into other medical facilities in Belgium and eventually Bastogne. By 0630hrs on December 20, it was officially confirmed that the bulk of the 326th Airborne Medical Co had been captured and the evacuation of future casualties would now be achieved through VIII Corps and the 429th Medical Collecting Co, who had recently relocated to a two-storey school building at Massul, near Molinfaing, 30 miles away toward Luxembourg.

One of the medics captured during the raid on the hospital was S/Sgt Ed Peterson, who recalls the events before and after the attack:

> We had packed and loaded everything at Mourmelon in a very short space of time. The tents were drenched with water and had to be drained before being "squared" away, and by about 1700hrs on Monday, December 18, everything was done. We left at 1900hrs and had only traveled about 5 miles when our convoy dwindled to about six vehicles and then two. Stopping constantly to check directions only served to delay us even further. S/Sgt Robert "Corky" Corcoran suggested several times that we should return to Mourmelon and try again the following morning. However, S/Sgt Stanley Rutter, who was up front in the cab, kept insisting that our colored driver knew where he was going.
>
> Around 0200hrs, we came across a vehicle which was being repaired, and the officer in charge told to us to stick around and follow him. The night was cold and we huddled together for warmth.

By dawn we caught up with our original convoy which was now parked bumper to bumper along the road. The early morning fog was now lifting, revealing a light dusting of snow, which had settled on the verges. Dozens of trucks and armored vehicles (some from the 28th ID) were heading toward the rear. Bastogne, we were told, was under fire so we stopped near a crossroads a few miles west of the town at a place called Herbaimont. Refugees from the north and east were running, riding, or walking as quickly as they were able and the look on their faces will be forever engraved on my memory.

S/Sgt John "Woody" Woodrich and I tried to discourage Capt Alvin Cohn from setting up our aid station in the field at Crossroad X but to no avail. Three tents were erected as a temporary measure, and by 1400hrs we were accepting our first casualties with another 50 on the way. Along with Corky, Woody, T/4 John Kalla, and T/5 Lark Meador, I was in the process of digging shelters close to the treatment tents but rain and other duties made the task impossible to complete before dark. At around 1700hrs we were able to get a cup of coffee and from then on everyone was flat out. Around 2100hrs, I went to look for some plasma with Corky and found Col Gold, Capt Ed Yeary, and Capt Jon Zumsteg standing beside a trailer deep in conversation.

The news wasn't great, and the boss informed us that the Germans were trying to encircle Bastogne which wouldn't be good for us. We returned to the tents and shortly afterwards heard the sound of heavy vehicles moving from north to south. For a moment we thought it was our own armor sent to protect us until a volley of .50cal [probably from the 801st] sent everyone diving to the ground. Bullets whistled through the canvas as more guns joined in the din. When the firing became more spasmodic, some of our officers shouted out in German that we were a hospital and totally unarmed. The Krauts paid no attention and continued with their attack. I was alongside Capt McKee, and can remember trying to keep a medical chest between me and the direction of fire. During one of the lulls, Maj Crandall asked me to help lower a patient on a nearby litter to the floor. As we did so,

T/4 James Query emerged from underneath the table, where much to our surprise he'd been hiding since the beginning of the attack.

More bullets ripped through the canvas above our heads. By now we could hear the enemy infantry outside calling to each other. Three or four trucks [part of the supply convoy ambushed at the crossroad] were now on fire as well as a German half-track, and although we had blacked out all the lights the whole place was lit up like a Christmas tree. The firing went on until around 2330hrs, at which time Col Gold was able to establish contact with a German officer, who accepted his surrender. We were told to board a group of vehicles and be ready to move out in 30 minutes after which time the firing would resume. As the patients were being loaded, a couple of us ran over to the foxholes we'd been digging earlier and grabbed as much personal equipment as we could find.

Those who had already boarded the trucks managed to get seats. When I called for everyone to shuffle forward and make more room, Capt David Habif chewed me out for appearing overly enthusiastic but I was just trying to make space for myself, Corky, Kalla, Woody, and Meador. While we were loading, ammunition on the burning vehicles opposite began to explode. One of my chums, who'd been busy with the patients, ran over and I pulled him up into our vehicle as it was pulling away. As we headed north toward Houffalize, the trucks passed small groups of enemy troops along the road. At one point we stopped and some of the officers were offloaded along with a few enlisted men and sent to care for German wounded. Our convoy continued through the night and at dawn halted for the first time. It was only then that we really had a chance to think about what had just happened. The boys who were in the other tents exchanged accounts and by piecing things together we figured that quite a few patients and staff had been killed and injured during the attack.

Some of the medics who had dug their foxholes in the nearby woods managed to escape back to American lines, using their prismatic compasses. "Along with two colleagues, we followed a southeasterly bearing for a couple of hours before stumbling across an isolated farm," recalls T/4 Lester Smith. "The family were kind enough to give us food and drink before we continued toward Bastogne." At first light, as the men approached Assenois, which was occupied by the 326th Airborne Engineer Bn, they were stopped by a sentry. "Of course we didn't know the password but managed to convince the outpost that we were Americans. After being called forward one at a time we were debriefed and eventually sent to the seminary."

Meanwhile the prisoners from the field hospital were now heading toward Luxembourg. The contents of Ed Peterson's musette bag, which he had thrown onto the trailer behind his truck, were about to fall out:

> I instructed Pvt Lucien Denis to stretch across and grab a hold before everything was lost. Half expecting my carton of cigarettes to be the first thing the Krauts were going to take, I handed a couple of packs to non-smoker T/5 Andy Roach for safe keeping, which turned out to be a wise move. I was wearing arctic issue clothing plus a pair of German officer's gloves, which I decided to keep in my possession despite being advised to get rid of them. Up until now no searches had been made and several of the men had pistols which they dismantled and threw away. The sight of the Germans using our vehicles back and forth along the way brought tears to my eyes… That day Wednesday, December 20, was one of the longest I've ever lived!
>
> Several times during the journey we had to leave the road, allowing the German armor priority. Dozens of wrecked American tanks and vehicles littered the fields and the bodies of our troops lay sprawled along hedgerows and on roads where passing traffic had ground them into the mud. At about 0300hrs on Thursday, we arrived in Luxembourg and detrucked at a small village. We were held in a school building which was surrounded by a large courtyard. After a couple hours' sleep they put us to work at first light unloading equipment from the trucks and trailers. The villagers

offered cookies and sugar and helped to refill our canteens. From here we were driven to Wiltz and herded into a theater, the walls of which were still adorned with posters advertising a "Christmas Dinner & Dance." Once inside we were lined up and searched and almost everyone went to great lengths to hide their valuables. When it came to me, one of the guards went through my musette bag and swiped a couple of packets of cigarettes, before throwing back my Zippo lighter which he declared was "kaput." As I walked across the room to join my buddies a young German officer, who spoke English, snatched away my gloves. I could see him discussing them with one of his colleagues who nodded affirmatively during the conversation. I thought they were going to give me a hard time, but the officer tossed them back and just said "Ja, German gloves." After being searched we were marched out of the building and lined up in formation, five abreast. Over the next couple of days we moved east on foot, across the German border, and joined around 500 other prisoners from the 28th and 106th infantry divisions. Our number had grown to about 1,800 by the time we reached a railway station at Gerolstein [some 30 miles from Wiltz] on Saturday, December 23.

We were marched to an old warehouse and each given a chunk of bread. The Krauts refused to speak to us in English but I understood enough to know that the building had just been vacated by another group of POWs who had been moved to the station to await transportation.

On Christmas Eve, the railway yards were attacked by the US Air Force. Toward evening we were lined up and searched again. This time the Germans made it clear that anyone subsequently caught hiding a lighter or matches would be shot. As an early "Christmas present" we were given a spoonful of sorghum [a cereal crop used for animal fodder], and as I was jostling in the "chow line" one of the other prisoners stole my belt kit and water bottle. At dusk two German ambulances drove up, loaded with GIs who had been injured during the attack on the railway. The poor devils had been trapped in boxcars and were slaughtered as the fighter bombers strafed the

> train. The guards finally unlocked the doors and the survivors used their blankets to form the letters "PW – US" in the snow. Although the fighters immediately called off the attack, 85 men were injured and 15 killed. Myself and several other medics went to work on the wounded as soon as they arrived – although the Krauts wouldn't lift a finger to help.

Shortly afterwards, the prisoners were marched to the station and placed aboard 40/8 boxcars before being transported to Stalag XII-A, situated 120 miles northeast of Bastogne, at Limburg near Koblenz in Germany.*

---

* Chapter 12 continues the narrative of life as a POW.

3

"Today is the only reality"

December 20, 1944

During the night many attempts were made by the enemy against 1st Bn at Noville to penetrate their perimeter using two or three tanks at a time supported by infantry. Heavy artillery and tank fire could be heard throughout the early hours, and at 0715hrs the reserve TD platoon moved forward to Noville. Accompanying the tanks were Lt Canham and the FOs from B Battery, 321st GFA, who had been ordered back to Foy the previous afternoon. The LOD was still covered in low cloud and dense fog that only served to amplify the sound of the enemy armor from 2.Panzer-Division now advancing on Noville from the east.

Luckily the German commander, Von Manteuffel, did not order Col von Lauchert, the CO of 2.Panzer-Division, to launch a frontal attack along the N30 against the southern edge of town. Instead, Manteuffel opted for a three-point envelopment (consisting of 20 tanks) that turned out to be a poor tactical decision. In a further attempt to close the net behind 1st Bn, Volksgrenadier-Regiment 78 were attached to the Panzers and sent several companies of infantry supported by more tanks to flank Foy and encircle Recogne. At 0800hrs, using all available roads, the enemy broke through the fog opposite H and I companies, while over on the western side of the LOD, G Co were hit hard by another small armored force.

In the afternoon, Tony McAuliffe drove to Neufchâteau for an emergency meeting with Gen Middleton about how best to coordinate the tanks from Combat Command B. Although the armor commander, Col Roberts, was also based in Bastogne at Hotel Lebrun, he was still under Troy Middleton's control. During the short conference, McAuliffe and Middleton discussed the possibilities of handing over responsibility of Combat Command B to the 101st. After returning to his CP, McAuliffe received a telephone call from Middleton, who gave permission for Tony to assume command of the tanks. Subsequently, Roberts relocated his HQ situated on Route de Marche to McAuliffe's bunker at Caserne Heintz. This dynamic change to the command structure would later prove vital to the outcome of the forthcoming battle.

That evening McAuliffe learned the enemy had crossed the Neufchâteau road and he was now completely surrounded and cut off from Gen Middleton and VIII Corps HQ. Before the encirclement only a handful of the 100-plus supply trucks that had been dispatched back to camps in France had returned to Bastogne. Although wire lines to Middleton had been cut, normal radio channels were still open; in addition, the specialist equipment maintained by VIII Corps Signal Co provided radio/telephone facilities throughout the forthcoming operation. The first air re-supply request was made but it was not possible to action due to the poor weather conditions.

Hotel Bastogne – feeding the prisoners

T/5 George Allen from the divisional Interrogation Prisoner of War team (IPW) was working 1 mile away from Caserne Heintz at the police station and recalls his first few days in Bastogne:

> Our nine-man team took over several buildings surrounding the Gendarmerie [along Route de Marche near the railway bridge] where the MPs had established a POW cage. During the afternoon of December 20, the tankers from Combat Command B started to bring in the first prisoners. Initially we arranged them by their regiments, battalions, and companies while lieutenants Vidor, Loeffler, and M/Sgt Charles Wahler (who was an Austrian political refugee) carried out the interrogations. The prisoners were telling us that most of

> their units were under strength and that they hadn't eaten properly for the last 48 hours. Most of the private soldiers were willing to talk while their senior NCOs and officers refused to cooperate. At the end of the day we had around 160 POWs in a large space above the stables with no chance of evacuating them due to the encirclement."

Virtually identical in construction to the Gendarmerie, the stable block (which included a number of small cells) was situated across a large courtyard from the police station (which in 2014 is being used for social housing). Allen continues:

> When I asked one of the MPs what plans they had for feeding the prisoners, he told me that they didn't have enough personnel for that sort of thing so the "Krauts" would have to go without.
>
> M/Sgt Wahler kindly gave me permission to establish a kitchen and scavenge for supplies. I discovered a large tub that had been used for laundering clothes which was ideal especially as it had a built in heating element. That evening I went over to the compound to see how the prisoners were doing. At the top of the stairs above the stables I came across a Volksgrenadier on a makeshift stretcher who had lost an arm and was in a bad way. I had no idea why the guy was not taken to the nearby aid station, but as I knelt down he whispered something about being hungry. One of the MPs handed over some crackers, which I placed in the man's mouth. I asked if he would care for a smoke. He nodded, and I lit and placed the cigarette between his lips. He inhaled several times and died in my arms.
>
> The next morning around 0800hrs, I went back to the POW compound and with permission from the MPs called for two cooks. In the event three men came forward and followed me downstairs to the laundry area in the courtyard. The prisoners set about scrubbing the tub with soap, using water from a nearby pump. I took the third guy and together we collected any food we could find from surrounding basements and cellars such as potatoes, oatmeal, apples,

> and purple-colored sugar beets. Nobody had seen this type of root vegetable before and we weren't sure if it was even edible. I decided to show the German officers, five of whom were locked up in one of the cells… They didn't know either and refused to sanction the sugar beet for use. When I got back to the "kitchen" the cooks had already tasted the white fleshy root and figured that it would make a perfect sweetener for porridge. As the men began to prepare the first meal we had time to chat. One came from Westphalia and had seen service in the Crimea. Another had been a steward on the airship *Hindenberg* while the third came from Austria like Wahler.
>
> As soon as the cauldron of food was ready, it was ladled into buckets and taken upstairs to feed the prisoners. All day long the three men cooked, dished up, scoured, and then prepared another serving. By 1600hrs, as it was starting to get dark, we had to call a halt to our makeshift restaurant for fear that the sparks emanating from the chimney would attract enemy artillery fire.

It was a slightly different story for the civilian population now trapped within the city. Several larger buildings that had underground cellars and vaults, such as the Pensionnat des Soeurs de Notre-Dame (Sisters of Notre-Dame Catholic Boarding School) located on Rue des Remparts in the center of town, and the French Franciscan Monastery, became safe havens for around 800 people during the siege. It is interesting to note that before the German breakthrough, Troy Middleton had planned to hold a dinner dance at the monastery to celebrate the first anniversary of VIII Corps. Bastogne's mayor, Leon Jacqmin, took control of the civilian crisis and appointed a team of volunteers, including two local doctors, to assist. Because of its facilities the boarding school became a bakery and food distribution point. Animals were collected from nearby stables and butchered before being delivered to the school. As the siege continued the cellars of Notre-Dame also became an overflow aid station for casualties. George Allen continues his account:

At first light on the 21st, more prisoners began to arrive in groups of varying sizes as we started the feeding process all over again. All the while German artillery grew heavier and the building behind ours was hit by a shell, killing two MPs who were taken to the cemetery for burial. A couple of days later we learned that two men from our team, Benoit and Herren, who had remained at the caserne with Divisional HQ, were also killed by shellfire. Both were replacements and had been with the division for less than a week. Around this time General Higgins visited the Gendarmerie to see how the prisoners were faring and I showed him the "kitchen." The prisoners kept coming and some were taken under guard to the cemetery to dig graves in the frozen ground. The burial detail allowed them extra rations so the Germans were happy to volunteer. I visited the site and witnessed Lt Duffield, our substitute Graves Registration Officer, bending over the body of a woman, trying to hack off her arm with an axe, so she could be conveniently placed into a crude coffin. Eventually he succeeded and the corpse was lowered into the solid ground, severed arm and all. Not long afterwards Duffield was badly wounded at the caserne and I never saw him again.

That night a number of German aircraft tried unsuccessfully to destroy the wooden bridge* situated no more than 200 yards away that separated us from the main part of town. Immediately the MPs decided to evacuate all prisoners into the basements of the houses, which we were now occupying. It was total chaos as they sent the POWs scrambling down the narrow basement steps of our house and we all sat there, while the raid against the bridge droned on overhead.

* The Germans had rebuilt the bridge over the railway after it was blown up by the Belgian Army in 1940. A short distance to the south along the tracks was the impressive terminus Gare du Sud. The railway system linked Bastogne's two stations: Gare du Sud to Libramont and Gare du Nord to Gouvy (through Bizory). Located at the eastern end of the bridge adjacent to a huge concrete water tower was the Hotel du Sud. The hotel acted as a tram stop where the single-lane track turned northwest through 90 degrees before continuing over the bridge along Route de Marche to Marche-en-Famenne.

Line of Defense, Foy – southeastern sector

Initially the sector protected by 3 Ptn H Co remained relatively untouched by Volksgrenadier-Regiment 78; however, the two other platoons were not quite so fortunate. Shortly after dawn on December 20, 2nd Lt Harry Begle was dozing in a haystack opposite the LOD when a burst of machine-gun fire ripped through the straw. "The stack caught alight and we ran for our lives. I leapt behind a nearby pile of manure as bullets tore up the ground behind me. A few moments later the clatter of enemy tanks became louder through the fog and we began to receive heavy mortar fire. The mortars were so close that we could hear the 'thump, thump' sound as they opened up." Clark Heggeness ran over and shouted in Begle's ear that Sgt Alex Spurr (3rd Squad) had been shot in the left knee over by the haystack and asked if he could help evacuate him back to Battalion HQ. The two men had only carried Spurr a short distance when Clark ordered Harry back to the LOD and told him to hold for as long as possible. The platoon was still dug in along the road and could not see the enemy due to the mist and smoke. Suddenly, Acting Sgt Ken Johnson and his 1st Squad spotted three tanks or SPGs supported by infantry directly opposite their positions.

The 75mm gun attached to the battalion from the 321st GFA accounted for at least one of the enemy vehicles. During the first contact, Johnson shot three enemy soldiers as Pvt Kneller sank to the bottom of the trench and curled up in the fetal position:

> Between shots I shouted for Kneller to pull himself together and he quickly gathered his wits, stood back up, and faced the enemy. I was glad that he did because moments later my machine gunner, Don Hegeness, was hit and began calling for help. Handing Kneller my M1, I sprinted about 70 yards through the fog and smoke to save Don. The tank shells were landing ahead of us and I could feel the pressure wave from the explosions against my chest. Bullets were whizzing above our heads and twice on the way back I was physically blown

> off my feet. At one point we were sent sprawling to the ground when a shell glanced off the side of my helmet, leaving a deep groove in the steel! An inch further and it probably would have taken my head off – someone was truly watching over me that morning!

Communications within the platoon quickly became an issue when Lt Heggeness disappeared with the SCR 536 portable radio handset or "walky-talky." "As we were expecting our own artillery at any moment," recalls Harry Begle, "I told the boys to pull back across the road and into the trees. Moving through the woods, I saw Capt Fred Anderson from I Co, who told me to watch out for the overhead enemy tank fire and to conserve ammo." At least one platoon from I Co had been sent through the Bois Jacques to support H Co's right flank with instructions not to engage any enemy troops unless they had a positive shot. Capt Jim Walker ordered Begle to take four men over to the railway embankment near Detaille Farm and give covering fire to Lt Wilkinson and his squad who were now trapped on the eastern side of the road in what was then open fields.

Begle took his men and followed a streambed along the edge of the tree line for about 300 yards until they reached the corner of the woods. From here the watercourse turned through 90 degrees and ran parallel to the railway before converging with the embankment. Once in position near the CP, Begle and his team had a clearer view along the tracks. Now, above the fog Begle was able to support Wilkinson who was crawling toward him along a fence line through the field next to the embankment. As Begle was observing Wilkinson, a couple of enemy shells burst into the trees behind them. Moments later a jeep (probably from the 501st) drove up and the men heard the driver shouting, "Tanks, tanks!"

A German tank was now advancing down the railway behind Wilkinson toward Detaille Farm. As the mist began to disperse an armor-piercing (AP) shell hit the CP and went right through the building. Another shell burst into the trees above Begle, badly wounding him. "That was the end of my war until March 1945," he recalls, "... one miserable morning of combat. I went over to our aid station which was next to the CP and Capt Walker told me to get on the next available medical evacuation jeep." Earlier, Clark Heggeness had been hit by a piece of shrapnel, which penetrated his thigh above the left knee. The two officers were loaded onto one of the Medevac jeeps belonging to the 326th with eight or nine other wounded and sent back to Bastogne. The men were taken to the divisional aid station inside the chapel at the Catholic Seminary located at the junction of Rue Pierre Thomas and Rue Gustave Delperdange.

Belonging to the seminary, the chapel was converted into a makeshift operating theater, while the floor of the beautiful arched-glass-covered courtyard became a recovery and ward area. At the time when the road to Neufchâteau was closed, over 100 wounded were awaiting evacuation to Massul and additional hospital space was now needed.

Capt "Shifty" Feiler, who had evaded capture at Crossroad X, had made his way back to Bastogne (most probably with Capt Patterson) where he established a secondary aid station for the "walking wounded" directly behind Col Sink's CP in the indoor rifle range at Caserne Heintz. The new facility was partially supported by doctors and medical personnel from the 81st AA Bn, 326th Airborne Engineer Bn and the 705th TD Bn, who had taken over the workshop building next door to the range. In the days that followed the medics at the workshop went on to establish an x-ray department as well as a secondary operating theater.

Back on the LOD 2nd Bn was ordered to take over the H Co sector and Detaille Farm. During the fighting 1st Lt Jerome Knight (2 Ptn I Co) was killed. Out of the corner of his eye, Sgt Harley Dingman thought he saw a German soldier dive into a nearby haystack. "This was the only time I fired my revolver in combat and squeezed off a round into the stack, which then caught fire, but I don't think the two were connected." Afterwards 3 Ptn pulled back to the woods adjacent to the embankment near the stream. "Up until then my guys had been using the spring so I went back to quickly refill my canteen," Dingman continues. "To my horror, looking down, I suddenly noticed the front part of a human skull and some brain matter in the water and immediately pulled back." Emptying the contaminated contents, Dingman instructed his men not to use the stream even if it meant going without water for the next few hours.

Acting Sgt Len "Sam" Goodgal (1 Ptn) was manning a .30cal light machine gun with privates first class Harvey Cross and Ray Crouch. As the team were engaging an enemy machine gun, a hail of bullets tore up the ground around them. Several rounds struck Harvey down the side of his body. "I was lucky," recalls Goodgal. "One of the bullets just grazed my cheek. Upon lifting Harvey's clothing, Ray and I realized he was critically injured." At that moment Goodgal spotted one of the medical evacuation jeeps coming up behind them through the murk along the Bizory road. With Cross unconscious in their arms, Goodgal and Crouch flagged the vehicle down and threw Harvey on an empty stretcher alongside three other wounded soldiers. "Later we heard that Harvey had died at the aid station in the seminary but I think he may already have already been beyond help when we loaded him onto the jeep."

Moments earlier, Richie Shinn was hit by machine-gun fire while crossing the road. Despite Shinn's agility one of the bullets passed through the palm of his hand. Harold Stedman saw his boxing buddy go down and ran through the heavy fire to assist. Shinn was still lying on the ground completely disorientated when Harold reached him. "I couldn't get any sense out of Richie, and as he didn't seem able to stand, I threw him over my shoulder and ran to the aid station. One of the medics saw that my legs were soaked with what he thought was blood and it was only then I noticed the crotch of my pants was shot away. It turned out that a bullet had penetrated both of my canteens, sending water cascading down the backs of my legs!" For saving Shinn, Stedman was awarded another "V" for Valor to his Bronze Star.

T/5 Eugene "Gene" Johnson was a radio operator with 3 Ptn H Co. "Lt Andros had sent me to make contact with our right flank when I spotted a group of Germans crawling through the woods. Returning with the bad news I ran into an officer from E Co who then took some of his men and went after the enemy troops." The officer Johnson spoke with was most likely 2nd Lt Richard Hughes (Ed Shames' new assistant). 3 Ptn had spent the night with I Co before redeploying to assist 3rd Bn. Alex Andros recalls, "2nd Bn [who had been in reserve] finally came through just as we were pulling out [around 1030hrs] and occupied our positions. We made our way back to the high ground [Bois Champay] west of the main road immediately south of Foy. As H Co were moving toward the ridgeline, 19-year-old Pfc Guy Jackson, who had joined 3 Ptn just before Holland, remembers passing five smartly uniformed and clean shaven German corpses, lined up on the ground in a neat row.

Due to the fog, smoke, and confusion, Ken Johnson and his 1st Squad were left behind when H Co withdrew. "I don't remember being relieved by E Co or anyone else from 2/506. Eventually we found our way back through the fog to the company where we had already been listed as missing."

When Harry Begle and Clark Heggeness arrived at the seminary there were a number of wounded Germans lying on the floor, recalls Harry: "The Krauts were moaning and carrying on so I called out, 'Shut your damn mouths, you bastards!'" Begle was luckier than Heggeness:

> I was evacuated on one of the last ambulances out of Bastogne along with 1st Lt Pat Sweeney [HQ Co 1/506] who had been hit through the shoulder at Noville. After arriving at a forward field hospital [probably Massul] the medics could only assess our wounds before tagging and moving us on. A few days later we ended up in a field hospital at Verviers near Liège [there were two medical facilities at Verviers in Belgium utilized by the US First Army – the 77th Evacuation Hospital and the 9th Field Hospital]. Pat and I had only been there for a couple of hours before the place had to be evacuated due to the close proximity of the enemy! Finally the medical services put us on a hospital train to Paris – up until then I don't think we'd slept for three whole days.

"When Gare du Nord was badly damaged by a German air raid in late December, we served a record 24 trains in 24 hours," recalls Helen

Briggs. "Most days we could expect four to five trains at Gare de l'Est, each carrying approximately 300 wounded. As the men were waiting to be unloaded we would serve coffee and donuts along with copies of *Stars & Stripes* magazine. Unfortunately my work as American Red Cross Director never really allowed me enough time to go onto the trains except for the odd occasion when I had prior warning about any soldiers from 3rd Bn coming through. It was heartbreaking to see those injured boys who really appreciated the company provided by our American girls."

Over the next week, as the German forces tightened their grip around Bastogne, the growing list of casualties trapped within the town grew to epic proportions. Clark Heggeness recalls: "Those of us cut off from evacuation were treated twice a day. The medics would dust my wounds with sulfanilamide powder [a strong antibiotic] and administer a shot of morphine [which, unlike C Rations, was in plentiful supply]. There was no food available and the only things I had to eat were apples."

The night before the first enemy attack, the positions occupied by 1 Ptn H Co in Foy had been hit a number of times by random shellfire, as 1st Lt Bob Stroud recalls: "Lt Smith was terrified and I spent most of the night telling him to go away, do his job and look after the platoon." Sgt Martin's squad sustained several casualties from incoming mortar and artillery fire including replacement privates Ralph Keene and Arthur McGinnis. "This one kid had been hit in the stomach and was evacuated back to my CP," continues Stroud. "I sent someone to the rear for a stretcher but he came back empty handed. So we found a ladder in an adjacent stable and covered it with a blanket. I then detailed two men to carry the wounded trooper up the hill to our aid station."

Watching from the upper windows of Gaspard Farm, Gordon Yates was monitoring communications chatter on his sound powered phone. It was just getting light as the communications sergeant squinted into the gloom across the street toward the outpost at Paquay Farm. Suddenly one of Hank DiCarlo's men manning the radio in the OP quietly alerted

Yates to the arrival of some enemy tanks and SPGs, one of which was now parked in a side street directly below the OP. As Yates was informing Lt Stroud, another tank came clattering around the corner through the mist along the road to his right. At that moment all hell broke loose as the Panzer began firing at random from left to right.

With tank shells exploding all around, Stroud decided to break down the radio equipment and abandon the CP. Before withdrawing, Bob moved forward to double check the situation at Paquay Farm. "After dislodging a couple of roof tiles, I was horrified to see the German tank still parked outside. A number of enemy soldiers were nonchalantly standing around the vehicle, so I ran back downstairs and grabbed a bazooka. Poking the barrel through the hole in the roof, I fired one rocket into the Panther's tracks." Rushing downstairs to get more ammunition, Stroud bumped into Pfc Wilber Johnson who had the foresight to bring up another projectile. In the meantime, the Panzer was backing away into the fog under a protective hail of small-arms fire.

Realizing the OP was compromised. Stroud issued orders to abandon the building. Ignoring Stroud's instructions, Hank DiCarlo, who was still on the other side of the property, began to shout fire control orders to his men who were dug in below. "I was more concerned about the enemy troops now appearing through the mist along the main road and northern edge of the perimeter in front of me. Although I still couldn't see any tanks, I shouted down to my squad: 'Watch my tracers' and began firing an M1 rifle at the advancing troops over on my right. Pvt Hargett and his Number Two landed several bazooka rounds into the lead group, and moments later Jack Grace's machine gun burst into life followed by the rifleman. I was continuing to fire at every target that presented itself until a German tank entered the perimeter with its gun aimed directly at me!"

This was probably the same Panzer targeted a few minutes earlier by Bob Stroud. Without hesitating, DiCarlo – still in the OP – turned and jumped down the grain shaft as the first round tore the top off the silo. Fortunately there was still enough hay in the basement to break his fall. After the enemy tank attacked the OP at Paquay Farm the crew focused their attention on the tracer rounds emanating from 2nd Squad's machine gun, as Lou Vecchi recalls: "The previous evening, I told my LMG crew to remove every red-tipped tracer round from their ammunition belts but they didn't listen. As I moved forward to have a few words, the enemy tank turned its turret toward us and fired. The shell exploded into a tree behind our position and severely damaged my hearing, leaving me totally disoriented. Just when I thought we were done for, a Sherman TD arrived [possibly one of the tanks left behind at Foy in reserve] and destroyed the enemy tank at extremely close range."

Hank DiCarlo managed to rejoin his squad, who were then handed another unexpected stroke of luck. "The thick curtain of mist returned and descended across the battlefield, causing all small-arms fire to stop for around 10 minutes. The fog slowly lifted and once again we were in full view of each other firing at close quarters. The fog descended again. A few minutes later as it was lifting we could see more enemy troops coming in, and word came down the line that we had to fall back about 700 yards to the high ground. What astonished me when I got around to counting heads was the fact that my squad had only two men with superficial wounds." The platoon withdrew under a hail of protective fire from S/Sgt Frank Padisak, who was crouching behind a woodpile pouring bullets from a Browning Automatic Rifle (BAR) into the oncoming enemy troops. The somewhat demoralized gray-clad infantry were now trying desperately to cut across the N30 while "the Slovak" (as Padisak was known) held his ground, buying precious time for the battalion.

At that point H and I companies reorganized on the ridgeline on the western side of the N30 above Foy. After re-forming in the Bois Champay, Guy Jackson reached into his top pocket for a cigarette case. "I was shocked to find the container (which I'd acquired in Holland) had been punctured by a piece of shrapnel and deflected off my GI spoon!" With his hearing now completely gone, Lou Vecchi was in agony and went over to ask Bob Stroud if he could be evacuated for treatment. Stroud agreed but as Vecchi was preparing to depart the company supply sergeant, Ferdinand Wilczek, demanded that he hand back his army issue combat wristwatch! "I couldn't believe it and promptly told him where to go," recalls Vecchi. Moments later a jeep driven by Pvt Charlie Kier, who was still on light duties after being seriously wounded in Holland, arrived and evacuated Vecchi to the rifle range at Caserne Heintz.

After Kier and Vecchi had gone, Capt Walker came over and informed Bob Stroud that the battalion was now on a warning order to mount a diversionary attack into Foy to help facilitate 1st Bn's escape from Noville. Hank DiCarlo was nearby and overheard the last words of their conversation, as Walker emphasized to Stroud, "They may be thinking they're heading for Bastogne but they are not going to get up THIS road. Do you understand me, Bob? It's here or nowhere. Pass that on to your men." At the time Stroud had just finished digging in with his runner Pvt Bill Brackett and Lt Smith, who was helping to cover the sizable hole with logs. Although the ridge was mostly concealed by woodland, the open field in front of the tree line dropped away in a short convex incline. Stroud was asked by Walker to move forward with a couple of men and establish an OP overlooking Foy. "We proceeded down the slope through a long finger of woodland to the edge of the trees, but as there seemed to be nothing happening I came back to grab a quick bite to eat. Sitting on the roof of our trench, searching through a ration pack, a shell exploded in the trees, wounding Lt Smith and myself. Smith was screaming in pain after losing the use of his arm. Although I was also hit in the shoulder my wound was nowhere near as painful as Smith's. Luckily Brackett escaped unharmed but was clearly shaken." After saying goodbye to the platoon, Stroud and Smith were evacuated by Charlie Kier to the rifle range. Unlike the two officers, Lou Vecchi remained at the range for less than 24 hours. "It was horrendous and the sand-covered concrete floor was freezing cold. I decided to hell with it – the front line has got to be better than this place – so I picked up my equipment and headed back to Foy, blood still trickling from my ears."

Earlier, further north in Noville, Maj Bob Harwick had been anxiously waiting and hoping that the fog would not lift: "Moments later the first of many enemy barrages screamed in, creating more smoke and dust which added to the mist, bringing visibility down to less than 20 yards. Word came back from the OPs that they could hear German tanks on the move. Within a few minutes the countryside became a confusion of clanking treads, dark shadows, and dirty yellow flashes as the tanks fired blindly into the town. The enemy formation disappeared and every engagement thereafter was a tank and a few men probing here, trying there. One of our tank destroyers held position and fired at such close range that the results were murderous. The fog was a mixed blessing, allowing the enemy tanks to slip through our defenses."

Over 20 tanks formed a U-shape around Noville and systematically pulverized the town with constant gunfire. Harwick continues: "One tank in particular was knocked out no more than 50ft away by one of ours, which although partially disabled was now protecting the CP. The shelling intensified and part of the wall from the church steeple came crashing down into the street."

Lt Canham and his small team of FOs from the 321st GFA had selected a stone-built barn on the northeastern edge of town as their OP, as Pfc Jay Stone recalls:

> Canham and Sgt Plummer were on the second floor observing through an open window. Canham was connected to a radio that I'd previously set up at the other end of the barn and was relaying fire missions to our Fire Detection Center [FDC] at Savy. The Germans were pounding Noville with everything they had and the piercing whistle of incoming projectiles was overwhelming. Suddenly a tank shell exploded right next to the barn and Plummer called me on the telephone to say that the lieutenant had been hit. Grabbing one of the aid men, we went upstairs to find the boss was dead. Amazingly the FDC urged us to remain in position and carry on, although we

> had no intention of going anywhere at that point as Sgt Plummer took over and successfully continued to direct our guns.

Due to the aid station being overwhelmed with casualties, 1st Bn opened another in a nearby cellar. "It was obvious that our losses were leaving gaps in the line that just couldn't be plugged and still we had no communications with Bastogne," recalls Bob Harwick. He continues:

> The CP personnel, switchboard operators, clerks, and the walking wounded were sent out to fight alongside the rifle companies. As the enemy tanks were regrouping there seemed to be a brief lull. A half-track that contained unserviceable radio equipment was loaded with the most critically injured. I designated a driver to try and force his way back to Bastogne along with a message: "Casualties heavy – no more armor piercing shells, request reinforcements, ammunition, and medical supplies." The vehicle departed but didn't return, although I subsequently found out that the driver had actually made it through to Bastogne.
>
> At about 1000hrs we briefly made contact with Regiment by radio. I was afraid to tell them of our true situation over the air, and the message we received was "Hold at all costs." It was at this point that another German tank attack punched through our forward positions and advanced down the road [N30] toward my CP. The TDs got their 20th tank which burned on the edge of town, setting fire to a building which up until that point had remained miraculously undamaged.

The radio belonging to the FOs became the only means of communication with the 506th via a link between the Fire Direction Center and Pfc Victor Sauerheber at the caserne. Any messages that came through were immediately passed on to Maj Harwick, who recalls, "The situation in Noville was now so acute that I called in all the company commanders for a briefing. Another couple of attacks, I explained, would finish us as a fighting force, and then discussed plans to fight a withdrawal. One of my men volunteered to drive a jeep carrying three of the wounded down the main road with a note for BrigGen McAuliffe that read, 'We can hold out but not indefinitely.' About 1230hrs a radio operator in one of the tanks picked up a message telling the armored units to assist the infantry in fighting out of Noville."

Forty-five minutes later the order came through on the FO's radio to withdraw. Sgt Plummer wrote down the short message and immediately handed it to Harwick, who continues, "I took this instruction as a legal means to do what I knew had to be done and ordered the withdrawal at 1330hrs, keeping the transcript as 'evidence.' Of the five tanks remaining [from the original taskforce of 15] I could locate crews for only two. My troops took over and drove two more. The disabled Sherman outside the CP was set ablaze and a 5-minute fuse put on what little ammunition remained. It was hoped that the resulting explosion would bring down the remnants of the church and block the road behind us [which failed]." First to depart were 1st Lt Mehosky and C Co, who had orders to push forward at all costs with a ramshackle convoy of four Shermans. One of the tanks was crewed by Mehosky's men, who had also commandeered a half-track, a truck, and a jeep.

"The tank destroyers with A Co formed the rearguard to prevent the Germans from following," recalls Bob Harwick. "The continuing heavy fog gave us much-needed cover and we set off as soon as the remainder of the wounded were loaded. Before long we could hear gunfire coming from the first group." As the last half-track left Noville a long burst of enemy machine-gun fire came ripping across the fields from somewhere over to the right, followed by direct and accurate artillery fire from the left (east). Jay Stone and the team from the 321st were traveling with Harwick and sent a "mobile" fire mission to Savy. While this was being processed the major ordered his column to leave the road and hide in the marshy dead ground to the west. "Our fire mission was successful enough for the column to continue," recalls Stone, "but the half-track in which we were now traveling kept getting stuck in the mud so we decided to make the rest of the journey on foot."

At the head of the first column, the lead tank had been hit on the approach to Foy but Harwick could not stop to help the crew who happened to be the volunteers from C Co. Meanwhile, supporting the withdrawal on the north-eastern edge of the village was another Sherman that had forced its way through the back of the Klein house and was now actively engaging enemy targets between Foy and Noville.

"Moments later, I sent a 'platoon' to the left (east), who quickly ran into trouble while I led about 30 men to the right toward 3rd Bn," recalls Maj Harwick. "Across the open fields from the road, tracer rounds from our machine guns set fire to one of the barns, and then killed a number of enemy troops as they emerged." During the chaos several 1st Bn soldiers were wounded by friendly fire emanating from 3/506. "We captured 32 prisoners including a major," continues Harwick. "Luckily the enemy troops pulled back, leaving the road clear through Foy. Our task force filed past me and began to regroup. With disheveled faces and torn, mud-caked clothing, the men had been through a tough couple of days, but they knew they had done a good job. Of the 600 who had originally gone into Noville, less than 400 now remained to tell the tale."

Jay Stone and the FOs arrived in Foy behind 1st Bn, with three German prisoners. "I eventually found our Liaison Officer, Capt Sam Skinner, who was working with 3/506 and handed him my POWs. Shortly afterwards, Lt Eugene Brooks from A Battery (who was seriously wounded the following day) took over our team, which had just been re-assigned to Col Patch."

By 1700hrs 1/506 had moved into a complex of barns around Blaise Farm (today called Sibret) at Luzery (recently vacated by 2nd Bn) on the outskirts of Bastogne as regimental reserve, where a couple of hours later they welcomed a hot meal, donuts, and coffee – although everyone wondered where on earth the food had come from.

Retaking Foy

As S/Sgt Frank Padisak was now the most senior rank in 1 Ptn H Co, it was up to him to gather the remaining squad leaders and assign them to their respective lanes of attack alongside I Co. After Stroud and Smith were evacuated, "the Slovak" flatly refused a recommendation from Capt Walker for a battlefield commission (BC). Frank had previously been put forward for a BC in Holland at the same time as Don Zahn, but he later discovered it had been blocked (probably by Walker – although Frank was never able to substantiate this). The Slovak was an immense asset to 1 Ptn and his patrolling, field craft, and weapon handling skills were instinctive.

Hank DiCarlo recalls:

> Our platoon was told to move forward with two squads down into Foy, with mine nearest the main road which was just over on my right. Sergeant Patterson and his 60mm mortar squad were to stay in the eastern finger of woods along with a couple of machine-gun teams to provide fire support. The attack started around 1100hrs, and advancing down the hill we came under immediate small-arms and automatic fire. Firing all our weapons, we reached the first outbuildings and began to push the enemy back. Breaking into smaller groups we systematically cleared each house, barn, and shed, leapfrogging between positions. T/5 Bill Gordon, who had been with us through Normandy and Holland, became the first casualty. I stopped to check but he was dead. Before moving onward, I took a pair of field glasses from his body.

Bill Gordon was a good-looking Jewish boy from a large family who always shared his care packages. After his death the Gordons continued to send parcels of sweets and sundries to the platoon.

"With the help of two tank destroyers from the 705th TD Bn," continues DiCarlo, "we drove the Germans back a couple of hundred yards into the fields north of Foy, clearing the main road in front of 1st Bn, who were now 'attacking' from the north."

Harold Stedman and Wayman Womack found themselves in front of their own rifleman when they came under fire from one of the buildings. The two mortar men took cover behind a wall and launched most of their 60mm rounds at the house. Just after Stedman sent Womack back for more ammunition, 1st Lt Don Replogle arrived with the rest of 3 Ptn. For a few minutes, sniper fire from the house held everything up until Womack returned with another ten shells, as Stedman remembers:

> Within a minute or two we were down to our last three rounds and it was my turn to get some more. As I crossed a small opening between two barns a bullet clipped my ear. Instinctively I threw myself on the ground and played dead for a few moments before attempting to move again. When I got back to Womack, the platoon had taken the house, killing three enemy soldiers. Two others were taken prisoner, one of whom was an officer. This guy was tall and looked mean and for some reason the boys thought he was the sniper who had just been shooting at us. The Kraut, who turned out to be Prussian, was refusing to put his hands in the air so I ran over and kicked him hard in the backside but he still refused to comply. One of the boys roughed him up and then asked the lieutenant if he could "take him to the coast" and was told under no circumstances was anyone going to shoot the man just for being arrogant.

3 Ptn H Co were in reserve and anxiously watching the first tank destroyer (belonging to the C Co group) as it ran into the German roadblock on the outskirts of Foy. "The Sherman was hit and immediately caught fire and I distinctly remember being horrified as the 'crew' scrambled for their lives through the flames," recalls Andros. During the battle the schoolhouse was hit and burned to the ground. Finally, around 1500hrs, the lead elements from C/506 were seen fighting their way toward 3rd Bn. Hank DiCarlo recounts: "As they passed through our lines, I saw my old platoon leader, 1st Lt Mehosky, for the first time since Normandy. 'Moose' was his old self, totally composed and in

full control of the situation. That day our joint forces destroyed over 20 enemy tanks and vehicles from 2.Panzer-Division and captured 113 prisoners, mainly from Volksgrenadier-Regiment 78. It was estimated that we inflicted casualties of up to 60 percent among the attacking force."

After consolidating, the battalion dug in a few yards north of the road to Recogne and waited for further orders. That night, hourly patrols were sent out to the 502nd. 2nd Bn did the same with the 501st. By 1730hrs LtCol Strayer's men were comfortably holding the eastern sector. 1st Lt Oswald and 2nd Lt Stapelfeld from 1 Ptn F/506 moved into the immediate area west of the railway embankment, while F Co established its CP at Detaille Farm. Locking in with Lt Richey and 3 Ptn, Ben Stapelfeld covered his sector along the road with two machine guns and a 60mm mortar, while 2 Ptn acted as security for a detachment of guns from the 321st GFA.

Ed Shames and the patrols platoon were assigned a sector alongside the Foy/Bizory road on the far northwestern edge of the Bois Jacques. The new area was close to the quarry where 2 Ptn H Co had previously held the line. "All I had at the time was a map of Foy I'd drawn by hand during our pre-deployment briefing," recalls Ed. "Thankfully the proper 1:50,000 maps were issued shortly afterwards." This area of the Bois Jacques was scattered with bricks belonging to an old hunting lodge that had been blown up by the Belgian Army in 1940. The forest partially overlooking Foy was to be Ed's "front room" and patrol base for the next two weeks. It is interesting to note that today, in 2014, the woods east and west of the Bizory road have been cut back, leaving a more exposed and open landscape. In 1944, the area occupied by 3 Ptn extended further northwest – as did the woods on the eastern side of the road which were then occupied by the enemy. Also of note is the fact that during World War II the forest directly behind Ed's position extended all the way back to the N30 – which afforded the platoon safe passage to 3rd Bn's CP and Main Line of Resistance (MLR). For the most part Shames took his orders directly from Regiment:

> Usually each afternoon I'd be briefed in the Jacques' Woods for the upcoming evening by either Maj Hester, Capt Leach, or Capt Gene Brown (CO Regt HQ Co). With things like listening patrols they'd give me a set of grid references that needed investigating. It wasn't unusual for us to have several three-man teams in Recogne and Foy on any given night. Generally I would lead one team while Sgt Darrell "Shifty" Powers, Pfc Robert "Popeye" Wynn, Earl McClung, "Skinny" Sisk, and Cpl Walter "Smokey" Gordon would take the others. Combat patrols were a different thing altogether and usually numbered around six people and were required to capture enemy soldiers for interrogation. My mortar sergeant, Paul "Hayseed" Rogers [who took over after Sgt Clarence "Crash" Tridle was wounded], would often remain behind in the bivouac area to oversee our defenses. Several of my guys were fluent in German, such as my armorer T/5 Forrest Guth, Rod Strohl, and Ed Stein.
>
> For the most part "Hayseed" worked with our platoon sergeant "Buck" Taylor and handled the base area administration and also the passwords for any checkpoint or OP that we would be encountering. S/Sgt Taylor had real authority and would have made one heck of an officer. This allowed me more time to concentrate on mission preparation and planning. Paul would often select the men for our patrols and made sure each individual was prepared for whatever job he was expected to do. Before leaving the area our guys would go through patrol order, hand signals, time limitations, and immediate actions for emergency RVs which we called "marking." Rogers and Taylor did everything expected of an officer and more – the only difference was that the men didn't have to call them "Sir."

Lt Richard Hughes was a wealthy and exceptionally well connected New Yorker who had been originally posted to 2 Ptn as 1st Lt Lynn "Buck" Compton's assistant. "I believe that his grandfather had been Governor and later Chief Justice to the US Supreme Court," recalls Ed. "During those first few days we began to notice alcohol on his breath, and when challenged, he openly admitted to drinking on duty. This to me was totally unacceptable behavior and couldn't be tolerated. So I knew he had to go at the first available opportunity."

G Company – the western sector: "Are we army or are we West Point!"

1st Lt Frank Rowe from 2 Ptn G Co had not performed well in Normandy, where he gained the title "Foxhole." West Point Military Academy graduate Turner Mason Chambliss had been the original platoon leader and had died on June 6 at the footbridge near Brévands. Lt Chambliss was a hard act to follow but eventually Rowe proved himself in Holland and was now a well respected and more than capable combat leader. "Rowe's assistant, 2nd Lt Sherman Sutherland, was a great guy who had won a BC and took time to listen to the enlisted men," recalls Jim Martin. When the enemy hit the G Co positions at dawn that first morning, 1st Lt Chester Osborne and 1 Ptn bore the brunt of the assault and 2 Ptn were sent across to assist. Pfc Ewell Martin and three other soldiers carried 1st Lt John Wiesenberger up the hill to the aid station.

The XO was mortally wounded and died later that same afternoon. Artillery accounted for most of the casualties suffered by the company on December 20. Sgt Andrew Hobbs and Pvt Joseph Laviolette both later succumbed to their wounds. Among the more seriously injured were Cpl Lester McNickle, privates first class Stan Davis and Ernie DeGarmo, and privates Clyde McCarty and Robert May.

During one of their first recon missions into Recogne – or the "Twilight Zone" as it came to be known – G Co had been tasked to make contact with H/502, as Jim Martin remembers: "Sergeant Bill Anderson (who was later wounded by shrapnel) and I had been manning the 60mm mortar, so we already had a pretty good idea regarding the terrain in front and to the left of us." G Co was defending a line that ballooned out to the northeastern edge of Recogne with everything to the west under the control of the 502nd, or so they thought. "As we didn't have much time, I suggested to 2nd Lt Sutherland that the others "stay put and wait" while the pair of us went forward to scout around the edge of the village. A regular officer would never have let me talk to him like that but Sutherland knew the score and was happy to accept my judgment. However, when the lieutenant and I moved westwards into Recogne the 502nd were nowhere to be found, and the mission took far longer than expected as we unsuccessfully tried to locate them." Lt Fitzpatrick assigned John Kilgore and Albert Gray for OP duty in Recogne, as Kilgore recalls: "Because Fitzpatrick knew Albert and me from the football team, it seemed to us that we were always the first people he picked if something needed doing. The following night we were sent out on patrol, and I remember saying before we headed off, 'Jesus Christ, Lieutenant, will you please learn someone else's name!' Albert Gray went missing during a night patrol on January 2, 1945, and we later learned that he'd been captured and then murdered several months later in Germany."

Directly behind G Co, lined by tall beech trees, was the Route Madame, marking the extreme western edge of the company area. The unmade road coursed downhill for about 600 yards to a beautiful farmhouse surrounded by five barns recently abandoned by the Degives family. Extending for about 250 yards and descending from the ridge alongside the Route Madame was a shoulder of woodland that would later become part of a permanent MLR for the company.

"After that initial patrol, I heard Sutherland was actually disciplined by Col Patch for not paying attention to his specific time limitations," recalls Jim Martin. "I suppose Sherman chalked it down to experience, but I know the information he provided meant that the gap was temporarily plugged until the 502nd could fully deploy." Although partially overlooked by the Château d'Hoffschmidt (which became the CP for H/502 until the end of December) Recogne was destined to become a no-man's land that could only be patrolled at night by either side.

4

"Epitaph for a generation"

December 21–24, 1944

The LOD at this time was no more than one man deep, and at 0330hrs the following morning 3rd Bn again came under attack. Enemy armor advancing down the N30 was met with bazooka fire and some well-placed rounds from the two Sherman tanks still attached from the 705th TD Bn. Sgt Harley Dingman and 3 Ptn I Co were alerted by an unidentified patrol moving toward them:

> We weren't quite sure who they were but had our suspicions. Immediately, I issued a challenge and asked for the password. It quickly became apparent that these soldiers were wearing hobnailed boots, but then an American voice responded from the darkness, "It's Lt Smith for Christ's sake; let us through." I hesitated for a split second and gave the order to open fire before picking up a loaded bazooka. Pulling the trigger, I was knocked off my feet and engulfed by fragments of flying masonry. In the panic I'd forgotten about the brick wall directly behind me. The blast pitched me forward, causing a partial malfunction, and the rocket barely made it across the road before exploding! Needless to say my guys were not impressed but we managed to disperse the enemy troops in our sector.

Due to the encirclement, the artillerymen had to conserve ammunition and were only permitted to fire on specific targets, such as the one described here by Jim Martin: "Before the battalion pulled out of Foy, we called in fire support, when through a gap in the fog I spotted a group of enemy soldiers moving into the village. The Germans paid dearly when the brief but effective bombardment blew them into oblivion." Because of the heavy mist, dozens of Volksgrenadiers, supported by a few tanks, succeeded in entering Foy. In several instances where the Germans had actually penetrated across the G Co LOD, 1 Ptn were forced to fix bayonets and fight hand to hand. At 0600hrs the order came for the company to withdraw into the Bois Champay. Before pulling out, 1st Lt Osborne asked 20-year-old acting sergeant Stan Clever and his squad, including replacements Pvt James "Dewey" Meriwether and Ewell Martin, to remain behind and cover the maneuver. Manning his machine gun, Stan Clever bravely continued firing at close range into the shadowy figures emerging from the mist. Clever and his squad held on for as long as they possibly could before making their way through heavy small-arms fire back to the edge of the tree line.

At least two machine guns from the machine-gun platoon were attached to G Co during the operation. As Cpl Jim Melhus recalls,

> I was manning a .30cal with Pvt Vince "Mike" Michael [G Co] alongside a couple of bazooka teams when the tanks attacked the village and blew the roof off the house we were using. At that point everyone pulled back to the woods. As we were withdrawing, halfway between the house and a large rectangular barn, "Mike" and I picked up an abandoned bazooka along with three rockets and decided to engage two Panthers that were by now only a short distance away on the road between Recogne and Foy. We were shaking in our boots as the first tank trundled closer but failed to spot us. "Mike" loaded and wired up the tube, and we waited until the tank passed the building so that its turret would no longer be able to turn in our direction. The bazooka round exploded into the engine compartment and a few seconds later the tank ground to a halt. As the second Panther drove up it stopped behind the one I'd just knocked out so we decided to regroup with the others.

Stan Clever's actions purchased G Co enough time to consolidate their new positions and earned him the Bronze Star for Valor. By 1100hrs, H and I companies followed suit, and the MLR was reorganized along the northern edge of the Bois Champay between Foy and Recogne.

On the slope above Foy, Hank DiCarlo and Pfc Bill Briggs knocked out the second Mk V Panzer seen earlier by Jim Melhus, as it advanced toward them:

> We happened to be in the finger of woods looking at the right flank of the tank. After borrowing a bazooka and a couple of rockets from 3 Ptn, we crawled within 20 yards of our intended target. The crew seemed oblivious to our presence and continued firing into the tree line behind us. Bill loaded the 30in-long projectile while I did my best to keep my hands steady before placing an AP round between the bogie wheels and the upper track. The tank was now close enough for us to be underneath the traverse of the turret. My lucky shot penetrated the side armor and began to set off the ammunition inside. Briggs and I ran into the shelter of the woods before looking back to check on our handiwork. I was half expecting to see the gun turn in our direction but instead the Panther started to reverse down the hill. As it moved away the crew jumped out and ran back toward Foy. We all cheered as Cpl Buck Bowitz from 4th Squad, who was covering us, shot and killed the commander as he dashed away from the vehicle… I think we all earned our Para Pay that day.

During the withdrawal Pvt Bob Kangas (3 Ptn I Co) was badly hurt and lying helpless out in the open. Ironically Kangas, who came from San Gabriel, California, had only just returned from hospital after being seriously wounded in Normandy. Pfc Ed Petrowski climbed out of his newly dug foxhole and ran over to Kangas, as DiCarlo recalls: "Petrowski was dragging the injured guy and just before they reached the tree line a mortar round exploded close by, hitting Ed. Despite being injured, Petrowski made sure that he got the wounded man into a trench and lay on top of the trooper, shielding him from further harm. Several of us ran over to help load them both in the back of a jeep for evacuation. These guys were total strangers, yet Ed risked his life to save the other fellow because he felt it was the right thing to do." Sadly Bob Kangas died a few hours later. In contrast, Capt Walker lacerated his hand on a tin can while jumping into a foxhole. "After reporting to the aid station for treatment, Walker's name was entered in the medical diary and he was subsequently awarded a Purple Heart, which we all thought was totally inappropriate," recalls Lou Vecchi.

Young Maguy Marenne was still sheltering with her family and around 40 other people from Foy in the basement of Jules Koeune's house. She recalls:

> Earlier that morning the fighting was going on right outside the house and we could tell that the troops were American because their boots didn't make as much noise as the German hobnails on the road. While looking through one of the slit windows facing the main street, I saw an American soldier fall to the ground. One of the men sheltering with us in the cellar ran out into the open to see if he could help the wounded paratrooper. In the time it took for him to reach the stricken soldier, the Germans had already removed the man's boots. Soon afterwards the enemy began shooting into the basement windows from the Gaspard house across the street – next door to the school. During the battle, a German AP tank shell fired from the direction of Noville penetrated the cellar, and passed through two rooms before coming to rest in a pile of fruit!

Had the enemy tank commander been using a high explosive (HE) projectile, then everyone sheltering in the basement would certainly have been killed.

The following day when things had calmed down, Maguy was allowed to go outside for a few minutes along with Héléne Gaspard and her two baby sons. Héléne's house, which was just across the road, had previously been used by Bob Stroud as his CP on December 20. Maguy continues:

> We played for a short time on the open area in front of the stable before I returned to the basement, leaving Mme Gaspard, eight-month old José, and two-year-old Guy outside. Moments later a shell landed on the road directly opposite the stable, killing Héléne and Guy instantly. Afterwards the Germans decided that they wanted to occupy the entire building and ordered everyone to relocate to the next farm owned by the Cordonniers. Conditions at Cordonnier were primitive, especially the toilet, which was a bucket in the center of the room. Teenage mother Ghislaine Bastin used the opportunity to break away from the group and go to Cobru, where she gave birth to a little boy on Christmas Day and called him Noel.
>
> Because of the poor sanitation, people started going down with dysentery but luckily we weren't starving. As kids we couldn't understand why the adults were constantly praying and the tone of their low mumbling voices is still with me today. The Germans gave us black bread, and the women were able to get enough fresh milk from the cows still in the dairy to feed the toddlers. On December 31, the Germans came in and told us to get out by midnight and those who remained would be shot! My mom didn't believe that they would actually do this, but around 8pm we finally convinced her to leave. That night we walked 5 miles to Hardigny with the Cordonniers along the N30, which had been blocked at regular intervals by blown telephone poles and trees.

Back in Noville on December 21, a number of officials from the Sicherheitsdienst (SD) arrived to question the locals. Staffed by political idealists, the SD was an intelligence-gathering and security organization with close links to the Gestapo. After establishing their HQ in the school which was previously Desobry's CP, the SD visited every house in the village to interview the occupants. While carrying out searches photographs were found that had been taken during the liberation on September 10, depicting certain families celebrating alongside American forces. A slogan was also discovered in the church affixed to the wall above the altar which read "*Vivent la Belgique et son Roi / Vivent la France et les Allies*" (Long live Belgium and the King and long live France and her Allies).

Several members of the SD team were French and seemed particularly well informed as to whom they wanted to bring in for questioning. During their search the SD arrested 16 civilians, including priest Louis Delvaux, local schoolteacher Auguste Lutgen, Fernand Beaujean (whose house had been used by 1/506 as an aid station), Fernand's two sons Blaise and Roger, and Michel Stranen, a 22-year-old from the town of Troine in Luxembourg. Ironically Stranen, a "diver," was on the run and hiding locally with friends at the time while evading the German forced labor program. Escorted by German troops, the men were lined up in front of the church whereupon ten were taken to the school for interrogation.

When Mme Gilis found out where the SD had taken her husband Louis, she rushed to the schoolhouse to protest the men's innocence but was told to go home. As she left the building, shortly before midday, all 16 villagers were standing outside the church under armed guard. The "prisoners" were then ordered to clear the N30 of debris. Some, including Louis Delvaux, initially refused and were forced by the SD to continue. As Delvaux walked into the road, he whispered to Louis Gilis, "It's all over brother – repent your sins." A few hours later, satisfied that the road was clear, the SD reassembled the 16 civilians in front of the school. A German officer then produced a list from his pocket and sent home eight people, including Fernand and Blaise Beaujean and Louis Gilis, before adding, "The rest of you, hands on head and follow me." Delvaux, Lutgen, Roger Beaujean, Stranen, and the remaining four men were marched to a patch of open ground behind the church, where three pits had been dug. As Fernand Beaujean was walking away he heard a number of shots and immediately knew that those left behind had just been executed, including his 21-year-old son Roger.

3/506 Main Line of Resistance December 21, 1944

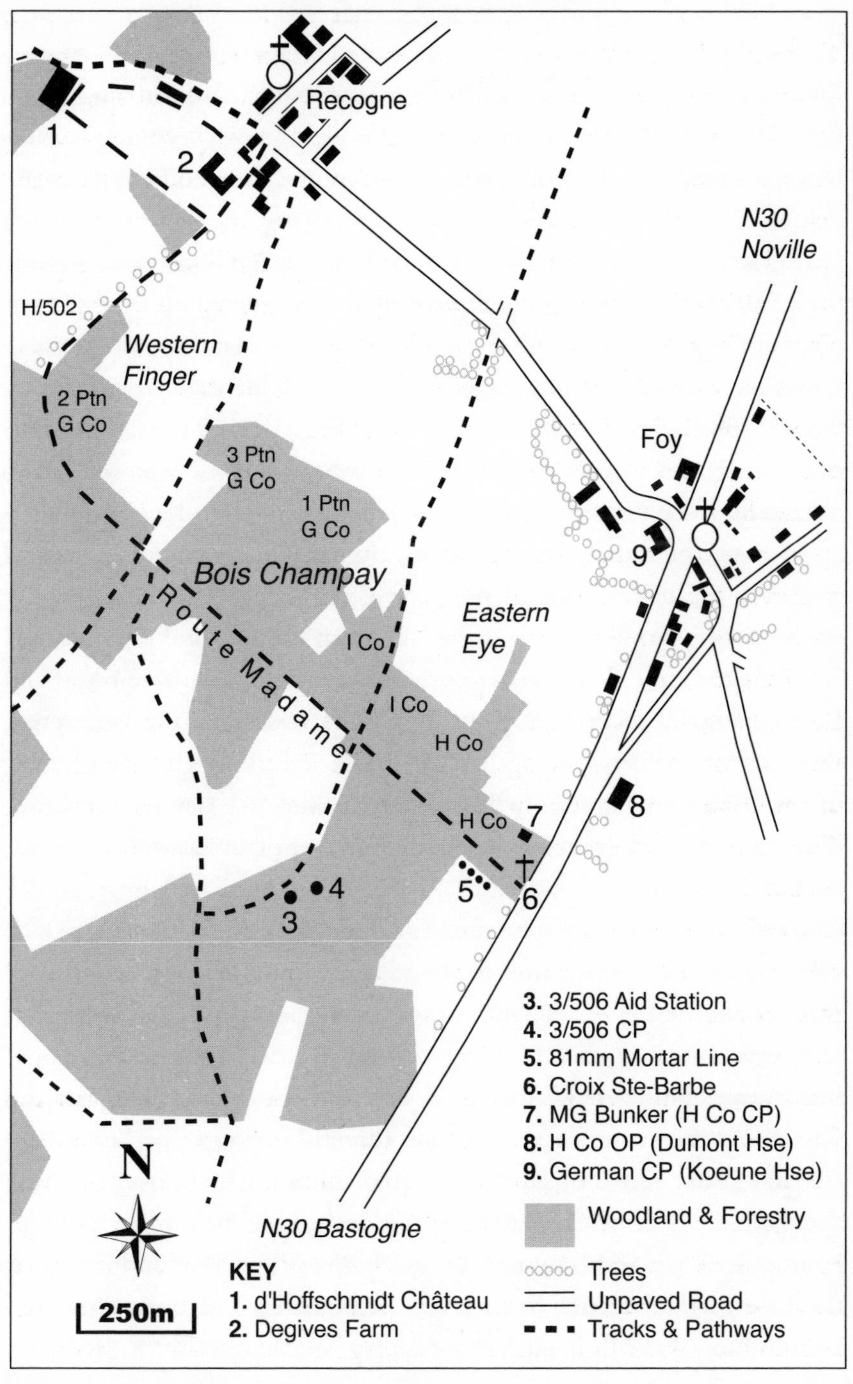

Oblivious to the situation unfolding in Noville, 3rd Bn dug in at Foy along the edge of the Champay Woods somewhat envious of the Germans who now had the luxury of sleeping in the houses and barns below. Capt Walker, 1/Sgt Gordon Bolles, and the officers from H Co took over "Château Foy," a small concrete pillbox overlooking the N30. The machine-gun emplacement was situated on the extreme northern edge of the woods, near a local religious landmark known as Croix Ste-Barbe. The bunker was one of three identical fortifications built by the Belgian Army around the village during the 1930s. The other structures were located further northeast and close to the farms owned by Joseph Bastin (father of Ghislaine) and Camille Dumont.

In 1944, the trees covering the 3rd Bn MLR were planted in such a way as to create two long, dense protrusions – these vitally important features are referred to here as the "Western Finger" and the "Eastern Eye." At the time G Co was responsible for the largest section of the Bois Champay, covering a front 800 yards wide running east across three sectors before locking in with I Co. 2 Ptn (G Co) were based in the "Western Finger," which when viewed from above formed a distinctive stepped shoulder pattern in the shape of an outstretched "W."

The "Eastern Eye" was located in the sector shared by H and I companies and ultimately became the doorway into Foy for the 506th PIR. Being the closest point to the village, a number of forward OPs were established here, including the 81mm mortar platoon (who had four tubes located in a clearing behind Route Madame). A single line of trees ran northwest midway between the lookout area and the village. At the center of this feature, directly opposite the "Eye," the tree line broke into a number of isolated clumps, which, over the next three weeks, became forward listening posts. Like most of 3 Ptn I Co, Harold Stedman and Wayman Womack dug in together and insulated the base of their trench with layers of branches and ferns. "As rifle ammunition was still in such short supply," recalls Stedman, "we took what we had and what could be recovered from the dead and divided it up equally along with other items such as food and candy."

S/Sgt Ralph Bennett (3 Ptn H Co) was digging in near the concrete bunker (150 yards east of the "Eye") with radio operator Gene Johnson, medic Pvt Irving Baldinger and runner Pfc Elmer Swanson. "I'd decided to create a trench big enough for all four of us and we were taking it in turns to dig. The earth was solid and we'd only gone down about 1½ft, when I had the desperate idea of using a hand grenade to soften up the ground. We all ducked down and braced ourselves as the grenade exploded. Unfortunately, the other guys around us weren't impressed by my brilliant notion. That being said it did the job and nobody got hurt so we ignored the negative comments from rookie replacements privates George Hart and James Sowards, Jr, who were struggling to dig in nearby."

The German probing attacks continued on and off throughout the day as Sgt Sam "Dud" Hefner, who had taken over from Ralph Bennett as 60mm mortar sergeant on October 5, recalls: "The crew of a 37mm antitank gun, attached to us from the 81st AA Bn, opened up at about 550 yards on a German tank, which responded by pouring fire directly into our positions." The first tree burst killed Jim Sowards instantly. Bennett could hear George Hart crying for help and crawled over with Hefner to see what had happened. Hart was lying face down in a shallow shell scrape with a huge gaping hole at the base of his spine and seemed paralyzed from the waist down. The two men carefully eased Hart out of the shallow hole and called over to Baldinger (who was known as "Blackie") for assistance. Baldinger made the decision to support George's spinal column and carry him back to the battalion aid station. Reaching Route Madame, the men flagged down a passing medical jeep that happened to be returning to Bastogne. "None of us thought Hart would make it but he did – only to spend the rest of his life in a wheelchair," recalls Bennett.

Five minutes later during another barrage, Pvt Ralph King, who was manning a machine gun, started to scream. Gene Johnson went over to help and was horrified to see that part of King's left shoulder had been torn away, exposing the bone:

> Grabbing hold, I dragged Ralph back to the ridge [Route Madame] and sat him against a tree before returning to help the others who included Pfc Adolph Nicolato. In all we evacuated about ten guys out of the immediate danger zone. Before the medics arrived, I did my best to help Ralph, who kept trying to glance down at his injured shoulder. As he slipped deeper into shock, I slapped him across the face shouting, "Don't you dare pass out on me… Don't you dare!" At that moment he began to focus and pointed out that I was also bleeding profusely from a head wound. "That's not mine … it's probably yours," I replied, but as I reached up to feel my face he was right … the blood was mine!
>
> Shortly afterwards the medics arrived and took us all down to the rifle range, which was rapidly filling up with wounded lying all over the floor. It was bitterly cold in that place and the only thing that kept us from starving was bullion soup.

Hefner's assistant in 4th Squad, Cpl Jim McCann, adds, "After the barrage we were sounding off names and when it came to Pvt Mike Eliuk there was no response. I scuttled across to check if he was OK and it seemed to me like Mike was asleep. I tried to wake him but he was dead – I couldn't believe it … he looked so peaceful."

Much time was now being spent on improving defenses, as Hank DiCarlo recalls: "The most lethal of enemy action were the 'tree bursts' sending shrapnel of all shapes and sizes ripping through branches into our foxholes. Everyone started to cover their trenches with logs, using soil to fill the gaps before pouring on water (mostly urine) that would then freeze to form an almost impenetrable barrier." H Co established their permanent OP in a farmhouse diagonally opposite the concrete bunker on the eastern side of the N30.

Number 40 Route de Houffalize was a two-storey building owned by Marcel and Julia Dumont, who had abandoned the property shortly before the battalion arrived. One-half of the house was for domestic use, while the other encompassed a barn containing a small dairy herd. The

Dumonts had been proud of their animals but were especially fond of their stunning white horse. When H Co took over, most of the animals except for a few chickens had been killed by artillery. The cows were still in the stalls hanging dead from their nose rings, and the white horse so cherished by the Dumonts was lying outside decapitated in the paddock.

Twenty-two-year-old Sgt Charles "Chuck" Richards was a squad leader in 3 Ptn at the time and recalls:

> One night "Dud" Hefner, myself, and couple of others were at the OP when two German soldiers approached the house along a side road. In a short burst of gunfire we killed one guy but the other slipped away. After dragging the body into the garden, we took his ID for Capt Walker and left the corpse lying on its right side with one arm outstretched. In the morning when I turned the guy over to check for unit insignia the man's right arm immediately extended upwards into the air. From then on it became a kind of ritual to shake hands with the Kraut every time we came in or out of the house. I guess we all figured that by doing so it made us feel a lot better off than he was, and not long afterwards somebody took the dead man's boots.

On December 23, when the first snow began to fall, the corpse was quickly covered by a thin layer of snow, leaving the extended arm exposed in a pathetic, frozen, Nazi-style salute.

Over the next 48 hours Hank DiCarlo found himself on constant night patrol:

> I knew we were short on manpower but I just couldn't believe we were that desperate. Patrols, at least for me, were a nerve-stretching activity. Creeping across fields, freezing in the glaring light of German flares, always expecting an ambush, got me so keyed up that it took a couple of hours to unwind before I could even think about getting any sleep. By then it was time for the next patrol, but I guess it was the same for everyone. Physical discomfort was a given but constant exposure to

> the elements began to take its toll. By this time we all had wet feet and those who took their boots off to change socks found it difficult to put them back on due to the intense swelling. I was afraid to remove my boots after seeing so many guys hobbling around on makeshift footwear or having to bind their feet with salvaged blankets.

Deeply troubled about the patrol situation, Hank spoke to 1/Sgt Fred Bahlau, whom he had known since the early days at Toccoa. Fred had nothing to do with making up the rosters and informed Hank it would be best to speak to the S3 who now happened to be 1st Lt Derwood Cann – who had previously loaned $500 from DiCarlo. "I hiked over to the battalion CP for a little *tête-à-tête* with the lieutenant. 'Sir, we're even. Please cut down my patrols … you won't owe me a cent!' He stared at me for a while before responding, 'I'm sorry you think I would intentionally put you in that kind of danger for a few bucks? I swear on my life that I will pay you back as soon as I'm able, but the truth of the matter is we need guys like you to get the replacements through what is happening out there.' On that note I saluted, apologized, and sheepishly made my way back to the 1 Ptn lines."

Located about 350 yards south of Route Madame, the battalion CP was well hidden in the Bois Champay behind H Co on the site of an old quarry about 250 yards west of the N30. In another pit 70 yards further south, Barney Ryan established his aid station, alongside a track that originated from Foy and ran up the hill through the MLR, before eventually joining the N30.

At over 10ft deep, the two ancient pits were ideal and measured about 25ft in diameter. Although they were covered by a thick layer of logs it was possible to stand up inside and the natural bunkers soon became a safe haven for Col Patch and his staff as Fred Bahlau recalls: "Whenever my guys were in reserve, I always had everyone remove their boots and massage toes and feet to promote circulation." Casualties with early-stage emersion foot or frostbite were stabilized inside the aid station by means of a coal-fired brazier before being sent back to their foxholes.

"On the MLR, the men were not really allowed to light fires. However, during daylight those of us dug in around the battalion CP were able to boil water and melt shavings from D-Bars and make our own form of airborne 'hot chocolate.' Every morning one of my duties as HQ Co first sergeant was to visit the battalion command post and report any casualties that had occurred during the previous 24 hours." A few days into the campaign, HQ Co began to send men across to the rifle companies in an attempt to make up for their acute loss of manpower.

Shadows in the mist

Sometime after midnight on December 21, a patrol from 2/506 discovered dozens of footprints near the railroad tracks around Detaille Farm and traced them to a patch of woods behind the eastern MLR.

The enemy troops were part of a reconnaissance group from Regiment 77, 26.Volksgrenadier-Division, who had previously been supporting Panzer-Lehr-Division around Margeret and were now in the process of attacking Bizory. At the time 2nd Bn were holding the MLR from the eastern edge of Foy through the Bois Jacques to the railway embankment at Detaille Farm (F/506 CP). With E and F/501 dug in around Bizory, the ground east of the tracks was virtually undefended. D/501 were still occupying a bivouac position in an isolated L-shaped block of woodland about half a mile southeast of the farm. At this point the fissure was extremely vulnerable, especially when heavy fog led to poor visibility. It would appear that the Volksgrenadiers were part of a spearhead whose job was to punch and consolidate a hole along the railway, enabling the Panzers clear route into Bastogne. D and F/506 were dug in along the edge of the Bois Jacques, with D Co now holding the line west of the embankment.

During the early hours of the morning, 250 Volksgrenadiers crossed the fields adjacent to the Bizory road. Avoiding the 506th CP, the enemy group slipped through the mist and swung northeast before reaching the railway embankment close to the D/501 bivouac area. Realizing the woods were occupied and with daylight fast approaching, the Germans decided to cross over and find shelter in dense woodland on the other side of the tracks. The forest here was scattered with trenches previously dug by the Belgian Army in 1940 and US forces in September 1944, which was a blessing in disguise for the Volksgrenadiers. After establishing their harbor area the Germans sent out recon patrols and OPs to protect the flanks. At 0830hrs D and F companies heard German voices coming from the woods and immediately formed a containment force with the 501st to block all possible escape routes.

Thirty minutes later, 1st Bn was mobilized and dispatched from nearby Luzery by Col Sink to eliminate the enemy force. As Bob Harwick recalls, "A and C companies were sent in, while B Co was placed between the target area and Luzery. Leaving 2nd Lt Don Zahn's platoon in reserve, I led 1st Lt Dick Meason's A Co and 1st Lt Mehosky's C Co and at 0900hrs carefully started in a southeasterly direction from the main road [N30]. We moved through the woods to try to chase the enemy into B Co led by 1st Lt Herbert Minton, who were now waiting in ambush." The forest was made up of dense woodland, the branches of which went down to the ground, forcing the men onto the single-lane logging tracks that criss-crossed the Bois Jacques.

The two assault groups advanced cautiously toward the railway as Bob Harwick continues:

> We experienced a limited amount of enemy shelling which mainly fell behind our line of advance. As the men moved onward, orders were issued by a whisper or hand signal. A shot rang out and everybody hit the ground wondering where it had come from. This was followed by a burst of machine-gun fire that ricocheted from tree to tree. A Co spotted a few low mounds of freshly dug earth marking the outer line of enemy defenses and put in a joint assault with C Co. A few moments later, above the noise, I heard someone shout for a "medic."
>
> At this point [1100hrs] C Co was still advancing to contact, when I moved forward past Lt Zahn to make sure that both companies didn't

> become separated in the forest. Another long burst of enemy machine-gun fire ripped through the trees as C Co closed in for the fight. A wall of noise erupted as the company engaged the enemy at close range. I came upon one of our boys who'd been killed earlier – face down in the dirt, helmet to one side – still holding his rifle. Two prisoners were brought back under close guard by one of my men. Both Germans were terrified and kept ducking their heads as stray bullets whipped through the trees. A burst of automatic fire sent them diving into a nearby foxhole. Taking no chances the guard threw a grenade in after the prisoners and followed up with four shots from his carbine before returning to the fight.

Maj Harwick crawled over to a wounded man in need of assistance. Next to him was the body of another soldier who had been shot in the head and killed while trying to apply a field dressing to his injured comrade. In total C Co lost four men during the attack. "More POWs were coming in – one of them, gibbering in German, half scared out of his wits, kept falling to his knees, eyes darting around like a lunatic. Finally in English he began to repeat 'Don't shoot me' before collapsing to the ground sobbing. The rest of the prisoners had a similar attitude except for one lieutenant who stood cold and aloof. His arrogance soon crumbled after one of our guys punched him in the face leaving his nose pouring with blood."

While this was happening, the support platoon from C Co were skirmishing northeast alongside the railway embankment and captured another 30 prisoners. "We counted 65 German bodies scattered amongst the trees. Most had been killed as they were falling back to a secondary defensive position," recalls Bob Harwick. "One of the 'dead' Krauts was found trying to operate the radio he was lying on … needless to say his communication came to a very abrupt end. Not all of the enemy troops were accounted for so we decided to sweep the woods towards B Co. It wasn't long before we found more along the edge of the tree line where they had hastily tried to dig in. Afraid to fight in the open, the Germans fired on our scouts." One squad from 2 Ptn A Co worked its way around the flank, killing four Volksgrenadiers, wounding three, and taking another prisoner, as Pfc Don Burgett recalls: "On our way back to the main road Pvt Don Brininstool, Pvt Charles Horn, and myself were covering the left flank of the company." Horn was a few yards behind Burgett and Brininstool when the beleaguered Volksgrenadiers opened up with a machine gun. The first burst went high but the second was more accurate, as Don recalls: "As the string of bullets ripped toward us we hit the ground and rolled away but Horn was too slow and died instantly after being hit in the face."

Moments after Horn was killed, Burgett and Brininstool were able to skirt around the enemy position and neutralize the gun crew and two riflemen. During the course of the morning, Dick Meason was shot in the abdomen and seriously wounded. A Co also lost privates Emanuel Fell, John Bielski, and Siber Speer, who were all from 2 Ptn. The remaining German troops, 13 in all, fled their positions and ran into B Co, who promptly took them prisoner. The 501st captured a further 85 soldiers in their sector as what was left of the Volksgrenadiers (some of whom were only 15 years old) withdrew east across the tracks. Around 1800hrs, upon returning to Luzery, 1/506 discovered that the 57 men who had been wounded during the attack had no hope of being evacuated as Bastogne was now completely surrounded by enemy forces.

Three days later at the rifle range, Meason developed acute peritonitis. Luckily, due to the abundance of penicillin and sulfadiazine (which was administered intravenously), he survived and eventually made a full recovery. Blood plasma was also in plentiful supply, thanks to VIII Corps, who had left behind most of their medical depot at Caserne Heintz.

Back on the 3rd Bn MLR, Capt Joe Doughty had been surveying Recogne together with Sherman Sutherland. As the two officers were standing along the edge of the 2 Ptn sector, the "Western Finger" came under intense fire by an enemy mortar barrage. Something struck Sutherland in the right temple and the men could only look on in horror as he fell, convulsing, to the ground. Jim Martin recalls, "Bizarrely, as

Capt Doughty was trying to revive Sherman, a bullet slipped from a gaping wound on the left side of the lieutenant's forehead!" (Martin thought Sherman had been killed instantly, but according to official company reports he actually died two days later.)

Cpl Don Skoglund (2 Ptn) was also killed while running messages to 1 Ptn, which suffered around a dozen casualties, including Stan Clever, Sgt Elden Gingerich, Sgt Vic Szidon (communications), and Cpl John Hildebrandt. Clever was sent back to Bastogne along with the rest of the walking wounded for treatment. Stan had not gone far when a heavily armed German patrol crossed the trail ahead. "They didn't see us and disappeared into the woods. A little further along the track we came across a group of GIs sitting beside a Sherman TD, brewing hot chocolate on a small campfire. They seemed unconcerned when we told them about the Kraut patrol and responded, 'So what – we don't have any ammo anyway!' Shrugging, we carried on to Bastogne, where I was treated by Capt Feiler, who suggested as my wound wasn't serious that I return to the front line the following morning. That night the town was bombed, so in all honesty, I was glad to be going back to the MLR."

The continuous patrolling by 2nd and 3rd battalions acquired dozens of potential targets for mortar and artillery in the vicinities of Recogne, Foy, and the Bois Jacques. 3 Ptn E Co would often use Route Madame as their highway into Recogne, moving out through 2 Ptn G Co and H/502. Ed Shames and his men spent many nights creeping around the village trying to figure out where the enemy-held positions and buildings were located.

One night Pvt Ray Calandrella was on guard duty and could not believe what he was seeing. "Somebody was using a flashlight around the battalion CP. Whispering angrily into the darkness, I asked for identification and that they extinguish the light immediately! 'Where are the candy bars?' came the response. I recognized the voice; it was 1st Lt John Williams. Although we were behind the MLR the lieutenant seemed clueless to the danger he might be exposing us to… I still can't believe that someone could be that stupid … totally unbelievable." The following morning, LtCol Patch was sitting outside the CP shaving, when a barrage of German shells came hurtling overhead. Unconcerned by the explosions, Patch carried on with his admin and shouted above the din, "Those bastards will never get me!"

Some nights, when things were quiet, Lou Vecchi would detail a couple of men to head down into Foy and collect fresh water from a well, located on the western side of the N30 between the houses belonging to Alphonse Degive and Jules Koeune. The route was protected by a shallow dip lined by a long hedge that provided good cover. One evening a Sherman tank was observed moving along the N30 from the direction of Bastogne. Bizarrely, the tank trundled slowly through the MLR down into Foy and straight into the path of a German Panzer hidden in the dip of the road. The longer gun of the German tank smashed into the side of the Sherman's turret, prompting its commander to traverse his shorter barrel before firing several rounds at pointblank range into the Panzer, incinerating its occupants. "The Sherman then backed up the hill to our positions, whereupon we learned from the crew that they were in fact lost and had missed the left turn for our battalion CP," recalls Hank DiCarlo. "The enemy in Foy began firing everything they had at the Sherman so we hunkered down in our foxholes and rode it out."

After returning to the Bois Jacques from a night patrol into Recogne, Ed Shames noticed a glow coming from one of his platoon foxholes. "Earl McClung and I wondered what the hell it was. As we approached the trench we discovered our armorer Forrest Guth, aka 'Goody,' underneath a raincoat reading a book by electric light! After a brief exchange of 'words,' we made him cut the wires to make sure he wouldn't compromise our position again. After calming down we inquired as to how he'd managed to do this. 'Goody' was a resourceful man and we weren't surprised to learn that earlier in the day he'd salvaged an old generator and headlight from a German motorcycle to form the basis of his 'in trench' lighting system."

During the morning of December 22, Hank DiCarlo was sent back to Bastogne with a detail to collect ammunition. "I decided to look in on Ed Petrowski at the seminary to see how he was doing. Although Ed appeared to be in some pain, he was quite coherent and we talked for several minutes. Turning to leave, Ed grabbed my sleeve and pulled me toward him – 'Hank, if something should happen to me I want you to promise to go see my wife and little girl and give them these.' Ed then handed me a set of rosary beads and a medal he'd 'acquired' when we were in Holland from a church at Uden. Assuming I would return at a later time, I patted his hand, told him not to be so stupid, and assured him everything was going to be OK."

Moving along the N30 on his way to Foy, DiCarlo was passing by the back gate of the caserne when he noticed bodies being carried into the indoor range. Entering through a set of double doors, Hank found himself in a target store at the end of the range. Continuing down a short but steep flight of stairs, DiCarlo entered the butts through a large sliding door. The sight that greeted him was deeply shocking. Spread across the sand-covered floor and sloped bank were numerous dead bodies, American and German, plus dozens of amputated arms and legs.

Over the next 48 hours the regimental CP at the barracks took a number of direct hits, resulting in yet more casualties as T/5 David Phillips from the regimental S3 (ex Co HQ 3rd Bn) remembers. "Around 0130hrs on December 23, a 105mm shell landed in the corridor close to our room. Two men were wounded and we were covered in dust and debris. My immediate boss, M/Sgt John Senior, brushed himself down and gave us all a large shot of cognac which helped to steady our nerves." That same evening the Luftwaffe arrived overhead and began to bomb the town. Nearby in Luzery Maj Bob Harwick was in his CP at Blaise Farm and recalls, "Immediately I abandoned my room on the second floor and moved downstairs to the living room. One of the bombs landed in the field opposite about 100 yards away, leaving a huge crater."

"Nuts" and the fortune of war

The previous morning (December 22), along the Arlon road south of Bastogne, a party of four Germans had approached the American lines at Kessler Farm (which was occupied by F Co 327th GIR) from the direction of Remoifosse, under a "white flag" of truce. It is likely that the commander of the 47.Panzerkorps, Heinrich von Lüttwitz, personally drafted a letter asking for the Americans to surrender. The party consisted of Major Wagner from the 47.Panzerkorps, Leutnant Helmuth Henke from the Panzer-Lehr operations section, and two enlisted men possibly from Panzergrenadier-Lehr Regiment 901.

Leutnant Henke, who spoke English, asked to see the commanding officer and was directed toward S/Sgt Carl Dickinson, T/4 Oswald Butler, and medic Pfc Ernest Premetz. Henke pointed to the briefcase he was holding and explained to Dickinson that he had a written message for the American commander in Bastogne. Leaving the Panzergrenadiers behind, Wagner and Henke were blindfolded and taken to the F Co CP located in a wooded area about a quarter of a mile away. Capt James Adams (F Co CO) made several telephone calls before he was able to speak with his regimental S3, Maj Alvin Jones, who was asked by Divisional HQ to retrieve the message and bring it to Caserne Heintz.

The surrender demand was written in both English and German and read:

> To the U.S. Commander of the encircled town of Bastogne: The fortune of war is changing. This time the U.S. forces in and near Bastogne have been encircled by strong German armored units. More German armored units have crossed the river Our near Ortheuville, have taken Marche and reached St. Hubert by passing through Hompré-Sibret-Tillet. Libramont is in German hands. There is only one possibility to save the encircled U.S. troops from total annihilation: that is the honorable surrender of the encircled town. In order to think it over a term of two hours will be granted beginning with the presentation of this note. If this proposal should be rejected one German Artillery Corps

> and six heavy AA Battalions are ready to annihilate the U.S. troops in and near Bastogne. The order for firing will be given immediately after this two hours' term. All serious civilian losses caused by this artillery fire would not correspond with the well-known American humanity.
>
> Signed: The German Commander.

Maj Jones and LtCol Ned Moore (divisional G1 and acting chief of staff) took the message to Tony McAuliffe, who at the time was trying to sleep. Jones explained the situation to the general, who much to everyone's surprise exploded in anger, threw the note on the ground, and shouted "Us surrender? Aw nuts!" At that point he left the building to visit a unit on the western perimeter to congratulate them for destroying a German roadblock.

Puzzled by the response, Jones returned to his Regimental HQ to brief Col Bud Harper (CO of 327th GIR). Almost 2 hours later, when McAuliffe came back from his trip, he was informed that Harper had telephoned to say the two German officers were still waiting at the F Co CP. In front of his staff, McAuliffe wondered aloud what to tell Wagner and Henke. It was only then that Harry Kinnard spoke up and suggested that what the general had said earlier would be hard to eclipse. Everyone agreed and McAuliffe scribbled a line on a message pad with instructions for it to be typed up by T/4 Ed Ihlenfeld. The message read simply: "To the German Commander, 'N-U-T-S' – The American Commander."

Col Harper, along with Maj Jones, was summoned to Caserne Heintz and instructed to personally deliver the message to the German officers waiting at the CP. Harper told Henke that he had the American commander's written response and gave it to Wagner before driving them blindfolded back to Kessler Farm. During the short journey, Henke asked if the reply was affirmative, and added that, if necessary, they were empowered to negotiate further terms. Harper told them that the reply was most definitely not affirmative and consisted of a single word. Henke translated the word "NUTS" to Wagner who was naturally confused by the slang terminology.

When they arrived back at the farm, the officers were reunited with their waiting colleagues. The order was given for the group to remove their blindfolds and Wagner opened the letter. One of the soldiers from F Co who spoke German translated Harper's previous explanation as "Go to Hell." As the German party was walking away, Harper shouted after them, "If you continue to attack, we will kill every goddamn German that tries to break into this city." Wagner stormed off, throwing his blindfold at a nearby BAR position; the time was recorded as 1400hrs. The threatened heavy artillery barrage was delayed due to other German operational commitments around the perimeter, and subsequently Von Lüttwitz was reprimanded for ordering the artillery to refocus its attention back on Bastogne.

Operation *Repulse* – rising from the ashes

The following morning (December 23), despite the light covering of snow, the overcast weather began to disperse, and by early afternoon, hundreds of vapor trails from Allied bombers (bound for Germany) began to appear in the clear blue sky. The first day of good weather also gave the Allies an unlimited ceiling and a free hand across the battle area. Air panels were displayed on the ground, marking friendly positions, while American P-38 Lightnings, P-47 Thunderbolts, and P-51 Mustangs attacked German tanks, troops, and artillery positions, alongside Typhoons, Hurricanes, and Spitfires from the Royal Air Force.

The improvement in weather also brought another surprise. The first of two ten-man teams from the 101st Pathfinder Co began dropping west of the railway line close to the Neufchâteau road and Isle-le-Pré, 1 mile southwest of Bastogne. Twenty-four-year-old 1st Lt Shrable Williams was in the lead aircraft flown by LtCol Joel L. Crouch. Williams had simply "cut cards" with 1st Lt Gordon Rothwell to see whose team would go in first. Rothwell lost the bet and was ordered to circle over the drop zone (DZ) until receiving the all clear from Williams. "Initially the mission had been scheduled for the 22nd but it was temporarily postponed at the last minute," recalls Williams. "On the flight over France we picked up our fighter air support, which was a blessing." For some reason Crouch overshot the DZ and decided to circle while Rothwell's stick took the initiative and jumped. Gordon's team consisted of Cpl Richard Wright (E Co), Cpl Lavon Reese (E Co), Pfc Carl Fenstermacker (E Co), Pvt Lachlan Tillman (D Co), Pvt Charles Partlow (D Co), Pfc Martin Majewski (Regt HQ Co), Pfc Nathan Ferster (HQ Co 1st Bn), Pvt Thomas Floyd (A Co), and last but not least, Pvt Irvin Schumacher (H Co). After making contact with friendly ground forces Rothwell popped smoke grenades to signal Williams to commence jumping. Williams was first out of the door, followed by Sgt Jake McNiece (Regt HQ Co), Sgt John Roseman (A Co), Sgt Cleo Merz (C Co), Sgt Leroy Shulenberg Jr (B Co), Cpl John Dewey (Regt HQ Co), T/5 George Blain (HQ Co 1st Bn), Pfc John Agnew (Regt HQ Co), Pvt William Coad (Regt HQ Co), and Pfc George Slater (B Co). While the enlisted men were servicing the Eureka signaling equipment, Rothwell and Williams went straight to Caserne Heintz to establish where exactly division wanted the supplies to be dropped.

The Pathfinders were directed to set up their Eureka transmitters and signaling equipment on the high ground west of the city near Grande Fontaine. Within an hour of landing, the two teams established contact with the first 16 aircraft from Operation *Repulse* – now coursing through heavy enemy antiaircraft fire toward Bastogne. Flying in from the direction of Sibret, 3 hours and 40 minutes behind the first wave, were 40 aircraft belonging to XVIII Corps Pathfinder Group, as George McMillan recalls:

> We took off from Membury in Oxfordshire at the head of the column along with B-24 and B-26 bombers plus fighter cover. I was working as an air dispatcher alongside two crewmen from the Air Force. As we flew over the DZ [at 1150hrs], I was standing behind the pilot and could see the fluorescent "T" panels [known as AP 30s] and colored smoke marking the DZ. I returned to my post just as the green light

> came on and helped shove three big containers out through the door of the aircraft. After our drop we had a ringside view of the other planes as they delivered their loads. It was an amazing spectacle to behold and later we learned that over 90 percent of the supplies dispatched were recovered.

As an example of the kind of loads delivered, 21 C-47s from 441st Troop Carrier Group (TCG), flying in three-ship Vics, were carrying, in order of priority: 66,800lb of ammunition, 15,600lb of rations, and 800lb of medical supplies. In total, on December 23, around 238 aircraft reached the target; however, six misdropped loads elsewhere, four (including three from 441st TCG) were shot down, and three more were forced to turn back before reaching the DZ. The last plane arrived at 1606hrs, signifying the end of a historic day for the defenders of Bastogne.

Lt Mehosky and 1st Bn were in reserve at Luzery when the parachute drops began: "C Co was still in possession of the vehicles I'd requisitioned from Noville. We sent every available truck and jeep out to the drop zone to help collect and transport supplies for Regimental HQ. Consequently, the company gathered dozens of parachutes as well as canvas sheets and felt liners from the packing crates. Layered onto logs, this waste material drastically improved our living conditions and provided warm bedding for the battalion. Many, like me, were having problems with footwear as our soles began to come away from the uppers. The leftover felt was tied together with paracord and formed into makeshift overshoes that kept our feet dry and considerably warmer."

More supply missions followed on December 24, 26, and 27. Due to bad weather all flights were suspended on Christmas Day. The follow-up drops brought in a variety of items ranging from artillery shells and telephone cable to cigarettes, candy, and mail – during which time over 40 aircraft were either damaged or shot down. For the most part the parachute insertions were accurate, but there was a slight problem. The

Col Robert F. Sink, Commanding Officer, 506th PIR, 1942–45. (Donald van den Bogert)

LtCol Lloyd Patch successfully led 3rd Bn through Bastogne to the end of the war. (Currahee Scrapbook)

The Commanding Officer of H Co, Capt James "Skunk" Walker. (Currahee Scrapbook)

Regimental XO LtCol Charles "Charlie" Chase, pictured before Normandy in the United Kingdom while on exercise at Marridge Hill training area. (John Reeder via D-Day Paratroopers Historical Center, St-Côme-du-Mont)

Mourmelon, December 1944, Sgt Bob Martin (right) and senior NCOs from 1 Ptn H Co, joking with newly commissioned Don Zahn. L to R: 2nd Lt Zahn, Sgt Lou Vecchi, Sgt Hank DiCarlo, and S/Sgt Frank Padisak. (Hank DiCarlo)

American Red Cross Club Gare de l'Est Paris, December 1944. L to R: Sgt Lou Vecchi, S/Sgt Ralph Bennett, T/5 Bruce Paxton, Helen Briggs (ARC), Pfc Spencer "SO" Phillips, and Sgt Hank DiCarlo. (Mark Bando)

Pfc Ken Ross joined the 101st at Mourmelon after his older brother, Don, had been captured on D-Day while serving with 3/506. (Ken Ross)

Pvt Bob Izumi, 3 Ptn G Co, photographed in August 1945, Paris. (Bob Izumi)

Pfc Jim Martin, 2 Ptn G Co, shortly after qualifying as a military parachutist in January 1943. (Jim "Pee Wee" Martin)

S/Sgt Harley Dingman, 3 Ptn I Co and later Battalion HQ, Austria 1945. (Harley Dingman)

Sgt Harold Stedman, 3 Ptn I Co, pictured here in the USA during early 1943. (Harold Stedman)

Pvt Richard "Richie" Shinn, 1 Ptn I Co. During his military career, Shinn represented the regiment at least 30 times and after the war became famous as a professional fighter. (George Koskimaki)

The 501st PIR were among the first to leave Mourmelon for Bastogne. Members of 2/501 can be seen here waiting to board. (NARA via Joe Muccia)

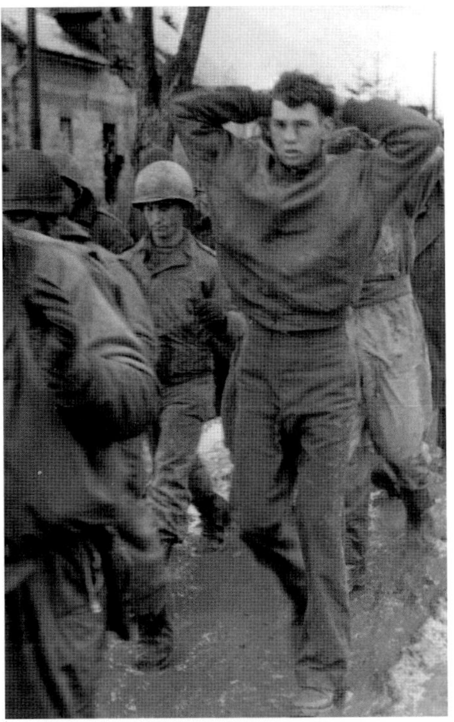

American soldiers captured during the opening German attack. (NARA via Donald van den Bogert)

Artillery Commander BrigGen Anthony "Tony" McAuliffe was in charge of the 101st Airborne Division for the first nine days in Bastogne. (NARA)

Doctor John "Jack" Prior, 20th Armored Infantry Bn, Task Force Desobry, 1944–45. (Robert Clam)

3rd Bn medic T/5 Johnny Gibson worked from the aid station in the Bois Champay throughout the campaign. (Reg Jans)

M1 155mm Field Gun "Long Tom" and crew in the Ardennes. (John Gibson via John Klein)

Pvt Ray Nagell (center) and his crew from B Battery 321st GFA manning their 75mm Pack Howitzer in training. (Ray Nagell via Reg Jans)

Paratroopers from the 506th PIR advancing passed Caserne Heintz (right) through the rain along the Route de Houffalize (N30) to Noville. (NARA via Reg Jans)

2/506 turning onto the N30 from Route de la Roche bound for rearguard positions behind the Main Line of Defense in the Bois Jacques. (NARA via Reg Jans)

Men from the 506th PIR moving north out of Bastogne along the N30 towards Foy and Noville. (NARA via Reg Jans)

TOP: The remains of the schoolhouse at Foy after the battle. (Joël Robert)

MIDDLE: Noville's ruined church (l'Église St-Étienne) and presbytery as seen from the Bourcy road in 1945. (Reg Jans)

BOTTOM: View north along N30 towards Houffalize from Noville in late January 1945. Detritus of the conflict litters the crossroad outside the presbytery (right). A German Stug III can be seen in the foreground. (Reg Jans)

The chapel at the Catholic Seminary became one of the first medical facilities to be established in Bastogne. (Reg Jans)

Abandoned tents belonging to 326th Airborne Medical Co near Herbaimont after the surprise German attack at Crossroad X. (Reg Jans)

German Commandos taking a break somewhere along the Belgian border next to an abandoned US M8 Greyhound Scout Car. (NARA via Donald van den Bogert)

Young German soldiers surrendering somewhere in the Bulge. (Joël Robert)

Stragglers from the 28th ID (Keystone Boys) at Sibret possibly being sent to support the 101st at Bastogne before the encirclement. (NARA via Donald van den Bogert)

Soldiers from the 501st PIR searching German prisoners outside the stables behind the Gendarmerie in Bastogne. (André Meurisse)

German prisoners burying bodies in the town cemetery opposite Caserne Heintz. (Reg Jans)

TOP: Stream where 2nd Lt Harry Begle (2 Ptn H Co) led his men. In the distance can be seen the railway embankment and Detaille Farm (3rd Bn CP). In 1944 everything right of the watercourse was woods and the area on the left open fields.

MIDDLE: A mixture of American casualties gathered somewhere inside the encirclement, possibly Bizory. (John Gibson via John Klein)

BOTTOM: Wounded arriving at the makeshift hospital in Caserne Heintz. The soldier on the stretcher appears to be German. (Reg Jans)

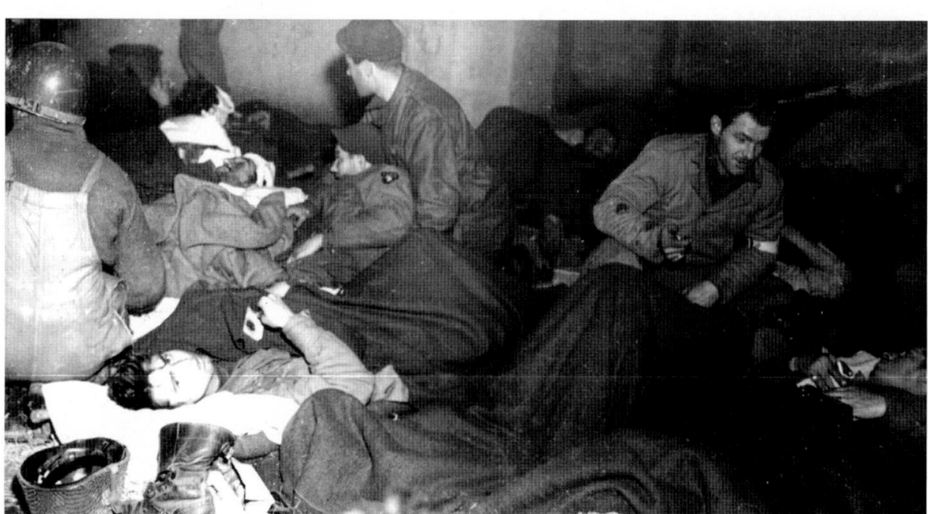

CO of Regt HQ Co Capt Gene Brown is pictured here during the winter of 1943 in his room at Littlecote House, England. (John Reeder via D-Day Paratroopers Historical Center, St-Côme-du-Mont)

1st Lt Chester Osborne, G Co, led 1 Ptn through Bastogne before being reassigned to HQ Co in late January 1945. (Dan & Laurie Uhlman)

Sgt Sam "Dud" Hefner, 3 Ptn H Co.

New Englander Pvt Mike Eliuk, 3 Ptn H Co, who was killed in action on December 21, 1944. (Alex Andros via Mark Bando)

This picture taken in central Bastogne opposite Hotel Lebrun shows two members of Combat Command B awaiting Team SNAFU deployment. (NARA via Donald van den Bogert)

Post-Christmas view looking north through the Bois Champay towards Route Madame and the 3rd Bn MLR. The battalion aid station was located foreground (right) just inside the tree line. (Currahee Scrapbook)

Bastogne's devastated town square during the early part of the siege. (Reg Jans)

Lt Helmuth Henke from the Panzer-Lehr operations section was a member of the German delegation sent to discuss surrender terms with Tony McAuliffe. (Reg Jans)

Pathfinder 1st Lt Shrable Williams jumped with his stick on December 23 to help facilitate the relief operation of Bastogne. (Roger Day)

First air re-supply coming in on December 23, 1944. (Reg Jans)

Pathfinder Pfc Jack Agnew (Regt HQ Co) operating signal equipment for the next re-supply drop at the Brick Factory along Route de Marche, probably on Boxing Day. (NARA via Donald van den Bogert)

Paratroopers recovering equipment from a later supply drop. (Currahee Scrapbook)

Divisional medics recovering supplies from the DZ. (Reg Jans)

color-coding of the canopies had been changed. This difference only served to confuse the ground troops as to what supplies were packed in which containers. Over the next few days, Shifty Feiler organized a number of work parties to go out to the DZ (which was only a few hundred yards west of the barracks) and collect medical supplies. Many parachutes were also gathered and brought back to the rifle range where they were used for blankets, bedding, and bandages. In total over 2,000 parachutes were dropped during the operation carrying a total of 481 tons of supplies. After their work was done and the siege lifted, the Pathfinders were trucked to Reims, from where they were flown back to the 9th Troop Carrier Command HQ in Britain.

Jim Martin has good reason to remember the first and subsequent parachute drops, which brought letters from home. He recalls:

> We were dug in on the eastern side of the "Finger" above Recogne when a jeep arrived behind us. Completely oblivious, the driver emerged with a sack of mail and handed it to the nearest person before tearing off at considerable speed. Moments later a German mortar barrage came crashing through the trees. Everyone ran for cover and I made it to the nearest foxhole closely followed by Pfc Mike Nassif, Jr. We were lucky as a shell exploded close to the trench, covering us both with dirt and cordite.
>
> After the attack everyone was still cursing the mail guy when we discovered that Sgt Dean Christensen had been mortally wounded. Dean had crawled under the back of a nearby Sherman TD only to be ripped to shreds when one of the shells exploded less than 2ft away from the rear of the tank.

That evening another mail truck using the main road overran the MLR and went down into Foy where it struck a mine on the outskirts of the village. The joy of receiving mail far outweighed the risks, and under cover of darkness a patrol from 2 Ptn H Co was able to reach the vehicle and bring the mailbags back to the MLR for distribution.

5

"The deep six"

The worst winter in 50 years

By holding a tight and well-connected perimeter that became known as "the hole in the donut," the 101st Airborne Division was able to keep the enemy infantry and armor away from Bastogne. After the divisional defense force was regrouped, the 506th PIR combat team was augmented by A Battery (Antitank), 81st AA Bn, and 1 and 2 platoons C Co, 705th TD Bn. Luckily, so far the Germans had chosen not to focus their strikes in any one particular place but instead used small probing attacks to try to locate US weak points. Despite the German ultimatum of total annihilation, nothing really changed, which came as a welcome relief to the troops. However, the regiment did not know that the enemy was building up strength in Recogne, Cobru, and, perhaps more importantly, on the eastern side of the MLR. At 0830hrs on Christmas Eve, the Volksgrenadiers launched a company-sized reconnaissance attack from their positions in the Bois Jacques against E and F companies. German casualties were heavy, and although the assault failed, it showed that the scaled-down enemy force was still active and ready to engage.

Ed Shames' platoon had just spent an uncomfortable day fighting off one particular enemy patrol that had managed to infiltrate into the edge of their harbor area. The acting squad leader, "Smokey" Gordon, was shot and severely wounded while manning a machine gun during the early stages of the attack. The bullet entered Cpl Gordon's chest just below the clavicle (collar bone) before exiting through his back. One of the Germans was now lying adjacent to Ed's foxhole, as he recalls:

> The dead Volksgrenadier made a nice addition to our "front room," and we subsequently used his frozen body as a kind of makeshift sofa! Afterwards everyone got into the habit of shaking the Kraut's hand every time we moved in and out of the patrol area. Sometime around this period a rumor began to circulate that a soldier from another company had been stabbed by a German night patrol. It was said that the Germans were specifically looking to murder or capture anyone they found asleep in a foxhole! All joking aside, the threat of being knifed shook me up so much that afterwards I spent most nights on top of the ground shivering like a lunatic in my sleeping bag.

The first heavy snowfall came at midday on Christmas Eve. At the time only 50 percent of the division had overshoes, and most of those never reached the front lines. As a stopgap, burlap bags (sandbags) were issued and all available white cloth requisitioned for camouflage purposes. Up until this point the men figured the weather could not get any worse – but they were in for a big surprise. In a desperate attempt to combat the falling temperatures, Ed Shames wrapped sacks around his boots and managed to "liberate" a German greatcoat along with a pair of fingerless mittens. "Despite looking like scarecrows, every morning I'd have my people shave no matter what the situation or temperature," recalls Ed, "because I figured if they looked like soldiers, they might behave like soldiers."

The deep white blanket now forming was powdery and dry and brought with it thousands of leaflets packed within specially modified artillery shells from the enemy that read:

> HARK … the HERALD ANGELS sing! Well, soldier here you are in "No-Man's Land," just before Christmas, far away from home and your loved ones. Your sweetheart or wife, your little girl, or perhaps even your little boy: don't you feel them worrying about you, praying for you? Yes old boy, praying and hoping you'll come home again, soon. Will you come back – are you sure to see those dear ones

> again? This is Christmas, Yule-time … the Yule log, the Mistletoe, the Christmas-tree, whatever it is, it's home and all that you think fine to celebrate the day of our Savior. Man, have you thought about it, what if you don't come back … what of those dear ones? Well soldier, "PEACE ON EARTH GOOD WILL TOWARDS MEN" … for where there's a will there's a way … only 300 yards ahead… MERRY CHRISTMAS!

Late in the afternoon, Pvt Herb "Junior" Suerth, who had joined 3 Ptn at Mourmelon, decided to visit a chum in the next sector, which at the time was under control of 1st Lt Lynn "Buck" Compton's 2 Ptn. It was common knowledge that Compton was undergoing some sort of breakdown due to combat fatigue. Rightly or wrongly, Ed Shames was intolerant to Compton's situation, believing that he should have stepped down days ago if only for the safety of his men. After what had recently happened with the enemy attack everyone was now feeling the strain, although they dealt with it in different ways. As Suerth trudged through the dense, snow-covered forest into the 2 Ptn area, Co§mpton strode over and verbally dissected him with such anger and venom that "Junior" was almost brought to tears. The tirade contained words such as "how dare you … without permission … who do you think you are … what do you think you are doing," and even "desertion." Of course, before leaving, Suerth had made sure he had permission from S/Sgt Taylor, and as "Junior" was not experienced enough to be on the patrol roster, it didn't really matter just as long as he came back before nightfall.

Shortly after Suerth returned to the harbor area, McClung reported the incident to Shames. "Man, I was livid, and ran through the woods to confront Compton. Buck didn't know what to do as I pushed him up against a tree and in front of his platoon screamed in his face, 'What the hell is the matter with you? How dare you chew out one of my men without talking to me first – he was only trying to wish someone a Happy Christmas!'" About one week later, Buck was taken off the line with battle fatigue and replaced by 2nd Lt Jack Foley.

Due to the activity in the Bois Jacques, 3rd Bn increased its night patrolling between Recogne and Foy. During one G Co patrol toward Recogne, Jim Martin, S/Sgt George Diebolt, and Lt Rowe passed a badly wounded German who had been left behind during an earlier incursion. "The guy was in a bad way and kept calling out for his mother over and over again," recalls Jim. "It was clear that he wasn't going to make it so Diebolt, who was my platoon sergeant, went back and put the man out of his misery with a single shot to the head." 1 Ptn were nearby and also heard the cries of the wounded Volksgrenadier along with the ominous sound of tanks, as Pfc Ewell Martin recalls:

> Our squad formed a line out in front of the MLR during the night. Early the next morning one of the guys who was dug in behind me called across that we were pulling back. I decided to go down the hill and check that the squad next to us who were located behind a hedgerow had also received word – which was a big mistake! As I stepped through the fence next to the hedge, a burst of enemy machine-gun fire, which I believe came from one of the tanks, forced me to dive for cover. The nearest hole was still occupied and I remember cussing the guy out for not digging it deep enough. The tracers were "walking" just above the ground toward me along the hedgerow and one of the bullets actually ripped through my trouser leg! After a while, I crawled back to the MLR and informed the crew of a 75mm gun where I thought the tank had gone but they couldn't get a visual and didn't have enough ammunition available to take the chance.

Hank DiCarlo's squad was down to eight men and starting to feel the effects of the last few days. At this point rations were becoming scarce, forcing the men to scavenge from the bodies of German infantrymen, as DiCarlo recalls: "We did our best to glean whatever rations we could from the corpses that were by now littering the patrol area in front of the MLR. Many of them had these little round wooden vessels that resembled soap dishes but contained butter. I really liked the tins of Argentine beef, but despite trying my best I couldn't tolerate something the Germans called 'blood pudding.'"

At the time most of the men on the front line were rationing themselves to one tiny meal per day. "Pretty soon my pants began to get loose," recalls Manny Barrios. Drinking water was always a problem, especially for Manny, who spent a lot of time on OP in the "Eastern Eye." "Melting the snow was often our only option but not always easy to achieve under the conditions as usually it took five helmets-full of snow to melt down enough water to fill one canteen."

During the late afternoon, Capt Jim Morton visited the G Co positions and stopped for a moment to speak with Jim Martin, who recalls: "Captain Morton had been our original XO so I knew him quite well. The captain told me that due to the shortage of officers in H Co he was now doubling up as temporary XO for Capt Walker. As we were casually discussing our individual hunger issues he noticed the body of a German soldier lying in front of my position. I couldn't believe what he said next – 'Jungle Jim' suggested that we go out under cover of darkness and cut the backside out of the Kraut and fry it as a 'steak supper.' 'Sir,' I replied, 'surely you are joking?' He looked at me, smiled, and retorted, 'It was only a suggestion,' before disappearing back into the woods… I never did find out if he was being serious."

Home to S/Sgt Ralph Bennett was the four-man foxhole, carved out three days earlier with a little help from a grenade.

> Before leaving Mourmelon, my parents sent me a package containing, amongst other things, a large tin of sweet peas along with a cryptic note saying, "Do not open until your 22nd birthday," which was … Christmas Eve. The guys in 3 Ptn were always very liberal with their care parcels and everything was shared whenever possible. Everyone in the trench wished me a Happy Birthday as I punched a couple of holes in the tin and placed it to heat on our squad stove. As the can started to boil we noticed an odd smell, and it suddenly dawned on

> us that the container was actually full of liquor, so I poured a little into our cups before passing it around to the rest of the platoon. It certainly gave us something to smile about, and for once I toasted my dad for doing the right thing. Later that evening we got our first hot meal, which was brought up from Bastogne – so my birthday couldn't have been any better!

2 Ptn H Co were still holding the line on the eastern edge of the Bois Champay when Frank Kneller stood up and attempted to sing "Silent Night" – very badly. Ken Johnson was not impressed, especially after one of the less compassionate enemy troops in Foy decided to take a potshot at them. The bullet passed between the two men, and Kneller was so angered by the response that he immediately got on the radio and called for mortar fire: "I could see some movement on the southern outskirts of the village and when the shells came in we looked on as a couple of German soldiers suddenly ran screaming into the open with their clothing on fire. I still feel guilty about my impetuous actions, which caused so much pain and suffering on this of all days."

To counter the enemy propaganda leaflets, LtCol Kinnard wrote and printed a special Christmas message on behalf of Gen McAuliffe, stating: "The Allied troops are counterattacking in force. We continue to hold Bastogne. By holding Bastogne we assure the success of the Allied Armies. We know that our Division Commander [who was still on his way back to the front] General Taylor, will say: 'Well done!' We are giving our country and our loved ones at home a worthy Christmas present and, being privileged to take part in this gallant feat of arms, are truly making for ourselves a Merry Christmas."

While Hank DiCarlo was in Bastogne collecting ammunition, the Luftwaffe bombed the town. "We were just about to leave when the air raid began, forcing us to spend several uncomfortable hours in a cellar before we could return to the MLR. When I got back, the boys informed me that Ed Petrowski had died from his wounds back in Bastogne. Despite our primeval living conditions it didn't stop us from being human. A wave of emotion crashed over me and I had to walk away for a few moments." Clasping Ed's medal, sitting alone with his back to a tree, Hank's face was soon wet with tears. "In a moment of weakness I wept for his wife and baby whom I'd only known from snapshots." Threading the religious icon onto a piece of string, DiCarlo's hands were shaking as he hung the medallion around his neck for safekeeping before returning to face the next challenge.

During the afternoon elements of H Co were ordered northwest to the sector operated by 2 Ptn G Co as the 502nd had been contacted by enemy forces. At the time Lt Ed Wierzbowski from H/502 had his CP inside the Château d'Hoffschmidt and recalls, "On at least two occasions the Germans sent in dogs trained to identify our forward OPs." A request was sent by Regimental HQ to gather more information about the potential enemy strength in Recogne. A group from H/506 drew the short straw for the initial patrol specifically designed to solicit fire. Jim Martin recalls:

> As their first scout passed through our position into the open field above the village, an enemy machine gun opened fire and he fell to the ground. We presumed that the guy had been hit and were not expecting him to stand up but by some miracle he did. Seeing that he was unharmed the officer [probably Ed Wilkinson] ordered the soldier to continue forward, whereupon this time he was struck by a bullet and collapsed. The entire patrol then exited through the tree line in groups of twos and threes and headed down the slope [parallel with Route Madame] toward the eastern edge of Recogne. The men had only gone about 100 yards when they came under fire again and several of them were wounded.

Back in the tree line, T/5 Walter Pelcher from the medical detachment (who had been attached to G Co at Mourmelon) began to remove his pack. Jim and some of the other men inquired what he thought he was doing. "I'm the guy who has to go out there and give first aid," replied

Pelcher. The men responded, "You'll be no good to anyone if you go and get yourself killed." Ignoring their advice he ran out into the snow toward the soldier farthest away. Throwing the wounded man across his shoulders, Pelcher returned through heavy small-arms fire to the relative safety of the "Finger." "We all felt it was an incredibly brave thing to do and told him so," recalls Jim, "but he didn't seem to think he'd done anything out of the ordinary at all."

G Co were soon mobilized to assist H Co when the mission began to unravel. Jim Martin recounts:

> As we pushed beyond Recogne some 15 enemy tanks supported by infantry attacked our left flank and looked as though they might get behind us. We pulled back into the village but were unable to hold against the tank fire and tried to withdraw to our positions on the MLR. Our officers and NCOs were desperately trying to steady the line. As we were about to fall apart, 1st Lt Derwood Cann (battalion S3) turned up and by his sheer weight of command forced us to become soldiers again instead of a routed rabble. At the time we were under a great deal of pressure and had been driven to the point of physical exhaustion by hunger. I'd not always seen eye to eye with Cann since he broke his ankle in '43 at Camp Mackall. Cann was very "GI," and as Col Sink held him in such high esteem we always called him "Golden Boy." He always thought I was a "Smart Aleck" but the thinly veiled animosity he frequently showed never stopped me from thinking that what he did in Recogne was one of the finest acts of military conduct anyone could imagine.

When the situation escalated, 1 Ptn H Co were also committed and Sgt DiCarlo took privates Bill Briggs, Vernon Timm, Wilber Johnson, and T/5 Jack Grace from his 1st Squad and ran through the woods to lend a hand. On approaching the positions belonging to 2 Ptn G Co, Hank's squad could hear the roar of tanks coming up the hill toward them. Using several unmade roads and logging tracks emanating from

Recogne, the enemy armor had successfully managed to outflank G Co and circle around the Château d'Hoffschmidt and were now looking for a route into the western Bois Champay. "An assortment of around 20 armored fighting vehicles came into view accompanied by infantry," recalls Hank, whose men took shelter inside the tree line belonging to 2 Ptn. The Panthers split into smaller groups, each taking a different route toward the ridge. Totally exposed, the German infantry were decimated by the 502nd, who were firmly entrenched further to the west along the semi-circular tree line overlooking the château. A number of tanks then began to converge on a single-track road that crossed the Route Madame on the right-hand edge of the G Co sector.

From here the road ran through the forest behind the MLR and coursed south to Savy and the edge of Bastogne. Hank's small force combined with a rearguard from G Co were able to neutralize the German stragglers now trying to catch up with the Panthers, but were unable to stem the advance. Upon crossing the MLR the enemy tanks were cut off by four Sherman TDs, which forced a couple of the Panthers into an adjacent field where they were knocked out. With their exit now blocked the other tanks had no choice but to continue forward through the woods toward Savy, where they were picked off one by one by antitank guns. Back in the field behind the MLR, the tank turrets flipped open, and rather than surrender, the crews ran toward the forest where they were cut down by H/502. Fighting was fierce around the château and the intense enemy shelling caused several deaths among the paratroopers.

Finally, around midnight on Christmas Eve, the gunfire subsided. High above the MLR, Sirius – also known as the "Dog Star" – stood out in the night sky, twinkling brightly. The star encapsulated the "Holy Night" as it would have done 2,000 years before during the birth of Christ at Bethlehem. It was a sobering thought for those who had just participated in the battle, who now must have been wondering what the next few days would bring.

"Hark the Herald Angels Sing"

The day before the Christmas Eve attacks on the 502nd and 506th MLR, Maj Bob Harwick and 1st Bn were still in reserve at Luzery when they heard the sound of gunfire and artillery coming from the southwest, where the 327th GIR were holding the perimeter. By 1900hrs the battalion was placed on 30-minute alert for a possible move to support the glider infantry. "Meanwhile we waited and told incredibly bad jokes that we'd heard countless times before but still seemed hilarious. At midnight the staff formed a quartet at the CP and I called each company commander in turn and sang 'Silent Night' to them over the phone."

In an attempt to lighten the mood, LtCol Paul Danahy (divisional G2), from Minneapolis, sent a spoof situation report to all command posts. The overlay, marked up with a red circle around the town, outlined the enemy positions, while in green were the words "Merry Christmas" scribbled over the American defenses. Meanwhile, 12 miles away to the north at Warnach, Combat Command B were moving in from the west, while Combat Command A from 4th Armored Division were heavily engaged against elements of the German 5.Fallschirmjäger-Division (Parachute Division).

Divisional interrogator George Allen was still based at the police station in Bastogne and recalls, "Between December 20 and Christmas Day we received 537 German prisoners. The POWs usually arrived either late morning or early afternoon, and one captive who witnessed the supply drops remarked, 'What can we do with an army that can put on such a spectacle?' The air supply had no immediate effect on me, the IPW team, or the prisoners, as we were still groveling around in cellars looking for food. For the most part the POWs were dependent on the gruel we regularly dished up, containing turnips and potatoes, sweetened with sugar beet. Enviously we looked on as the trucks went out to the DZ and brought bundles back to a nearby supply dump where they were collected by their designated recipients."

During the afternoon, Allen walked into Bastogne looking for supplies and stopped for a moment to watch one of the Forward Air

Controllers (FACs) at work. "From a jeep in the center of town, the Air Force officer was busy calling in air strikes. I watched with fascination while the captain checked his map, as an enemy tank was described by one of our regiments holding the perimeter. Seconds after requesting the next available ground-attack aircraft, a pilot came on the radio to confirm the grid coordinates before engaging. I was amazed how efficiently the system worked and how quickly a plane could be directed onto each target." Captains Jim Parker (himself a pilot) and Richard Cherie, and Lt George Woldt made up the 101st Airborne Air Liaison Team. The three men worked closely with the FACs, and from their converted Sherman played a vital role during the siege. When the weather was more favorable, it was possible for the team to coordinate anything up to 19 squadrons of Thunderbolts at any one time.

"On Christmas Eve, after another enemy bombing raid against the railway bridge on Route de Marche, our prisoners emerged from the cellars and began to sing a number of hymns including '*Stille Nacht, Heilige Nacht*' (Silent Night, Holy Night)," recalls George Allen. "One of the MPs requested '*Wiegenlied*' (Cradle Song) by Brahms, which was beautifully delivered by our guests." Allen continues:

> At 0230hrs on Christmas morning the Germans launched an attack against the northeastern side of the perimeter that was contained after some tough fighting. Later that day, after I'd made sure the German cooks had enough food and coal, I went for a walk to see the damage that the Luftwaffe had inflicted on the bridge. Two dead soldiers from the 28th ID were sprawled on the ground about 50ft away from their antiaircraft gun. One of them had the top of his head missing, exposing the brain. Returning to the Gendarmerie, I sat down with my three cooks, who now called me "*Unser Kaporal*" [Our Corporal] and chatted about what we traditionally did on Christmas Day. We wondered what our loved ones would be doing at this precise moment back home and discussed the two dead GIs.

Many stragglers from the 28th Infantry and 9th Armored had recently been reconstituted by VIII Corps and sent back into action with the 101st around Bastogne. The small mobile reserve known as "Team SNAFU" (Situation Normal All Fouled Up) was created to reinforce positions around the perimeter. Stan Clever recalls one particular incident with a SNAFU replacement who had been assigned to him from the Quarter Master Corps: "I had a truck driver in my squad who managed to shoot himself in the foot while cleaning an M1 carbine. Some of my guys thought this was intentional but I believe it was just inexperience and poor weapon handling skills." One night Lou Vecchi led a group of around 15 soldiers out to a forward OP. "They were all replacements of one sort or another and begged me not to leave them alone. They were so inexperienced and scared that I had to stay with them until it was time to return." Certainly, at night the MLR could be a terrifying place, especially when the cries and moans of the wounded could be heard echoing across the battlefield.

Merry Christmas from no-man's land

At 0525hrs on Christmas Day, 1st Bn was once again placed on alert and 3 hours later moved west from Luzery to Savy in support of the 502nd. That same night the Luftwaffe hit the caserne yet again, this time injuring several men from the S2, including Pfc Vinnie Utz, who lost his left arm. The bombing forced Col Sink to cut his losses and relocate along with Regimental HQ to Blaise Farm at Luzery, which had up until that point been occupied by Bob Harwick, who recalls: "We took off across the snowy fields and came across four enemy tanks that were still burning, marking the 'high water mark' of their recent attack from Recogne. Not long after our arrival at Savy we received further orders to dig in and form a second line of defense." Ex-tanker Jack Grace and several colleagues from 1 Ptn H Co decided it would be a good idea to drive one of the enemy tanks abandoned during the failed Christmas Eve attack to Bastogne as a trophy.

Despite the siege, before the move to Luzery, Regimental HQ were able to print and distribute the regimental tabloid *Para-Dice Minor.* Most popular with the men on the front lines were the writings of Dave Phillips as he recalls: "At the time I was based at the barracks working as a draftsman with the regimental S3. If we were quiet, SgtMaj Senior had me produce several news bulletins in which I wrote my own column – 'Society Notes from Here and There' – under the pseudonym of 'Miss Champagne Belch.'" Dave's Christmas offering was remembered by all those who had the opportunity to read it:

> Your society editor offers the following tips on where to go for dinner and dancing on your special night out… The Bastogne Bar & Grille is featuring a tasty little luncheon menu consisting mainly of "Ratione de Kay avec Café GI." Gerald Kraut and his "88 piece" band furnish lively and varied entertainment during cocktail hour. After sundown, the club occasionally bills Mr Looft Waffe and his famous "Flare Dance"… "The Blue Bosche" up the street furnishes a clever program of native folk dances. The most entertaining is the renowned "German War Waltz" in which the chorus performs intricate circles with hands raised while singing the hit number of the show, as popularized by the "Wehrmacht Playboys," entitled "I'm Forever Shouting Kamerad."

Further west, Ken Ross and the 502nd were on the receiving end of a regimental-scale assault from the 26.Volksgrenadier-Division, who were augmented by one battalion of tanks and two artillery battalions from Panzergrenadier-Regiment 15. "I happened to be out walking our dog, a stray that Regimental HQ had adopted, when the shelling began," Ross recalls. The attack that followed was overwhelming and at one point even reached LtCol Steve Chappuis' CP, forcing him to take up arms alongside his staff; and several enemy soldiers were cut down and killed in the orderly room. Two hours later, 1 mile further southwest, 18 enemy armored fighting vehicles broke through, carrying infantry supported by Panzergrenadier-Regiment 77 and attacked the line being held by 327th Glider Infantry between Champs and Hemroulle hoping to bypass the 502nd. During the course of the day six tanks were destroyed and two American TDs knocked out. Only after the FACs assigned to the 502nd called in air support from Ninth Air Force was the assault finally driven off.

Toward the end of the day the Germans withdrew, leaving the woods and fields northwest of Mande-St-Étienne littered with bodies and wrecked vehicles. The joint action between the 327th and 502nd (who were formed into a task force by BrigGen Higgins) resulted in 165 enemy dead and 208 prisoners. The schoolhouse at Champs had seen much fighting as witnessed by this chalk message scribbled by one of the teachers across a classroom blackboard: "Let the world never see such a Christmas night again. To die far from one's children, wife and mother, under artillery fire, there is no greater cruelty. To take away from his mother a son, a husband from his wife, a father from his children, is it worthy of a human being? Life can only be for love and respect. At the sight of ruins, of blood and death, universal fraternity will rise."

The anticipated follow-up attack did not come, and 1st Bn held their foxholes over Christmas in very cold and uncomfortable conditions, as Bob Harwick recalls: "By dawn on the 26th, I started rotating my men into local barns to catch up on some much-needed sleep. Shortly afterwards the attacks in our sector began to weaken as the Germans relocated their forces elsewhere to try and stop the Third Army relief now moving up from the south."

Back on the MLR, Cpl Bob Webb and S/Sgt Leroy Vickers from 3rd Bn communications platoon had been called out to repair a broken cable at the 81mm mortar OP in the "Eastern Eye." Short and stocky, Leroy came from Silsbee in Texas, a small town north of Beaumont, where Bob grew up. Both men had enlisted at the same time and became great friends. Webb recalls:

> The wind was gusting and whipping up the snow, forcing it horizontally into our faces. At around 0200hrs, after taking care of

the wire, we returned to the OP, which looked more like a log cabin than a hole in the ground. You could almost stand up in this thing, which had three or four bales of hay spread across the floor. The guys had a Coleman burner on a low heat and it was warm as toast. Taking off our equipment, we both sat down to get warmed up. The mortar boys offered us "clear coffee" served in a number ten fruit can. You'd bring your water to the boil and add coffee powder before dropping a small snowball into the cup, which immediately sank to the bottom, leaving you with "clear" coffee – it was such a neat trick.

Over the last few weeks I'd been suffering from intense stomach cramps that seemed to be getting worse and had to go outside and use the toilet. Squatting over the nearby latrine, I noticed a figure moving toward me. I could just make out the shape of a man wearing a heavy overcoat carrying a rifle. "Oh God no," I thought and slowly reached into my jacket for my pistol. The shadowy figure came closer and muttered something in German. Raising my .45, I carefully aimed at the man's head before realizing it was Vickers! Thinking I was unarmed, that SOB thought he'd play a trick … boy did he ever get a surprise – thank heavens I didn't pull the damn trigger.

The 20th Armored Infantry Bn (Combat Command B) aid station run by Capt "Jack" Prior was still operational along Route de Neufchâteau. He recalls: "Living in a city with no electricity, food, or proper medicine was a constant challenge. My men scrounged anything they could from deserted homes." Luckily Prior had the assistance of his battalion S1, 1st Lt Herman Jacobs, who had moved heaven and earth to find medical supplies and additional personnel to help treat, care, and cook for the patients. Among these were two young Belgian nurses, Renée Lemaire and Augusta Chiwi. A native of the Belgian Congo, Augusta had an exotic coffee-colored complexion and beautiful thick black hair. Augusta, whose uncle was a local doctor, was very capable and helped with all manner of procedures such as splinting, wound dressing, and hemorrhage control – unlike Renée, who preferred lighter duties like sponging and feeding. Dr Jack remembers:

> The combat units sent whatever food and medical supplies they could spare. Lack of water was a serious problem, although melted snow helped enormously. However, champagne seemed to fill the gap, which we often used to wash and shave with! Although there were at least three other battalion surgeons with the armor, I was the only doctor from Combat Command B operating any kind of aid station. We were now holding over 100 patients, 30 of whom were very seriously injured. To prevent gas gangrene, those suffering from extremity wounds had to be irrigated with hydrogen peroxide. Sadly, due to the lack of surgeons and operating equipment, those with head, chest, and abdominal wounds faced a slow and almost certain death.

Previously, on December 23, Capt Prior made his first visit to the caserne where he met the acting divisional surgeon, Maj Douglas Davidson, from the 502nd PIR. "I requested that he make an effort to bring in some sort of medical help for us. Davidson listened as I detailed my situation and then assured me that it was currently impossible to bring in a glider surgical team, at least not until the weather improved." To illustrate the scale of the problem facing the 101st, Davidson showed Prior around the rifle range and adjacent workshop building. Prior could not believe the staggering number of casualties spread across the two facilities and was moved to tears as he watched Father John Maloney give last rights to the dying. It seemed odd to Jack that a Catholic priest should be carrying a .45 semi-automatic pistol in a shoulder holster, but that was the nature of things at Bastogne. "Someone announced that Third Army was only a few miles away, which evoked a huge cheer from the patients," recalls Jack. "After the tour, I returned to my post feeling quite depressed. The next day, I was told that Maj Davidson made a trip into the German lines, under a white flag, in an attempt to arrange a truce for medical evacuation. Davidson had proposed to take out one German casualty for every two Americans, but the idea was refused by the German commander."

Ironically, on Christmas Day, despite the bad weather, surgeon Maj Howard Sorrell from Third Army was flown in ahead of his team by Piper Cub. Twelve hours earlier, the Luftwaffe had inadvertently bombed the 20th Armored Infantry aid station, killing 20 patients and nurse Renée Lemaire. Jack Prior was in the next building with Lt Jacobs and Augusta Chiwi when the enemy aircraft attacked a convoy in the street opposite. "After the raid we ran outside and discovered the aid station was now a flaming inferno. The magnesium flares dropped by the plane were still burning as we clawed our way through the debris. The pilot saw what was happening and came back to strafe the crowd."

Although injured by falling masonry, Herman Jacobs helped evacuate the patients and organized firefighting parties to extinguish the blaze. After the aircraft had gone, Capt Prior and several others were able to gain entry through a cellar window and recover two or three casualties before the entire building collapsed. After gathering together the remaining patients, Prior had them transported to the rifle range at the caserne. At around 0300hrs on Christmas morning, another raid totally destroyed the building next door to the smoldering medical facility. "Before my unit left Bastogne on January 17, we picked our way through the debris and managed to recover and identify most of the bodies, including Renée Lemaire's, which I wrapped in a white parachute and took back to her parents. Later I wrote a special commendation for her and forwarded it to my commander, MajGen William Morris."

Things were relatively quiet up on the MLR, and many people like Hank DiCarlo spent their time improving foxholes and visiting friends in other platoons. On Christmas morning, Ed Shames sent Earl McClung to Bastogne with several others to collect supplies that had been dropped by parachute the previous day. Ed recalls:

> When they returned, McClung came over and said "Cap, there's a package for you." I was ecstatic and imagined a pair of gloves, a hat,

> or a muffler. Enthusiastically, I tore open the small parcel that was from Ida Aframe – a gorgeous girl I'd known back in Virginia – and was underwhelmed to find a fountain pen along with a neatly folded letter. Somewhat frustrated, I threw the pen into the snow and went about my business. A couple of hours later Rod Strohl came over and said, "Here Lieutenant, you dropped your pen." "No," I replied. I threw it away in disgust. "Well, you better take another look, sir, because this thing is fabulous and made of solid 14-carat gold." Sure it is, sure it is – I thought he was joking because the boys were always pulling pranks, but he was quite right. I told him to hell with the pen and that he was welcome to keep it. When I read Ida's letter it was clear that after taking advice from my sister Anna, she presumed that we were well catered for and that the beautiful high-quality pen – manufactured by Eversharp, engraved "Lt E. D. Shames" – which cost her an astonishing $245.00 would make an ideal gift! The next day Rod gave the pen back to me and this time I was man enough to accept the "gift" for what it was – a wonderful gesture from my future wife, although I didn't know that at the time!

Meanwhile "Sharkey" Tarquini (1 Ptn H Co) received a forwarded letter from an English gentleman, as Lou Vecchi recalls: "Sharkey had got this guy's wife pregnant and was dumb enough to leave her his APO address. Her husband wanted to know what he was going to do about it, and I remember when things calmed down, Sharkey sarcastically writing back, 'If you can get me out of here right now, then I am more than willing to help you and your wife, in any way possible!' I've often wondered what that kid would have looked like, as Sharkey was not blessed with good looks." Harold Stedman distinctly remembers being handed packets of DDT powder that had been parachuted in with the medical supplies. "I guess that as we were covered in fleas and lice the army decided to do something about it?"

At 0905hrs on the 26th, enemy aircraft appeared above Foy and proceeded to bomb and strafe the 3rd Bn MLR. Although there were no casualties, the raid reminded the paratroopers that they were still vulnerable and defenseless against the Luftwaffe. Harley Dingman remembers the attack:

> Orange air panels and parachutes had been placed in the snow along the edge of the woods. At the time I was standing under the trees with some of my guys and could only hear the engines and presumed they were ours. Then suddenly one of the planes came screaming toward us. We could just make out something dropping a short distance away. Looking up, I recall saying to the boys, "Christ Almighty – it's a bomb." The guys were already piling into one of our pre-dug air-raid trenches as the bomb bounced through the trees and hit the ground no more than 50ft away from where I was standing. Luckily the concussion blew up and over my head, forcing me down into another hole. Bizarrely there was no sound; everything in that instant was completely silent, almost like I was in some sort of vacuum.

Doctor Ryan received several boxes of medicinal alcohol, which had been air dropped before Christmas. Barney had far more than he was ever going to use, so as a gesture of benevolence he decided to distribute the excess spirit among the men. The platoon sergeants were called over to the aid station, where they were each allocated a number of the small bottles. Ryan stressed that because of the alcohol's strength and purity only a tiny amount could be rationed to each man and even then it had to be drastically watered down.

It would appear that some people ignored the doctor's advice, including Col Patch. When Fred Bahlau reported to the warm and cozy battalion CP, one of the officers handed him a green jar with what he thought contained a hot beverage. Col Patch fell about laughing as Bahlau struggled to catch his breath and nearly collapsed after taking two small sips. Harley Dingman recalls having to mix the spirit with melted snow before adding lemon powder to taste. "Even then it was far too strong but seemed to hit the mark." At the time, Johnny Gibson was sharing a foxhole next to the aid station with fellow medic John Eckman. "Eckman drank far too much alcohol and around midnight began vomiting everywhere. Not only did 'Big John' throw up all over me but also my emergency telephone connected to the battalion CP. The smell was so bad that I opened the hessian drape covering the entrance to my cozy trench. I couldn't stand it any longer and in sheer desperation crawled over to a nearby unfinished foxhole and spent the rest of the night shivering in the open." Eckman was luckier than S/Sgt Alexander Engelbrecht (I Co 1 Ptn), who subsequently developed Dry Beriberi, which affected his nervous system, and had to be evacuated.

Silent wings

Between December 26 and 27, 61 gliders from the 439th and 440th TCG (which had dropped 3/506 into Normandy on D-Day) brought in heavier supplies and equipment, such as gasoline, plus a nine-man surgical team from Third Army. The volunteer medics were Maj Lamar Soutter, Capt Stanley Wesolowski, and Capt Foy Moody, plus technicians Clarence Matz and John Knowles from the 4th Auxiliary Surgical Group. The remaining four medical personnel, Capt Henry Mills, Capt Edward Zinschlag, and technicians John Donahue and Laurence Rethwisch, came from 12th Evacuation Hospital. The surgical team immediately went to work alongside Maj Sorrell (who was assisted by Jack Prior), operating on patients with abdominal and chest injuries to stabilize them for the inevitable forthcoming evacuation.

Unusually, the GC4A glider carrying the surgical staff made not one but two landings on December 26, as pilot 1st Lt Charleton Corwin Jr (96th Sqn) recalls: "After being briefed by our CO, LtCol Frank Krebs, I took off with my co-pilot, Ben Constantino, from our base in Orleans behind 'The Trusty Township,' a C-47 tow plane flown by Capt Roy Ottoman. After being released we landed on a fighter airfield at Etain, where the medical team were waiting for us. From here we headed for the operations office, who informed us that we would have at least one P-47 escort. After loading the medics and all of their equipment, we re-attached to Roy Ottoman's plane and lifted off for Bastogne. During the last leg of the flight a Thunderbolt pitched up, and the pilot waved at us before disappearing into the distance."

On December 27, five C-47s from 95th Sqn, 440th TCG, were shot down, resulting in the loss of nine airmen. Herbert Ballinger was a navigator in 93rd Sqn, 439th TCG, who volunteered to pilot one of the 50 gliders selected for the mission:

> I'd been assigned Glider Number 35, which was loaded with 105mm artillery shells. Flying without a co-pilot, it was cold, but I was wrapped up in suitable clothing, flak suit, and parachute. For the first part of the trip the air was full of ice crystals constantly rattling against the windshield. The glider wouldn't trim properly and had to be constantly maneuvered to maintain position. As soon as we crossed enemy lines the flak began to intensify, but most of it was exploding way above our formation. At that point I felt the urge to urinate but couldn't leave the flight deck to use the "relief tube" situated toward the back of the aircraft. I soon lost the urge when a couple of C-47s were hit and went down, taking their gliders with them. Moments later my tow ship was struck in the left aileron and then the glider was peppered by shrapnel which penetrated my windshield, rear-loading door, and elevators. It was terrifying knowing I was carrying high explosives even though the fuses had been removed and stored separately.

The glider missions all came in on a northeasterly course to the landing zone (LZ) northeast of Savy. "Not long after we made it through the flak belt, a white light flashed from the astrodome of my tow ship, signaling me to release the cable in 1 minute. I quickly checked my map against the terrain below and realized we were in the wrong place, so I didn't cut away." Standard operating procedures dictated that if a glider did not release after 60 seconds, the tow plane would then show a green light. If that failed then a red light was flashed to signal that the cable would be jettisoned after a further 60 seconds. Ballinger continues:

> Looking down, I could see what looked like enemy tanks, so there was no way I was going to disconnect. After receiving the green and red lights my C-47 jettisoned the cable. Turning into the LZ, I took a fair amount of small-arms fire as I slowed the glider during my descent. Trying to keep the nose up I came to rest in a bank of snow about 400 yards inside our lines!
>
> The paratroopers soon arrived with a jeep and trailer and had to unload through the rear door instead of the usual front access. Before they had finished another jeep turned up and took me to Divisional Headquarters, where I joined the other glider pilots and some of the power boys [slang for aircrew flying piston engined aircraft] who'd previously been shot down. After the siege was lifted we were evacuated by truck and acted as escorts for the German prisoners in Bastogne who were then handed over to the army. As for us we ended up at a railway station [probably Libramont] and spent a bitterly cold night waiting for a train that eventually arrived in the early hours of the morning. We were then taken to an airfield and flown back to the UK.

6

"Steel whirlwind"

Post-Christmas breakthrough

Despite the weather conditions, three columns from Third Army simultaneously converged on Bastogne from Martelange, Witre, and Neufchâteau. At 1645hrs on the 26th, supported by 105mm and 155mm artillery, C Co 37th Tank Bn, led by LtCol Creighton Abrams, and C Co 53rd Armored Infantry Bn (4th Armored Division) were the first unit from "Combat Command Reserve" to make contact with elements of 326th Airborne Engineers near Assenois. Early the following morning (December 27), the road between Neufchâteau and Bastogne was officially declared open. Although supported by troops from the 35th ID it would take another two days for the main body to clear a wider and more secure corridor along the main road from the border with Luxembourg at Arlon to Bastogne.

The American tankers were surprised to see the countryside surrounding the city littered with over 170 knocked-out German armored vehicles. By late afternoon, a convoy of ten trucks and 22 ambulances evacuated 260 priority patients to the 635th Clearing Co at Villers d'Avant. During the epic week-long siege a total of 943 American and 125 German casualties were dealt with by the medical facilities in Bastogne. Amongst those being evacuated was Clark Heggeness, who recalls, "I was sent by ambulance train to Paris before being flown to England for treatment. Back in the UK, I underwent skin graft surgery and after several months of recuperation was sent back to the 506th in southern Bavaria."

Despite bringing in reinforcements from Mourmelon, the regiment was still desperately short of manpower and began to draft in troops from other units such as the 327th and 401st GIR – while existing front-line personnel were reshuffled. Five L-4 spotter planes were also flown in and put to immediate use by the Air Liaison Team.

When the first relief tanks from Third Army arrived at Foy, Hank DiCarlo was shocked to see an old friend from back home. "One of the crewmen, Phil Bonelli, was from my hometown of Wildwood, New Jersey. Phil's dad ran the local grocery store just around the corner from my parents, who owned a small hotel. It was astonishing to see him – I just couldn't believe it." Harley Dingman was also surprised when an old buddy, 2nd Lt Joe Wetzig, tapped him on the shoulder: "Last time I spoke to Joe he was a garbage collector from West Carthage [New York] and now I had to salute him! We only had a chance to talk for a few minutes before Joe was called back to his platoon."

For T/5 George Allen at the police station, there were no cheers of joy.

> We simply went about our business as usual. By mid-afternoon the trucks arrived with trailers to collect the prisoners and take them to a new camp at Neufchâteau. I said goodbye to my three cooks, who offered me no thanks for my efforts – although I never really expected any. Just as the POWs were being herded onto the transport by our MPs and glider pilots, a captain from the "Order of Battle" [OB] section came over and asked if I could take over while he returned to Mourmelon to pick up replacements. The rest of the divisional IPW team were brought back to the caserne to run a small POW compound next to McAuliffe's HQ. The OB job was simple and consisted of me staying in the cellar at the divisional CP and keeping a map which showed the enemy and our own dispositions so that visiting liaison officers could see an up-to-date view of our divisional lines!

With the road from Neufchâteau now open, the 801st Ordnance Co, who had been "locked out" since December 20, were sent to the indoor range, which had been cleared of dead and wounded the previous afternoon. Sharing the facility with the 801st was a bomb disposal unit and a small team from the intelligence section. "We also had use of a smaller building nearby and the target store, which became our kitchen and mess area," recalls 1/Sgt Bob Higgins.

When the first A rations began to arrive, the divisional mess sergeant visited the 801st and asked if he could relocate his kitchen to the target store, where he could more easily serve three decent meals a day. During the siege the 101st kitchen had been located in one of the barrack buildings, next door to Div Signal Co, facing the square. The cookhouse was vulnerable to artillery and on Christmas Eve had been hit by a 280mm shell from a rail gun hidden in a tunnel at Schimpach east of Benonchamps (which luckily failed to detonate). However, a smaller projectile had passed through the signal office and exploded in the next room, killing cooks Pfc Ben Childs and Pfc Floyd Goad. "The mess sergeant wanted to move in right away," recalls Higgins. "But because we had so many other problems to resolve, I told him it would have to wait until the next day. No more than 1 hour later a shell penetrated the target store. Luckily the place was empty at the time and nobody was hurt, but if I'd agreed to the mess sergeant's idea it may well have been a different story. Around the same time, one of the intelligence guys, an officer – I never knew his name – was killed in an adjacent building by shellfire." Later, another 300lb shell fired from the railway gun landed close to the range. "The enormous blast lifted me bodily in my sleeping bag completely off the ground," recalls Higgins. "The following morning we were astonished to see an antiaircraft team arrive [from Combat Command A] and park their 'quad fifty' in the crater."

Up on the MLR ammunition became more plentiful and the cooks from the front-line units were now able to produce a variety of food. The 3rd Bn catering staff, S/Sgt Tony Zeoli and Pvt Bob Penner (ex I Co), were working from a field kitchen close to the battalion CP, providing regular hot meals for the men. Finally MajGen Maxwell Taylor reached Bastogne and took command of the division. Before leaving Neufchâteau, he offered a lift to several journalists, including Cornelius Ryan and Mary Monks.

Monks (who married Ernest Hemingway in 1946) was known as Mary Welsh when she worked for *The Daily Express.* Although Ryan refused due to the high risks, Mary threw caution to the wind and became the first reporter to interview Anthony McAuliffe. Subsequently Tony (who was replaced by William Gillmore) did a brief publicity tour before being posted to the 103rd ID in Alsace Lorraine (McAuliffe finally left Bastogne on January 9). Two days before McAuliffe's departure, leaving behind a forward section at the barracks, Gen Taylor relocated his Divisional Headquarters 2 miles southwest of the town, split between Ile-le Pré and Ile-la Hesse. Each HQ was completely self-sufficient and capable of independent function should either be affected by enemy action.

After going AWOL and being sent back to Mourmelon on Christmas Eve, Bob Rommel discovered that the battalion had already departed for Bastogne. "For obvious reasons we had to wait until after Christmas before being transported to Belgium with reinforcements. It was standing room only in the trucks and the temperature was off the scale. At one point, due to the treacherous conditions, our driver skidded and the back of the truck hit the side of a house, putting a huge crack in the front wall. The owner appeared and angrily shouted and shook his fist in the air as we drove away. That first evening on the MLR, despite the freezing cold, I got so snug and warm in my foxhole that I even took my boots off and fell into a deep sleep – although this never happened again."

It had been quiet for a few days, but despite the general feeling of exhaustion, Alex Andros still had his men "stand to" before first light. "One morning during this lull as it was getting light we noticed the front of an enemy tank protruding from behind a house on the edge of Foy. We still had the 37mm antitank gun located with us, so I instructed the crew to fire one shot, but it fell short by about 50 yards. The crew readjusted and fired another two or three rounds which bounced off the tank's glacis plate straight up into the air. Moments later the tank moved forward, traversing its turret, and fired several rounds of AP toward our position before backing away. We all dove for cover into our foxholes as the shells cut straight through our positions and continued on into the woods behind us."

The Dominique family, who had migrated west from Recogne, decided to head back and check on their livestock. Roger Dominique recalls:

> Making our way through the Fazone Woods, we passed a number of enemy positions. When we arrived at our farm a German soldier was on guard next to the barn. The sentry let us enter the house, where we found the roof riddled with holes but the building still habitable. Miraculously, the cows and horses were still alive so we took them to a nearby water point that wasn't frozen solid. My mom went ahead with one of the other horses and managed to upset a squad of Germans by inadvertently walking through their "roadblock" at the crossroads near d'Hoffschmidt Château. Mom was so busy looking around at the damage to the village that she failed to notice a string of daisy mines scattered across the road! We had about 20–30 German troops in Recogne and one of these was an NCO who constantly ordered my mother to make hot meals for his men. We called him "Prima," because he always repeated the word to express his satisfaction regarding the "forced labor" we were providing.

The improving weather conditions allowed the Air Force to fly several missions during the day against Noville, Foy, and Recogne. Once again the battalion placed orange marker panels along the edge of the MLR to keep the Allied aircraft north of the Bois Champay. Earlier, taking full advantage of the clear skies, Bastogne was bombed and strafed for the eighth time by the Luftwaffe. Shortly after the attack, it was announced by Patton's Third Army that respirators were to be issued due to growing fears that the Germans were contemplating the use of chemical weapons. The ground troops were now being supported by dozens of newly arrived heavy guns from Third Army that also provided much-needed additional firepower for their own 4th Armored Division.

At 0710hrs on December 30, a number of enemy planes bombed the area across the road from the regimental CP at Luzery injuring several people, including Clarence Hester. Later that night, the Luftwaffe flew one of their most concentrated missions against Bastogne, and as a result many of the last remaining civilians were evacuated.

It was business as usual for Alex Andros and 3 Ptn H Co, although New Year's Eve would be a day he would always remember. "A squadron of P-47 Thunderbolt ground-attack aircraft flew in low overhead. It was like watching a movie as they dropped a couple of bombs and strafed Foy before heading west toward Noville, hitting several enemy tanks along the way." Andros had previously noted a re-entrant southwest of Vaux, where the Germans had positioned a number of their antiaircraft guns. "Needless to say, the draw took a bit of a hammering during the raid and it looked to us like one of the planes was hit by ground fire from this area as it banked away, leaving a long trail of smoke. At the same time we watched one of the German tanks painted in white winter camouflage moving perpendicular to our lines at about 700 yards."

The action performed by the Panzer was a standard protective drill as its commander desperately tried to maneuver his chassis broadside toward the oncoming threat. The Thunderbolts were based at Mourmelon and came from the 513th Fighter Squadron, 406th Fighter Group. The pilot of the P-47 hit by ground fire may well have been 1st Lt Harry Krig, who recalls the events before and after the attack:

> We had orders to neutralize a German tank convoy on the road to Bastogne. Our first wave attacked and, as expected, received heavy fire from the flak guns. As part of the second wave we were advised because of the antiaircraft fire to begin our attack runs from behind a nearby hill. I came in so low that my propeller blade hit the tops of the trees. Before launching my rockets, I had to gain altitude and

> then dive back down to get a decent firing position. Aiming for this one particular "white" tank, I pulled up into a turn to avoid flying through the explosion. At this point the engine of my plane was hit by 20mm cannon fire. Turning toward Bastogne I was alarmed to see a large hole in my left wing and a belt of ammunition dangling from it. As I began to climb the engine burst into flames and, before cutting out, caused the cockpit to fill with dark acrid smoke. We knew that the 101st were holding the perimeter below and had orders when hit, to jump, if possible, within their main line of defense.
>
> The standard operating procedure was to open the canopy at the lowest possible speed and jump toward the trailing edge of the wing. Rapidly losing altitude, the plane was accelerating, and as I stood up the wind pressure threw me back against the cockpit. Clambering out, I managed to slide a short distance along the fuselage but as I leapt off, my left leg smashed into the leading edge of the tail plane. Tumbling in freefall, I managed to deploy my parachute with only seconds to spare before landing heavily in the 12in-deep snow [the plane crashed 1 mile southwest of the MLR alongside the N30 near Luzery]. While unbuckling my 'chute, I noticed my left leg seemed paralyzed and numb. It was late morning when I heard voices but couldn't quite make out what language they were speaking and decided to cover myself with the white canopy.

Krig had in fact come down on the edge of Foy, adjacent to the "Eastern Eye" and the 3rd Bn 81mm OP.

"Not long after landing I noticed a medic waving to me from the edge of the woods about 250 yards away," Krig continues. "I couldn't stay in the field and began to drag myself under cover of the parachute toward the friendly tree line. After what seemed like an eternity my strength ran out; the medic and another trooper ran across, grabbed underneath my arms, and dragged me into the woods. After being covered with a blanket they placed me in a log-covered foxhole as protection from incoming enemy mortar fire. After being given a shot of morphine I was told by the medics that I would have to wait for nightfall before it would be safe for evacuation."

Harry was handed a rifle and told to point it toward the direction he had just come from. 3 Ptn G Co were dug in nearby, and just before dark Bob Izumi went over to see if there was anything he could do. "We got the pilot onto a stretcher and carried him back to a waiting jeep," recalls Bob. From here Krig was taken to the seminary. He describes his arrival there:

> One side of the building had been hit by a shell and was covered by a tarpaulin. The wounded – both military and civilian – were lying in rows on stretchers. Behind a screen at one end of the hospital was a brightly lit operating theater. As the medic who had been treating me said goodbye I handed him my pistol as a token of appreciation. The woman on the stretcher next to me died during the night and her place was taken by a young soldier fresh out of theater. Morphine seemed to be plentiful, and after being dosed up I closed my eyes and went to sleep.
>
> The next day, New Year's Eve, was spent in a corner out of the way waiting to be evacuated, feasting on crackers and cheese. That night I was loaded into an ambulance that stopped constantly for tank and truck convoys which had the right of way.

At dawn on New Year's Day, Krig arrived at the recently established divisional clearing station in a school at Cobreville situated halfway along the main road to Neufchâteau. He continues his account:

> Because my leg was badly swollen, it was splinted, and I was issued a pair of crutches in readiness for a medevac flight to the UK. Not wanting to leave my squadron, my buddies, or the war, I hitchhiked about half a mile down the road to a makeshift airfield. After chatting to a pilot of a spotter plane, he agreed to fly me to Mourmelon in exchange for two bottles of Scotch whiskey stored at the base in my footlocker.

> Returning to the hospital, I told the administrator of my plans and strangely he didn't seem to object. The following morning I returned to the airfield, and as we were preparing to leave, nine ME109s raced in low overhead and began strafing a row of C-47s. Leaving me struggling like an idiot, everyone ran toward a sandbagged antiaircraft battery. I abandoned my crutches and crawled toward the emplacement. After three runs the ME109s departed, leaving the L-4 intact and inflicting only minor damage to the transport planes. My pilot, who was a sergeant, took off and flew all the way to Mourmelon at treetop height. After paying the agreed fare I made my way to the squadron operations tent, where the guys were shocked and amazed to see me alive. Our surgeon, Doc Neel, took me to a hospital in Metz where my leg was finally placed in a plaster cast. After a brief spell at a Forward Air Control Center, I came back to Mourmelon to have my cast removed before returning to operational flying with the squadron.

Up on the MLR, Harold Stedman had not taken his boots off for a week. "We had a small fire going in our CP and I was able to warm my feet, which were completely numb, over the hot coals. Within a few minutes, the heat twisted my boots into a 'U' shape and burned the soles of my feet. Luckily one of the boys managed to get another pair of boots from a dead colleague who had no further use for them." Meanwhile, from his four-man dugout on the 81mm mortar line, Bob Dunning was sitting with Herb Spence's frozen feet firmly tucked into his armpits. Pfc Carlos DeBlasio was cooking a small can of cheese and had forgotten to puncture the lid. A few minutes later the tin exploded with a loud bang, showering the three men with its scalding contents. Dunning and the others broke into fits of laughter as they reflected on the ridiculous situation they now found themselves in. At 1 minute past midnight, both sides welcomed in the New Year with several barrages of artillery and mortar fire. However, in Berlin, Hitler had already begun to make plans for a new offensive in Alsace Lorraine.

The "Relief Corridor" into Bastogne had been considerably widened, taking the pressure off the MLR. German activity along the front had slowed down to a point that it was almost nonexistent. Manny Barrios was ordered to mount a three-man patrol to bring back a prisoner from 26.Volksgrenadier-Division, who were still holding the area around Foy and Recogne. Information from POWs and captured documents enabled the artillery to disorganize any possible enemy troop concentrations or potential attacks. Manny recalls the details of the search:

> The following night we moved out through the MLR and down into Foy without any problem. After 2 or 3 hours of searching, we spotted something glowing in the distance. Quietly we approached and watched two German soldiers warming their hands over a small field stove. The man closest to the cooker had a rifle lying on the snow next to him. Another rifle was resting against the stump of a tree that we figured belonged to the other guy.
>
> We must have spent an hour or so trying to decide how to get at least one of them out alive without making too much noise. Finally it was decided that I would circle around to the rear while the others jumped the two Volksgrenadiers from the front. Everything went as planned until the Kraut who'd left his rifle against the stump suddenly raised his hand and said something. His buddy picked up the weapon that was on the ground, turned, and pointed it directly at me. Thankfully the gun malfunctioned but by that time I was close enough to smash the soldier across the face with the butt of my rifle. My two colleagues subdued the other guy and we were able to restrain and gag them both. Before retracing our steps back to the MLR, I picked up and turned off the stove before sliding it into the cargo pocket of my trousers. Over the next few weeks the Kraut cooker came in plenty useful and 70 years later it still works.

On New Year's Day 1945, while drawing water from the well in Foy, several unidentified American troops had been observed by members of H Co. Ed Shames and the regimental patrols platoon were alerted and moved west from their bivouac area in the Bois Jacques to the 3rd Bn MLR. Here the men split into their respective mission groups and waited for nightfall. As Ed Shames' patrol was tasked with observing the well, he moved forward to the "Eastern Eye" of the Bois Champay.

Stepping out in single file, Shames led his men under cover of darkness to the edge of Foy. Using foliage for cover, Ed pushed forward through a small orchard and positioned his patrol along a slope overlooking the well. "We lay there for several hours trying to keep warm but nothing was happening. I remember feeling peckish and struggled with frozen fingers to open a tin of corn pork loaf with apple flakes." Just as Shames was about to withdraw, a figure appeared and approached the well. Ed quietly moved forward with "Skinny" Sisk, who made it clear that he would cut the man's throat if he uttered a single word or sound. Ed noted that the individual was wearing an American uniform, but the real surprise came when they got him back to the MLR. "I was shocked to hear the prisoner conversing with me like any other dogface American soldier."

Under duress, before Shames sent the prisoner back to Regiment, the soldier revealed that he belonged to an eight-man commando team now working from the basement of the Koeune house. It is entirely possible that the Germans were part of Operation *Greif* ("Griffin") set up by legendary SS-Obersturmbannführer Otto Skorzeny to infiltrate and create chaos behind enemy lines. In a desperate attempt to plea bargain, the prisoner revealed the names of his colleagues and that they had all lived in the States before the war. "Orders came back for us to stake out the house over the next two nights," recalls Ed. "The planning was left to me and I selected the same five guys who had accompanied me the previous evening. You would have imagined, knowing their colleague had disappeared, that the men working from the basement might have suspected they had been compromised. But bizarrely they remained in situ, maybe because the cellar provided a warm and therefore more comfortable place to stay. On the second night it got so cold that I had to inject my leg with morphine to numb the pain from the frozen ground. We had seen enough to know that there was no immediate security around the building so I gave the order to move in."

Walking along the side of the house with Sisk and Stein, Ed arrived at the sunken entrance to the cellar and tapped lightly on the heavy wooden door. It is interesting to note that by this stage in the campaign enemy forces fighting around the pocket had been scaled down by around 50 percent, which may explain why Shames and his team were able to access the Koeune house without challenge.

Speaking just above a whisper, Stein uttered a few words in German, and moments later a man appeared in the doorway. Shames continues: "Initially the Kraut thought we were another German patrol before I told him in English that they were surrounded and we knew exactly who they were. The Feldwebel [corporal] was informed that if he or any of his men didn't come quietly then we would cut their throats. We counted and disarmed the soldiers as they emerged from the cellar and ordered them to keep their mouths tightly shut before returning to the MLR."

Shortly after passing through one of the I Co OPs in the "Eye," the senior man (who had answered the door) arrogantly began talking to his comrades in rapid German. "After telling him to shut the hell up, I called the guy forward and asked him to kneel on the ground. Again I asked for information but he flatly refused. The intelligence was vital and it didn't matter how we got it; after all, these troops were by no means conventional."

In front of the other prisoners, Ed placed the muzzle of his .45 automatic on the man's forehead. Once more Shames requested information: "I made it clear that if someone didn't speak up within the next minute I'd give the Feldwebel the 'deep six' treatment.* The Kraut snapped at his men to remain silent so I gently squeezed the trigger and blew the back of his skull off. That really got the attention of the others, who quickly told us everything we needed to know.

* In military terms, this refers to human annihilation, and is derived from the traditional depth of a grave: 6ft.

Afterwards, I sent the prisoners over to Regiment but was never told what became of them." The decision to kill the enemy soldier certainly did not come easily but these were times of extreme duress and almost unimaginable combat stress. Ed Shames feared for the lives of the men under his own command as well as the greater American force surrounded in Foy if they were to be infiltrated.

Word quickly spread about the capture of the German imposters. "Before first light on January 2, after all our patrols had returned safely, the MLR went on to high alert," recalls Jim Martin. "This was followed by a 2-hour 'window,' during which any unscheduled 'American' activity coming from the area in front of our positions could be instantly targeted without challenge."

Previously Capt Doughty had turned a blind eye to S/Sgt James West (1 Ptn) making regular unsanctioned trips down to Degives Farm on the southern edge of Recogne. Although the farm had been abandoned two weeks earlier, Nestor Degives had left behind a well-stocked wine cellar. Despite the "lockdown," West, accompanied by Pvt Charles Hunton, decided to ignore what was going on. Route Madame was the boundary between G/506 and the 502nd. As usual, West informed whoever was manning the OP before passing through. However, while the two G Co men were relaxing down at the farm, the H/502 OP shift changed and the new guard was not updated with the situation.

An hour or so later, as Hunton and West were returning along the beech-lined road, the soldier in the OP opened fire with a machine gun and both men were killed instantly. The stupidity and risk of Jim West's actions almost beggars belief but death and horrific injury on the front line around Bastogne were something that everyone became accustomed to. A few miserable days later, Ed Stein was also badly wounded by shrapnel while on OP duty with Shames.

By early January on the eastern MLR, 2/506 were preparing to cross the Bizory road in preparation for a frontal attack northeast alongside the 501st, through the Bois Jacques into the Bois des Corbeaux (Crow Wood). The idea of the maneuver (which commenced at 0930hrs) was to advance through 1,000 yards of dense forest to an old farmer's road that ran from Foy to Ourbourcy. At 0600hrs on January 2, 1st Bn moved forward from Savy to take over the 2/506 MLR. During the move Maj Harwick's battalion came under attack from the Luftwaffe and suffered a number of casualties.

Initially resistance was light until the paratroopers reached the road. By late afternoon the objective had been taken and a new MLR established with F Co on the left and E Co in the center. Ed Shames and 3 Ptn were designated to patrol the right-hand flank of the incursion and took up positions alongside D/501 near an iron bridge over the Bastogne/Gouvy railway. By this time 2nd Lt Hughes was having difficulty walking and removed his boots for a foot inspection by Ed Shames, who recalls: "Both of Hughes' feet were black and we tried to warm them gently over a small fire in the bottom of a foxhole. The man was in so much pain that I had absolutely no choice but to call the medics, who evacuated him immediately. We learned later that another day or two on the line and Hughes would have lost both feet."

The iron bridge (scrapped in 2009) was utilized by local farmers for moving produce and livestock from Foy and signified the entry into "bandit country" for Shames, who recalls, "We would have to approach the bridge from the west through the dense forest alongside the old drover's road and then claw our way down the embankment onto the tracks." The enemy were holding the woods on the other side of the bridge where Shames was instructed to carry out combat patrols to keep the Germans on the eastern side of the tracks.

At night the area around the bridge was pitch black and the trees that lined the steep embankment either side of the line difficult to traverse. "'Skinny' Sisk used to throw pebbles through the gap under the bridge to solicit any possible response before deciding if it was safe to continue," recalls Ed. "One night we came back off patrol and it had been so cold that I could feel the chill deep inside my bones. McCardle, my runner, came over and said, 'Sir, we've got a hot meal for you!' I was speechless and inquired how on earth they'd managed to prepare such a thing. McClung had shot a jackrabbit but I just couldn't bring myself to eat the meat because of the disgusting smell permeating from the carcass. This was crazy because although I was starving hungry I couldn't swallow a single mouthful of that hideous concoction without retching."

Thirty-six hours later the 501st took over the newly established front line and 2nd Bn began to exfiltrate in several phases toward an area of woods recently vacated by 1/506. 1st Bn had been held in regimental reserve directly behind the original 3 Ptn E Co positions and had departed for Savy late the previous afternoon (January 3).

Over on the western MLR, things had been relatively calm for 3rd Bn except for the usual incoming artillery and mortar fire, as Bob Rommel recalls:

> I swear that we could never see or pinpoint any muzzle flashes when we came under regular artillery fire. For this reason we suspected the enemy must have been firing through dampened burlap sacks or something similar. This wasn't the case with the *Nebelwerfer* rocket launchers or "Screaming Meemies," one of the most devastating weapons we experienced after New Year. When 2/506 re-occupied the Bois Jacques on our right flank, they came under the most horrific attack. From where I was it looked as though the entire ridgeline behind Foy erupted in smoke and flame. The rockets made a terrible noise and we could actually see the projectiles traveling through the air into the 2nd Bn positions over on the other side of the N30.

Back in the Bois Jacques, D and E companies were in the process of crossing the Foy/Bizory road when they were hit by the "Screaming Meemies." The initial devastating attack lasted 5 minutes. Ed Shames and Paul Rogers frantically organized a human chain to evacuate the wounded, which was abruptly cut short by a second, even more deadly, saturation. It was around this time that "Buck" Compton finally imploded after seeing two of his men, Sgt Bill Guarnere and Sgt Joe Toye, horrifically injured. As 3 Ptn were reorganizing one of the men ran over to inform Ed Shames of an officer from another platoon who was nearby and behaving strangely.

Shames dashed across and found 2nd Lt Ernie Mann from 1 Ptn sitting at the bottom of a shell crater staring blankly into space. "I'd known Mann since Toccoa. 'Ernie, Ernie can you hear me, it's Ed, Eddie Shames. I was in I Co with you … remember?' Nothing I said seemed to connect and he just sat there motionless like a zombie, his unblinking eyes looking right through me. There was nothing I could do except keep him warm and tell our company commander." Norman Dike quickly arranged for Ernie Mann (who had won a battlefield commission in Holland) to be evacuated and Ed never saw him again. Further along the road to the east around 1530hrs, elements of D Co were caught out in the open as radio operator Cpl Richard Gleason recalls: "I was with Sgt Allen Westphal moving down the road along the edge of the woods when the first rockets screamed in. We all hit the deck, and in the ensuing panic Westphal managed to wedge his boots against my face. A chunk of twisted casing whistled past and glanced off Westphal's leg before piercing the tire of a jeep parked on the road. 1st Lt Robert Gage was just beyond the vehicle and got another piece of shrapnel in his right hip. It went quiet for a few moments and Westphal rolled up his trouser leg to check that he was OK."

As the men began to move off there was a big explosion from the other side of the railway near Detaille Farm followed by a rising column of black smoke. Moments later two tattered and bleeding tankers appeared over the embankment and staggered toward D Co. Suddenly Cpl Gleason and the others came under fire again. "Crawling on my hands and knees, I had just made it to a small clump of trees when it felt like someone had punched me in the ribs." Dropping the radio Gleason began to remove his equipment. "I knew I'd been hit but couldn't figure out where. Then something struck my helmet and blood began to run down my face." After a quick inspection Gleason discovered a jagged half-inch hole through the steel, but that was the least of his worries. "My left shoulder had been penetrated by shrapnel and was now beginning to stiffen. Fording a nearby stream, I made my way to a half-track ambulance and was evacuated an hour or so later."

Shortly after Jack Foley took over Buck Compton's platoon he stormed into Ed Shames' area, complaining about a small fire they had burning in one of the foxholes. "After the recent rocket attack," recalls Shames, "I turned to Foley, who I figured was only trying to make a point, and replied sarcastically, 'Lieutenant, you think they don't know where the hell we are? Now if you don't mind I have patrols to organize – remind me again what it is exactly that your platoon does?" Foley's face was like thunder as he turned around and went back to 2 Ptn, spitting nails. Like Compton, the E Co commander, 1st Lt Norman Dike, had not performed well over the last few days and was now under close scrutiny. After being relieved by the 501st, 2nd Bn were finally pulled out of the Bois Jacques at 2130hrs on January 4, before rotating into regimental reserve in the Bois Champay behind H/506 and later G Co.

One morning in early January a German ambulance came trundling through the mist out of Foy and stopped on the N30 opposite the H Co lines. Ken Johnson recalls the vehicle pulling up opposite 2 Ptn. "When the German orderly clambered out and put his hands in the air, I promptly told him to get back in and keep going up the hill under a white flag of truce!" The driver, who had become disorientated, followed Ken's orders and continued to the Route Madame, whereupon the medical detachment took his surrender and commandeered the vehicle. Afterwards the ambulance was put to good use as a temporary shelter for the growing number of frostbite victims.

A couple of days later Johnson was working at the H Co OP in the Dumont house, when he managed to trap a malnourished rooster. "I brought the bird back up the hill to treat the squad to a nice chicken broth. Sitting down on my steel helmet, I began to pluck the bird when a mortar barrage exploded around us. One round landed a couple of yards away, wounding two tankers who were parked up with their Sherman. Thank goodness I wasn't resting directly on the ground because a piece of shrapnel made a 3in hole in my helmet! However, another penetrated my left ankle and lodged in the bone." As Ken was being evacuated, Pfc Frank Malik took over and melted some snow in a rusty old bucket before adding in the chicken and a handful of rotten vegetables. As the stew came to the boil another barrage slammed in and Lt Wilkinson grabbed the bucket by the red-hot handle and carried it cursing all the way to his foxhole. After the shelling, Malik placed the stew back on the heat to cook. Before Ken departed for Bastogne, Lt Wilkinson trotted over to wish him luck and jokingly said that he would be sending the recipe home to his wife!

The same day Johnson was wounded (January 5), 13 men from the 501st Demolition Ptn were killed at the seminary in Bastogne. The soldiers were most likely unloading a truck full of mines and dead bodies when the vehicle exploded. It would seem that a random artillery shell might have hit the vehicle, causing a chain reaction. The only identifiable remains to be found were an arm and head belonging to S/Sgt Leon Brown. Completely unaware of the accident, Johnson passed through the town and was taken by ambulance to the 40th Evacuation Hospital before being sent to Paris by train, where the shrapnel was removed. "For a few days, I was on a ward full of amputees. The nights were horrendous, with guys constantly crying out in pain. From here I was sent to England before being shipped home to the USA on the RMS *Queen Elizabeth*. I was on the promenade deck at the stern with eight other guys, opposite the bar, which unfortunately remained shut during the entire high-speed voyage. I was discharged in September 1945, after a long stay at Hammond General Hospital in Modesto, California."

I Co maintained a strong presence along the edge of the "Eastern Eye," as Harley Dingman recalls: "Captain Anderson was dug in nearby and suffered the same deprivations that we did. Anderson and I worked closely on company administration, general assignments, and daily passwords. The passwords were vital and were mainly for the benefit of other patrols moving in and out of our area." Sgt Manny Barrios and Pvt Bill Chivvis were on constant OP duty although they were working in different parts of the "Eye."

Chivvis was over in the 1 Ptn area and recalls the following:

> As so many of the guys were getting sick, myself and Pvt Jim Meade volunteered to stay out there almost permanently. During the early part of January, Pfc Don "Duffy" Susak was badly wounded and I recall a couple of replacements that were sent to us – Pfc Eugene Smith and Pvt Florensio Valenzuela. Eugene was such a nice boy but there was some doubt in his mind as to whether or not he could pull the trigger. We called him "Vic" because he had chiseled features like the Hollywood actor Victor Mature. A few days later I heard that Vic missed his chance and was shot dead while still trying to decide. As Bob Chovan had been wounded in December, Valenzuela was offered his old job of second scout but wasn't in the least bit interested.
>
> Subsequently, Valenzuela was put forward as a machine gunner (because David Dillon had also been wounded in December). He knew that both jobs were risky, so Florensio opted to be our platoon runner. Jim Meade eventually took over on the machine gun and like me continued through the war unscathed, which is more than can be said for Valenzuela.

7

"Hell night"

Clearing the Fazone Woods – January 9, 1945

Since the siege was effectively broken on December 26, the regiment had been preparing for an all-out assault on the enemy lines. For the past week, Gen Patton's Third Army had been working hard to widen the main arterial road and clear the route. During the epic advance, 4th Armored had inflicted over 2,000 enemy casualties, and it was reported that the road to Bastogne from Neufchâteau was littered with .50cal cases that in some places were over 3in deep. By January 5, the 506th PIR had begun to step up its patrolling and small-unit activity in a determined effort to regain control of the hills and woods surrounding Bastogne. Over the next few days, in order to keep up with the fluid tactical situation, Col Sink relocated his CP several times. Firstly Sink went to Sonne Fontaine Farm (where 3/502 also had their HQ) and then Hemroulle, before moving to Col Patch's CP in the Bois Champay.

After being relieved by 3/501 at 0500hrs on January 9, 3rd Bn moved through the Bois Champay southwest from the MLR to an assembly area near Sonne Fontaine. At the time, Guy Jackson (3 Ptn H Co) was on OP duty in Foy at the Dumont house. "For some reason the signal to leave my post never arrived. Later in the afternoon an enemy tank began firing at my location from the north. As the shelling became more accurate I decided to abandon the property and return to the MLR where I discovered, much to my horror that the battalion had already pulled out. Not really knowing quite what to do, I walked south along the main road toward Bastogne." A couple of hours earlier, 2nd Bn had advanced north, accompanied by tanks from Task Force Cherry. Their mission was to clear and occupy the woods at Fazone and the ground southwest of Vaux, in preparation for their forthcoming attack on Noville. The northeastern edge of Fazone was already part of the 506th MLR. This area of woods had previously been the domain of 1/506 but they were withdrawn during the early afternoon, and placed in mobile reserve behind 2nd Bn.

Over at Sonne Fontaine, Cpl Jim Brown (2 Ptn I Co) visited 3 Ptn looking for Harold Stedman, who recalls:

> He sat down beside me, opened a packet of sweets, and began to talk. Jim had a bad feeling about the forthcoming attack and that he wasn't going to make it. I told him not to be so ridiculous and focus on the job. After a few minutes of soul searching he shook my hand and returned to his own lines. Turning to leave, Jim said "Goodbye" and then insisted on thanking me for my friendship and always looking out for him when things got rough. "Don't worry," I reassured him, "Everything is gonna be just fine – I'll be right there; now get the hell out of here." Like most of the guys in our outfit we knew everything about each another – flaws and possible weaknesses and even families who, for the most part, we had never even met.

Meanwhile back on the western MLR, E and F/501 were in the process of attacking and reclaiming Recogne, and by 1230hrs had reached a line with the Château d'Hoffschmidt, which had been reoccupied by the Germans in early January. During the assault, crossing open ground west of the Bois Champay, the commanding officer of the 501st PIR, Col Julian Ewell, was seriously wounded.

A fresh fall of snow around 8in deep lay on top of the frozen crust, as 3rd Bn moved out toward Fazone at 1110hrs on January 9. 2/506 had crossed the first phase line 10 minutes earlier, and within half an hour had overrun a German OP, capturing a small number of

Attack into Fazone Woods
January 9, 1945

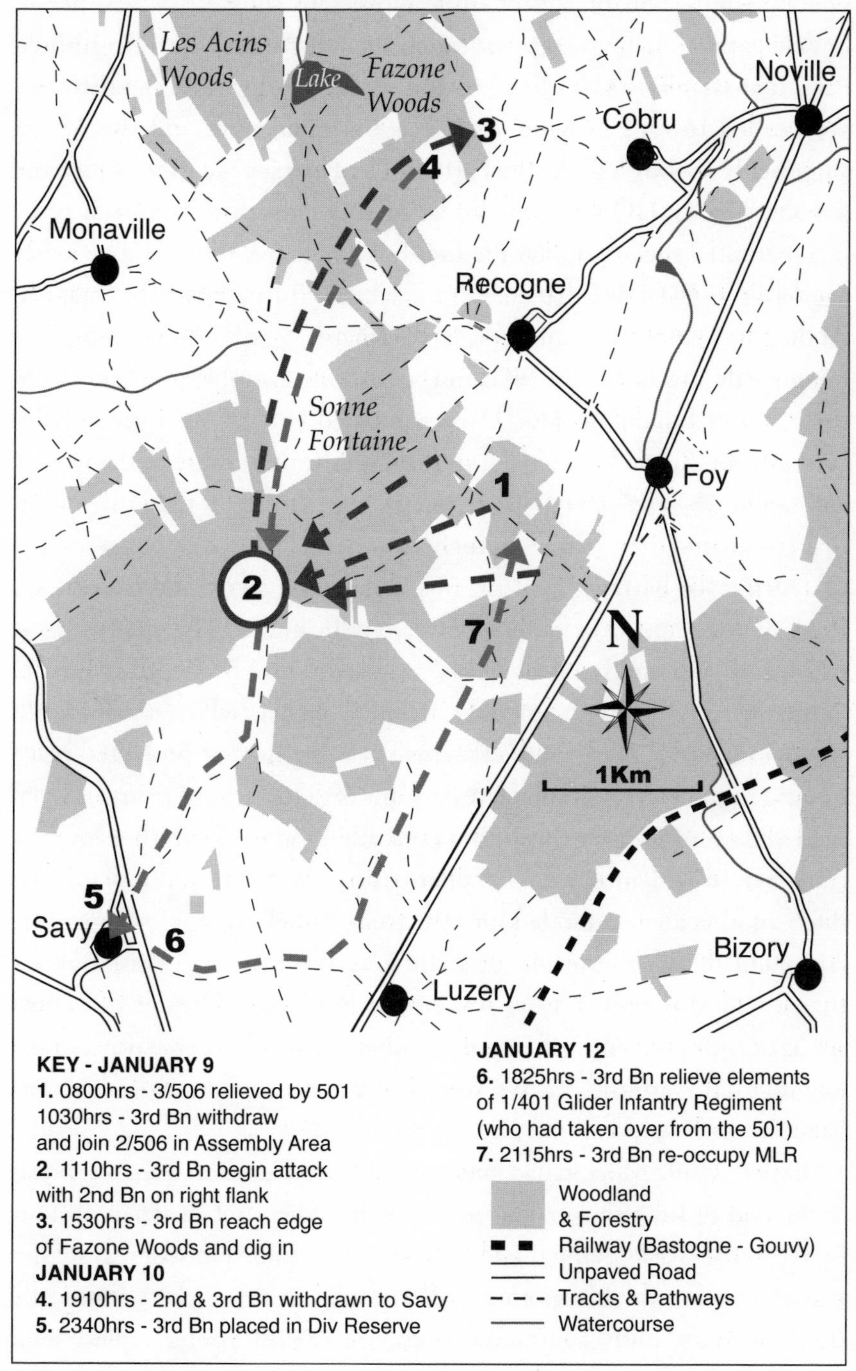

Les Acins Woods
Lake
Fazone Woods
Noville
Cobru
3
4
Monaville
Recogne
Sonne Fontaine
Foy
1
2
7
N
1Km
5
Savy
6
Bizory
Luzery
KEY - JANUARY 9
1. 0800hrs - 3/506 relieved by 501
1030hrs - 3rd Bn withdraw
and join 2/506 in Assembly Area
2. 1110hrs - 3rd Bn begin attack
with 2nd Bn on right flank
3. 1530hrs - 3rd Bn reach edge
of Fazone Woods and dig in
JANUARY 10
4. 1910hrs - 2nd & 3rd Bn withdrawn to Savy
5. 2340hrs - 3rd Bn placed in Div Reserve
JANUARY 12
6. 1825hrs - 3rd Bn relieve elements
of 1/401 Glider Infantry Regiment
(who had taken over from the 501)
7. 2115hrs - 3rd Bn re-occupy MLR
Woodland
& Forestry
Railway (Bastogne - Gouvy)
Unpaved Road
Tracks & Pathways
Watercourse

enemy troops. During the 1½-mile move, 3rd Bn were to advance in a wide parallel maneuver, pivoting on the left flank as part of a limited objective assault, as Capt Jim Morton recalls: "After veering northeast, we headed toward Noville with 2/506 to our right and the 502nd supposedly on our left. As the battalion began to make its way into the Fazone Woods, HQ Co came under intense and accurate mortar fire."

The initial shelling killed Pfc Len Lundquist (MG Ptn) and seriously injured 2nd Lt Ken Beard (battalion S2), who was hit in the arm by shrapnel. At the time, company mail clerk, Pvt Richard "Swede" Stockhouse, was temporarily attached to the MGs and became inconsolable after witnessing the death of Lundquist. Doc Dwyer grabbed hold of Stockhouse (who was only 5ft 2in) and marched him through the mortar fire to the nearest aid station. "Swede" had good reason to be in shock – Lundquist was his first cousin and they were extremely close.

During the barrage, Morton was blown over twice and his runner, Pvt Charles Coppala Jr, badly wounded in the knee. "The poor guy was in a lot of pain and lying in a very exposed position," recalls Morton. "Upon retrieving his helmet, I carried Coppala (who was short but stocky) toward a nearby culvert which was the nearest protected place I could find." Here a drainage ditch runs into the woods from an open field and continues on through a concrete pipe underneath a logging track before widening into a deeper basin. "As we moved towards the ditch another shell exploded into the trees, knocking us to the ground. Although the blast tore off my helmet and sunglasses, I wasn't aware that it had also ripped away my entrenching tool. During this short space of time, the company took another six or seven casualties so we couldn't hang around. As we were leaving, I came across a shattered bazooka with blood all over the ground."

Earlier, while Morton had been attending to Coppala, Bob Webb was at the end of his tether trying to maintain radio contact when all four SCR310 backpacks being used by the battalion ceased to work. A soldier was crying out for his mother as Webb and Leroy Vickers frantically tried to re-establish communications. Nearby, a young replacement holding a bazooka took a direct hit and was blown to pieces. At that point Bob's nervous system went into overload, bringing on a form of Neurogenic Shock. For a moment, everyone thought Bob had lost his mind, but Vickers and T/4 Ed Sokolosky managed to calm him down to a point where he was once again able to function and continue forward.

The Germans had booby-trapped most of the main pathways along which the battalion were now advancing. 1st Lt Alex Andros recalls: "We were constantly stopping to carefully step over tripwires. The temperature had dropped off the scale and I don't remember it ever being quite as cold as it was that day." As 3/506 moved closer toward its final objective (a crossroad west of Noville at Cobru) they passed through several open areas, as medic Johnny Gibson remembers: "The group I was working with stopped along a small track on the edge of a wood to let a jeep pass by. Moving slowly through the snow, the vehicle struck a landmine with its left front wheel and parts of the engine and dashboard hit the driver in the chest. I was 40ft away and went over to help. Moments later, the driver, whose name was Herbert A. Derwig, died, but luckily his passenger whom I treated for shock escaped unharmed."

Avoiding the logging tracks, H Co pushed ahead through the woods toward Cobru, taking several casualties on the way due to friendly artillery fire. The ground at the edge of the Fazone slopes away in a long undulating curve toward the German-held villages of Vaux (on the left) and Cobru (on the right). Beyond the two hamlets on the high ground in the distance was the final prize – Noville. Even today, the dense woodland at the edge of the forest has a dark, sinister feel, with one or two original foxholes from January 9 still in existence. The oppressive atmosphere along the edge of the tree line is sobering and strangely uncomfortable.

Soon after leaving the relative "safety" of the Fazone, Alex Andros received orders to pull back:

> As we turned to leave three or four shells slammed in and everyone hit the ground. Pfc Anthony Busone was lying next to me as I struggled back to my feet, "Come on, Tony, let's go!" I shouted, but he didn't

move. After rolling Busone over we noticed a tiny hole where a piece of shrapnel had entered his temple, killing him instantly. After Busone lost his life we withdrew back along the road toward Foy. The path was so icy that the tracks of the tanks (which were accompanying us) were unable to grip the surface, causing them to slip and slide uncontrollably. We all wondered what we were doing and if there was even a strategy to our actions. I guess they were trying to coordinate us with the armor but at that time it was so chaotic it seemed almost futile.

Johnny Gibson was still behind the main body and recalls:

> There was more shelling up ahead, and while crossing an open clearing I came across a soldier sitting in the snow with his leg missing below the knee… The man's foot and part of his leg were still contained within his boot, which was lying on the ground no more than 20ft away. Although the casualty was pale and suffering from traumatic shock, he was still able to support what was left of his leg with both hands. Taking out a large compression bandage and some sulfa powder [sulfanilamide], I bent down to dress the mangled stump but the man refused treatment. Instead he requested a cigarette, so I retrieved one from his pocket, lit it, and placed it between his lips. Again the trooper refused treatment but asked me if I would be kind enough to collect his severed leg. At that moment a patrol came by and I spotted a couple of medics and handed the guy over to them before leaving to catch up with the battalion.
>
> Trudging away, I turned around to see the casualty struggling physically with the medics who were desperately trying to treat his injury. Moving deeper into the forest the shelling seemed to intensify and shrapnel began to pick off our men, one by one.

Following dozens of footprints through the woods, Gibson came across two soldiers from I Co face down in the snow and stopped to check. Both were dead.

It was just about to get dark when John rejoined the main force and was told to dig in by Col Charlie Chase. Before doing so Gibson went over to see Capt Anderson to inform him about the two casualties. Much to Gibson's surprise, "Andy" broke down in tears. Although the soldiers were replacements, the captain seemed overwhelmed by their loss and the real prospect that his cherished company was now facing total annihilation. Shortly afterwards Anderson was transferred to the battalion staff and replaced Blaine Pothier as XO.

Earlier, around 1300hrs, the battalion had attacked and neutralized four German outposts, taking a number of prisoners. "As we were moving forward, I happened to notice a badly wounded German soldier on the ground waving at me," recalls Cpl Jim Melhus (MG Ptn). "I'll never forget this kid, who was very young and had bright red hair. The lad pleaded with us to help, but as we were about to move him to the aid station my section leader, S/Sgt August Saperito, came by and ordered us to keep moving." Two hours later, unable to make contact with the 502nd, Jim Morton and Sgt Wester went on a patrol to the western edge of the forest and found the battalion's left flank completely exposed (at the time the 502nd were actually further west, attacking enemy positions in the Acins woods).

Col Patch halted the advance on the northeastern edge of Fazone and ordered the battalion to dig in. Cpl Bobbie Rommel was instructed to take a couple of machine-gun teams and move forward to establish a firebase on the edge of the tree line overlooking Cobru. "Moving through the dense woodland with Cpl Fred Sneesby," Rommel recalls, "I bumped into my buddy Harold Stedman, who I'd known since high school in Modesto, California. Harold was standing in the snow with a 60mm mortar barrel slung over his shoulder, wearing an enormous Kraut greatcoat that went clear down to the ground. I mean, he looked so ridiculous that I had to laugh." Harold could not understand what Rommel found so funny: "Bob lived right around the corner from me back in the States and was one hell of a great guy who never asked anybody to do anything that he wouldn't do himself."

Still laughing, Bobbie told Harold that he'd see him later, shook hands, and carried on his way to the edge of the wood where the machine gunners hunkered down to form a defensive line. "As we were digging in, a Sherman tank came up behind us, which we knew would get someone's attention," recalls Bob. "Predictably the artillery came in and the shells burst into the trees, covering us with snow. After digging ourselves out, a piece of shrapnel from another burst whizzed past, narrowly missing my knee. During the next barrage I wasn't so lucky and another tree burst, about 6ft above our heads, and sent a chunk of shrapnel through my overshoes and boots, penetrating deep into the arch of my left foot. The pain was excruciating, and it felt like I had been struck with a baseball bat."

A 1in piece of white-hot metal shattered the bones in Rommel's big toe before lodging underneath his foot. "Guys were getting hit all around and hollering for medical attention," remembers Rommel. Incredibly, thinking they were going to be fed, the German prisoners who had been captured earlier were standing around holding their mess tins. Some of the Germans inquired if they would be sent to New York. As a joke one of the paratroopers suggested Hollywood might be more appropriate, but surprisingly many of the prisoners did not seem to know where it was. Suddenly another barrage hit the treetops, scattering the prisoners in all directions. "I could only crawl, and as Fred Sneesby was such a little guy he struggled to support my weight," continues Rommel. "Fred ordered a couple of the Krauts to help carry me to the aid post where I was loaded onto a jeep and taken to Bastogne."

Barely 10 minutes after Bob Rommel was manhandled to the evacuation point, two enemy tanks broke through and came within spitting distance of Harold Stedman:

> Between explosions we could hear German voices talking and laughing like they were on dope or some sort of drugs. Womack was beginning to lose it and asked me, what in God's name were we gonna do? The only thing we could do was move away from

> the tanks. Running through the woods we got split up and the last thing I remember is diving or being blown into a crater. When I regained my senses several hours later, I was missing seven teeth and had a lump of shrapnel embedded in my shoulder. Thankfully the heavy German greatcoat I was wearing kept me from freezing. It was getting light as I tried to find my way back to our lines when I was jumped on by a sentry who was about to cut my throat, thinking I was a Kraut. Shortly afterwards I reported to the medics who promptly sent me off to the nearest hospital.

Previously, Barney Ryan and senior medic S/Sgt Harold Haycraft had just pulled a wounded soldier from his foxhole when they heard the sound of the first enemy tank approaching. Ryan remembers: "Swearing under my breath, I turned around to see a German Panther threshing up the snow practically looking right down our throats. Just as we dragged the wounded man away, the Panther put a round in exactly where we had just come from!"

Although still in reserve, 1st Bn had been moving up behind 3/506. Maj Bob Harwick recalls: "So far the advance for 1st Bn had been easy and we processed around 50 prisoners who had been sent back down the line. Then we came under the most intense shelling I have ever experienced. I didn't hear the first shell – it was more like a pressure wave – but I felt something hit me in the stomach, immediately followed by a sharp tearing pain to my side. Turning slowly to the right, I fell on my knees and face into the snow, then crawled a few feet to a small tree. As I rested my weight against the trunk, snow from the branches tumbled down onto my face."

XO Knut Raudstein was wounded at the same time and shouted across to his boss to see if he was OK. "I tried to answer Raudstein but couldn't get my breath and it was only then that I realized just how badly I'd been injured," Harwick continues. "I think my runner then came over and said, 'Don't move sir; I've sent for an aid man.' He then proceeded to cut open my clothing, and when I saw the mess in the center of my chest, I felt a rush of emotion, anger, frustration, and perhaps a little regret." Maj Harwick quickly said a prayer for his daughter Bobbie, the same devotion that he'd repeated every night since being posted overseas. "Other than that I numbly lay there in the snow cursing softly at the pain, helplessly awaiting my fate. A medic arrived and gave me a shot of morphine closely followed by a doctor who proceeded to bandage my wounds. As the morphine began to take effect, I was placed on a stretcher and carried to an evacuation jeep."

The ride through the woods along the logging tracks to the aid station was a gut-wrenching experience due to the deep ruts churned over by the 30-ton Shermans. Shells were exploding all around. One mortar landed so close to the jeep that Bob instinctively covered his face with both hands. Harwick was given a brief examination by Doctor "Shifty" Feiler at the forward regimental dressing station next to the main road at Luzery. "Doc Feiler sprinkled sulfa powder over my wounds, handed me some pills, and said, 'For Evacuation.'" When Bob arrived in Bastogne he was greeted by regimental medical officer Maj Louis Kent, and Catholic chaplain John Maloney, who encouraged him to take Holy Communion. Shortly after Bob Harwick was evacuated, Maj Charles Shettle was temporarily re-assigned from 2/506 to take command of 1st Bn.

Back in the Fazone, as 3rd Bn were establishing their foxholes along the edge of the woods, Jim Morton decided to take Bahlau and Wester with him to check the nearby mortar platoon positions. Before they left, Morton made sure that any gaps between the rifle companies were covered by machine guns: "Satisfied that the line was secure, we returned to our 'Company Headquarters' located next to the battalion CP." By that time it was getting dark and almost everyone except Morton, Bahlau, and Wester had dug in. Capt Joe Doughty was nearby and sharing his position with 1st Lt Frank Rowe. "I remember looking enviously on Doughty's foxhole," recalls Morton, "a real plush job lined with pine boughs and covered with heavy logs for overhead protection. Joe could have easily held off a German battalion from that position!" It would need to be, as over the next 18 hours of heavy fighting G Co suffered one KIA – Pvt Garland Cline – and 14 wounded, including sergeants Oscar Saxvik and Clair Mathiason.

It was then that Morton reached for his shovel, only to find a torn remnant of canvas, and informed Wester that they would now have to take turns with his. "To save time we decided to open a trench big enough to accommodate all three of us," recalls Morton. "Around 1700hrs, I asked Bahlau to leave his shovel and take an overlay of the battalion MLR across to Pete Madden and the mortar platoon. Fred had only been gone a few minutes when the enemy tanks arrived and began to blast our positions."

The shrieking crash of shells tore open the dense canopy, uprooting trees and anything else standing in the way. Shrapnel skipped through branches, buzzing everywhere as soldiers cowered, trying to dig deeper into the frozen earth. Between each barrage the plaintive calls for "medic" could be heard, growing more piteous as the fear of being overlooked in the growing darkness began to take hold. Between flares and the flashes of gunfire it was difficult for the senior NCOs to keep track of their men, let alone comprehend whether the enemy was advancing, retreating, or holding ground.

As Bahlau desperately tried to make his way back toward the HQ Co CP he passed Pfc Ray Calandrella hugging the snow, frantically stabbing away at the solid earth with his entrenching tool. As the barrage intensified Fred threw himself to the ground to take his chances alongside Calandrella.

Back at the CP the first round hit Wester and Morton plus three or four others. "We were all temporarily blinded by the blast and part of my lip was blown off," recalls Morton. "I was still dazed when Gibson ran over to assist. It was a very brave thing to do because he knew the risks, especially after leaving the safety of his foxhole." A large splinter of metal had penetrated Morton's left leg, leaving a 6in gash in the ankle and a gaping comma-shaped exit wound. Another smaller fragment lodged next to the artery in his thigh. "A few minutes later, as John was applying a tourniquet, another shell exploded, hitting me again, seriously wounding Gibson, whose immediate first aid probably saved my life, as left unattended I would have without doubt bled to death."

"After hearing the calls for a medic," recalls Gibson, "I made my way through the chaos to find Morton face down in his foxhole. Straddling his body, I cut away the captain's clothing to gain access to his wounds. As I was rendering medical assistance more shells began to erupt around us – all of which I chose to ignore. One round struck a few yards away, killing my friend and fellow medic T/5 Robert Evans [who was attached to I Co]. Another shell exploded directly overhead, perforating my back with white-hot shrapnel."

As Gibson collapsed, another razor-sharp piece of steel penetrated his right lung and diaphragm. Upon exhalation Gibson could now hear the oxygenated bubbles emanating from the thoracic cavity and felt a trickle of warm blood running down his spine. Morton continues: "One of the fragments that hit Gibson lodged in my leg after passing through his body, tearing a hole in my thigh about the size of a teacup. Gibson's weight pinned me to the ground and another medic, Pfc Andy Sosnak, pulled his colleague to one side and continued to patch me up."

After dealing with Morton, Sosnak turned his full attention to Gibson and placed a wide strip of surgical tape over his friend's back to seal the wounds. Before being evacuated, Morton made sure Fred Bahlau received his personal sheepskin vest and original-issue M1 Thompson submachine gun, complete with 50-round drum magazine, mumbling that he would no longer be in need of them. Both Morton and Gibson were placed on stretchers and evacuated by jeep to Luzery along with several others, including 2nd Lt Denver Albrecht (2 Ptn I Co), Bobbie Rommel, Sgt Bill Pershing (Bazooka Ptn), and Cpl Leonard Schmidt (S2), who had also been badly hurt in the same shelling.

"When we reached the forward aid station it was under mortar fire," recalls Morton. "Doc Feiler happened to mention that he was having trouble locating the morphine in the dark so we told him to forget about pain relief and just get us the hell out." Next stop for Morton, Gibson, and Rommel was the regimental aid station in Bastogne where

Louis Kent (regimental surgeon), Father John Maloney, and medic Owen Miller from 1st Bn were in charge of triage.

Maj Kent informed Morton that his left foot was nearly severed at the ankle and would probably need amputating. At the time Jim did not care one way or the other; he was just glad to be alive. The next morning, January 10, Barney Ryan visited Morton and told him that the previous 24 hours had been the worst of his army career and that the regiment had sustained 126 casualties. During the conversation, Ryan mentioned that he had personally dealt with 15 severe cases at the battalion aid post, including Charlie Shettle, who had been wounded in the foot. Shortly after Shettle left the battlefield, Maj Clarence Hester was posted in from regiment and took over 1/506. The day had been somewhat of a record for 1st Bn, having had three commanders in the last 8 hours.

Throughout the night, mortar, artillery, and tank shells continually hammered into the woods, making medical evacuation next to impossible. Ben Hiner remembers seeing Pfc Jose Suarez from HQ Co remove his clothing and equipment before rolling around in the snow babbling like a lunatic.

At 0230hrs an enemy combat patrol supported by two platoons attacked the woods but failed to break through. Shortly afterwards the men from 326th Airborne Engineers were brought in and cut a considerable amount of logs that were used by the troops to cover foxholes, which undoubtedly saved further lives.

Because of the exceptionally high wind chill factor the temperature on January 9 dropped to -17 degrees Celsius and was, for the 506th PIR, the coldest night experienced during the campaign. The extreme cold "burned" the skin on the men's faces like never before. When Bob Webb opened his eyes the next morning he was shocked to find lateral icicles had formed between the wall of the shallow shell scrape and his mouth. Webb was feeling much better after his brief "meltdown" the previous morning – unlike veteran combat medic Tom "Mutt" Collier, who, during the night, decided he could no longer cope with the responsibility and "resigned," knowing full well that he would be charged with desertion or, even worse, cowardice.

At dawn the following morning Ryan's aid post looked like an image from Hell. Several dead bodies were piled outside and trails of blood marked the snow where the wounded had dragged themselves, desperately seeking medical attention. Despite the chaos and confusion of the previous night the enemy had successfully been pushed further north beyond Cobru – which at least was something positive.

After spending the day on line at Fazone, the remnants of 3rd Bn were replaced by 1/506, and at 1830hrs the battalion moved to Savy as divisional reserve. Before the battalion pulled out, Guy Jackson, who had been left behind in Foy, reported for duty after sheltering all night in a barn along the N30 at Luzery: "When I arrived the ground was frozen solid and it was almost impossible to dig in. That evening before we went to Savy the outfit came under a sustained barrage of enemy artillery and mortar fire. The shelling lasted around 30 minutes, during which time my best friend Pfc Charles Kiefer was killed." As the battalion was making its way back to the reserve area, Jim Melhus passed by the German youth he had tried to help the previous afternoon. "The red-haired kid's body was frozen solid with his left arm pitifully raised in the air. It was a real low point for me, even after what we had just been through and I really began to wonder what it all was for."

Earlier on the 10th, as 2nd Bn (who had also been withdrawn) were heading south, Ed Shames decided to stop his platoon for a few minutes to regroup. Buck Taylor thought he would use the opportunity to make contact with 1st Bn, who were now in regimental reserve (waiting to be relieved by 2/506) somewhere over on 3 Ptn's left flank. As Buck turned to leave the 1st Bn area he was hit by a bullet just above the ankle and had to be evacuated by stretcher. "I'd been grooming Paul Rogers in readiness for such an occasion as this, and therefore the reshuffle was seamless," recalls Shames. "Even before Paul became platoon sergeant, I gave him more responsibility than the other squad leaders so I knew he was the right man for the job." After Buck Taylor was wounded, 3 Ptn rejoined 2nd Bn, who were now on the southern side of the Champay Woods near Savy. Later that evening the enemy blanketed the area with artillery, killing Sgt Warren "Skip" Muck and Pfc Alex Penkala. After dark, Ed Shames sent Junior Suerth and several others back to Luzery to collect stretchers. On the way the men stopped to speak with the crew of a tank whose unit was parked in the woods. During the brief conversation one of the crewmen foolishly lit a cigarette. Coincidentally, moments later a number of German shells exploded around the tanks. During the attack four people were killed and Suerth was badly injured in both legs by shrapnel.

Cpl Bob Webb had spent January 10 trying to service the radio equipment. Every single antenna had been blown off during the move through the Fazone. When the battalion pulled out, Webb decided to walk into Bastogne and look for some replacement aerials: "I came across a road junction clogged with traffic and the last thing I remember was running for a ditch as a shell exploded 20 or 30ft in front of me. After being unconscious for some time, I awoke to discover that I was virtually blind and could feel blood seeping from my ears, nose, and mouth. The battalion never got the radio antennas it so desperately needed as ironically I was diagnosed with severe concussion and evacuated for treatment."

Suffering from frostbite, Manny Barrios was sent to Luzery. "As there seemed to be no doctors available I was seen by one of the medics working from a large open barn," he recalls. "Apart from frostbite I also had some shrapnel in my right leg. The aid man placed both of my feet in hay-filled sacks before disinfecting my leg wound. That evening I stayed in the warm barn and had my first decent night's sleep in almost two weeks. The penetrating cold had affected my ankle – damaged six months earlier in Normandy. As the temperatures dropped the pain grew worse but I never said a word for fear of being taken off the line and letting my 'squad' down."

While Sgt Barrios was recovering at Luzery the battalion was heading out through deep snow toward Savy, each soldier following the footsteps of the man in front. 1st Lt Chester Osborne and 1 Ptn G Co remained on line to assist 1/506 in taking over the area. During the early hours of January 11, a German patrol came through the position, as Ewell Martin recounts: "We were dug in on a point of woods. I was manning a machine gun with Sgt John Luse who, as it happened, was also from Mississippi. We were rotating every 2 hours, and as I was sleeping, John nudged my shoulder and pointed out the enemy patrol in snowsuits quietly entering the woods behind us. Gently lifting the gun, we moved after the enemy patrol but had only gone a short distance when a volley of shots rang out and the Germans disappeared into the night."

The gunfire came from Pvt Haynes Knox, who had been dozing in his sleeping bag as the soldiers passed within a few feet of him. The zip of the bag jammed, trapping Knox, who panicked and loosed off a couple of rounds through the material with his pistol!

"Shortly afterwards we began to exchange machine-gun fire with the enemy troops in the woods opposite," continues Ewell Martin. "Not long after Knox's brush with death we came under intense artillery fire which badly wounded Cpl Gabriel Sonoqui and Sgt Merville Grimes, who were both hit while sheltering in their foxholes [Pfc Harold Martin and Pfc John Krupa were also seriously hurt in the shelling]. During the barrage we also lost several M1 rifles that happened to be above ground and also our precious supply of fresh water stored in a large insulated container, which was an enormous blow to our morale." Despite the overwhelming abundance of snow, fresh water was still essential. Tactical conditions dictated that fires were not allowed. Eating snow was not an effective option as it only served to lower the core temperature, forcing the human body to burn more energy to keep warm.

The following afternoon, January 12, 1 Ptn pulled out and headed for Savy only to be told on arrival that the battalion had just departed for Foy. Ewell Martin recalls: "We marched like crazy men trying to catch up, and after going without water for the last 24 hours we were badly dehydrated. My platoon sergeant, Flint Brown, was carrying four rifles that belonged to some of the guys who were having a hard time keeping up. Before long even Flint began to struggle, so as I was nearest he handed one of the M1s to me." As the men crossed a bridge over a small stream, Pvt "Duane" Meriwether broke ranks and scooped up a canteen full of water before running back to share the precious liquid amongst the squad.

For whom the dice rolls

Along with scores of wounded, Harwick, Morton, Wester, Gibson, and Rommel were probably sent to the 429th Medical Collection Co at Massul near Luxembourg. Because Bobbie Rommel's wound was not immediately obvious, Maj Kent ordered him to walk to a waiting ambulance. "The pain was so overwhelming that I began to pass out and it was only then that the medics helped me into the back of the vehicle." When Bob arrived at the schoolhouse in Massul the doctors removed the shrapnel from his foot before sending him to Paris for further treatment. "After several operations and skin grafts, I spent a total of 119 days in various English hospitals… When released I had to cut my boot open to physically get it on my foot and subsequently the doctors decided not to send me back to the 506th. Instead I was placed on 'limited service' and sent to France where I drove a truck for a USO show. Another GI was driving a second vehicle containing the wardrobe, while I transported the piano and all the stage equipment. The show had seven gorgeous girls and very quickly we learned not to carry anything for them; otherwise those chicks would have worked us both to death."

Nearly six decades later Bob Rommel finally received his Purple Heart, Good Conduct Medal, Presidential Unit Citation, and Victory Emblem in a plain paper envelope. No salute, no shaking of hands, no flags fluttering in the breeze.

When Johnny Gibson arrived at the 429th, he was immediately prepared for surgery and had a tube inserted through the chest wall to allow blood, air, and fluid trapped within the pleural cavity to escape. He recalls:

A day or two later another casualty, Lloyd Molina (who had been shot in the abdomen), was brought in and placed in the bed opposite. Lloyd and I had known each other since before Pearl Harbor and had worked together at several Civilian Conservation Corps camps in northern Arizona. Lloyd asked how I was feeling and I replied sarcastically, "strong as a bull." For some reason it struck us both as being hilarious, and despite the excruciating pain we couldn't stop laughing for a good 10 minutes.

A few days later, I was transported by ambulance to Paris. The two black drivers were real gentlemen, and they could see I was in agony from the shrapnel still embedded in my liver. The pain became so acute that they had to stop off at an army hospital for two days in order for the doctors to stabilize me. When I got to Paris the surgeons removed the shrapnel from my liver and lung and some bone splinters that had originated from my ribs. I wanted to keep one jagged piece of metal about the size of my fingernail as a souvenir but one of the French domestics threw it away. Seventeen days later and after battling severe infection, I was transferred to England (Taunton) and then back to the USA, eventually ending up in Birmingham General Hospital, Van Nuys, near Los Angeles.

It was here that I came across Robert Evans' address in my notebook and decided to write to his widow and explain her husband's last moments. Two years earlier Bob and I had shared a room at Camp Mackall and became very close friends. During a night out in Fayetteville, I had met up with Bob and his wife in a bar. Between drinks, she surreptitiously gave me her home address and asked me to write if anything serious ever happened. It seemed a lifetime since that night and after what I'd been through. Writing that letter was agonizingly difficult.

Jim Morton was put on an ambulance with four other patients. "As we left Bastogne a couple of shells struck the road and blew in the doors of the vehicle, peppering everyone except me with shrapnel! From my hospital bed near Paris, I drafted letters to Bob Sink and Charlie Chase to recommend Fred Bahlau for a battlefield commission. I told Sink of Fred's leadership skills and devotion to duty and recalled that he had twice been awarded the Silver Star for gallantry in action. However, I was too sick at the time to recommend Johnny Gibson for the Silver Star – although I knew he deserved it – which I regret." 1st Lt John Williams agreed to take over as temporary commander of HQ Co until a worthy replacement for Morton could be found. One week later, Ed Harrell (who had been promoted to captain) accepted the job and was transferred from G Co, where he had previously been temporary XO after John Wiesenberger died.

Many, like John Gibson, were never officially recognized for their courage due to the fact that the officers who would have recommended specific bravery awards were either dead or seriously injured. At the end of January Jim Morton arrived at Woodrow Wilson General Hospital in Staunton, Virginia. "The chief surgeon was able to put his entire hand through the hole in my leg and told me it was a miracle that I hadn't lost the limb – although it would take another two years and many operations to fix."

Shortly after midnight on January 10, Bob Harwick arrived at Massul, where he was given two pints of plasma before undergoing emergency surgery. Two days later, Bob was transferred to a hospital train and moved to Paris. He recalls: "It was so cold during the journey that ice formed on the floor and frost appeared on the bolts that extended through the walls of the compartment." On arrival, Helen Briggs came aboard to look for her boyfriend. The couple had last seen each other in December when Bob and Helen spent two blissful days together before the recall went out for Bastogne. "I had been informed the day before that Bob would be on this particular train," recalls Briggsy. "No wonder he was so cold – the poor guy was completely naked except for a belly band and a hospital destination card." After a brief but emotional reunion, Helen kissed her lover and wished him luck, not knowing when or where she would ever see him again.

8

"Salute the new dawn"

The final attacks on Foy and Noville – January 13–17, 1945

On the evening of January 12, after relieving 401st GIR (who in turn had taken over from the 501st) on the ridgeline at Foy, Col Patch briefed what was left of his officers at the battalion CP in the trees behind the Bois Champay. The idea was to secure the village without damaging the N30 (therefore no artillery was to be used), enabling Shermans and M18 Hellcats from the 11th Armored Division to pass through unimpeded toward Noville. Due to the high number of casualties on January 9, the remaining senior NCOs were shuffled between rifle companies, which, for the most part, were down to fewer than 30 men each with the exception of G Co, which had around 50 soldiers available for duty. What the regiment did not know was that parts of their communications network had been compromised and the enemy were expecting them.

For the first phase, although 2nd Bn were now in regimental reserve behind the MLR, E Co had been attached to 3rd Bn and would join I Co for the attack that was due to begin the following morning. As he had been working so closely with Lloyd Patch, the CO of Regt HQ Co, Gene Brown, was asked to take temporary command of I Co after Andy Anderson had been re-assigned to the battalion staff. I Co were split into two composite squads, the first led by 2nd Lt Roger Tinsley (1 Ptn) and the other (numbering 16 soldiers) by Sgt Harley Dingman, whose platoon leaders, Milo Bush and Don Replogle, had both recently been evacuated.

G and H companies were tasked with holding the line while maintaining fire support along with the 81mm mortar platoon. Alex Andros thought the idea was unworkable due to the lack of available manpower. He recalls: "Other than myself, Capt Jim Walker and 2nd Lt Willie Miller were the only officers remaining in H Co, while I Co were in a worse state than we were. The battalion as a whole was nothing more than an oversized platoon and Patch didn't really know how he could effectively deploy us, but orders were orders." During the briefing, 1st Lt Pete Madden was told that he would be providing mortar support to suppress a number of suspected enemy machine-gun positions located on the high ground beyond the village. During the early hours of the 13th, Col Sink relocated his HQ from Hemroulle to the 3rd Bn CP along with reinforcements from Regt HQ Co.

After a night of light enemy shelling the American attack began as planned at 0900hrs, as Madden recalls:

> We were waiting for the signal from regiment to commence our fire missions. Several minutes went by but we received no such instruction. By this time, I could see puffs of smoke coming from the German machine-gun nests so we knew they were now actively engaging our troops from E Co who were spearheading the assault.
>
> Suddenly the radio crackled into life: "STAND BY – WAIT – OUT." Clearly I was familiar with Col Patch's radio operator, but I didn't recognize the voice on the end of the line so called for clarification, and the reply came back, "THIS IS KIDNAP BLUE – HOLD YOUR FIRE MISSION." "What target do you want me to hit first?" I inquired. "JUST HOLD FIRE – THE MISSION IS NO LONGER NECESSARY." I could still see the smoke from the enemy machine guns up in the woods to the north and couldn't figure out what was going on. I called back again only to be told, "HOLD YOUR FIRE – THAT IS A DIRECT ORDER." We knew something was wrong, so I asked for identification. There was a long pause and I repeated the request but received no answer. That

> was all I needed and immediately called all four batteries onto our pre-recorded targets.

Madden ran back to the battalion CP to advise that the enemy were now tapping into the communications network. Sink had no choice but to order complete radio silence, making command and control during the attack and also over the next few days very difficult.

While Madden had been puzzling over the fire control orders, 1 and 2 platoons from E Co had crossed their jump off point (start line) and were now proceeding down into Foy. Earlier, Ed Shames and 3 Ptn had been sent across the N30 to the extreme western edge of the Bois Jacques (then held by the 501st), where they were supposed to be the lead platoon in a diversionary attack. Shames' mission was to push down to the crossroad and draw the enemy forces away from the center of town. Simultaneously, at the Bois Champay, 1 and 2 platoons, led by 1st Lt Tom Peacock and 2nd Lt Jack Foley, had emerged from either side of the "Eastern Eye" to begin their advance, keeping the Route de Houffalize on the right. Once into Foy, Peacock and Foley had been ordered to link up with Shames and form a blocking force along a line approximately 300 yards in length, south of the road leading to Recogne.

Ed Shames and 3 Ptn were to employ the same tactic by capturing and holding the other side of the road leading to Bizory. Unknown to the 506th, a German minefield was now covering the N30 at the southern edge of the village. Enemy forces had also established a defensive firebase at the Koeune house. Located at the strongpoint was a mortar fire controller who had all entry routes into the village covered. Several machine-gun crews were located on the upper floors, with uninterrupted views towards the "Eye." Another gun group operating nearby at Cordonnier Farm had superb fields of fire along the road to Recogne.

The machine guns were also protecting a Mk IV Panzer parked in the dip directly outside the Koeune house. Here the road dropped sharply away, leaving the turret barely visible from the N30. The tank created a formidable barrier and ultimately prevented Shames from

Final Attack on Foy, 0845–1100hrs January 13, 1945

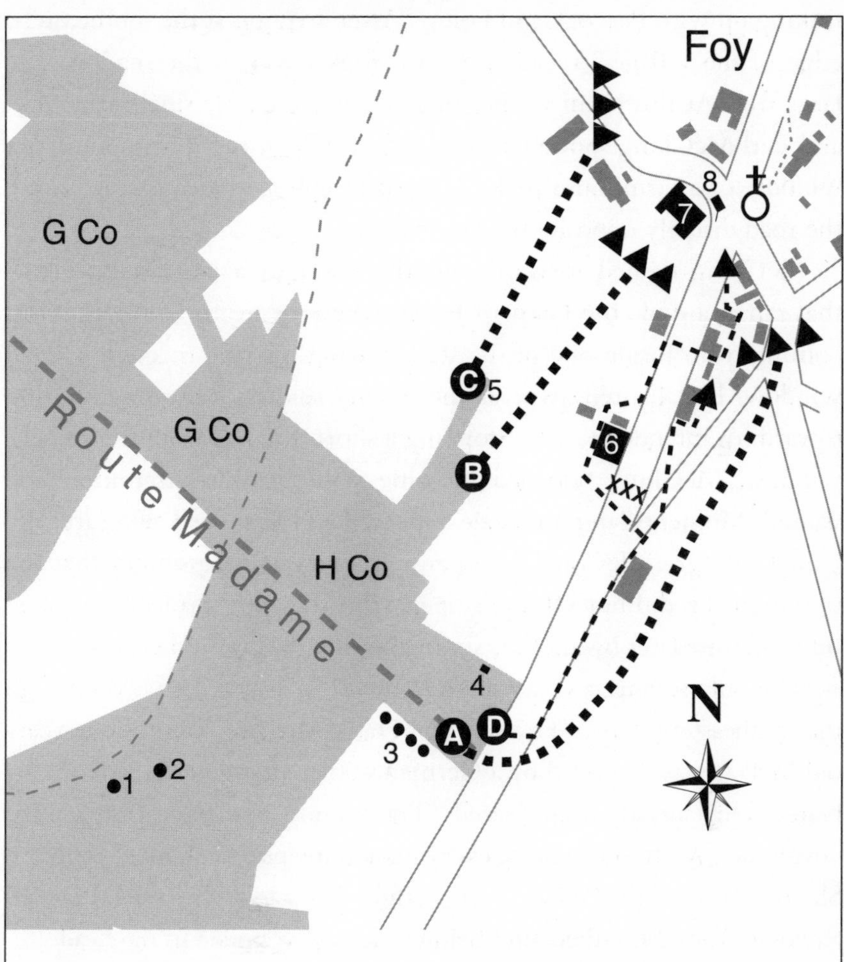

KEY

A. 0830hrs:
2Lt Ed Shames & 3 Ptn E Co
Commence with a diversionary assault

B. 0900hrs:
1Lt Tom Peacock & 1 Ptn E Co

C. 2Lt Jack Foley & 2 Ptn E Co
Advance to form a Blocking Force
(NB: Assumed B&C line of attack)

D. 1015hrs:
Capt Gene Brown & I Co

1. 3/506 Aid Station

2. 3/506 & 506 RHQ CP

3. 81mm Mortar Line

4. MG Bunker (H Co CP)

5. 81mm Mortar OP (1Lt Pete Madden)

6. Forward Aid Station established by Dr Barney Ryan at Albert Koeune's house (where Joe Madona was killed)

7. Jules Koeune's house used by Germans as a strongpoint and CP

8. Mk IV Panzer (using dip in road for cover)

XXX German Minefield

250m

linking up with Peacock and Foley. "After arriving at the southeastern edge of the village," recalls Ed, "we took cover in the shadow of a large tree. At this point we began to receive accurate small-arms fire, and Earl McClung spotted a muzzle flash which came from an upper window of a farmhouse [belonging to Joseph Gaspard] further along the road directly opposite the church."

McClung dashed forward into the cover of a large stable block that ran alongside the Gaspard Farm, where he heard German voices coming from inside one of the stalls. Firing his rifle through a small window, Earl blasted away at the enemy soldiers before continuing toward his intended target. Stopping a short distance from the sniper's window, McClung reloaded his rifle with blank ammunition and waited. Moments later a muzzle appeared and Earl fired two carefully aimed rifle grenades into the opening. There is a possibility that the two grenades did not kill the sniper, who was most probably finished off sometime later by another shot from Sgt "Shifty" Powers.

The only serious casualty suffered by 3 Ptn as it skirmished through the southeastern part of Foy was Cpl Frank Mellett. Twenty-four-year-old Mellett was shot dead by a German soldier after entering a house he believed had already been cleared. "Frank's unnecessary death made me vow to do my utmost to bring every man in my platoon home," reflected Shames. Beyond the Panzer, over on the other side of the street, Pfc Carl Sawosko from 2 Ptn died after being seriously wounded in the head.

Gene Brown was tasked by Col Sink to lead I Co for the second phase of the assault. He was assisted by Tinsley and Dingman – the idea was to advance down the eastern (right-hand) edge of the N30 and link up with Ed Shames' platoon at the crossroad. As the only medical officer available, Barney Ryan was attached to Brown along with medics Walter Pelcher and T/5 Eugene Woodside. Shortly after 1015hrs, as Brown's small force got to within sight of the crossroad, his drive came to an abrupt halt.

Dozens of booby traps had been scattered by the Germans across the N30. Moments later, the leading elements of Brown's column came under intense machine-gun fire, forcing the men to take cover along the embankment on the left side of the road. Doctor Ryan, who was following behind, received word that a number of casualties were now gathering up ahead around a three-storey house (owned by Albert Koeune). "I decided that this building would become our aid station and ominously upon entering discovered abandoned German equipment, including grenades and a *Panzerfaust* [antitank grenade launcher] stashed in the kitchen. There were also a number of mattresses lying around which came in useful for the wounded."

Dead ground

Bypassing the "minefield," Pvt Al Cappelli (2 Ptn I Co) was sixth in line moving down the edge of the road when the first scout became pinned down by the machine gun from the Mk IV Panzer. From here the road beyond la Vieille Forge (meaning "the old smithy") dropped away to the crossroad at Foy where the tank was waiting in the hollow outside the Koeune house. Cappelli was called forward and adopted the prone position on the steep snow-covered bank directly opposite a large house owned by the Collard family. "Suddenly I felt a burning sensation in my left knee and looked down to see two blood-soaked holes in my pants." After being instructed to outflank the Panzer, Cappelli limped back across the road, clutching his bazooka, toward the Evrard house. Moving behind the property and over a connecting footpath, Al found himself virtually opposite the well and close enough to get a clear shot at the tank. The first rocket struck the target (which immediately lost power), but before he could load another round Cappelli was hit again. A few yards away, at the Evrard house, a German soldier with a 9mm Walther pistol was watching from a ground-floor window. "I couldn't believe that one of the bullets from the P-38 hit me 6in above the wound I'd received moments earlier!"

Lt Tinsley saved Cappelli's life when he charged the window and killed the enemy soldier. The now-stranded tank was eventually overrun after it ran out of ammunition. Leaving the barrel of their 75mm gun pointing toward Bastogne, the crew evacuated through the rear escape hatches. The turret was later blasted by one of the American TDs, making sure it was no longer serviceable.

A colleague helped carry Cappelli back across the road to the aid station, and with help from Pelcher and Woodside many more casualties were collected and brought in. However, the wounded could not be evacuated by vehicle due to the mines blocking the road opposite the aid post. S/Sgt Joe "Shorty" Madona, who was now platoon sergeant for 2 Ptn I Co, arrived and moved to the rear with Dr Ryan hoping to get a situation report from Capt Brown.

Gene had broken radio silence and was sheltering behind a nearby stone barn. Ryan and Madona listened intently as Brown told Col Patch that I Co had hit a "hornet's nest" and he needed immediate back up. As Madona and Ryan walked back toward the doorway they were hit by a sudden burst of machine-gun fire. "It felt like I'd been struck in the chest with an axe," recalls Ryan. "S/Sgt Madona was killed instantly and crumpled to the floor. The burst ricocheted off the solid stone frame surrounding the door, striking me in the chest and Joe (who was much smaller than me) in the forehead."

Later Madona was awarded a posthumous Distinguished Service Cross for his actions at Bastogne. He had developed into a fantastic leader and was greatly admired by everyone, especially Ed Shames, with whom he had been best friends since the early training days in the USA.

"I felt myself breaking into a cold sweat," recalls Ryan, "and although weakened, I managed to walk into the house and lie down beside the others. Blood had begun to trickle down my back as Woodside cut away my British tanker overalls (given to me on January 9 by Charlie Shettle) and applied a Carlisle bandage. Surprisingly there wasn't that much pain, so I refused morphine." Shortly afterwards, Ryan sent word to Capt Brown, who notified the regiment that the battalion needed another medical officer and Louis Kent was sent forward to keep things under control.

Unbeknown to Ryan, four Germans had been trapped in the cellar when he occupied the house. Uncertain of what to do next, the enemy soldiers remained silent as blood from the wounded lying on the floorboards above began to drip through the cracks. In the darkness one of the young Volksgrenadiers started to panic and knocked over a shelf. "On hearing a German voice, Walter Pelcher sent someone down into the basement with a weapon, and 30 seconds later the four young men appeared with their hands raised in surrender," recalls Ryan. "I heard someone say, 'Let's shoot the bastards.' 'Hell no,' I screamed. 'We'll use them to carry the wounded back up to the MLR' (no doubt thinking of my own self- preservation at the same time!). Pelcher put the prisoners to work carrying the more severely wounded out on stretchers through roadside ditches to a hastily organized jeep collection point."

Ryan was taken to Bastogne before being evacuated by ambulance to the 60th Field Hospital at Neufchâteau. By the time he arrived, Barney was in deep shock and underwent immediate surgery. "I awoke the next morning to find myself under the care of an old classmate from medical school, Larry Kilham, who presented me with a battered 7.92mm bullet that the surgical team had removed from my lung."

Last gang in town

On the MLR, at around 1100hrs that same day, just like a scene from the Alamo, Bob Sink and Lloyd Patch ordered Andy Anderson and Jim Walker to gather all available spare manpower and join forces with 1 Ptn F Co to relieve the pressure on Gene Brown. The enemy shelled the woods while the composite group was being assembled behind the "Eye" on Route Madame. The intense barrage delayed the relief mission and wounded several people, including S/Sgt Richard "Red" Falvey from HQ Co 2nd Bn. Shortly before the relief force left the woods, Capt Dick Winters (who had just taken over as 2nd Bn XO from Charlie Shettle) ordered 1st Lt Ronald "Sparkey" Speirs to go on ahead with a handful of troops to personally inform Norman Dike what was about to happen. At the time Speirs, formerly with D Co, was temporarily un-assigned. However, steel and fortitude were now needed and clearly "Sparkey" was the best man for the job.

After being attached to 3rd Bn, F/506 took over the positions vacated by H Co as Walker ordered Alex Andros to take 3 Ptn and make a flanking movement across the N30 along the outskirts of the village (the same route previously taken by Ed Shames and his men). Walker then split his 1 Ptn equally on either side of the main road and was about to move out when Fred Bahlau ran over to offer assistance. Moving forward, the men passed a dead German frozen in the snow, who looked like some ghoulish form of traffic calming measure. Before reaching the edge of the minefield, Walker's team came under heavy artillery fire and ran for cover.

Down in Foy it was complete chaos – Brown and Tinsley were now desperately trying to coordinate I Co, who numbered fewer than 20 men, including replacement Pvt Alvin Viste: "Our 'squad' was on the right flank next to H Co, when we came up against stiff resistance from a machine gun near the aid station, which was now clearly marked by a large Red Cross. There was another German MG firing from a nearby farm building. Using our light machine gun, Cpl Wilbur Fishel began pouring fire into the enemy position until his weapon jammed due to a stoppage in the feed tray. To enable Fishel to safely sort out the malfunction, Florensio Valenzuela and I agreed to swap positions with him. As we began to move forward, a mortar shell exploded on the spot I had just vacated, killing Valenzuela (who was just behind me) and seriously injuring Fishel."

Nowhere was safe from enemy machine-gun fire, and without Harold Stedman around to watch his back, Cpl Jim Brown was killed after being struck in the left eye. Both Cpl Harry Watson and Pvt Wayman Womack (Harold's Number Two on the 60mm mortar) were badly wounded, and T/5 Gene Kristie and Pvt Howard Cleaver captured.

After Joe Madona was killed, Alvin Viste and his squad overran the enemy machine-gun team who then tried to surrender, as Viste recalls: "Pumped up with anger we took no prisoners and finished the crew off with our trench knives. We then began to work our way toward the aid station, joining with other troopers from H Co who were now coming in from the east, where, for most part, the cleansing action was complete. While clearing one of the buildings we came

Final Attack on Foy, 1100–1530hrs January 13, 1945

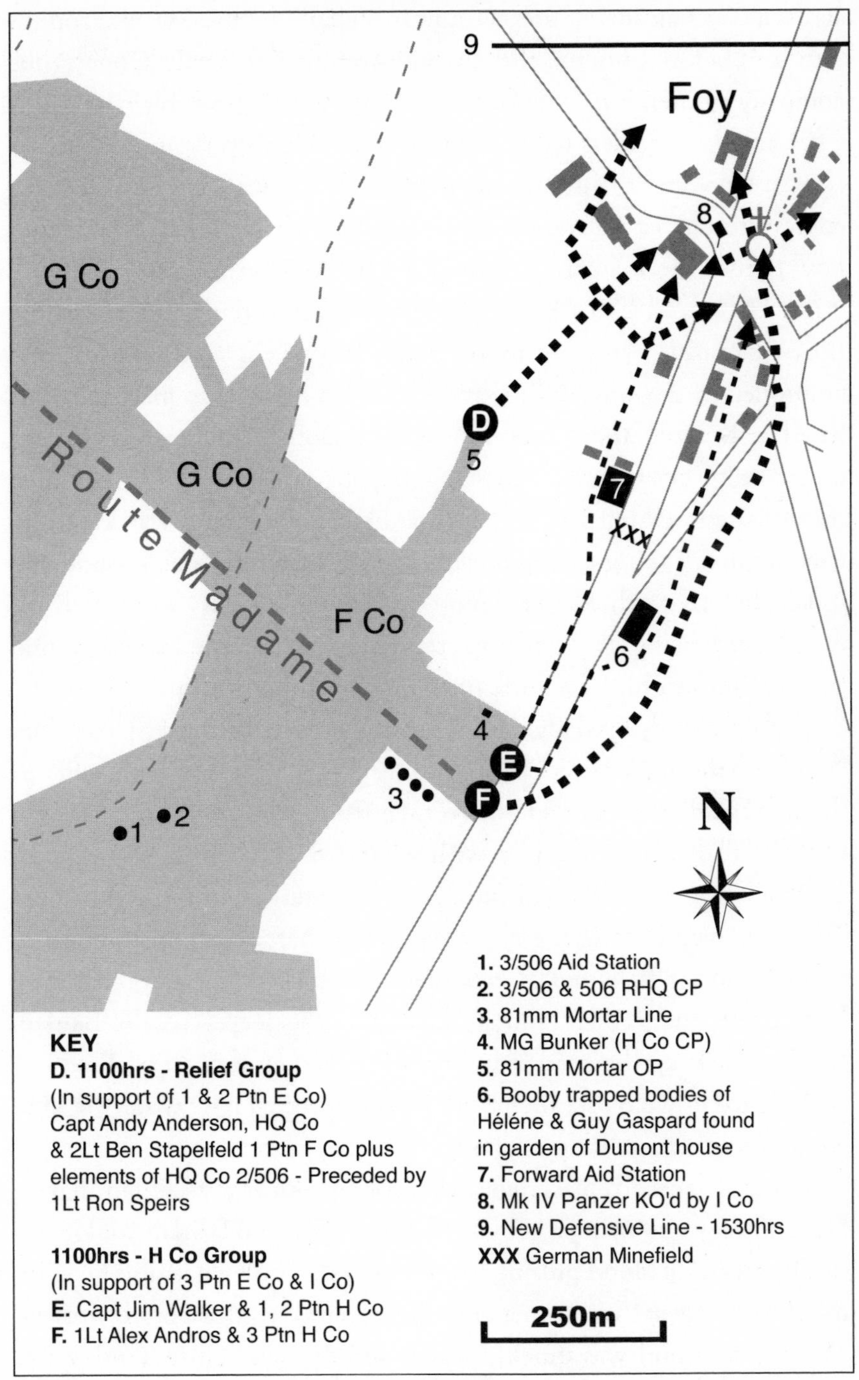

9
Foy
8
G Co
D
5
G Co
Route Madame
7
XXX
F Co
6
4
E
3
F
2
1
N
KEY
D. 1100hrs - Relief Group
(In support of 1 & 2 Ptn E Co)
Capt Andy Anderson, HQ Co
& 2Lt Ben Stapelfeld 1 Ptn F Co plus
elements of HQ Co 2/506 - Preceded by
1Lt Ron Speirs
1100hrs - H Co Group
(In support of 3 Ptn E Co & I Co)
E. Capt Jim Walker & 1, 2 Ptn H Co
F. 1Lt Alex Andros & 3 Ptn H Co
1. 3/506 Aid Station
2. 3/506 & 506 RHQ CP
3. 81mm Mortar Line
4. MG Bunker (H Co CP)
5. 81mm Mortar OP
6. Booby trapped bodies of
Héléne & Guy Gaspard found
in garden of Dumont house
7. Forward Aid Station
8. Mk IV Panzer KO'd by I Co
9. New Defensive Line - 1530hrs
XXX German Minefield
250m

across a German sitting bolt upright in a chair and fired several rounds into him before noticing that the guy was already dead. 'Dopey,' our company runner, burst out laughing and it was then we realized it was a sick joke … needless to say the rest of us weren't very amused."

As I Co were still attempting to clear the houses along the southern edge of town, 1st Lt Alex Andros and his men were halfway around Foy. Earlier the main relief group led by Andy Anderson, including 2 Ptn H Co and 1 Ptn F Co, headed down into the village from the Bois Champay. Hindered by the radio lockdown, Anderson became embroiled in crossfire with E and I Co plus the enemy machine guns based at Koeune and Cordonnier farms. Both companies were now under heavy mortar fire and struggling to maintain their individual missions. Something had to be done before somebody was killed by friendly fire. Taking a deep breath, Speirs ran across open ground and spoke directly with Roger Tinsley, who immediately instructed his men to stop firing. As Speirs was returning to E Co he looked around and saw Tinsley hit by a burst of enemy machine-gun fire.

Just up ahead, Fred Bahlau, who was now with the H Co group, could see the medical collection point close to the southern edge of the minefield and watched as two men from 326th Airborne Medical Co loaded an evacuation jeep with wounded. As more shells began to explode, one medic dashed into a nearby house, while the other hid under the jeep leaving their two wounded charges strapped helplessly on stretchers. "Incensed, I ran over and kicked the guy cowering underneath the vehicle and jumped into the jeep," recalls Bahlau. Driving back up the road away from the danger area, "Fast Freddie" was flagged down by six men from I Co who asked if he would be kind enough to evacuate Roger Tinsley.

Being a recent replacement, the young officer was unfamiliar to Fred. Tinsley's combat jacket was hanging open and Bahlau could see a steady stream of blood pulsing from his chest. Tinsley had also been hit in the head, but at that moment in time it seemed the least of his worries. The chest wound was quickly sealed and dressed before Tinsley was leant across the hood. Bahlau instructed two of the lieutenant's men to climb onto the jeep and hold their platoon leader down before heading to Bastogne – where, the following day, 2nd Lt Tinsley died.

During the next hour or so, 1 Ptn from F Co played a vital role in mopping up. This was illustrated by the fact that 2nd Lt Ben Stapelfeld, who had been deafened by concussion, personally dispatched two enemy soldiers hiding in a cellar. Further east, 3 Ptn H Co came under heavy shellfire near the church. "I concluded that the rounds must have come from a wooded area we could see in the distance," recalls Alex Andros. As 3 Ptn maneuvered to envelope the buildings on the western side of the road, the intense shelling suddenly lifted. Realizing the enemy must have been communicating with their own artillery from the basement of Jules Koeune's house, "Dud" Hefner moved forward past the Panzer (which had been abandoned earlier) with a couple of men. Hefner approached the property and fired a burst from his submachine gun through one of the 2ft-wide slit windows near the entrance.

Hearing the challenge issued by Hefner, the enemy troops sheltering in the cellar moved back to another compartment, as the bullets tore into the wall and ricocheted across the ceiling adjacent to the door. "Moments later, around 20 Germans emerged, hands on heads, and surrendered. As we double-timed the prisoners back to a temporary compound, our medic, Irvin 'Blackie' Baldinger (who spoke German), came over and told me that one of the younger Krauts was being particularly difficult and kept swearing at me. I wasn't in any mood for this nonsense and ran over to the kid, cocked my Thompson, and tapped a few rounds into the ground around his feet. I'm pleased to say he sprinted away like his life depended on it … and truthfully it probably did."

Later in the afternoon Alvin Viste encountered a couple of unidentified civilians who were protesting about what they thought was indiscriminate American gunfire during the attack. "This was totally untrue and I believe that these people, whoever they were, may have actually contributed toward the deaths of my comrades. At that point I felt that there were far too many troops milling around and decided to move away and find cover before we all became a target for further enemy mortar fire. Not long afterwards I learned that Cpl Fishel had been dragged to safety and subsequently evacuated."

2 Ptn H Co had cleared one particular house and were now using it for an OP. It would appear that after the village was back in American hands, radio silence was briefly lifted, as Frank Kneller recalls: "Two hundred yards or so further to the north, we observed smoke rising from the chimney of a small farmhouse. Within seconds, I'd been patched through via our phone network to the Air Force. To me, as a lowly 7745 [payslip code for a private soldier], it seemed amazing that I was now talking directly to the pilot of a P-47 Thunderbolt circling overhead." Kneller tried his best to direct the aircraft toward its target but the last bomb fell short and blew him down a flight of stairs.

The wrecks of several burnt-out German tanks and fighting vehicles lay scattered through Foy. Although the Germans continued to shell the village the area was now clear of enemy troops. In total around 70 prisoners were taken during the 7-hour operation. By 1630hrs, shortly after 3rd Bn regained control, E Co returned to 2nd Bn, leaving H and I companies in defense, with F Co on the far northeastern edge of the village.

At this point Norman Dike was promoted and Ron Speirs given charge of E Co. F Co were now firmly connected to the left flank of 3/501 (along the old drover's road), who were still occupying the Bois des Corbeaux. H Co secured an area around the center of the village, while I Co held the northern approaches near the two concrete bunkers on a line between the properties belonging to Leon Dumont and Joseph Bastin. Lou Vecchi recalls a few of his guys from 1 Ptn sheltering inside the church for warmth, which was one of only a few buildings left standing that still had a roof.

Later on the afternoon of January 13, the remainder of the wounded were evacuated. Behind Joseph Gaspard's house on the eastern side of the main road, Alex Andros discovered a ruined barn containing dozens of frozen corpses, both American and German. "I suppose the Krauts must have used the place as a temporary morgue, but what took me by surprise was the way in which the bodies were so neatly stacked and separated." Ralph Bennett remembers seeing a number of starving pigs feasting on recently deceased German bodies.

Under cover of darkness the assault pioneers cleared the main road of mines to make way for the Sherman TDs and Hellcats from 11th Armored. F Co established its CP at the Evrard house and set up a defensive line facing east toward Bizory. Adjacent to the "minefield" in the back garden of Marcel Dumont's house, the engineers made a gruesome discovery. The bomb squad came across the corpses of Héléne Gaspard and her two-year-old son Guy in makeshift coffins. Héléne and Guy had been killed by shellfire almost three weeks earlier. Despicably, their frozen corpses had been booby-trapped by the Germans.

Lift up thine eyes – January 14, 1945

All three remaining companies (F, H, and I) prepared to spend a cold night in Foy. The remains of the village seemed peppered with abandoned enemy trenches and defensive positions full of lice and human feces. That night, on the northern edge of town, Alex Andros was trying to get some rest in a barn behind one of the farmhouses when Pfc Tom "Pat" Fitzmaurice, who had been on outpost duty, informed him that he could hear enemy armor gathering on the edge of the village: "I grabbed a couple of guys and went forward with Fitzmaurice to the OP and sure enough we could hear about four enemy tanks trundling around no more than 50 yards away. For some reason the crews decided to open up with machine guns but every round they fired went way above our heads." The German tanks were attempting to draw fire and ascertain American strength. Andros reported the build-up and before the regiment had a chance to react, German artillery activity began to intensify.

Around 0415hrs the enemy counterattacked with six tanks, each supported by six or seven infantrymen who bayoneted every foxhole they came across. Emile Dumont's house (on the northeastern edge of town) had become the CP for 1 Ptn F Co. Ben Stapelfeld and one of his NCOs, John Taylor (who was later awarded the Silver Star for his actions), were watching a side road from the kitchen window when they saw a tank and around 12 infantrymen heading their way. After a brief exchange of fire (which killed four enemy soldiers) Stapelfeld and his colleagues escaped through a rear window and made their way back to the church where they hooked up with H Co.

Sgt Harley Dingman was ordered to report to the forward CP, located near the crossroad, most probably at the Gaspard house. As Dingman walked in, Gene Brown, Jim Walker, and Alex Andros were weighing up their options. After a brief discussion Brown told Dingman in no uncertain terms that he was volunteering his eight-man squad to cover a controlled withdrawal. "It wasn't up for discussion," recalls Harley. "The rifle companies were then ordered to bring all their remaining ammunition and medical supplies to the CP." After Dingman and his squad had "bombed up," he split his men into four two-man teams and deployed them on a line in the Wilkin, Gaspard, Koeune, and Cordonnier houses. Over the next 2 hours, under cover of darkness, the men kept up a continuous volley of small-arms fire as Dingman ran from house to house shooting into the air. "I had my guys moving between windows firing randomly on a low trajectory toward the oncoming threat," recalls Harley. "The diversionary rearguard action worked and fooled the Germans into thinking we still had a sizable combat presence in the village." However, this did not stop the enemy tanks from carefully advancing in parallel down the N30 and along a side road leading into Foy.

Gene Brown received orders via runner (as the regiment was back on radio silence) to withdraw and reorganize with 2/506 up on the ridgeline. 2nd Bn had been ordered forward to take up positions extending from the 3rd Bn CP in the Bois Champay to the N30. At the same time the first American tanks began to move down into Foy. "As it started to get light we began to exfiltrate but still kept up the rifle fire until we were out of the village," recalls Dingman. Harley was later awarded the Silver Star for his courage, leadership, and initiative during the mission, which gained some vital time for the 506th. He adds, "After what was left of my patrol regrouped back on the MLR, I looked into their haggard faces and felt momentarily overwhelmed by the terrible responsibility of leadership."

Earlier, just before 1 Ptn H Co withdrew, Lou Vecchi received last-minute instructions to abandon his line of precious 60mm mortars. "To leave the tubes in situ seemed a ridiculous idea, so I decided to remove each C2 sight and throw it as far away into snow as possible. At this point, Tom Beasley came running over in a panic, shouting, 'Cpl Myers is dead!' I couldn't believe what he was saying because I had only spoken to Luther a few moments earlier. After disposing of the sights, I went to check on Myers, who thankfully was still very much alive after being hit by shrapnel."

A few hundred yards away to the west the forward sector occupied by G Co had also received some attention from the enemy, as Jim Martin recalls: "At around 2300hrs, 2 Ptn (who numbered about 26 men) were on OP duty 1,000 yards in front of the ridge when two enemy tanks supported by infantry pushed into our area, and the firefight continued deep into the night. Illuminating rounds fired from the 81mm mortar line up on the MLR kept troop movement to a minimum. A Sherman TD came trundling down the hill in the darkness and began spraying the enemy with heavy machine-gun fire. When the tracer rounds started to ricochet at right angles into the air, the TD crew knew that they had located the lead enemy tank."

Seconds later, the Sherman fired two rounds in rapid succession, both of which deflected upwards after striking the glacis plate of the German tank, directly below the front turret. "Bizarrely, as the first shell left the barrel it was followed by a luminous green smoke ring that slowly disappeared before our eyes," recalls Jim. The lead enemy tank returned fire, knocking out the TD. Another Sherman rolled up and pumped a couple of rounds into the first tank, which immediately caught fire. At this point the second German tank opened up on the newly arrived Sherman and disabled its turret before withdrawing. Jim Martin continues:

> It looked to us like the bedrolls strapped to the side of the German vehicle had caught fire, ignited by sparks from the other tank.
>
> Although it became a kind of stand-off we could clearly hear the sounds of more enemy armor building up in the distance. As it began to get light we spotted one of the tanks from the night before parked up about 75 yards in front of our positions. The remaining Sherman TD had moved away in the early hours toward Foy, which, despite the fog, left us vulnerable and exposed. If we were going to get out in one piece we had to do something.
>
> 1st Lt Rowe called me over to his foxhole and said, "Martin, I'll put you in for a Silver Star if you'll go out there and plant a demolition charge under the tank." "Lieutenant," I replied, "are you crazy? Sergeant Anderson and I will put you in for one if you go." Rowe wasn't impressed and gave me permission to call in smoke to mark and record the surviving enemy tank and also the approximate position of the German troops who were in the trees opposite. The first rounds fired for effect landed accurately, so we gave the artillery boys permission to go ahead and send in the 155mm HE. Around 0600hrs, when we were certain the enemy were pinned down, Lt Rowe gave the order to withdraw. I've never been so scared, and luckily, despite coming under random small-arms fire, nobody was seriously injured as we ran back through the mist toward the "safety" of the MLR.

Dawn was breaking as H Co moved out of Foy in extended line. "As the fog was clearing," recalls Alex Andros, "I happened to look round and saw Fitzmaurice (who had been on OP duty) about 300 yards away slipping and sliding up the slope trying to catch up with us. It transpired that despite my clear verbal instructions nobody had told him we were leaving!" Up on the ridge Pete Madden was attending an officers' meeting at the battalion CP. "Afterwards, as I was preparing to return to the mortar line, I bumped into one of the cooks I knew from HQ Co, Sgt Tony Zeoli, and stopped for a quick cup of coffee. As we were talking a shell exploded in the trees and a piece of shrapnel tore through

Zeoli's groin and kidneys. Another fragment hit me in the upper chest but luckily was stopped by a box of C-rations in my top pocket."

Bob Dunning happened to be there at the time and recalls, "It looked like Zeoli's penis had been injured and he was screaming over and over that he'd been ruined for life. We really didn't like Zeoli, whose nickname was 'Blackass,' and as Doctor Kent was taking him back to the regimental aid station, one of our replacements, Charlie Smith, called after him and said, 'Don't worry Sarge, the Doc might be able to cut off a piece of your nose (which was pretty large) and replace your pecker with it!' He didn't appreciate our humor and disappeared into the distance shouting abuse with all the venom he could muster."

"After Zeoli was sent off to the hospital," recalls Pete Madden, "another barrage came in and shrapnel rained down all over the place. I crawled under a Sherman tank that was parked nearby and lit up a cigarette. In the middle of the barrage the tank drove off toward Foy. I sprinted to my CP, which was covered with heavy logs. Ironically, as I entered the bunker, a piece of shrapnel came flying through the entrance and tore into my knee. The wound was serious enough for me to be evacuated to Paris. After the splinters of metal were removed from behind my patella I was shipped to a hospital in the UK."

2nd Bn were diverted to an assembly area in the woods above Recogne in preparation for a hastily organized attack on Cobru, which they subsequently secured. With Allied armor now consolidating in Foy and Recogne, the last few remaining enemy tanks were destroyed.

What was now left of 3rd Bn was ordered northwest to the southern edge of Fazone near the lake to make contact with 1st Bn and the 17th Airborne (who were scheduled to take over from the 101st), as Alex Andros recalls: "We marched through deep snow in single file and upon reaching the woods came under artillery bombardment. The barrage seemed to originate from somewhere to our rear so we knew it had to be friendly. About half a dozen rounds exploded before someone realized they had made a mistake but not before one of our replacements was badly injured. I don't think the new guys reacted in the same way we did to counterfire. Maybe they froze for a few extra seconds… I mean, we were still just as scared but somehow those of us who had survived one or more campaigns seemed to instinctively know what to do."

Due to the shelling G Co suffered four casualties when Pvt Franklin Ely was killed and privates Abner Liggett, Chester Shaffer, and Tim Clifford were seriously wounded. With 2nd Bn now in control of Cobru, E Co moved forward to the high ground on the southeastern edge of Noville between D and F Co to maintain the regimental front – which was once again under radio silence.

Guts and drive – January 15–20, 1945

After digging in for the night, 3/506 relocated to the northeastern edge of Fazone Woods, where they had previously suffered so much damage during "Hell Night." The battalion re-occupied the fortifications recently vacated by 1/506 – now in the process of attacking and capturing a wooded area directly northwest of Cobru. During the "cleansing" action, Capt Roy Kessler was killed leading A/506. Kessler had been seriously wounded in Holland when he was XO for H Co. As 2/506 were attacking Noville, Col Sink moved forward and relocated his CP to the Château d'Hoffschmidt in Recogne, which had only recently been cleared by S/Sgt Keith Carpenter and the regimental demolition platoon. Back in Bastogne the town was still under intermittent attack by the rail gun, which had an effective range of over 11 miles!

On January 14, two platoons from E Co and one from F Co took cover for the night in an old, abandoned quarry overlooking the church at Noville. The quarry pits were covered with logs and anything else that could be found for protection. A dawn attack was planned for the following morning that would simultaneously coincide with 1st Bn's assault into the woods directly northwest of Cobru. During the pre-mission briefing, carried out by Capt Winters and 1st Lt Speirs, 1/Sgt Carwood Lipton was tasked to take 2 Ptn (because Jack Foley had been wounded at Foy) and clear the western (left-hand side of town), while

Ed Shames and 2nd Lt Ben Stapelfeld (1 Ptn F Co) were to come in from the east. Still under radio blackout, the force was told to expect support from 11th Armored, who were operating a number of M36 "Jackson" tank destroyers that had only just arrived in theater. With its low silhouette, the Jackson, weighing 29 tons, was fitted with a long, 90mm gun complete with a muzzle brake. At a glance it could quite easily be mistaken for a German Mk V Panther.

Pfc Jay Stone and Sgt Plummer from 321st GFA were attached to 2/506 for the assault albeit in different FO parties. There was no evidence to suggest that the 321st communications network had been breached, so the two groups were able to provide the artillery and close air support vital to the assault. Because the church was so badly damaged the enemy were unable to use its steeple as an observation post. For this reason 2 Ptn were able to move forward to a fence line from where Lipton could just make out the rear of several large properties situated on the western side of the main road.

As the buildings seemed unoccupied, Lipton carefully advanced with his radio operator (probably tuned to the 321st network) to a barn from where they could clearly observe the N30. From here it was just about possible to make out the outline of a Sherman and a half-track. Thinking 11th Armored could already be in town, Lipton decided to patrol toward the crossroad for a closer look. Trying hard not to disturb the frost-covered snow, Lipton picked his way into town only to find that the American vehicles had been knocked out on December 20 during Team Desobry and 1st Bn's epic withdrawal. Fearing the worst, he decided to pull back and report his findings to Speirs.

Shortly before first light the assault platoons moved out to their respective jump-off points. Ed Shames crossed the N30 with 3 Ptn ahead of Ben Stapelfeld and moved his men into position behind the Beaujean house (previously the 1st Bn aid station on December 19/20) situated on the southern edge of Noville. Once again, the job for 3 Ptn was to punch toward the center of town and consolidate behind the church and await further instructions. Shames was somewhat concerned by the amount of exposed ground he and his men would have to cross before even reaching the church. In front of 3 Ptn, about 300 yards away on the other side of the field, was a line of trees that ran toward the back of the church and presbytery. Beyond the trees was a small group of buildings that included the milking shed belonging to Felten Farm.

Almost immediately 3 Ptn came under artillery fire. The shelling seemed to be coming from a nearby area of woods that overlooked the town from the northwest, as Ed Shames recalls: "I watched the shells come in and start to explode on a line, one by one, in front of us. As they dropped closer I thought, 'This is it; I'm dead,' but the last shell in the salvo failed to detonate and was still fizzing in the deep snow as we passed by." 2 Ptn encountered less resistance as they were partially protected by buildings but still lost Pfc Ed Joint (1st Squad) and Pfc Brad Freeman (60mm mortar squad), who were both wounded.

Quickly gathering momentum the platoon reached the tree line on the far side of the field and took refuge in the milking shed behind the church. After a brief respite, 3 Ptn went on the offensive and skirmished around the barn, neutralizing the few remaining pockets of enemy resistance as a flight of P-47 Thunderbolts arrived overhead. The attack ended as quickly as it had begun, with the enemy withdrawing northeast, leaving the area around the church clear. Minutes later Ed was somewhat surprised when a message came through on the radio: "Friendly armor on the right." "Shortly afterwards," he recalls, "we heard a terrific rumbling noise and I asked my radio operator Pvt Jim 'Moe' Alley to go outside with me and make contact."

So as not to become targets for the P-47s and because radio silence was still officially in force, the two men decided to leave their helmets, rifles, and equipment behind before walking around the corner into Route de Bourcy. Shames and Alley headed down the road a short distance to the crossroads, passing the stone wall belonging to the presbytery on their left. Upon reaching the main road, Shames looked both ways but saw nothing except for the Sherman, a German Stug SPG, and the half-track knocked out in December outside the church. Then Shames noticed the back of another tank parked between two gutted buildings on the right-hand side of the street in the direction of Houffalize. Thinking this might be one of the new M36s, Alley ran on ahead and yelled out a greeting to its commander.

As the two paratroopers approached they could now clearly see the NCO standing in the turret. As the man turned around, Shames and Alley stopped in their tracks. The tank was not an M36 but a Panzer V armed with a powerful 75mm gun. It would appear that the vehicle and its five-man crew had been left behind, possibly due to some sort of communications breakdown.

The enemy tanker panicked and immediately attempted to traverse his turret toward Shames and Alley. "It was a terrifying moment as we turned on our heels and ran for our lives," recalls Shames. The tank reversed out and lurched forward in pursuit, firing its 7.92mm machine gun as the two men sprinted back toward the presbytery. Helpless over on the other side of the street, 2 Ptn looked on, open mouthed, while the 46-ton behemoth chased down their comrades. As the tank (which had a top speed of 38mph) was turning into Route de Bourcy, Shames and Alley took a leap of faith over the 5ft-high presbytery wall, which, luckily for them, tapered at that point into a small embankment. No more than a second later, as the Panzer turned the corner, it fired into what was left of the building before continuing westwards toward Bourcy. The concussive blast of the gun made everything shudder, and the resulting explosion lifted Shames and Alley bodily off the ground.

Ben Stapelfeld's 1 Ptn from F Co had been attached to E Co for the assault. Ben led his men in behind 3 Ptn, past a burned-out Mk IV Panther, toward the graves of the eight civilians murdered by the SD on December 21. Ben and his men were pinned down by enemy machine-gun fire and forced to take cover in a nearby pigpen. Cpl Robert Stone was ordered by Stapelfeld to fire his 60mm mortar onto the enemy tank as it moved along the road toward Bourcy. Ben hoped that one of the shells might hit the commander but it was futile. Just when they were about to give up, the men cheered as one of the circling P-47s flew in low and destroyed the Panzer as it raced over a nearby hill.

A perimeter defense was established shortly after midday when the cleansing action was complete. At this point F Co withdrew to the southern edge of town close to the newly established E Co CP. Everyone was convinced that this was the final objective of the campaign, but there was still more to come. Shortly after the town was taken, Maxwell Taylor and Gerald Higgins arrived to get a situation report from Col Sink and Capt Winters. Due to the continuous radio lockdowns over the last 30 hours, Divisional HQ had been for the most part unaware as to what was happening and where. Taylor was horrified by the state of the town and asked Sink what on earth he had done. Up until then, the general had had no real idea of the terrible damage previously inflicted against Noville.

From his temporary command center in Recogne, Sink began preparations for the combined regimental attack on Rachamps before relocating the following day to Vaux. With all radio channels now reopened, full command and control was restored. The simultaneous move northeast to capture Rachamps, Wicourt, and Neuf-Moulin was supported by two companies of tanks from the 705th and 811th TD battalions.

The main attack to push the enemy forces away to the east began on January 16 at 0930hrs, after 3rd Bn had advanced along the road from Fagnoux to Wicourt (supported by 3/501), while 1st and 2nd battalions put in their assault on Rachamps from Cobru and Noville. North of Noville, Rachamps was situated in a gently sloping valley. 2nd Bn pushed forward along the N30 from Noville. After occupying the high ground north of the town, 2/506 made their advance on Rachamps, which fell on January 16. That same day, after 2nd Bn reclaimed Rachamps, First and Third armies were able to link up further north at Houffalize, spelling the beginning of the end of the German action in the Ardennes.

Meanwhile 1st Bn had moved onto the left flank of 3/506 to launch its own assault back toward Noville. 3rd Bn advanced further west and then drove north beyond Noville toward Wicourt. With 11th Armored supporting the drive, 1/506 sent spearheads across the N30 north of Noville and above Rachamps. This action cut off the remaining enemy forces, which subsequently began to surrender in ever increasing numbers.

It was late in the afternoon by the time 3rd Bn reached the high ground at Neuf-Moulin (2 miles northeast of Wicourt), as Alex Andros recalls: "The Germans had only just withdrawn and left most of their wounded behind for us to deal with." The mass of churned up mud surrounding the recently vacated artillery positions led the men to conclude that horses had been used to move the guns. Andros continues his account:

> The abandoned dugouts were deep and well constructed, with plenty of headroom, so we selected one for our CP. Leaving Capt Walker, Willie Miller, Ralph Bennett, and a few other guys in the new position, I walked over to the edge of the wood to survey the valley through my binoculars.
>
> From where I was standing about 4 or 5 yards inside the tree line, I had a commanding view to the east, about half a mile across a shallow valley to the woods on the other side, where I could see what looked like tanks in the trees. Suddenly there was a blinding flash from the edge of the woods opposite and then everything went black. I awoke to find my helmet lying beside me with the fluorescent green identification flag that I kept inside the liner protruding through a ragged exit hole. Disorientated and bleeding – despite suffering from concussion – I realized that a shell fragment had ripped through the upper part of my helmet, narrowly missing my skull. I yelled for a medic but nobody came, so as it was getting dark, I crawled back to the CP where Willie Miller administered first aid and arranged for me to be evacuated.

After Andros had gone, Miller assumed command of 3 Ptn. Later that night, during a battalion commanders' meeting, Col Patch got up and told the handful of officers who were left that he was planning a possible attack the following morning. At that time, apart from Capt Walker, Willie Miller was the only officer left from H Co and he was not impressed by the order. When excited or agitated, Willie's voice went up several octaves as he squawked, "Hell, sir, I've only got 11 men at my disposal – what on god's earth are you expecting me to do with them?"

Jimmy Martin had been ignoring the symptoms of emersion foot for the last ten days because he did not want to leave his post or let anyone down. "Eventually my feet turned black, and on January 15, I asked Capt Doughty for permission to leave the front line and gingerly walked about half a mile to the nearest aid post. I later learned that another few days in theater and I would have lost my toes." Despite the dreadful losses suffered by H and I companies, G Co still had 56 men available for duty. However, over the next seven days the company would lose a further 30 percent of its remaining strength (including Capt Doughty) to trench foot and other non-battle-related injuries. Jim Martin was evacuated to the United Kingdom by Norwegian hospital ship and spent several weeks in Cirencester, where an entire hospital wing was dedicated to emersion and cold injuries. "For many like me, the condition was so painful and sensitive that we were made to lie in bed with our lower limbs exposed. Any draft or movement, such as a nurse walking by, caused an intense burning sensation to the feet … which was pretty grim at times."

Where dead men sleep

Finally, the regiment handed over control to the newly formed 17th Airborne Division, and 3rd Bn spent their first stress-free night under cover in a warm barn at Luzery. "When my jump boots came off for the first time since December 17, I found that my socks had completely disintegrated below the tops of my boots," recalls Hank DiCarlo. "The dry hay in the barn felt softer and sweeter than any luxury mattress."

By January 18, the regiment was in corps reserve at La Petite Rosière, 6 miles south of Sibret. Frank Kneller remembers being taken by truck to a frozen lake, where water was being pumped to a row of showers. "We took one look at the facility and refused to get off the vehicles. After many protests, eventually we were taken to a nearby town where we were allowed to wash and bathe in a proper bath house with hot water – the ultimate luxury." It was here that Kneller was evacuated with advanced trench foot and was lucky not to have both feet amputated.

During this time around 500 men from the 101st were selected to attend a Silver Star ceremony at the main square (which had recently been cleared of debris) in Bastogne, hosted by Troy Middleton, Maxwell Taylor, Gerald Higgins, and BrigGen Charles Kilburn from the 11th Armored Division. Also in attendance was Mayor Leon Jacqmin, who, after delivering a short but emotional speech, presented Taylor with a flag representing the official colors of the city. Frank Marchesse and Alden Todd from F/502 were part of the small group chosen to represent their regiment still fighting at Bourcy. As the two men were walking through Foy, Todd stopped at the Chapelle Ste-Barbe and retrieved a small handbell from the ruins as a souvenir. Some 50 years later Alden returned the bell, which now sits in its rightful place on the altar.

In total five soldiers were honored on the 18th, including the commanding officer of 1/502, Maj John D. Hanlon, Lt Frank R. Stanfield, S/Sgt Lawrence F. Casper, and Pvt Wolfe. Before reviewing the troops, Middleton, Taylor, and assembled staff officers posed for the press beneath a sign on the wall of a nearby building. The sign, posted close to the main road junction, aptly summed up the siege experience: "This is Bastogne, Bastion of the Battered Bastards of the 101st Airborne Division."

After a couple days' pampering, the men were informed that they were moving to a defensive area in Alsace Lorraine. "Everyone thought we had just got out of one so-called 'defensive' position," recalls Hank DiCarlo. "It was rumored that we were going to outpost a relatively inactive part of the line, but hadn't they told us the same thing before Bastogne?"

Continuing bad weather hampered the First and Third armies' advance, but by January 28, the enemy were pushed back to their original point of departure and the thrust into the Ardennes was declared officially over. During the coming weeks and months American and French forces attacked into Luxembourg and Germany, but the war was by no means finished for Hitler and his fanatical commanders.

Capt Fred Anderson reflects: "I Co went into Bastogne with 150 men and came out with 28. G and H companies fared little better." Bob Webb adds: "After the final attack on Foy, Col Sink lost one of the best battalions he ever had and he knew it." During the four weeks on the line at Bastogne the 506th PIR suffered over 40 percent casualties (although the 501st suffered the highest): 119 men were killed, 670 wounded, and 59 missing in action – total 848. The division as a whole lost 525 KIA, 2,653 WIA, and 527 missing or captured – total 3,705. Combat Command B lost 73 KIA, 279 WIA, and 116 missing or captured – total 468.

The Battle of the Bulge was arguably one of the most important events of World War II and signified the beginning of the end for Germany. The Wehrmacht had suffered some 110,000 casualties, while the total American losses had risen to 80,000, of whom approximately 19,000 had been killed. It was said that no other battle had caused so much American blood to be spilt.

Addressing the House of Commons in London, Sir Winston Churchill was quoted as saying, "This is undoubtedly the greatest American battle of the war and will, I believe, be regarded as an ever famous victory."

The devastation to the civilian population was also immense, with around 2,500 people killed, and towns and villages such as Foy, Recogne, Noville, Wardin, Sibret, Chenogne, and Villers-la-Bobbe-Eau all but destroyed. Along with the massacres of US forces at places such as Malmedy and Wereth, 164 civilians were also murdered at Stavelot and Bande. So ended Operation *Watch on the Rhine* and the now legendary Battle of the Bulge.

9

"After the storm"

Alsace Lorraine and the Colmar Pocket – January 21–February 25, 1945

Alsace and Lorraine are two separate regions in France's northeastern corner bordering Belgium, Luxembourg, Germany, and Switzerland. Alsace follows the river Rhine north from Basel, while Lorraine rises from the plains of Champagne before converging at the Vosges Mountains. Historically, most of Alsace was German speaking when awarded to France by the Hapsburg Empire. In 1871, after France was defeated in the Franco-Prussian War, Germany annexed Alsace and the Moselle Department of Lorraine and reintroduced a program of forced Germanization. At the end of World War I the region reverted back to French control only to be re-occupied in 1940 by Germany, who over the next four years conscripted around 130,000 Alsatian men into their armed forces.

The Western Front, in early 1945, was divided into three army groups. Northernmost was 21st Army Group, under Field Marshal Bernard Montgomery. Omar Bradley and his 12th Army Group were situated centrally, with 6th Army Group commanded by Gen Jacob Devers to the south around Alsace Lorraine and the Swiss border. Devers' group was part of a joint force comprising Seventh Army (XV and VI Corps) under LtGen Alexander Patch and the French First Army (I and II Corps) commanded by Général d'Armée Jean de Lattre de Tissigny.

Unlike some of the towns and villages further north, the French were initially unable to push the enemy back across the Rhine. Therefore, in late November 1944, the Germans forced a bridgehead along the western edge of the Black Forest between the ancient towns of Pfaffenhoffen, Haguenau, Colmar, and Basel. Before Christmas the Nazi war machine began to threaten the rear of George Patton's Third Army and also Seventh Army. When Patton was redirected to the Ardennes, part of Seventh Army moved south to assist the French. During the early stages of the battle, the Germans tried desperately to break out and drive north to link up with their forces around Bastogne. The threat to the supply lines was real, and if the enemy had not been contained in Alsace then Gen Patton would have struggled to maintain his push to reach Bastogne (which lay 125 miles to the northwest).

It was here in Alsace at the crossroad of Europe on January 1, 1945, that Hitler decided to reinstate his offensive. Operation *Nordwind* was similar in execution to *Watch on the Rhine* and generally became known to the Allies as "The Battle of the Colmar Pocket." Commander-in-Chief West, Generalfeldmarschall Gerd von Runstedt, who had been the driving force behind *Watch on the Rhine*, was completely opposed to this new plan. Subsequently, Hitler asked SS Commander Heinrich Himmler to take charge of the southern front with instructions to ignore Von Runstedt and report directly to him in Berlin. Hitler's idea was to cut off the regional capital, Strasbourg, with two pincer movements from Haguenau in the north and further south at Colmar. Over the next three weeks the attack shifted back and forth before finally grounding to a stalemate near Strasbourg.

Firefighting in Pfaffenhoffen

After being relieved by the 17th Airborne, the 506th was placed in reserve by XVIII Airborne Corps at La Petite Rosière, a few miles south of Bastogne. On January 20, the 101st was temporarily attached to MajGen Wade "Ham" Haislip's XV Corps and instructed to take over one of the more peaceful sectors of the old Maginot Line along the Moder valley in Alsace (allowing Haislip a better opportunity to exploit his divisions elsewhere). The regiment was mobilized and transported by truck to Diemeringen near Sarre-Union, 20 miles northwest of the small town of Pfaffenhoffen. Just like Bastogne the journey was cold and badly delayed by icy road conditions. With 16in of snow on the ground, the men were not looking forward to their new assignment.Ahead of the main body was the regimental IPW team led by Capt Alphonse Gion and M/Sgt Herman Coquelin, who had been tasked with securing billets in the villages of Diemeringen, Waldhambach, and Weislingen.

Traveling with the team was 22-year-old Dutchman Piet "Pete" Luiten, who recalls, "I came from the Stratum district of Eindhoven and had previously worked with 2nd Bn, 81mm mortar platoon, as their interpreter. By late September, I was promoted to 'lieutenant' and re-assigned to the IPW team before being wounded at Opheusden." After spending several months in hospital, Pete managed to hitchhike back to La Petite Rosière, where he was able to rejoin the regiment. On the 506th payroll Luiten was still officially under the British 21st Army Group as part of the Dutch Free Forces Corps of Interpreters. "I rode down to Alsace with Capt Gion, who knew that my excellent command of German and French would come in useful over the next few days."

With 3rd Bn stationed at Diemeringen (alongside Regimental HQ) the other two battalions were billeted nearby along a southeasterly line in the villages of Waldhambach (2/506) and Weislingen (1/506) – whereupon they were able to check and take stock of weapons, equipment, ammunition, and rations. Even before the regiment reached Alsace, information packs were distributed, reminding everyone that although this was "friendly" territory the area contained many civilians, for whom German was still their first language and who might also be sympathetic to the Fatherland. Despite these fears some people seemed more than happy to help the Americans, as Pete Luiten reflects: "Somewhere along the way I'd picked up a serious chest infection. I was surprised when one of the locals that we'd just given notice to vacate kindly made up some sort of alcohol-based linctus, which really helped me get back on my feet."

Five days later the 506th PIR relocated 30 miles further southeast to Wickersheim-Wilshausen near Hochfelden. The three battalions were deployed within a 2-mile radius of Wickersheim, with 3/506 being sent to the village of Geiswiller. By January 28, the regiment was still in divisional reserve when it moved closer to the river Moder and into the villages around Ettendorf in preparation to relieve the 409th Infantry Regiment (IR) from the 103rd ID now led by Tony McAuliffe (part of XV Corps). Initially the regiment was sent to three small villages just southwest of Pfaffenhoffen. 3rd Bn went to Lixhausen and 1st Bn to Bossendorf, leaving 2nd Bn behind at Grassendorf.

The heavily depleted regiment was enhanced by A and F batteries, 81st AA Bn, and C Co (less 3 Ptn), 807th TD Bn. From here the paratroopers were deployed along a 1-mile-wide front, overlooking the river, between a set of partially demolished bridges east from Pfaffenhoffen to the village of Niedermodern.

The ancient and once prosperous town of Pfaffenhoffen is situated in the Val de Moder – a shallow valley spanning the river which usually, at its widest, is no bigger than a main road. The basic plan was to send patrols across to the northern bank and disrupt enemy forces based at la Walck (a northern suburb of Pfaffenhoffen), plus the surrounding villages of Kindwiller, Bitschhoffen, and Uberach. Uberach was on the regiment's right flank and nestled along the edge of the Haguenau Forest. Overshadowing the northern banks of the Moder, the dense woodland covered a large area to the east as far as the eye could see.

On February 1, 2nd Bn was for the most part still in regimental reserve when 1st and 3rd battalions deployed onto the MLR. At the time Pfaffenhoffen was partly bandit country and virtually devoid of civilians, except for a few abandoned dogs and cats.

C Co set up its CP on the left flank at the railway station in the basement of a house that had once belonged to the stationmaster. The railway followed the Moder through the Haguenau Forest, crossing the river near Uberach, through Niedermodern, Pfaffenhoffen, and Obermodern, before turning northwest toward the Vosges Mountains at Ingwiller.

One rifle company from each battalion was sent forward to maintain an "Outpost Line of Resistance" (OPLR) beyond the raised road overlooking the river. Some foxholes had to be relocated to higher ground after they began to fill with water. "I was in charge of one makeshift squad," recalls Manny Barrios. "There wasn't much action at the time except for a big rail gun that fired a salvo every now and then." Alsace Annie was believed to be a 15in artillery piece hidden somewhere along the tracks in the Haguenau Forest and had a long enough range to target Hochfelden where Divisional HQ were now located. "It's strange but the sound those shells made as they flew overhead was really weird and scared the heck out of us," Barrios added.

Col Sink established his CP in a schoolhouse at Ettendorf. The small town was equidistant between Grassendorf and Ringendorf, situated around a crossroads along another railway line that meandered northwest before connecting with Obermodern. On the first night, a woman who had private quarters in another part of the school shot herself through the mouth after being exposed as a German spy. The woman's body was stored in a room next door to the S3 office where it remained for several days. It was a dramatic beginning to the redeployment.

Recently promoted to staff sergeant, George Allen, from the 101st IPW team, was posted to counterintelligence and recalls, "As predicted, any cordiality shown by the local population toward us seemed completely false. Despite this fact, enough information was gathered to uncover a small group of enemy soldiers who were trying to infiltrate the area dressed as civilians."

Several German units had previously been identified across the river, such as the Infanterie-Regiment 937 belonging to 245.Volksgrenadier-Division, which was predominantly made up of boys and older men. Other than that, this sector of the German West Wall was relatively peaceful apart from the rail gun, sporadic mortar fire, and occasional enemy patrolling.

By February 2, as the snow began to thaw, it caused extensive flooding, turning the ground into thick mud. Long overdue, a large consignment of rubberized winter overshoes arrived. Although thankful, the men were upset by the delay as many serious non-battle casualties could have been avoided if the "shoepacks" had been more widely available at Bastogne.

Bob Dunning from the 81mm mortar platoon was sent to Strasbourg for emergency treatment when the bullet still lodged in his left hip became a problem. "The surgeon who removed the 9mm slug was from Kalamazoo and recognized me … small world, eh? We'd both been camp counselors for the Kellogg's Corporation in Hastings, Michigan. Shortly after returning to the outfit I developed a dangerously high temperature and was diagnosed with blood poisoning. For 24 hours the doctors at Soissons deliberated over removing the leg. Luckily my temperature, which had been just above 110 degrees Fahrenheit, began to reduce and saved my leg from amputation."

Around the same time Bob Webb returned to the front line from hospital. "The doctors had sent me to a psychiatric ward, but my previous confused mental state (no doubt caused by the concussion I received in Bastogne) quickly cleared up. While in hospital, I bumped into Maj Charles Shettle, who was still recovering from his foot wound. After seeing one of the patients on my ward slashing his wrists with a razor, I just wanted to get out and return to the battalion. Shettle felt the same way and used his rank to commandeer a jeep so we were able to avoid any replacement depots and head straight back to the 506th in Alsace."

Shortly after Webb returned to duty he was promoted to sergeant. "I hadn't been back long when we had our first mail from home and received two packages from my girlfriend, containing drawing pencils, paper, food, a cake, billfold, Bible with metal case, and – best of all – a picture of Muriel in a snazzy blue leather folder." Bob was a gifted artist and had been looking forward to receiving the drawing materials to help him pass the time, sketching portraits, which were much sought after by his friends and colleagues.

At 0240hrs on February 4, 22 men from F Co, led by 2nd Lt Ben Stapelfeld, crossed the Moder and made their way to Bitschhoffen. The mission was ordered at the last minute, leaving Ben no time to plan or prepare. Before re-crossing the river opposite Pfaffenhoffen, Stapelfeld and his men were ambushed by enemy machine-gun and mortar fire. During the chaotic firefight, Sgt Bill Green was killed and six others wounded. For the remainder of the night I Co bracketed the area with 60mm mortar fire. Subsequently it was decided that all future missions were to be given two days to prepare and executed with full mortar and artillery support.

Haguenau, the southwest front – "no place for heroes"

The following morning orders were received by 1st and 3rd battalions that they were to be relieved by the 409th IR. During the early hours both battalions were pulled out and sent 9 miles east along the river to Haguenau. Their new job would be to assist MajGen Edward H. Brooks' VI Corps, who were going on the offensive north of Strasbourg.

Situated between Schweighouse-sur-Moder and Bischwiller, 25 miles from Strasbourg, Haguenau was and still is one of the largest towns in the region of Bas-Rhin. Straddling the meandering Moder, Haguenau had become a thriving industrial town with a wartime population of around 18,000 people, although most had fled by February 1945. From here the Moder twists and turns for around 10 miles in an easterly direction through Drusenheim, before filtering into the mighty river Rhine marking the border with Germany.

Along with its vitally important road network, Haguenau also boasted a major railway terminus and military airfield, located nearby at Kaltenhouse, which had been captured by the Allies in December, 1944. Over on the enemy-held bank, the massive Haguenau Forest swallowed the northern boundaries of the town, while further north the land rose steeply to mark the beginning of the Vosges du Nord mountain range.

After the earlier poor patrol performances, the 506th made sure that each battalion now had at least three five-man patrols on 24-hour standby and one specified platoon trained to operate independently as a large-scale raiding party.

By February 5, 1st Bn had been moved back to Bossendorf, while 1 mile further northwest, 3rd Bn reoccupied Lixhausen. At 1330hrs, 2nd Bn arrived and a temporary forward CP was established with the 313th IR (45th ID) at Harthausen, until Col Sink could establish his own HQ at Château Walk. The château was located on the southern side of Haguenau along Rue Député Hallez and had been a former German Youth camp. Close to the château was a heavily booby-trapped area of woodland known as the Weitbruch Forest, where the engineers were still working hard to clear the sector of "Schu mines." These small, wooden-framed, antipersonnel devices were undetectable and had recently caused several serious civilian and military casualties.

At 2200hrs, the 506th took over the MLR from the 313th IR with 1/506 on the left and 2/506 to the right. In addition to the previous attachments the regiment was assigned A Co and 1 Ptn from D Co 47th Tank Bn. Over the next five days the 506th remained in defense of Haguenau, conducting vigorous patrolling, both combat and recon, across the Moder while waiting for replacements.

Every rifle company underwent drastic changes to its structure and manpower as the new blood began to arrive at Château Walk. Manny Barrios wound up with a number of green replacements and instructions to provide security for I Co's left flank. Barrios and his squad moved into a building on the edge of town close to the river, which was now in full flood and therefore appeared much wider. Manny recalls:

> Here the edge of the river was quite shallow and it was possible to wade out some distance before it deepened and dropped away. I inherited a pair of binoculars and spent most of the time watching the opposite bank. There were no factories or bridges where we

ABOVE: Drop on December 26 as seen from the parade ground at Caserne Heintz. Col Sink's CP was located in the last block on the right. (NARA via Donald van den Bogert)

LEFT: Members of 3rd Bn's medical detachment celebrating Christmas Day outside the aid station in the Bois Champay. L to R (standing): Harold Haycraft, Talford Wynne, Walter Pelcher, John Eckman; (kneeling) Eugene Woodside, John Gibson, Robert Evans, Andy Sosnack. (John Gibson via John Klein)

Midnight Mass for walking wounded in one of the barrack blocks at Caserne Heintz. Moments after this photograph was taken a German air raid broke up the service. (NARA via Donald van den Bogert)

On Christmas Day the senior commanders took a few moments out to contemplate the festive season. L to R: William Roberts, Ned Moore, Gerald Higgins, Tony McAuliffe, Thomas Sherburne, Harry Kinnard, Carl Kohls, Paul Danahy, and Curtis Renfro. (NARA via Donald van den Bogert)

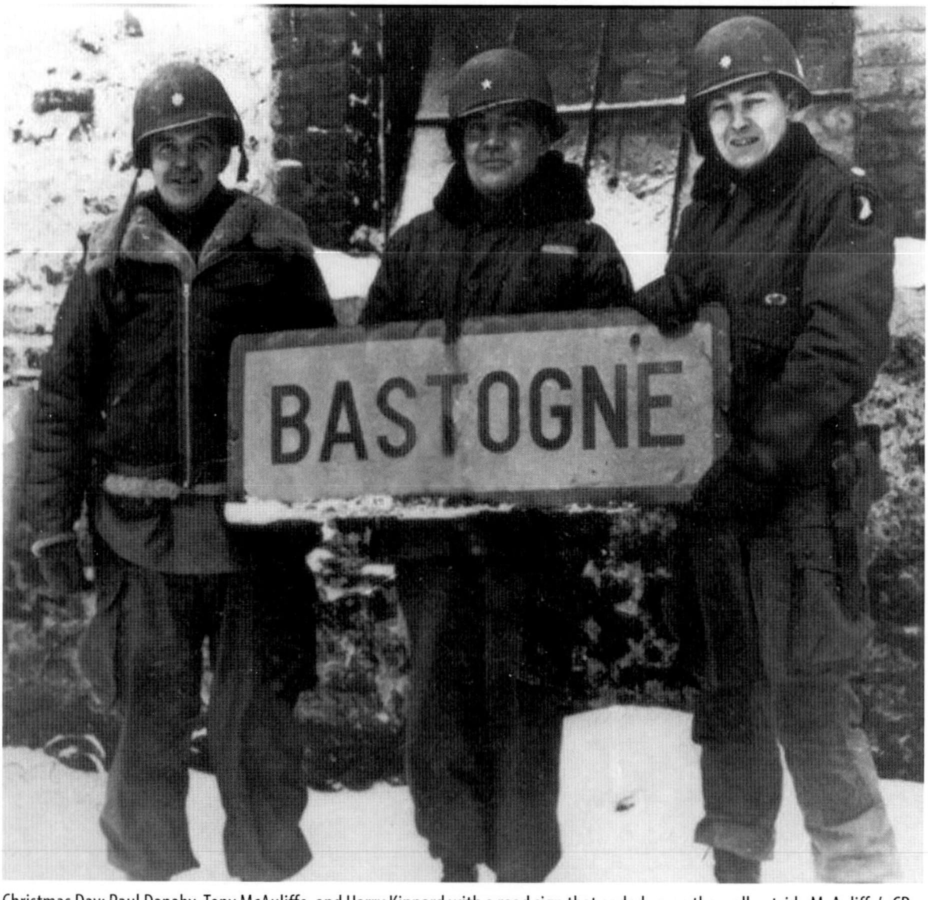

Christmas Day; Paul Danahy, Tony McAuliffe, and Harry Kinnard with a road sign that ended up on the wall outside McAuliffe's CP. (NARA)

Abandoned GC4A gliders and "Stardust," a C-47 that crash landed east of Savy being inspected by members of the 321st GFA who drained over 200 gallons of fuel from its tanks. (Don Straith via Reg Jans)

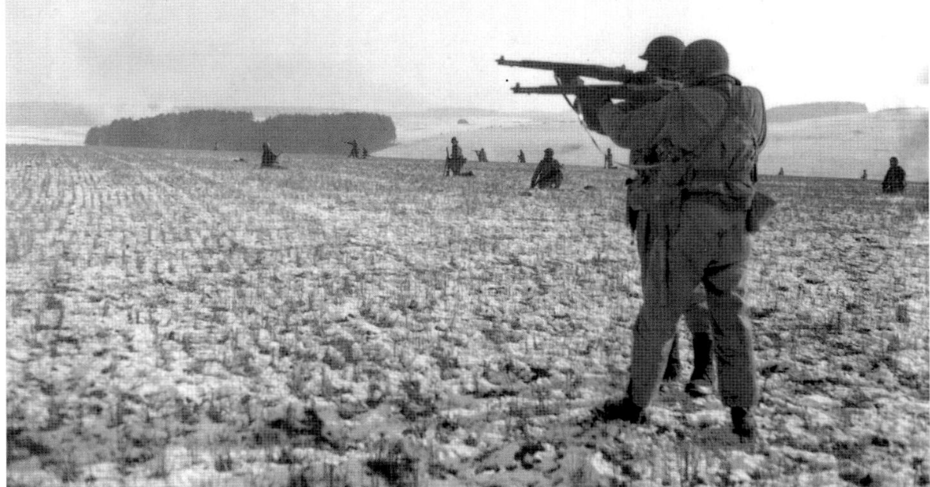

Troops from 10th Armored Infantry Bn, 4th Armored Division, on their way to Bastogne. (NARA via Donald van den Bogert)

Vehicle convoy moving up towards Bastogne. (John Gibson via John Klein)

A German Panzer V, also known as the Panther, abandoned by its crew somewhere around the perimeter. (John Gibson via John Klein)

Patton and Tony McAuliffe awarding the DSC to 32-year-old Steve Chappuis, CO 502nd PIR, at Château de Rolley for his incredible leadership during the German attack at Champs on Christmas Day. (Reg Jans)

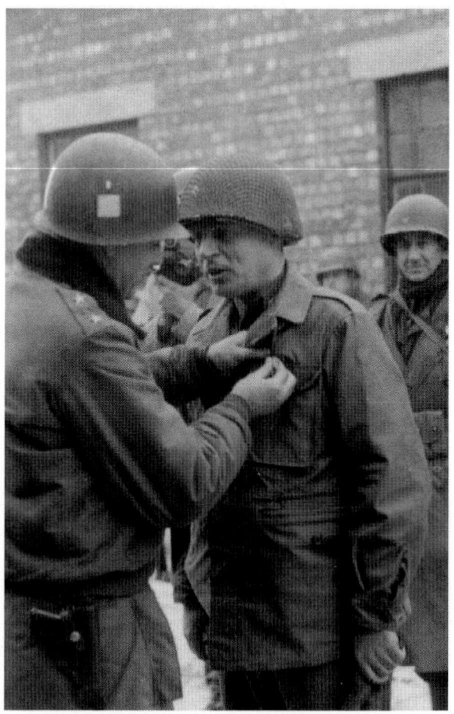

Shortly after arriving in theater, Gen Taylor presented Silver Stars at Caserne Heintz to the CO of 705th TD Bn, LtCol Clifford Templeton, and Col William Roberts (standing rear), CO of Combat Command B. (NARA via Donald van den Bogert)

Cpl Jim Brown from 2 Ptn I Co had a premonition that he was not going to make it. (Bill Galbraith via John Klein)

Cpl Bobbie Rommel, MG Ptn, was injured on January 9 in the Fazone Woods.

Pictured here in September 1945, T/4 Robert Webb from Communications Ptn was badly affected by the shelling in the Fazone Woods. (Bob Webb Jr)

1st Lt Peter Madden, CO of 81mm Mortar Platoon, seen here in May 1944 with Peter and Anne Mills at their home in Ramsbury where he was billeted before and after D-Day. (Peter Mills)

A paratrooper, probably from the 82nd Airborne Division, poses for a publicity picture while guarding German POWs. (NARA via Donald van den Bogert)

German prisoners being marched along the N30 above Foy close to the 3/506 MLR on January 13 in the direction of Bastogne. (Joël Robert)

A Panzer IV disabled by Pvt Al Cappelli (2 Ptn I Co) at the crossroad outside Jules Koeune's house in Foy on January 13, 1945. (Joël Robert)

TOP: Foy, January 14/15, 1945: the clean up begins. Note the edge of the chapel (left) and the Gaspard house on the right. The soldier in the jeep (right foreground) is from HQ Co 502nd PIR. (John Gibson via John Klein)

MIDDLE : M7 Priest SPG in action supporting the 506th PIR at Noville and beyond. (Reg Jans)

BOTTOM: View north towards Foy from Joseph Collard's house around January 14, along the N30, showing an M18 Hellcat from 11th Armored Division. (Currahee Scrapbook via Reg Jans & Robert Remacle)

Bastogne jammed with vehicles heading for the northern perimeter; note the seminary in the background. (NARA via Reg Jans)

Divisional meeting outside Noville Church, January 15. L to R: Maxwell Taylor, Dick Winters, Gerald Higgins, and Bob Sink. Higgins was one of the youngest brigadier generals in the US Army. (Reg Jans)

Silver Star Ceremony, Bastogne, January 18, 1945. L to R: LtGen Troy Middleton, Maxwell Taylor, BrigGen Charles Kilburn, Gerald Higgins, and Bastogne's Mayor Leon Jacqmin stand at attention. (Reg Jans)

Capt Derwood Cann took command of G Co at Mourmelon on February 28, 1945. (Currahee Scrapbook)

Fred Bahlau pictured here shortly after being commissioned as a second lieutenant and posted to 1/506. (Reg Jans)

2nd Lt Roy Gates joined 3 Ptn E Co at Mourmelon in early April 1945. (Joe Muccia)

Sgt Lou Vecchi (right) and S/Sgt Gordon Yates (H Co Communications Ptn) strolling along the seafront on Promenade des Anglais, Nice, French Riviera, March 1945. (Lou Vecchi)

1st Squad H Co, Nievenheim, Ruhr Pocket April 1945. L to R (standing): Pvt Frank Parker, Pvt Carl Henson, Sgt Hank DiCarlo, Sgt Bob Hoffman (DiCarlo's assistant), Pvt Vernon Timm; (kneeling) T/5 Jack Grace, Pfc Jimmy Igoe, Pvt Joe Novak, Pfc Wilber Johnson. (Hank DiCarlo)

Bob Hoffman, Pvt "Charlie" Kier, and Pvt Bob Willis from 1 Ptn H Co, constructively passing the time in between doing the laundry. (Lou Vecchi)

A photograph that appeared on the front cover of the March 1945 edition of *Yank* Magazine, showing Sonny Sundquist (center) a few weeks before he deserted. (NARA via Donald van den Bogert)

One corner of KZ-IV (Camp 4) at Hurlag shortly after it was liberated. (NARA via Gerhard Roletscheck)

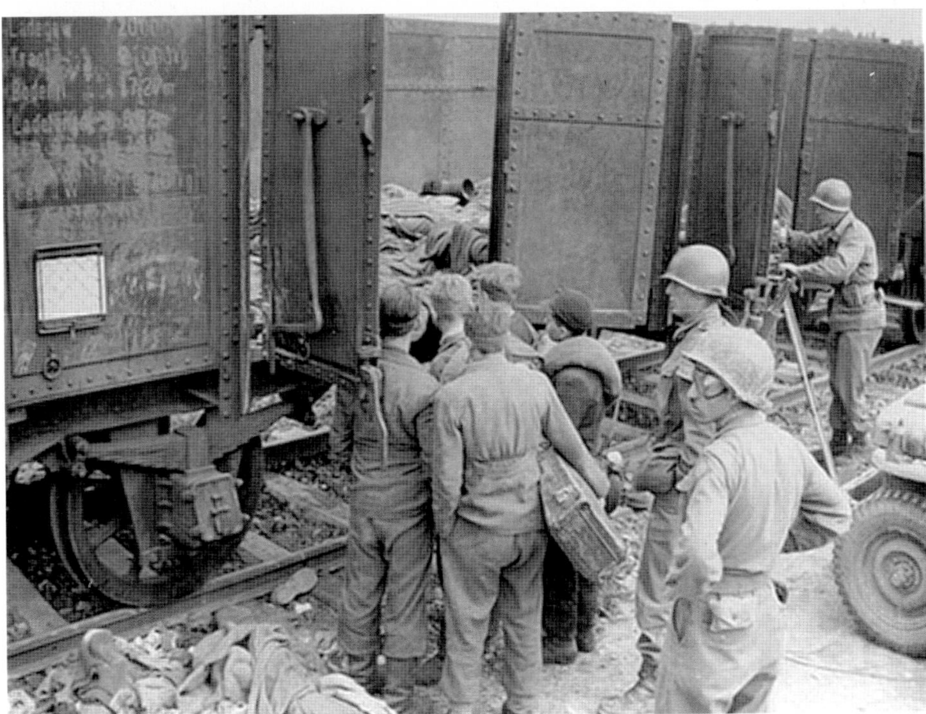

Troops from either 42nd or 45th ID. The same boxcars lined with bodies witnessed by 2nd Lt Ed Shames and Pfc Carl Fenstermacker from 3 Ptn E Co when they first arrived at Dachau. (NARA via Geoffrey & Gregory Walden)

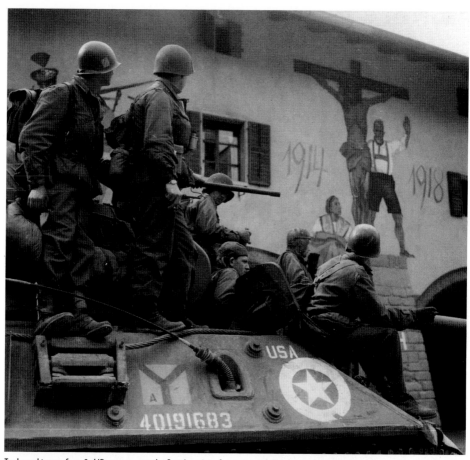

Tanks and troops from 3rd ID were among the first American forces to reach Berchtesgaden and are seen here at the town square opposite the World War I Memorial. (NARA via Geoff Walden)

The 506th PIR in their DUKWs en route to Berchtesgaden. (Currahee Scrapbook)

Hitler's Berghof, May 5, 1945: bombed by the British, burned by the SS, and then looted by the French. A soldier from 30th ID stands awestruck. (NARA via Geoff Walden)

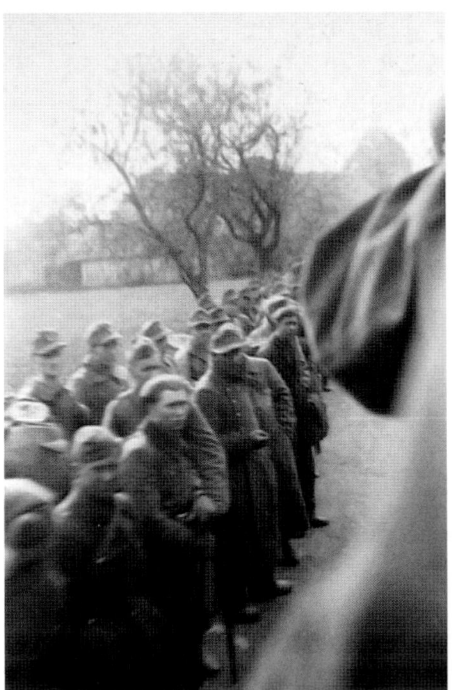
Surrendered German troops near Munich. (George Koskimaki)

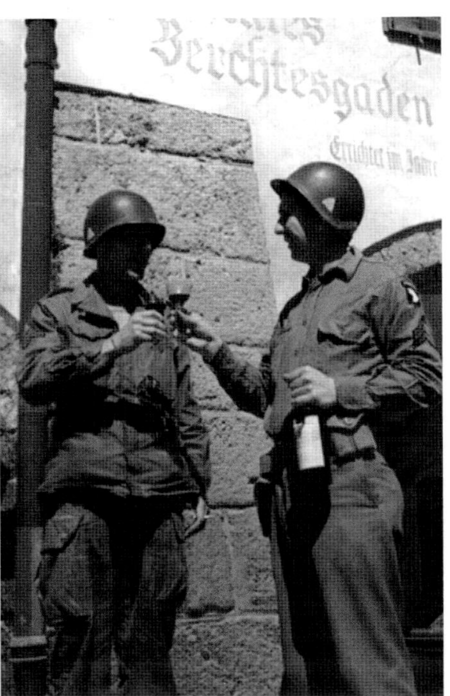

Two men from the 81st AA Bn toasting the end of hostilities at the World War I Memorial with a bottle of wine probably liberated from Göring's cellar. (NARA)

SS-Obergruppenführer Gottlob Berger (left) seen here leaving the Berchtesgadener Hof Hotel. The white armband worn by the other officer signifies that permission had been granted by the 101st for him to carry a sidearm for protection. (John Gibson via John Klein)

TOP: 2 Ptn G Co investigating a remote ski lodge northwest of Berchtesgaden. (Jim "Pee Wee" Martin)

MIDDLE: 2nd Lt Bahlau and members of C/506 enjoying the sunshine in the foothills above Bruck in Austria. (Fred Bahlau)

BOTTOM: 2nd Lt Alexander Hamilton and 2nd Lt Ed Shames (3 Ptn E Co) pictured here in the garden of the doctor's house at Saalfelden. (Karen McGee)

Bob Hoffman enjoying a stein of Bavarian Beer at Zell, July 5, 1945. (Lou Vecchi)

Saalbach, H Co officers. L to R (standing): 1st Lt Willie Miller, 2nd Lt Don Barlow, 2nd Lt Harry Begle; (kneeling) 1st Lt Bob Stroud, Capt Jim Walker, 1st Lt Ed Buss, 1st Lt Alex Andros. (Lou Vecchi)

US soldiers visiting the remains of Hermann Göring's house at Obersalzberg during the summer of 1945. (NARA via Geoff Walden)

Gathering of 3rd Bn officers June 1945. L to R (first row kneeling): 2nd Lt Bausman, 1st Lt Buss, 2nd Lt Bjorkman, 1st Lt Sutfin, 2nd Lt Berger, 1st Lt Walker, 1st Lt Replogle, 1st Lt Rowe; (second row kneeling) Hollbrook, 2nd Lt Wilkinson, 1st Lt Southerland, 1st Lt Raduenz, Bryant, Capt Walker, 1st Lt Albrecht; (third row standing) Capt Anderson, 1st Lt Miller, Capt Hollstein, 2nd Lt Barlow, Col Sink, LtCol Patch, Capt Cann, 2nd Lt Sardis, 1st Lt Osborne, 2nd Lt Schaefer; (fourth row standing) Capt Harrell, 1st Lt Heggeness, 2nd Lt Schroeder, Fortier, Holland, Lang, Harrington, Capt Doughty.

On September 3, 1945 a contingent from the 101st Airborne Division took part in a victory parade through Brussels to mark the first anniversary of its liberation. (NARA via Patrick Brion)

> were, just countryside scattered with a few single-storey buildings. During the day we would usually see one or two enemy soldiers moving around. A radio operator would come to our OP for 2 hours every day to report my observations, including troop movements and concentrations. I don't think we ever left that position because battalion would send our rations up every now and then by runner. Because of this, I instructed my "kids" how to scavenge anything and everything that could be cooked and eaten.

At the center of town, the river was overlooked on both sides by a number of tall, abandoned factory buildings. Many ideas were tested in an attempt to launch explosive devices across the river, such as grenades and 60mm mortar rounds. The most successful was created by Sgt Walter Kyle from G Co. With great ingenuity Kyle adapted the standard tail fin of a rifle grenade to screw into the base of a 60mm mortar shell, allowing it to be fired from an M1 rifle.

But George McMillan, who had just returned to I Co from Pathfinder duty, thought he had a better way. George built a catapult from shredded car inner tubes and attempted to launch a live grenade across the river. His first and only attempt failed in spectacular fashion as the primed grenade slipped from McMillan's grasp and rolled backwards, sending his colleagues scattering in all directions!

Bob Webb describes the river patrols:

> One or two bridges were still partially intact. Across from our positions was a large wine factory, where we and the Germans would both patrol. For the most part if they were there we'd leave them alone and they would do the same for us – although we did our best to procure as many cases of delicious red and white wine as we could. HQ Co was billeted in a lovely bungalow-style house that had a china cabinet with over 200 Champagne glasses made from the finest crystal I'd ever seen. The owners also had a fantastic cast-iron Aga stove in the kitchen so we always had a hot brew on the go.

> By this time I think we all realized the war was virtually over and just wanted to stay alive to see the end. One of the problems we faced was getting the proper intelligence back from our five-man patrols. Once across the river they were supposed to observe all the usual things, such as troop movements and activity around road junctions, etc., and then radio back the information to Battalion HQ. We had several communication cables running across the bed of the river for radio guys like myself to connect into.

3rd Bn were initially placed in reserve around Château Walk, where they followed a limited schedule, including training films and critiques on Holland and Bastogne. Harley Dingman accepted a new job offer from Andy Anderson to join him on the battalion staff as his sergeant major.

Dingman was somewhat surprised by his new posting to middle management and recalls, "The enlisted men called me 'Sir' and the officers addressed me as 'Mister.' I began to work closely with Anderson, specializing in procurement of billets and vehicles. Capt Anderson gave me a small team, which included Pvt Chester Molawa. Molawa had been in the army for over three years and was never promoted due to his previous criminal record. In early 1941, Molawa was caught driving a getaway car in a failed bank robbery. Instead of going to jail, the judge gave him the option of joining the regular army. Eventually, Molawa came to HQ Co as a replacement. Despite his somewhat dodgy background, Chester was a faithful and trustworthy member of the team and became my orderly."

T/4 Dave Phillips (regimental S3) was asked to interview members of G Co: "My old boss John Senior was now their first sergeant and really showed me a good time. The abandoned winery a couple of hundred yards away to the northeast kept us pleasantly intoxicated. The Kaiser family occupied part of the building now being used by G Co as their HQ. Paul Kaiser was an artist in his thirties and very intelligent. Being a talented artist himself, 1st Lt Frank Rowe seemed to get on well with Paul, who also spoke pretty good English." Like

Harley Dingman, Paul was also fluent in Latin. Harley had studied the subject at college and spent most of his down time at Paul's home practicing and discussing the subject.

On February 12, the 101st area was reorganized and each regiment tasked to defend a sector with a reinforced battalion. At 1800hrs, 1st Bn moved out to Hochstett, 10 miles further southwest, where they were placed in divisional reserve. At the same time H Co were attached to 2nd Bn and took over a sector on the left flank. "Patrol activity was reinstituted, although not with the frequency and intensity of the Ardennes," recalls Hank DiCarlo. "Almost every patrol we sent out returned with at least two prisoners. The German troops here simply weren't the same caliber as those we'd encountered at Foy." Light discipline was still paramount, especially at night where any breach would be met by a substantial enemy artillery or mortar barrage.

Sgt Audrey Lewallen returned to active duty with the machine-gun platoon after being injured in early October during the battle for Opheusden, as Jim Melhus woefully reflects:

> I remember this moment vividly as if it were yesterday. We had just returned to the CP after a failed mission across the river and went upstairs to collect our supplies that had been spread out on a large table. As I walked into the room, Lewallen was sitting on the floor and accidentally pointed a pistol at me while trying to eject a round from the chamber. I don't think that there was any malice involved, just negligence. For some reason he managed to pull the trigger and the bullet went through my right forearm, entering about 3in above the wrist (completely severing the radial bone) and into the floor, narrowly missing another guy's foot. The medics were called and gave me something for the pain before I was rushed away to a nearby field hospital. The first doctor I saw wanted to amputate but was overruled by a major who showed him an alternative procedure, which undoubtedly saved my arm. I had several things stolen during this period, like a beautiful diamond and ruby ring purchased in

> Paris. Plus, would you believe, my jump boots and a petite .25cal automatic pistol. At least the vultures left my old wristwatch – which was kind of ironic after nearly losing the arm that I wore it on.

One night Bob Webb went down to the river to assist a five-man recon patrol that was being led by a brand-new replacement officer:

> The idea as per standard operating procedure was to keep total radio silence until the men had deployed onto the northern bank. I was monitoring the network when the lieutenant leading the incursion accidentally placed his hand on the "talk switch." We could hear every word that he said. This went on for a few minutes until he whispered, "I think they've found us; what on earth are we gonna do now?"
>
> By this time, Col Sink had arrived and soon became frustrated by the lieutenant's incompetence. Finally, one of the guys on the patrol took control of the radio while another brought the officer back in the boat. Col Sink said he wanted another group ready to go within 10 minutes … then ordered one of the standby squads to deploy, and I foolishly decided to volunteer as their radio operator. Changing into a sweater and knitted cap, my face blackened, pistol loaded and safety catch on, I stuck some surgical tape over my dog tags before our equipment was checked for noise discipline.
>
> We crossed the river about 40 minutes before first light and upon reaching the northern bank had a quick look around for the three missing men but there was no sign of them. As it was getting light, the sergeant in charge decided to brazenly move further inland. As the sun came up we took cover in a barn not far from the road that the patrol we'd replaced was supposed to have been observing. Although we had good cover it was decided to move closer to the highway and go to ground in an abandoned farmhouse.
>
> I was able to climb up into the roof space, which gave me a commanding view across the surrounding area. As the day wore on we saw nothing. That evening the sergeant decided to take his men

in search of a better OP while I stayed behind with the radio and kept watch. Not long afterwards, I heard firing and about 90 minutes later one of the guys returned and told me to head back to the first barn. I don't know what happened to the rest of the patrol, but the guy who spoke to me did eventually make it back to our lines. After reporting the situation over the radio I was told to stay put and relay information for another 24 hours. That was fine, but I didn't really have enough food or water and reasoned that a nearby stream would help see me through. Forty-eight hours later, I was finally instructed to pull back to the river Moder under cover of darkness where a soldier in a rubber dingy was waiting for me. After being debriefed it was clear that the area I'd been watching was no longer a threat and the regiment could now concentrate on another sector.

Not long after the patrol, I became ill with acute diarrhea and sickness. Initially our medics thought it might be stomach ulcers and after a brief rest sent me back to duty. Over the following two weeks my condition continued to deteriorate, and by the end of the month I was sent to the UK for specialist treatment. After what seemed like dozens of tests, the 53rd General Hospital in Malvern diagnosed me with a virulent form of intestinal parasite usually only found in goats, which I'd probably picked up from drinking the stream water while on that last patrol.

Webb spent the next three months in hospital, during which time he lost and regained nearly 40lb before finally returning to duty in June.

After being posted to G Co at Château Walk, Pvt Ira Morehart's first experience of war was not one to be proud of. One of the members of his new squad, Pvt James Williams, was a serious cause for concern. Williams had been a sergeant until being demoted for dereliction of duty during the battle for Bastogne. Morehart and Williams were part of a five-man security patrol on the southern bank of the river Moder when they walked into a farmyard. Williams immediately spotted a young woman and immediately began to pester her for sex.

As she started to scream her husband arrived and proceeded to beat Williams into submission. Although Williams was dragged away by Ira and the others, he forced them to return the following morning. Perhaps looking for revenge in the ensuing fracas, Williams shot and killed the farmer before raping his wife. Ira and the other team members were bullied into silence after Williams threatened to kill anyone who breathed a single word about what had happened here. The incident was an ignoble stain on the hitherto untarnished war record of a fine and proud unit. Jim Martin believes that after the war, James Williams served a long jail term in Hamilton Prison, Indiana, after being convicted of several armed robberies, and died shortly after being released in the 1980s.

Sometime around the second week of February, spring came early with three days of clear weather and beautiful sunshine. The sudden change was not just an opportunity to sunbathe but also meant better visibility and therefore increased patrolling, which brought its own risks.

On the evening of February 15, 1st Lt Lawrence Fitzpatrick and several of his soldiers from 3 Ptn G Co were preparing to cross the river via a sector controlled by lieutenants Oswald and Stapelfeld from F Co. After a short briefing by Ben Stapelfeld, Fitzpatrick used the opportunity to observe one of the factories opposite what Ben said was a regular enemy OP. Further to the right was a timber merchants and cemetery. Over on the left, Fitzpatrick could see a row of houses, but at the time these were believed to be unoccupied. Sometime after midnight, as the lieutenant was leading his men across the Moder, he was killed instantly by a burst of enemy machine-gun fire, which most likely came from one of the "abandoned" houses opposite. The mission was quickly aborted, and under cover of automatic fire from F Co, the men frantically paddled back to safety.

At 0100hrs on the 18th, another patrol crossed the Moder. Despite suffering four casualties from Schu mines and enemy mortar fire, the group brought back three prisoners from Infanterie-Regiment 103 (47.Volksgrenadier-Division) and Pionier-Batallion 257, 257.Infanterie-Division. The following afternoon 1/506 moved from Hochstett to Château Walk. Two hours later B Co was attached to 3rd Bn, who were now assigned to take over the MLR from 2/506. Over the next few days, elements of the 143rd ID began to arrive in preparation to relieve the regiment.

By February 23, the 506th started moving out by road to a rear assembly area near Saverne, 50 miles southwest of Haguenau. Col Sink established his CP a couple of miles to the southwest at Marmoutier alongside 2nd Bn, while 1st Bn was sent southwest to Haegen. 3rd Bn bivouacked between the two villages at Schwebwiller. Forty-eight hours later the regiment moved by truck to the railway station at Saverne. The floors of the French boxcars were layered in straw and provided a comfortable bonus for the troops during the 200-mile rail journey back to Mourmelon.

Before 3rd Bn departed from Schwebwiller, Harold Stedman returned: "I'd been in hospital for the last seven weeks and was hardly able to recognize anyone in I Co, except Manny Barrios, Richie Shinn (who had also just got out of hospital), and Pvt Harvey DeVries, whom we all thought had been killed back in October up on the island." The constant combat in the intervening weeks had certainly taken a heavy toll on the battalion.

10

"Home alive in '45"

Return to Mourmelon – February 26–April 2, 1945

When the division returned to Mourmelon in late February, most of Camp Châlons had been taken over by a field hospital. After recovering from yellow jaundice, 1st Lt Bill Wedeking found himself assigned to the advance party helping organize "Tent City" and area cleaning. "At the time I was still officially the machine-gun platoon leader but never really had a chance to get to know any of the new men. A few days later, I began to experience trouble with my hearing, which had been damaged by an explosion in Normandy. Once the problem was diagnosed, the divisional surgeon took me off jump status. After being downgraded and reclassified, I was sent to Le Havre to take command of a German POW camp, which was very disappointing."

Medical and support staff were now occupying the permanent barracks that the 101st had so painstakingly repaired before leaving for Bastogne. "We were forced to live in a village of pyramidal tents," recalls Hank DiCarlo. "Still, it certainly beat the life we'd lived in the Ardennes, and at least every tent had a stove."

Around February 28, the battalion underwent several changes to the command structure. Capt Doughty transferred to Bn S3 and took over from the newly promoted Derwood Cann, who in turn was given command of G Co. After Bill Wedeking was posted to the 1486 Labor Support Co, 2nd Lt Lloyd Wills and Doc Dwyer took control of the light machine-gun platoon with staff sergeants Auguste Saperito and Darvin Lee as his section leaders along with gun sergeants Albert Duraso, Johnnie Prezas, Joe Mielcarek (who had previously escaped from the Germans with Marty Clark), Audrey Lewallen, Emmett McKeon, and several others.

Nathan Bullock was promoted to HQ Co first sergeant, after Fred Bahlau's commission and transfer to C/506 finally came through. Many of Bullock's close friends, like Richard Stockhouse, Fayez Handy, and Bob Webb, thought he let the rank go to his head. Sgt Handy could not accept the recent changes, especially after what Lewallen had done to Melhus in Haguenau, and opted for a new role as provost sergeant.

Ed Shames reflects on the changes:

> 2nd Lt Roy Paul Gates was posted to my platoon. Gates handed me his orders and I thought, "Just what did I do to deserve the oldest lieutenant in the entire army?" Roy attended Texas A&M University and had been part of 10th Armored Division before joining the 101st. His family was extremely wealthy and had sold their successful leisure business to The Disney Corporation several years before the war. I learned that his promotion over the last couple of years had stalled due to the fact that he'd struck a superior officer, who unfortunately turned out to be the son of a general. For a replacement officer, I figured, Gates might not be a bad fit after all. Roy spoke French, as did many Germans, which was a bonus. More importantly, it meant that he could travel to Paris and sell our "loot" on the "Black Market" without any language issues. And he was smart enough to let Paul Rogers run things when I wasn't around. Roy turned out to be a wonderful guy and also a lifelong friend.

Many were granted seven-day leave passes and hundreds of troopers were flown down to the French Riviera each Sunday. Capt Walker issued Hank DiCarlo, Lou Vecchi, and several others from H Co a seven-day furlough to Nice. "We were warned not to go out alone at night because local gangs would attack, rob, and strip any serviceman they came across," recalls Lou. "I was never much of a drinker – 7-Up and a little bit of whisky was about it – so I never really spent that much money, unlike some of the other guys who went through $500 or more. I was a little shy with women and didn't have the gift of the gab like Hank and for the most part spent my time sightseeing with Gordon Yates."

DiCarlo's furlough would be one that he would remember for the rest of his life. "When we arrived, I was pleasantly surprised to find that we were quartered at 'Le Negresco.' Situated on Rue d'Anglais, the Negresco was a five-star luxury hotel overlooking the Bay of Angels and the deep blue expanse of the Mediterranean. The beautifully appointed rooms were amazing, but, best of all, if you left your jump boots outside your door each night, the following morning you'd find them cleaned and polished like new."

After an amazing week out on the town, Hank and the boys reported to the airfield for their flight back to Mourmelon. However, due to bad weather and a last-minute emergency, the trip was postponed until the following weekend. As Lou, Gordon, and Hank were about to board the bus back to the hotel, Hank struck up a conversation with a couple of Air Force men. "The crew chiefs told me that there were always scheduled daily mail flights to just about every liberated major European city, including Rome. As it happened my mother, Anna, came from a small town near Rome called Teramo. One guy was scheduled for Rome the next day and said that I could bum a ride on his flight!"

Trip to Teramo

Hank DiCarlo reflects on his fortuitous trip:

> Bright and early on Sunday morning, the C-47 took off carrying 50 bags of mail and me. After an uneventful flight we were on final approach when the crew chief came over and said, "Bad news, Sarge. We just received instructions to bypass Rome and continue on to

Naples." This wasn't what I wanted to hear and shouted back in his ear, "Naples is out! No way I'm goin' there!" The crew chief shrugged his shoulders and hollered back, "You're with us, buddy boy, so you ain't got no choice." Putting a little rising anger in my voice, I said, "That ain't necessarily so … how about donating your chest 'chute and dropping me over the airfield?" He thought for a minute, went forward to the cockpit, and came back smiling. The pilot had agreed to notify us when we got close to Rome and would make one pass over the base at 1,000ft to permit me to "bail out." It was my first experience with this kind of parachute, but this was a minor detail to me at that moment in time.

The pilot decreased airspeed, and as we flew straight and level across the strip I leapt into space with my hand on the parachute release ring. After the canopy deployed I had time to admire the scenery for a moment before focusing on a vehicle rapidly moving toward my expected landing area. The instant my feet touched the ground, two MPs hustled me away to a guardhouse. I had a spirited conversation with the duty officer, a captain by the name of Louis Wallace. Capt Wallace listened intently while examining my furlough papers before telling me I was engaged in an illegal activity and would have to take a flight back to Nice the next day. "You mean you're not going to punish me, sir?" With the Battle of the Bulge still fresh in everyone's mind I don't think being a member of the 101st Airborne did me any harm. Capt Wallace suggested that I should get a meal in the transient troops' mess and then bunk down at their barracks. Thanking him profusely, I went over to the mess hall and got something to eat.

As I was tucking into my meatloaf, a GI sat down opposite and struck up a conversation. I found out that he was from Philadelphia and his name was Danny Infante and he was a driver for the Quartermaster Corps. When Danny heard my story he got all excited because he had a jeep at his disposal. Danny also knew where Teramo was and told me that if we left immediately we could be there by midnight at the latest. The idea sounded totally crazy but I went for it.

Before departing, Danny managed to "requisition" two cases of C rations and a few tins of coffee. Shortly before midnight we arrived at Teramo, which seemed to have escaped virtually untouched by war. I had no idea what my Uncle Tomaso Lolli's address was so we decided to knock on the first door we came across.

Initially there was no response. Then a sash window on the second floor slid open and an irate face appeared wanting to know who the hell we were and what the hell we wanted. I responded in Italian that my mother was a Lolli and asked if he knew where Tomaso lived. His attitude changed immediately, "Yes, of course," he replied. "They live in the third house from the corner on the next street. If you'd care to wait a minute, I'd be pleased to show you."

Moments later the man greeted us at the door, having hastily pulled on a pair of trousers under his nightclothes. By this time the rest of his family had awoken and came out to see Anna Lolli's son. Some of the neighbors were getting in on the act, with everyone now wanting to guide me to my uncle's. Luckily Tomaso's home was fairly large as it contained three families. Besides Tomaso, there were my uncles Salvatore and Gaspere. Twelve people in all – including wives and children – who, despite the late hour, made me feel like I was home.

More neighbors came across to wish us well and before we knew it the visit turned into a party. Uncle Tomaso introduced us to his secret stash of "Dago" red and we brought in the C rations and coffee and held *una festa* in and around the house. Danny became smitten by Tomaso's 17-year-old daughter, Modesta, and showed good judgment by never leaving her side the whole night.

The gathering broke up shortly after dawn and finally we had the opportunity to talk about the family. Tomaso had two sons in northern Italy, fighting with the Partisans. After losing his eldest son in the battle for Sicily, Salvatore's other two lads were currently being held as hostages by the Germans. Uncle Gaspere had no male offspring but three beautiful daughters. It was so good to meet them

> all and now I could truly satisfy my mother's desire to know if her siblings were surviving the war and how they were doing. Finally it was time to start back, which we did most reluctantly. All the excitement of that night had really drained me, and despite the appalling roads, I slept like a baby all the way back to the airfield. I couldn't thank Danny enough for his time and trouble but he'd procured Modesta's address and was more than happy. We said our farewells and I made my way to the dispatch office where I found out there was a plane leaving for Nice at 2200hrs.

A Presidential Citation

Jim Martin returned to Mourmelon on March 14, after being treated for the emersion injuries to his feet:

> I still hadn't fully recovered when I was discharged from hospital. At that time most of my friends had already gone on leave to the Riviera, Paris, or the UK. It seemed to me that our company offices were being operated by a handful of temporary personnel. Myself and several other "invalids" were told that we would be acting as instructors for new replacements who were expected to arrive over the next few days. None of us wanted that so we went AWOL the following morning, which also happened to be the day that the division received its Presidential Citation. The 506th had already received a Regimental Unit Citation for Normandy, and after what I'd been through in Belgium … I couldn't have really cared less.

Despite Jim's well-earned cynicism, March 15, 1945 was a significant day in the history of the 101st Airborne, as they were the first entire division ever to be awarded a Presidential Distinguished Unit Citation. Gen Eisenhower presented the award "for extraordinary heroism" during the defense of the key communications center at Bastogne between December 18 and 27, 1944. The day was bathed in sunshine as 12,000 men stood sharply to attention in line along the edge of the airfield as dozens of transport aircraft buzzed about overhead.

Absent from the podium was Anthony McAuliffe, who had recently been promoted to major general. At the time McAuliffe and the 103rd ID were still fighting hard along the Siegfried Line west of Wissembourg in Alsace. Those who were present on the podium alongside "Ike" were Supreme Headquarters Allied Expeditionary Force (SHAEF) members of staff MajGen Lowell Rooks and LtGen Sir Frederick Morgan. Also included were senior members from the First Allied Airborne Army, LtGen Lewis Brereton and his chief of staff BrigGen Floyd Parks, as well as commander of XVIII Airborne Corps Matthew Ridgeway, MajGen Paul Williams (IX Troop Carrier Command), White House secretary Steve Early, Eisenhower's naval aide Capt Harry Butcher, and representatives of the Oise Base Section. Next to the stand, adding a touch of glamor, was German-born actress and singer Marlene Dietrich who happened to be performing at Mourmelon in a USO show.

Speaking via a public address system Eisenhower declared:

> You in reserve were hurried forward and told to hold that position. All the elements of battle drama were there. You were cut off and surrounded. Only valor, complete self-confidence in yourselves and in your leaders and a knowledge that you were well trained, and only the determination to win could sustain soldiers under those conditions. You were given a marvelous opportunity and you met every test. You have become a fighting symbol on which all citizens of the United Nations can say to their soldiers today: "We are proud of you." It is my great privilege to say to you here today, to the 101st Airborne Division and all its attached units: I am awfully proud of you. Just as you are the beginning of a new tradition, you must realize that from now on the spotlight will beat on you with particular brilliance.
>
> Whenever you say you are a soldier from the 101st, everybody, whether it is on the street, in the city, or in the front lines, will expect

> unusual conduct from you. I know that you will meet every test of the future just like you met in Bastogne. Good luck and God be with you.

As the Supreme Commander stepped back from the microphone, the divisional flag – now adorned with its sky-blue-colored Citation ribbon – suddenly fluttered in the breeze. The US Army band struck up a march as the troops began to pass by in review. For almost 70 minutes, the men passed by the podium while Ike, MajGen Maxwell Taylor, and the other dignitaries proudly took their salute.

Hank DiCarlo was present and recalls: "Directly after the parade, it was announced that the army was introducing a point system which would ultimately lead to some of us 'old timers' going home. In the meantime, those like me who had been through Normandy, Holland, and Bastogne would be entered into a lottery for a limited number of 30-day furloughs to the USA – which as per usual I didn't win. However, S/Sgt Frank Padisak (who was wounded during the last few days at Bastogne) was among the lucky few to be awarded one of the 'golden tickets.'"

Amongst the recipients were Cpl Stanley Stasica (H Co) and also 1/Sgt Albert Miller from Regimental HQ. In Padisak's absence, Lou Vecchi was promoted to platoon sergeant. Like many others, 1 Ptn received more replacements and underwent a management reshuffle. Sgt Bob Martin became "platoon guide" to work alongside Vecchi as his assistant. Walt Patterson took over 2nd Squad, while Luther Myers and Buck Bowitz were both promoted to sergeant and given charge of 3rd and 4th squads, respectively. While relaxing over a coffee in the senior ranks' mess, Hank happened to pick up the latest edition of *Yank* magazine and nearly choked when he saw the front cover: "The picture showed some troops walking in the snow during the Battle of the Bulge and right up front with a big smile on his face was Sonny Sundquist. I can't tell you how much we despised that man. Sundquist had been transferred to 1st Bn before Bastogne and was listed as 'Missing in Action' during the heavy fighting at Noville – that was until the SOB was picked up later in Marseille trying to blag his way onto a troopship!"

Strange times

By the time the parade finished, Jim Martin and a couple of the others were safely on a transport plane bound for the United Kingdom. At the time, getting a flight was fairly easy owing to the enormous buildup of aircraft for Operation *Varsity*, which was set to take place within the next two weeks. Jim continues his account, a touch of bitterness in his voice:

> Nobody really cared because most of the crews flying re-supply missions between the UK and Europe were making a small fortune for themselves by importing British spirits and exporting French wines. But what can you do? At that moment I needed them, which was all that mattered.
>
> We flew into RAF Bovingdon (USAAF Station 112) near Watford, Hertfordshire, the center of operations for the Air Transport Service and only 20 miles from central London. Having no cash to speak of we headed for the Base Finance Office and spoke to a major who initially refused assistance. During the conversation I reminded him of a little-known fact that where necessary "troops in transit" were entitled to a "partial payment," which was something I'd learned before Normandy. We presented our pay books and played on our newfound fame and the major begrudgingly issued us with our "holiday" pay.
>
> After spending a day in London, I caught the train to Hungerford, Berkshire, with the idea of getting a place to stay at Chilton Foliat, but the camp was overflowing with replacements. In a way I'm glad because I headed over to Ramsbury and stayed with my friends, the Barretts, who lived in a row of cottages along the road leading up to the airfield. Mr and Mrs Barrett had three young sons (Tony, Theo, and Archie) and also provided a billet for Agnes McNerney, who was a member of the Women's Land Army. Agnes came from Liverpool and was a lovely girl with whom I had dated a couple of times before Normandy but it was nothing serious. However, my relationship with Molly Studdy was very different. During the last

few days of my "vacation," Molly and I spent a lot of time together. Tall, fair, and buxom, 32-year-old Mrs Studdy lived along the High Street at the Malt House not too far from the Malt Shovel pub. She was married to a dentist and had a six-year-old son called Anthony. It seemed to me that Molly's marriage was a loose arrangement due to the fact that her husband was seeing another woman and didn't mind Molly spending time with me or anyone else for that matter. These were strange times indeed.

When I arrived back at Mourmelon, Capt Cann called me into his office and asked where the heck I'd been. "Nowhere really, sir," I replied. "Is it something I'm going to hear about Martin?" "No, sir, absolutely not." "OK," he replied, "go ahead and rejoin your platoon – dismissed." With that, I came to attention, saluted, and marched out of the office. As I have previously stated Cann always thought I was a bit of a smart aleck but I guess on this occasion after what we'd all just been through he was willing to let it go.

On the morning of March 24, the 17th Airborne Division, commanded by MajGen William Miley, took off from Mourmelon as part of Operation *Varsity* – to assist Field Marshal Montgomery's 21st Army Group in their crossing of the Rhine (itself codenamed Operation *Plunder*). The 17th Airborne dropped on the eastern bank at Wesel along with the British 6th Airborne Division, commanded by MajGen Eric Bois. Both divisions were part of XVIII Airborne Corps, and despite heavy casualties bravely opened the way for the Allies into Germany. In one day the joint force dropped 16,000 men onto one DZ, dwarfing Normandy and Holland and making *Varsity* the largest single airborne assault in military history.

By the end of March all four US armies fighting in Western Europe were east of the Rhine, while First and Ninth armies followed through to encircle and neutralize enemy forces in the Ruhr. With the "Gates of the West" now firmly open, the 101st Airborne went on to provide security and establish military law wherever and whenever required.

The officers' mess at Mourmelon had a ballroom on the second floor, and the regiment organized a dinner dance with a band just before it was put on standby for the Ruhr. "I was friendly with 'Captain Anne,' who was one of the senior nurses at the field hospital," recalls Fred Bahlau. "Anne agreed to be my date and also organized a group of nurses to come along. On the evening of the dance I sent a truck fitted out with comfortable furniture and plenty of wine. Climbing the staircase to the ballroom, Anne and I were just ahead of the girls when I noticed Col Sink smiling at us from the top. As I introduced my date to the boss, the sly old devil slipped his hand under Anne's arm and walked off with her. Before he turned away, I'll never forget what he said: 'Mr Bahlau, you've just learned a valuable lesson in officer protocol … enjoy your evening, Lieutenant … dismissed.'"

Ed Shames also fondly remembers the party but for a slightly different reason:

> Many of the senior guys kept sending me to the bar to get their drinks… I didn't mind; it's just the way it is. The party was in full swing when LtCol Strayer passed out in front of Sink. I'd had four or five strong vodka martinis when the colonel asked me in no uncertain terms to remove Strayer. "What shall I do with him, sir?" I inquired. "Anything you like; just get him out of here!" I called over 2nd Lt Alexander Hamilton who had only recently been posted to E Co's 2 Ptn. As we carried Strayer (who was now acting regimental XO) out by his hands and feet, Hamilton asked where we were going to put him. I was pretty drunk, and feeling slightly mischievous suggested we stick him in Bob Sink's tent under the bed!
>
> I heard when Sink awoke the following morning and discovered our little "gift" still fast asleep, he kicked Strayer straight out the door and into the street! Thankfully Strayer never found out it was me – otherwise I'm sure he would have made my life much worse.

11

"Setting sons"

The Ruhr, western Germany – April 3–24, 1945

On April 1, 1945, the 101st Airborne was attached to MajGen Ernest Harmon's XXII Corps, part of the Fifteenth Army now under command of LtGen Leonard Gerow.

The advance party left Mourmelon on Saturday, March 31, and was followed two days later, during the early hours of the morning, by the main body. Consisting of 117 officers and 2,006 enlisted men, the regiment traveled via Maastricht in an impressive convoy of trailer trucks – a distance of some 200 miles. The 506th took over from the 387th IR (97th ID) and were deployed south of Düsseldorf around the town of Nievenheim and the villages of Stürzelberg and Zons, 50 miles east of the border with Holland and Belgium.

Situated on the western tip of the Ruhr valley, the ancient city of Düsseldorf straddles the Rhine. At the beginning of World War II, with a growing population of some 540,000 people, the city had become an important industrial center for the Nazi war machine. Around 60 percent of the city had been destroyed during recent strategic Allied bombing raids that forced around 200,000 civilians to flee into the surrounding countryside.

The nearby town of Gohr became the central hub where Col Sink established his regimental command post for the next three weeks. Bordering the river Erft, on the regiment's extreme left flank, were the troops from the 327th GIR. On the right, at Worringen, was the 504th

PIR, part of the 82nd Airborne Division. The MLR for the 506th was roughly a 10-mile front along the Rhine that meandered north from Worringen, through Himmelgeist, before reaching Düsseldorf. The 387th IR handed over its sector to the 506th on April 4, whose job it now was to keep contact between the 327th and 504th and carry out regular recon and combat patrols across the Rhine. In addition the three battalions were tasked with maintaining military government in their own specific areas. Attached to 3rd Bn during this period were F Battery from the 81st AA Bn, with overall rear-echelon security being provided for the first week by the divisional recon platoon.

All the bridges across the Rhine in the regimental sector had been destroyed, isolating around 5,000 troops from 176. and 338. Volksgrenadier-Divisionen on the eastern bank of the river. Despite these fragmented pockets of resistance the war was really over and the German will and means to fight all but exhausted. As part of the blocking force, 3rd Bn were allocated the northern sector, tying in with the 327th GIR. 2/506 took control of the eastern sector, while 1st Bn were placed in regimental reserve at Nievenheim.

As usual the 321st GFA were supporting the 506th with their 105mm guns. The troops were billeted comfortably in private houses and farms. 3rd Bn were sent to Norf, a small town due north of Gohr. "The first night, there was no sign of the 387th IR," recalls Hank DiCarlo. "So we simply outposted the river without anyone there to guide us in. The next morning the battalion straightened out the lines and bracketed in its mortars and artillery."

At the end of March 1945, around 300,000 enemy troops, mostly belonging to Feldmarschall Walther Model's reconstituted Heeresgruppe B (Army Group B), were encircled east of the Rhine along the Ruhr valley. The area that became known as the "Ruhr Pocket" was almost 80 miles deep and 50 miles wide.

As "Hitler's Fireman," Walther Model was directed by him to fight for every last inch of German soil. After failing to destroy a vital bridge spanning the Rhine at Remagen, Heeresgruppe B soon found that it had been outflanked by American ground forces. Due to the tenacity of the US Ninth and Fifteenth armies, the "pocket" was quickly reduced to a 25-mile front bordering the Rhine north from Cologne to Düsseldorf. The job of cleansing the western edge of the pocket along the river had been given to units from the Fifteenth Army.

Model, who had led the unsuccessful German offensive in the Ardennes, was ordered by Hitler to destroy the factories and turn the region into a fortress. Although he ignored the "scorched earth" directive, Model's attempts at defense ultimately failed when, in the middle of April, Heeresgruppe B was split in half by the Allies during their final penetration of the pocket. Unwilling to submit, Model discharged his youngest and oldest troops, while informing the remainder to either surrender or attempt to break out through the encirclement. Berlin denounced Model and his army as traitors and ordered SS units within the pocket to seek revenge on any soldier or civilian refusing to stay and fight.

Despite the chaos on the other side of the river, the first week in theater was quiet for the 506th, with many still being sent on leave. For the most part, combat activity consisted of patrolling or crossing the Rhine in small boats to assess enemy strength and capture a few prisoners for intelligence purposes.

"During that time there was a lot of looting and not much action, although we were shelled from time to time by the big guns across the river," recalls Jim Martin. "Some of our guys went on one patrol and were amazed to find themselves walking through an industrial area where the factories were still producing items for the German war effort!"

"The enemy troops we encountered preferred to surrender rather than fight," recalls Hank DiCarlo. "We saw very little evidence of German activity and as our presence became more aggressive there was hardly a time that I can remember when a patrol didn't return without capturing one or more prisoners."

On April 12, 3rd Bn were relieved by 1/506 and sent to Nievenheim as regimental reserve. Shortly after 1st Bn took over the MLR, a large-scale raiding party from A Co, made up of seven officers and 125 enlisted men, was sent across the river to destabilize any enemy troops still in the area. At the same time the regimental intelligence officer, Maj Bill Leach, led a five-man patrol from the S2 into the southern sector between the villages of Stürzelberg and Zons, to reconnoiter a suspected enemy observation post near a suburb of Düsseldorf called Benrath.

Between the two villages, the Rhine bends acutely eastwards, and it was along the Stürzelberger Strasse near Zons that Leach decided to launch his night mission. Over to the major's immediate right were three squads from F Co controlled by sergeants Joe Flick, Bob Stone, and Gaston Adams.

Whether he realized it or not, on the way back across the river, Leach and his men were paddling toward Bob Stone's squad when a nervous replacement opened up with an automatic weapon and killed every man in the patrol. Five days later, on April 18, the bodies of Leach and Pfc Robert Watts were recovered from the river opposite the F Co CP at Stürzelberg. It was a tragic incident during a relatively quiet period of the war.

The authorities established collection centers at Nievenheim for refugees or displaced persons (DP centers). Many civilians had escaped from their own troops across the Rhine into the American sector and now had to be sprayed with DTT before being processed, as Jim Martin recalls: "While we were in reserve we watched with interest as hundreds of semi-naked women were being deloused. G Co requisitioned private houses for our billets and we stayed there for around seven days. The occupants were thrown out with very little notice and I know they despised us for doing it." It became Harley Dingman's job as sergeant major to evict German civilians from their homes, as he recalls: "I spoke only a few words of German but at least it was enough to get the message across that the property was about to be occupied. I think for the most part the civilians were actually relieved that we were American and not Russian or French."

"In reality we were being used as a kind of military fire brigade," recalls Lou Vecchi. As they had plenty of time on their hands Lou and the boys dressed up and posed for snapshots wearing Nazi uniforms liberated from a local military outfitters. 1 Ptn H Co ended up living in a number of private houses around Nievenheim. "Walking toward one of our squad billets, I noticed a bone china plate come flying out of a window, followed by several more, all shattering on the road in front of me. When I inquired as to what on earth was going on … the boys just laughed and said, 'Sarge, we are the occupying force so there will be absolutely no damn washing up for us!'"

"Several members from our platoon decided to play a terrible prank on Pfc Tom Beasley," recalls Hank DiCarlo.

> Tom had a reputation as a sexual adventurer. I'm almost ashamed to say but this event occurred on the day President Roosevelt died. It was mid-afternoon and we had just returned to Nievenheim from a memorial service. My squad were hanging around in front of this farmhouse cleaning weapons and generally shooting the breeze. There was a two-storey building next to the house, the first floor of which was a stable with an outside staircase leading to what looked like some sort of servants' quarters.
>
> While we were thus engaged, Walt Patterson came down the steps and said, "Hey you know there's a dead woman lying on the bed up there … it looks like she shot herself." Of course we all had to take a look and what he told us was correct – there was a dead woman, I would guess in her early thirties, lying on a bed with a gunshot wound to her head. We could only surmise that she'd committed suicide.

Thousands of German civilians took their own lives during April and May 1945, believing the puerile propaganda being broadcast by Goebbels – that the Americans would rape and murder anyone or anything they came across.

"The guys closed the heavy blackout curtains and climbed into a large wardrobe," recalls Hank. He continues:

> One of Beasley's squad mates, a recent replacement named Fannia, was sent to find Tom and tell him that there was a woman who'd agreed to have sex with the members of the platoon in exchange for cigarettes. As he wasn't one of the guys who had initially made the deal, Fannia advised Beasley not to open the curtains. Most of us sitting around outside still had no idea what was transpiring as Tom dashed past and charged up the stairs. It was quiet for about 5 minutes and then we heard a God-awful scream and then Beasley came bowling down the steps, pistol in hand, demanding to know where he could find Fannia.
>
> We later learned the details of what happened. As advised, Tom didn't open the curtains and felt his way to where the woman was lying. He climbed onto the bed and was heard to remark, "Geez lady, you're pretty damn cold." At this point the guys figured the joke had gone far enough and leapt from the wardrobe to find Tom straddling the woman's body, staring into her dead eyes … hence the scream. Ignoring the four other men in the room, Beasley drew his pistol and went in search of Fannia. Tom never forgave the kid for being the triggerman on that trick and Fannia had to be transferred to another company for his own safety. After that I don't think Beasley ever really trusted any of us again, but you should've seen his face when he came back down those steps.

A liaison party from the 97th ID reported to the regimental CP, confirming that elements of their division had occupied Baumberg on the eastern bank of the Rhine. Shortly afterwards the 506th was informed that elements of the 94th ID would soon be relieving its front-line battalions.

Official contact was made with the US infantry on the eastern bank by a patrol from the 506th who crossed the river under a white flag. Not long afterwards 1st Bn and 2nd Bn were relieved by 1/303 and 2/303 from the 94th ID and sent to Weckhoven, Horrem, and Dormagen. The next two days were spent training, while military control passed to the 94th ID. It was during this period that 3 Ptn H Co suffered one of its biggest tragedies when Sgt George Montilio was killed accidentally by a nervous replacement. Montilio's death came as a heavy blow to Ralph Bennett and Alex Andros, who both worshipped the ground the New Englander walked on.

The last pocket of resistance at Düsseldorf did not stop fighting until Feldmarschall Model committed suicide near Duisburg on April 21. By the end of the month, around 325,000 German troops had been taken prisoner. On April 21/22, the 506th was transported by truck and rail to Jagsthausen in support of Seventh Army. Three days later, Col Patch established the 3rd Bn CP at Rossach while G, H, and I companies settled in nearby Untermessach. At the same time, 1/506 went to Oberkessach, Service Co to Olinhausen, while 2/506 made themselves at home in Widdern.

On the 26th, while Harley Dingman was visiting Regimental HQ at Von Berlichingen Castle (now Hotel Die Götzenburg) near Krautheim, he noticed a pile of promotion papers outside Col Sink's office. "As there was nobody around, I added Chester Molawa's name to the list. Because of his criminal record he was never going to get a promotion but he'd been doing such a great job for me that I figured he needed a break. The paperwork sailed through without any problems and a few days later Chester was made up to T/5!"

Before leaving the Ruhr, Ed Shames developed a problem with his teeth. The pain became so acute that Col Sink sent him to a mobile dentist in Cologne. "When I arrived, there was a long line of people waiting to be seen. Dressed in combat clothing, .45 on my hip, I jumped to the front of the line, causing a massive argument with the officer in charge. I told the man that my unit was in the process of pulling out and that I couldn't wait and eventually he gave in. A week or so later, Sink got a letter from the dental people complaining about my attitude. All Sink could say was, 'Not again, Shames. The rear echelon are there to support not hinder us, so in future please, please, please be nice to them!'"

12

"Striking back"

The plight of the 3rd Battalion POWs – June 1944–May 1945

Although Ed Shames was now beginning to enjoy his new life as an officer, he was often reminded of his early days with Col Wolverton and 3rd Bn. "Occasionally, when I saw S/Sgt Joe Gorenc, we would talk about the old days and our friend Pfc Don Ross, who'd been captured in Normandy but, unlike Joe, wasn't lucky enough to escape."

When Don Ross arrived at Limburg in Germany he was billeted with fellow D-Day captives Pfc Billy Weimer, Pfc Don Armenio, and Sgt "Bud" Estes from H Co, along with Pfc George Rosie and Cpl Jim Bradley from HQ Co and I Co's T/Sgt Joe Beyrle. The next part of the POW journey was usually by rail and could take days or even weeks depending on the final destination. In August, after a short stay in Stalag IV-B at Mühlberg, many private soldiers like Ross were sent to other camps, where they were used as *Arbeitskommandos*, or labor details. Don (now prisoner number 80427) was sent east by train with Weimer and Armenio and ten other men. After several long stops and delays the group finally arrived at Stalag IV-C, near Wistritz in the Sudetenland on the Czech border.

Established at the beginning of the war in a former porcelain factory, IV-C provided a 23,000-strong labor force to local industry. Many British, French, Polish, American, and Russian prisoners were forced to toil at the Sudetenland Fuel Works, where petrol was synthesized from coal. Shortly after arriving, Don was sent to work in the camp's blacksmith shop:

I helped two Americans escape after providing them with a stolen hacksaw blade. Later, one of the men was killed and the other recaptured and brought back to the Stalag. A few of the guards made the poor wretch run into the "forbidden area" between the barbed wire. Many of us were forced to stand and watch while they machine-gunned the escapee to death.

A week or so later, I was re-assigned to a local open cast coalmine. If the opportunity arose everyone did their level best to sabotage anything and everything they could lay their hands on. It was my job to separate any waste material from the coal, and whenever possible I'd place the spoil in the coal wagons and vice versa. One day a civilian worker saw what I was doing and deliberately ran a wagon into me, injuring my back. However, a few days later the same guy was "accidentally" crushed to death, but none of us were ever suspected.

Two months later, Don was moved into Czechoslovakia to Falknov nad Ohri. Today the town is known as Sokolov and is situated in the Karlovy Vary region northeast of Cheb. The Germans called the small facility "Falknov an der Eger," which was a subunit of the infamous Flossenbürg concentration camp. Ross was forced to work through the coldest winter in 50 years:

We were standing on frozen rivers, breaking up ice, allowing the water to flow more freely through a nearby hydro-electric dam. Most of us went down with emersion injuries, and I suffered severe frostbite to my hands and feet. Sometimes we were ordered to a nearby railway to unload goods wagons, which was always a great opportunity to steal a few potatoes and carrots.

One of the guards was an older fellow who clearly sympathized with our situation. After returning from an unloading detail, the German would often pat us down at the gate and jokingly say, "Been putting on any weight lately lads?" before letting us pass. There was another German NCO who was decent enough to keep us informed on any Allied progress and how close they were to the camp. On several occasions the "Little Corporal" saved my life by intervening as I was about to be beaten for some misdemeanor or other … and we didn't forget his kindness. During early March, with the Allies on the doorstep, we rose up and disarmed our captors. Those that we didn't like were beaten and locked in one of the camp buildings. However, we left the older guard and the Little Corporal alone. After leaving the camp through the front gates we all went our separate ways.

Don and another man opted to join the Czech guerrillas and, despite the language barrier, fought with them for the next two months. He continues:

We didn't take any prisoners, and to us every dead enemy soldier was a "good comrade." We soon met up with the Russians, who were brilliant, and it was while working with them in early May that we finally hooked up with the American 1st ID. To be honest many of us wanted to continue fighting but were told that it just wasn't an option. So we were sent to Camp Lucky Strike at Le Havre to await shipment home. At that time I had long hair and a full beard and weighed around 115lb. When I enlisted on September 12, 1942, I weighed 180lb! The quartermaster at Lucky Strike issued us with cash and new uniforms, and for the first time we had access to decent food and regular showers.

We were given 48-hour passes to Paris and spent a wonderful couple of days exploring the city and its restaurants. My prison buddy and I met up with two American Army girls and spent an afternoon enjoying the sights. It was strange to think that only one year earlier we had been paraded through the streets like criminals. The Parisians we came across seemed slightly distant, but at least it was better than being spat on. It is fair to say that the behavior of some American servicemen at that time wasn't particularly good, which probably didn't help the situation.

The following day we intervened at one restaurant when a drunken soldier stood on a table and began to sing lewd songs in front of the other customers. We told the man and his friends that they were a disgrace to our uniform but nobody seemed to give a damn. By this time I was fuming and through gritted teeth responded, "You might want to be careful when you leave." "Why?" came the reply. "Because somebody might be out there waiting for you." At that point, I turned and walked outside, expecting at least one of them to follow, but the cowards decided to make a run for it and left through a back door.

After returning by train to Le Havre we boarded a passenger ship for the voyage home. Two weeks later, at the end of June, we docked at Newport News and were sent to a large military base in West Virginia. Here, I was given two months' leave and said goodbye to most of the POWs before heading home to the west coast with my three remaining "muckers." There were a lot of young women with small children on the train, and we offered our overcoats as blankets and pillows for some of the kids. When we reached Marysville, California, I said a final farewell to my buddies and never saw them again.

From here I hitchhiked to San Francisco and caught the bus to San Rafael. Since I'd been away my parents had moved to a new address – 28 Hart Avenue – so I took a cab (the taxi driver never charged me) and arrived at their house around midnight. Although my folks were asleep the front door was unlocked. Walking into their bedroom, I picked my dad out of bed and said, "Hi Pop," before hugging the life out of him. During the commotion my mother awoke and burst into floods of tears. We stayed up the rest of the night talking … reaching across every now and then just to touch my Mom's hand… It was good to be home.

On August 15, 1945, six days before Don's leave expired, the Japanese surrendered and World War II officially came to an end.

On April 25, the link-up of US and Russian troops at Torgau on the river Elbe affected the dynamic of many POWs in northeastern Germany. The situation on the enemy flanks after this momentous event ceased to be of any further importance, and the only justification to Germany for continuing the war was to allow their divisions in the east time to fight their way back into the areas held by British and American forces.

At one point Hitler actually considered using a threat to execute 35,000 POWs (there were around 270,000 prisoners in Germany in 1945) unless the Allies agreed to broker some kind of peace deal. However, SS-Obergruppenführer und General der Waffen-SS Gottlob Berger (who had been appointed general commander of POW camps in 1944) convinced Hitler that using the prisoners as hostages might be a better idea. Thankfully, neither option materialized, although the resulting forced migration from east to west caused the deaths of thousands of Allied POWs and concentration camp inmates.

Dozens of 3rd Bn men like Ross were captured during the first few days of Normandy, including Capt John McKnight and his radio operator Joe Beyrle, Pvt David Morgan, and Jim Brown's twin brother Jack, who all came from I Co. Others previously mentioned, such as George "Doc" Dwyer, Ray Calandrella, Johnny Gibson, Marty Clark, and Joe Gorenc, along with Joe Mielcarek, Jim Sheeran, and Bernie Rainwater, eventually managed to escape and return to the United Kingdom before the invasion of the Netherlands. Most of these, including Ray, would eventually return to active service and fight at Bastogne.

Following D-Day, after a brief spell at Dépôt de Remonte, all of the POWs including those from 3/506 ended up at the Hôtellerie Notre-Dame ("Starvation Hill") south of St-Lô, where they were eventually split into three distinct groups. The main body, numbering around 700, was sent southwest by road to a military base at Rennes (Frontstalag 221). This group included Dwyer and Gorenc, as well as Brown and Calandrella, whose footwear had been stolen by the Germans. Two smaller groups were also mobilized for movement (southeast) to a temporary facility at Alencon. The first departed by truck around June 10, and the other followed on foot two weeks later.

Shortly after their arrival at Alencon, a number of men from the first group were selected for a march through Paris. Among those forced to participate were John McKnight, Joe Beyrle, Bernie Rainwater, Jim Sheeran, Pvt John McKinstry (81mm mortar platoon), Marty Clark, George Rosie, Jim Bradley, and Don Ross, who recalled the march when he was finally a free visitor to the city.

Dwyer, Brown, Calandrella, and Gorenc fared better and as part of the main body were sent by train to Frontstalag 194 at Châlons-sur-Marne (near Mourmelon). The circular route from Frontstalag 221 lasted 23 days and followed a convoluted course through the Indre-et-Loire region of central France – where Dwyer and Gorenc made good their escape.

In total, some 2,000 Allied prisoners converged on Paris for the "Walk of Shame" that took place around June 20. Flanked by armed guards, the heavily bearded prisoners were formed into three enormous columns and marched past the Arc de Triomphe in a long meandering procession en route to Gare de l'Est railway station. At the head of the column were two German officers and dozens of cameramen, all eager to photograph every aspect of the "humiliated" servicemen. Loudspeakers were placed along the route, broadcasting propaganda stating that all paratroopers were in fact convicted criminals and rapists who had been given the option of joining the army rather than go to jail (which was partly true in Chester Molawa's case). The column came to a halt beyond the iron footbridge spanning Rue d'Alsace, alongside the station. From here the POWs, including the 3rd Bn men, were loaded aboard dozens of 40/8 boxcars and sent via Château Thierry to Reims and then Châlons-sur-Marne.

Ray Calandrella remembers the living conditions at the barracks:

> Sanitation at the former French cavalry barracks was not great and the water was even worse, but we did receive one Red Cross parcel between two men each week. The parcels were incredible and

> contained tins of salmon, meat roll, and condensed milk, as well as cigarettes, cheese, candy, and other delicious products. We had many air raid alerts, especially when the railway station was being bombed. Some like me were sent on work parties to the station to help clear up after the raids. I'd heard from one of the French civilians down at the station that the Allies weren't far away and expected them to be here in about ten days. The work parties were issued extra rations of soup plus one food parcel per four men. On August 19, I made plans to escape with a boxcar buddy called Elmer Draver from the 29th ID.
>
> Two days later, after we'd gathered enough rations to last until September 10, I helped Elmer climb up into the attic at the barracks. During morning roll call, Elmer was listed as missing, and despite a rigorous search, the Germans didn't bother to look in the loft – which wasn't really surprising as the ceiling hatch was about 15ft from the floor. I carried on working down at the station for a couple of days, gathering more water and rations. On August 23, I joined Elmer by means of a rope he lowered made from knotted blankets.

Coincidentally, that afternoon, with Paris on the verge of liberation, around 1,000 POWs were moved to Limburg Stalag XII-A and XII-D/Z Trier in Germany. With the barracks now empty, Calandrella and Draver remained in hiding for the next six days until Châlons was liberated on August 29. Two days later, on September 1, they were evacuated by air back to England, where Elmer opted for "ZI" and Ray returned to the battalion at Ramsbury.

In January 1945, after several disastrous attempts, Joe Beyrle and Pfc Arnaud Rocquin (506th Regt HQ Demolition Ptn) successfully escaped from Stalag III-C Altdrewitz, near the Polish border at Küstren. Wading east toward Poland along the banks of the river Warta, Beyrle managed to shake off the dogs and their handlers who had been following him. "Two days later, after walking toward the sound of advancing artillery fire, I ran into a Soviet tank squadron who, much to my amazement, were using 'Lend-Lease' Shermans. The only Russian words I knew were

Amerikanskii Tovarisch [American Comrade], which at least stopped them from shooting me. The Russian troops quickly found an officer who spoke a little English and I was able to explain my situation. Somewhat reluctantly the Russians gave me a submachine gun and a brief lesson on how to look after it. I was assigned to one of the tanks, whose commander was a woman, and became one of her supporting infantrymen." It was a similar story for Rocquin, who also managed to hook up with another Soviet unit and spent the next few weeks fighting with them.

Ironically Stalag III-C was liberated a few days later, after a 48-hour tank battle, and around 25,000 Allied POWs set free, as Pvt Bob Hayes from B/506 recalls:

> After the Russians led us out of the camp we found out that we were on our own. Initially I was in a group of about 300 Americans but we decided to split up into smaller groups of 8–10 men.
>
> My group was heading for Moscow and hitched rides on military vehicles whenever we could. For once, fresh food wasn't a problem as the Germans had abandoned their farms and houses in the rush to evade Soviet forces. The Russian troops seemed friendly enough to us but it was clear that we were still on our own. By hopping trains through Poland we made it as far as Warsaw, where the Russians finally took action and began to round everyone up. I mean by then there were hundreds if not thousands of liberated prisoners mingling in the streets. The Russians provided accommodation and made sure that we were well fed. Eventually, after two or three weeks, everybody was sent 600 miles southeast to the Black Sea port of Odessa in the Ukraine for repatriation.

Incredibly, the Russian tank unit that Beyrle was working with arrived at the now abandoned III-C. "I was still shaking my head in disbelief when one of the Soviet soldiers asked me to come with him to the commandant's office. In the room was a safe and my Russian chums were trying to figure out how to blow it using some quarter-pound blocks of US nitro-starch. When we got the safe open the guys helped themselves to all the shiny stuff and didn't seem interested in the American, Canadian, French, and British currency … which I happily piled into a large satchel, thank you very much. While in the office, I was also able to locate my POW record card and picture, which ironically turned out to be one of the few things I managed to bring home!"

One month later Beyrle was wounded in the groin. "While recovering in a Russian field hospital somewhere in Poland, Georgi Zhukov, the Russian commander-in-chief and all round Soviet hero, visited the facility. I couldn't stand upright like everyone else on my ward which kind of got Zhukov's attention. Through an interpreter we had a short conversation during which I asked if it would be possible for him to write me a note of safe passage as I had no formal means (except for my record card) of identifying myself." Years later Beyrle learned that his tank commander, who was only a year older, had been killed just one month after he was wounded. When Joe was discharged from hospital, he tried to make his way to Moscow, heading east in a Russian medical evacuation convoy toward Lodz, Poland. Inevitably he was redirected to Warsaw and joined the thousands of other Allied servicemen awaiting shipment to the Black Sea.

The men spent about two and a half weeks at Odessa while the port was being cleared of German mines and booby traps. Bizarrely, the first ship to arrive was His Majesty's Troop Ship (HMTS) *Samaria*, the same passenger liner that had brought the 506th PIR to the United Kingdom on September 15, 1943.

After the *Samaria* unloaded its precious cargo of sugar, the POWs were allowed to board, as Bob Hayes recalls: "We set sail for Port Said in Egypt, where we were issued new uniforms and $100 cash." From here the ship continued to Italy, where Beyrle underwent surgery to remove more shrapnel from his groin. On April 1, 1945 the *Samaria* left Naples, bound for the United States, and ten days later arrived in Boston.

Interestingly, within a month of the *Samaria* leaving Odessa, the Russian authorities closed the port and held thousands of liberated

POWs against their will for "political screening." Those found to be of Russian descent or whose families had left the Soviet Union seeking political asylum were detained by Stalin, who planned to use them as collateral in the postwar European carve up.

"I recall the date of our arrival vividly because it was the day before President Roosevelt died," Hayes remembers. "After being processed at Fort Sheridan, Illinois, we were all given a 60-day leave and I went home to Indiana to see my folks and get things straightened out with my girlfriend, who had married another guy!" Joe Beyrle was reunited with his family on April 21, who showed him the official notices they had been sent about his mistaken "death" in Normandy and another letter from a 1st Lt R. B. Stevens representing the "Army Service Forces Office of The Fiscal Director," demanding that they refund the $861.60 awarded to them as a "death gratuity!"

The road to Dresden

During the early stages of their captivity, George Rosie, Jim Bradley, and the others were sent into the streets of Alencon to excavate unexploded bombs. Afterwards the prisoners were moved a few miles further east to another transit camp at Chartres, located in a block of warehouses. "There were about 300 Americans in our part of the building," recalls Rosie. "As the floors were covered with straw most of us soon became infested with fleas. Two days later we were on our way to Paris for the big march. In certain places there were hundreds of people lining the streets, men and women side by side, jeering … and on several occasions I saw guys getting punched as they passed by." Most of these civilians were right-wing Vichy supporters placed along the route at specific points to abuse and antagonize the prisoners. Rosie was walking behind Jim Bradley and recalls, "One girl was running down the column ahead of me spitting at the men who were nearest. She got to Jim and was just about to let loose when he hawked up in her face … she wasn't expecting that! I thought, boy we are going to catch hell now, but the guard just pushed her back into the crowd and we carried on." Not long after the POWs' unmarked train departed Paris, the locomotive was strafed by Allied fighters and badly damaged. The men spent the next few hours anxiously waiting inside the boxcars until a replacement engine could be found. Some of the bullets from the attack struck the first few carriages and Rosie and his friends prayed as the new locomotive was hooked up.

The laborious journey that followed spanned a couple of weeks due to constant track repairs before finally arriving at Châlons. On August 23, Châlons itself was evacuated and the prisoners sent to Limburg XII-A for processing. Limburg XII-A was situated south of the Ruhr valley a few miles east of Koblenz close to the border with Belgium and France. As a transit camp the primary function of XII-A was to process all newly captured POWs before sending them on to other camps deeper inside the Fatherland. Traditionally, the new arrivals would be interviewed, documented, and issued prison numbers. Due to the transient nature of the camp, no letters or Red Cross parcels were possible. However, the men were allowed to fill in one postcard containing the most basic information, which was then sent via the Red Cross to their next of kin. The Stalag held around 20,000 men who came from all corners of the globe, including Africa, France, India, Italy, Russia, Great Britain, and America.

"We were assigned to three large marquees with straw scattered across the ground and for the first time in almost 50 days I was able to wash in fresh water," recalls Rosie. He continues:

> Our captors issued us with an identification tag perforated down the center apparently so the metal could be split and one half placed in your mouth if you died!
>
> During the interview process the Germans asked what our former occupations had been. You can imagine some of the answers: "Rum Runner," "Pimp," "Cowboy," and so on and so forth. Back in our tent we learned that an Air Force sergeant had been worked

> over pretty badly by one of the guards using a rubber hose. We soon found out that when the Krauts said "Move," we moved. And fast! A few days later while we were on parade about 400 names were called, mine included. After being directed to a wooden barracks we were showered and deloused before being sent to the railway station, where once again they took away our footwear.
>
> After boarding the boxcars we were surprised to find some bread and corned beef on the floor. The guards sarcastically told us that this was more than enough to feed us for the next three days! Although crowded and stuffy we traveled through the night, which at least gave us some feeling of security. [The paratroopers were heading 240 miles east across Germany to the town of Mühlberg on the river Elbe.]
>
> We stopped early the next morning and the doors were opened. Stepping down onto the tracks into fresh air was wonderful as we went to empty our latrine buckets. As I was replenishing the drinking water the guard nearest me said that we could expect to reach our new camp by next morning.

Situated 30 miles northwest of Dresden Stalag IV-B was one of the largest in Germany, covering 74 acres. Rosie continues his account:

> After arriving at 0700hrs, our boots were returned and we marched into camp. After being inoculated against typhus and several other diseases we were issued two blankets, 12 cigarettes, and a Red Cross parcel before being shown to our barracks. The Canadian sergeant major (WOII), who ran our compound, was known to all as "The Man of Confidence." This meant that he was the duly elected liaison between the POWs and the Germans. During my time as a prisoner, IV-B was by far the best run, no doubt thanks to the efforts of that Canadian warrant officer. To us the additional Red Cross supplies were all valuable currency and could be readily exchanged for other more luxurious items that were available for the right price.

> I'm not saying that the Germans fed us well but we were receiving three small meals a day and began to get some strength back. Although the Russian area was off limits, Jim Bradley and I would walk over to the other compounds occupied by the Dutch and French. At that time camp life wasn't too bad and we joined in with some of the sporting activities that were on offer such as basketball. One of the men from the 82nd Airborne, Patrick Bogie, was recruited for our "team." Pat soon became our "mucker," pooling food and cigarettes. Bradley didn't smoke so he traded his ciggies for extra rations and collectively we exchanged all of our duplicate items.

Over in the Canadian compound there were five or six Americans who had joined the Canadian Army, only to be captured at Dieppe.

"While the weather was good the camp set up a basketball league, and Bogie and I qualified for places on the Canadian team and guess what? We won the competition. Most of the Canadians had been at IV-B for nearly two and a half years and were now receiving between ten and 12 cartons of cigarettes regularly per month! The Canadian press printed lists of its POWs along with their respective prison camps and invited people to send gifts to them through the International Red Cross. Of course these guys were now betting large amounts of 'smokes,' and because our team was doing so well they would reward us with two or three cartons every time we won." Luckily for Rosie, the "Man of Confidence" also played on the Canadian basketball team and made sure that George's prison records were changed from "Private First Class" to "Corporal."

By November it had begun to turn cold, as Rosie recalls: "With no heating, Jim, Pat, and I took to sharing a double bunk with six blankets. Every now and then we would rotate our positions so we all had a share of the 'warm spot' in the middle." By December 1944, around 7,500 US POWs arrived from the Battle of the Bulge, although 3,000 were quickly transferred to other camps.

"Some were paratroopers but most were from the 106th ID," Rosie continues, "and of course we were all shocked by what they had to say about the Ardennes. Around January 5, due to overcrowding, we moved again but this time in Wehrmacht boxcars installed with coal stoves." Thankfully, the journey was only 70 miles to the US NCO camp at Fürstenburg III-B, situated on the river Oder, southeast of Berlin. Rosie recalls:

> Our barracks were in a terrible state and hadn't been used for some time. The bunks didn't have enough slats so the next day we found an empty block and scrounged every bed plank we could find. That evening they issued each one of us 20 cigarettes. After reveille the next day we had hot showers, clean underwear (which was a minor miracle), and were issued one Red Cross parcel between two people… The rations at Stalag III-B were probably the best food we'd had so far. Trading with the guards was quite normal and we were always able to swap cigarettes for a loaf of bread or butter. One of the guys had a secret radio so we knew that the Russians were fast approaching from the east.

On January 31, Rosie's world turned upside down. Since December, to prevent repatriation, the Germans had been evacuating the main camps in Poland, Silesia, Czechoslovakia, and East Prussia. Thousands of POWs were herded east along three routes. The northern route emanated from East Prussia and followed a course through Pomerania to Fallingbostel. The southern began at Teschen near Auschwitz and continued through Czechoslovakia to Moosburg in Bavaria. The central route started in Silesia via Görlitz and finished at Luckenwalde III-A. The event became known as "The Long March," and thousands died on the much longer northern and southern routes, with many covering 500 miles or more.

In retrospect, prisoners like George Rosie and Bud Estes were lucky, as the distance from Stalag III-B to III-A at Luckenwalde on the Elbe was no more than 60 miles. But the extreme cold and their worsening physical condition caused many problems, as Rosie recalls:

The authorities decided to march around 4,000 of us to Luckenwalde. The painfully slow journey took six days and it was colder than hell. We had been given some old overcoats, which believe me was a blessing, but none of us had a hat or gloves or in some cases even boots! We trudged along into the afternoon and through the night with only three short breaks. The guards were constantly pushing to keep us moving. At first light we were given another rest stop but no food. Everyone had to rely on what little rations they had brought with them. By this time we were really struggling and up ahead I could see people throwing things away because they no longer had enough strength remaining to carry them.

We stopped at a complex of barns where one of the prisoners approached an elderly woman for food. As he was in the process of exchanging a bar of soap one of the guards walked up and butt stroked the man across the back of the head. A few minutes later as we were entering the building, I looked down at the body and could clearly see that the man's skull had been completely smashed in. We all thought, 'You bastards – the poor kid was just trying to feed himself!'

The following morning we were all cold and stiff… I could hardly move and eventually got to my feet feeling like a 90-year-old. Back on the road we were joined by hundreds of civilians who were also moving west. Later that afternoon we stopped near one of the concentration camps. We hadn't seen anything like this before and were all shocked by the emaciated physical condition of the people. Our attention quickly turned to a camp guard who was beating one of the inmates with a club. As we moved off a POW at the head of the line hollered out, 'You lousy goddamn Krauts – God will get even with you some day… He will, he will, he will!' Others joined in and started shouting and swearing at our guards who completely ignored us and just carried on as if nothing had happened.

Later that day after passing several German gun emplacements being dug by Jews our group was halted for a rest break. As we were

> getting back on the road I heard a bang. Word came back down the line that one of the Airborne men had been shot in the head because he didn't get up quickly enough when ordered. I didn't recognize the guy who was lying face up by the side of the road as we filed past.*

At one point the prisoners stopped for the night at a small farming community. Rosie and about 30 other men were in a small barn when the owner, accompanied by a young Russian girl, came in with some soup and potatoes. It was not unusual for German women to have white Russian "slave" girls working for them as domestics. Most of these youngsters would eventually end up as displaced persons (DPs), unable to return to their families who for the most part, no longer existed.

Things go better with Coke

"I remember toward the end of the ordeal we passed through a small town where a number of locals had gathered to stare," Rosie reflected. "They never said a word – just stood in silence and looked on. We must have been a sorry looking bunch by that time."

As the prisoners reached the far edge of the town they were amused to see a Coca-Cola sign hanging from a wall. Everyone to a man saw the irony and at that moment dreamed of taking a long slurp from a bottle or two. "A few hours later we crossed a bridge over the eight-lane ring road around Berlin, which was completely devoid of vehicles." Eighteen miles west of Luckenwalde is the small town of Halbe, surrounded by the Spree Forest.

By late April, the entire area would be devastated by a terrific battle (that became known as the Halbe Cauldron), in which nearly 100,000 people perished. Of course, to those like Rosie and Estes, who were shuffling along during the first days of February, it was just another

---

* The murdered man may well have been Pvt Albert Gray (G Co 3 Ptn), who had been captured during a night patrol into Recogne on January 2, 1945.

town, as Rosie recalls: "At Halbe we passed another column of POWs heading for Luckenwalde. A few men in the other group had fallen out and were peeing by the roadside as we came by. Looking across I couldn't believe my eyes. One of the men was Mike Michaelson, with whom I'd played softball back in Chicago. After a quick 'Hello – see you later,' we carried on toward our final destination. I learned later that Mike had been fighting with the 106th ID when captured on December 20 at St Vith… A mile or so west of Halbe, a bunch of German soldiers were standing at the roadside handing out food … one loaf of bread and a can of cheese for every five prisoners."

The men stopped for the night at a "mock village," previously used by Germans troops for FIBUA training – Fighting in Built-up Areas. "The following day we reached Luckenwalde and were herded into an area containing seven enormous circus tents. I heard that only 2,800 out of the original 4,000 made it to III-A. Those of us who remained were divided into smaller groups of around 400 and each assigned to a tent." There were already 7,000 men at Luckenwalde, and the huge influx of extra POWs made living conditions increasingly difficult.

A few days later Rosie saw Capt John McKnight, who had been in command of I Co before he was captured during the early hours of D-Day. McKnight had just come in from Silesia via the central route, which made Rosie's trip seem like a walk in the park. Not much more than a skeleton, it would take McKnight (who weighed only 67lb) another three years before he returned to some kind of normal health, but he was never the same again.

By late February contrails from high-flying Allied bombers heading for Berlin were a constant feature in the skies above the camp. Incredibly, the small radio was broken down and smuggled from Fürstenberg to Luckenwalde. "I don't know how they managed it but the radio continued to provide vital information regarding the progress of Allied forces." The world-famous German prewar boxing champion Max Schmeling visited Luckenwalde during a tour of American camps, completely unaware of the resentment he was generating among the long-term emaciated and ragged prisoners like Rosie. "Some of the new guys rushed across to meet him and get his autograph, but to me, Schmeling, who had joined the *Fallschirmjäger* (German paratroops), was just another Kraut and I certainly wasn't going to welcome or treat him as any kind of hero."

Rosie continues his account of the POW camp:

> All through March the weather was horrendous, with high winds and plenty of rain that damaged our "big top." The Germans sent a Russian prisoner across to carry out repairs but he was slow and I don't blame him. That little guy was in no hurry to go back to his chums starving to death in the Russian compound [Germany maintained that as the Soviet Union had not signed the 1929 Geneva Convention it was not obliged to uphold its stipulations regarding treatment of Russian POWs]. At least we were getting some food and the odd Red Cross parcel. To cut a long story short, finally, as the Russians approached, the guards fled and we were liberated on April 23, 1945. Many of the Russian prisoners were absorbed back into the Red Army and sent off to fight in the battle to conquer Berlin. Can you imagine what those guys would have done to any Krauts, male or female, that they ran into?

Rosie and Bud Estes from H Co joined a small group and decided (against direct orders from the officers now running III-A) to leave the camp and walk west toward US forces fast approaching the Elbe. Some, like Jim Bradley and John McKnight, remained behind and were not repatriated until a week later. Bradley and McKnight were among the lucky ones.

Around the same time the Russians closed the camp and refused to release any more prisoners until everyone had been "politically screened." From the Elbe, Rosie and crew were flown to Mourmelon, where the 101st Airborne Division still had a rear-echelon presence. Rosie's old boss from the 81mm mortar platoon, 1st Lt Pete Madden, who was recovering from wounds received in Bastogne, made sure that the boys had everything they needed including transit passes to Camp Lucky Strike for final shipment home.

Guten Morgen Herr Morgan

Pvt David Morgan was only 19 years old when captured shortly after dawn on D-Day. Morgan and several other men from 2 Ptn I Co were selected as security and jumped in with the 3rd Bn Pathfinder Detachment ahead of the main drop. Dave's POW experience was altogether different from that of many of the others, as he recalls: "I arrived at 'Starvation Hill' on Saturday, June 10, with another colleague from I Co, Pfc Bill Harrington. The following day Sgt Sid McCallum and Pfc Jack Brown [who were also part of the security team from 2 Ptn] were brought in." A day or so later Brown was shipped out by truck to Rennes, along with Calandrella, Gorenc, and Dwyer. Morgan and Harrington remained at "Starvation Hill" for a further two weeks until the evening of June 25, when they were sent on foot toward Alencon. Along the way the prisoners, who included about 12 officers, were held in a hayloft in the grounds of a château.

Dave Morgan continues his account:

> As we were only allowed to move at night, it took us three days to reach the château, where we remained for nearly two weeks. During our stay we helped four guys escape so the Krauts temporarily removed our belts and bootlaces, which quickly put a stop to any further attempts to break out! On the night of July 11, we hit the road again, and during the march (which took us another week to complete) we stopped over at a school and spent the last 24 hours at a railway station.
>
> Early the next morning (July 18) the Germans provided some trucks and drove us the rest of the way to Alencon. At the camp we met up with another guy from I Co, Pvt Tom Jackson, who was

> happy to share his bread ration with us. Over the next three weeks we worked on a local railroad and also a German military hospital that seemed to specialize in burns. Our billet was well run by a British NCO who would get everyone up in the morning and take roll call, etc.
>
> We left for Paris on August 9, in eight large trucks, and just outside Chartres the convoy was buzzed by a Spitfire and a P-51 Mustang. Although we had been given white bed sheets to wave, the Spitfire still strafed the convoy, killing several people, including a German warrant officer. Our truck was badly damaged and one man, named Griffiths, who wasn't quick enough, almost had his leg severed by a cannon shell. Despite our best efforts to tourniquet the wound, Griffiths died a few minutes later in the back of the vehicle.
>
> About 5pm that afternoon we reached Chartres, where we stayed for the night. As we were sleeping more prisoners and trucks arrived. By first light our convoy had doubled in size to around 15 vehicles, and before we got onto the wagons each of us was given a Red Cross parcel and a small loaf.

A train was waiting at Gare de l'Est, and the prisoners loaded the following morning, 45 men to each boxcar. The lack of drinking water coupled with the hot summer days made for a stifling trip as the train trundled northeast through Château Thierry and Reims. At one point, when the doors were finally opened, the men were treated to the sight of a number of naked French girls taking a communal outdoor shower. However, before the train arrived at Châlons, several prisoners had managed to escape.

On August 15, Morgan and Harrington reached Frontstalag 194. "It was good to see Jack Brown and some of the others," Morgan recalls. Jack raised his foot to show Dave the wooden clogs he had recently been given by the French Moroccan POWs held in the adjacent courtyard. Morgan was only at Châlons for four days before he was sent with Brown and Harrington to Stalag XII-D/Z on the

Luxembourg/German border at Trier, 30 miles southeast of Bastogne. "We passed through Nancy and Metz before arriving at the camp on August 23," Morgan continues.

The historic city of Trier is situated in the Moselle valley, and Stalag XII-D/Z was located at the top of Petrisberg Hill overlooking the town. "Trier was the biggest camp we'd ever seen, and after living in a boxcar the steep walk up to the entrance seemed exhausting. The place was full of vermin and the food barely edible. We stayed at Trier for about ten days before being sent southeast across Germany by rail via Stuttgart to Memmingen VII-B in Bavaria. We had several stopovers, and one I recall was Stalag VII-A at Moosburg near Munich. As Moosburg was an NCO camp most of us weren't allowed to enter and had to stay in the boxcars, although the Germans did open the doors for us during daylight."

Despite being only 60 miles southwest of the satellite labor camps around Landsberg, living conditions at Memmingen were a world apart. "On arrival we had food and coffee waiting. The American prisoners were very welcoming and gave us a bunch of stuff, including cigarettes and a few bottles of beer. We were billeted in two large tents and surprisingly had a decent supply of Red Cross parcels. Most, like me, were soon sent to work in the town but a few days later, on September 25, the Germans selected 25 men, including Jack, Bill, and myself to go and work on local farms a few miles further south."

The three friends boarded a train to Kempten, from where they were trucked east into the foothills of the Bavarian Alps toward Friedrichshafen and Lake Constance to the town of Weitnau:

> From here our group went to Kleinweiler, where over the next seven months we did a variety of jobs, including tree felling, railway and canal repairs, plus snow clearance during the cold, hard winter.
>
> It's funny but we became quite friendly with the locals and I even got myself a regular girlfriend. I used to say hello to the kids as they went to school and they always replied jokingly, "*Guten Morgen Herr*

Morgan." There were many Russians and Italians working nearby under the forced labor program at a factory producing wooden handles for stick grenades. One of the Italian prisoners that we got to know made a lovely wooden box with the initials "M-B-H" burned onto the lid and gave it to us as a present. Strangely, our crew was liberated by French Moroccans on April 29, 1945; it was an amazing feeling to know we were free again.

A day or so later we were sent to a nearby airfield to be deloused and inoculated against typhoid and tetanus before being fitted out with new uniforms. From here we went to Strasbourg and had a wonderful night on the town. The following day, complete with brand new sleeping bags, we set off by truck for Camp Lucky Strike, stopping overnight in Epinal.

After spending four days at Le Havre we boarded a ship on May 26 and sailed for the States … my war was now over – thank God.

13

"Candle for the dead"

Southern Bavaria – April 28–May 3, 1945

The day before Dave Morgan was liberated an advance party from the 506th left for Ulm. The regiment, along with A and B batteries, 81st AA Bn, C/326th Airborne Engineer Bn, and 321st GFA, were to be attached to VI Corps (from Seventh Army), commanded by MajGen Lucian Truscott. The mission was not only to protect Truscott's flanks but also help stabilize southwest Bavaria behind Tony McAuliffe's 103rd ID.

Earlier, on April 22, Regimental HQ had moved to Götzenburg Castle at Jagsthausen in the Heilbronn region (previously liberated by Seventh Army) situated midway between Würzburg and Stuttgart. Capt Jean Hollstein from Fayetteville, North Carolina, was posted in and took over I Co from Gene Brown, who returned to Regt HQ Co. Several more officers also joined the battalion, such as Capt George Lancaster (battalion S1) and 2nd Lt Bruno Schroeder (battalion S2). Schroeder had previously been with Regimental HQ as a staff sergeant before receiving a battlefield commission. 1st Lt Robert Stocking (ex HQ Co) and second lieutenants Robert Bausman (ex Service Co), Carl Pinsky, and Cecil Fisher (ex I Co) were all assigned to G Co.

A few days later the regiment was sent by train to Ludwigshafen, near Heidelberg. During the seemingly endless journey from Gohr the train stopped at several towns to stock up on coal and water. Before crossing the Rhine, Lou Vecchi remembers one station in particular where there was a large supply of rations stored on the platform:

"Dozens bailed out of the boxcars to 'liberate' the food and the MPs were powerless to stop them. During later stops our people were running amok looting the nearest houses. A few of my guys came back with a wood-burning stove that we fired up and were able to cook with for the remainder of the journey!"

Before the 506th departed from Jagsthausen, Ray Calandrella went to see Capt Anderson to inquire if now it might be possible to take the ZI option and go home. "Andy Anderson was quite cynical but listened intently to what I had to say before commenting, 'Calandrella, what on earth do you mean *escaped*? Son, the way I heard you were damn well rescued. Now get your sorry face out of here … dismissed!'" Ray was a little taken aback by Anderson's response, but as usual Andy was only joking and let Ray sweat for a while before sending word that it had all been arranged and he would be going home the following morning!

Ray ended up with the 101st divisional rear echelon at Kaufbeuren (southwest of Landsberg) until May 3, when he received shipment orders to Camp Lucky Strike. He recalls:

> On the way, I diverted to Paris because I'd promised to see Helen Briggs before she was transferred to head up a new American Red Cross operation in Reims called "Club Lorraine." When I got back to the States, all the men who'd been POWs got a two-month furlough instead of the standard 30 days. Initially I felt a bit of a fraud having only spent three months in captivity, but when they offered me a choice of either Atlantic City, the Vanderbilt mansion at Ashville, North Carolina, or Lake Placid, I was more than happy to oblige. Luckily I chose Lake Placid, where although still officially in a military environment we were treated like royalty. There were all the outdoor adventure activities you could wish for. It was truly amazing. We were also interviewed by students who had been given the job of trying to ascertain what items of personal value may have been stolen from us by the Germans. Some people really pushed the boat out and made up all sorts of stories and were subsequently

compensated for things like expensive watches and jewelry that never existed.

Landsberg – the gates to oblivion

On April 28, as the 506th Battle Group was traveling through Bavaria behind LtGen Alexander Patch's Seventh Army, they were ordered south toward the medieval walled town of Landsberg am Lech, 40 miles west of the regional capital, Munich. At the time the division was stretched to its furthest geographical limits. The Germans had established a stop line (15 miles long) west of the mighty river Lech, from Obermeitinge in the north to Erpfting, 3 miles southwest of Landsberg.

A full 24 hours before the 506th occupied Landsberg, the 12th Armored Division (commanded by MajGen Roderick Allen) was in the process of pushing enemy forces back across the Lech. As the Germans withdrew they demolished all road and rail bridges behind them. However, one crossing point remained partially serviceable near Beuerbach at Schwabstadel but could only be used by infantry. In the meantime, 4 miles further south at Kaufering (next to the damaged railway bridge), the engineers were working frantically to build a pontoon crossing for the tanks but this would not be ready for at least another 48 hours. Later that day the 103rd ID, supported by the 10th Armored Division, attacked the southwestern edge of Landsberg. As the name suggests Landsberg am Lech straddles the river, which courses south downhill through a series of impressive weirs and hydroelectric dams.

Previously the town had played an important role in the development of National Socialism. Adolf Hitler had been imprisoned here in 1923, and while serving a five-year term for "high treason," began to write the first part of *Mein Kampf,* his political directive for the future Nazi state. Nine months later, due to growing popularity and political pressure, Hitler was released. Several years afterwards when Hitler finally came to power, Cell No. 7 at Landsberg Prison was made into a shrine. The party had a plaque placed on the door that proclaimed "Der Führer" as Germany's "greatest son."

While engaged in combat operations the troops from Seventh Army began to notice a thick stifling odor permeating around the town. One by one the 92nd and 101st cavalry regiments from Combat Command B, 12th Armored, discovered three slave labor camps designated by the SS as "Kauferings" due to their close proximity to the railhead at Kaufering.

These three facilities were KZ-I, III, and IV, but there were seven more camps still waiting to be discovered. A total of ten labor facilities had been established in June 1944 to house 21,000 slave workers whose job was to build three enormous factories (partially underground) west of the Lech, codenamed "Walnut II" (Walnuss), "Vineyard II" (Weingut), and "Diana II." The factories were built to produce the new twin-engine push-pull Dornier Do335 A-1 "Pfeil" (Arrow) fighter-bomber as well as the Focke Wulf FW190 D9 and the Messerschmitt ME262 jet fighter. A testament to the workforce, Weingut II is still in use today by the German Air Force. However, a total of 6,364 people died during the construction of the three factories and other associated regional forced labor programs. It is also incredible to note that, by 1945, nearly 20,000 labor camps were scattered throughout the Third Reich.

By the time US forces arrived, a vast majority of the slave force had already been evacuated eastwards by train or on foot. KZ-IV (Camp 4) at Hurlag was a sick camp and served as a ghoulish "hospice," where those no longer able to work were sent to die. Normally these unfortunate individuals would have been sent back to Auschwitz for extermination but that option had ceased months ago. At Kaufering itself, a short distance south of the camp was a rail junction that acted as the central hub for slave labor continuously arriving from larger camps across the Reich. Up until this time names such as Auschwitz/Birkenau, Buchenwald, Mauthausen, Flossenbürg, and Dachau were still largely unknown to the advancing Allies.

Shortly after dawn on April 27, Capt John Paul Jones of C/134th Armored Ordnance Bn was helping to recover a broken-down tank when he noticed a handful of emaciated people emerging from woodland who told him about the barracks that were smoldering nearby.

Later that morning a small team was sent to investigate and what they found was sickening. Over 300 disease-ridden skeletal corpses had been partially dragged from the huts and dumped in piles at collection points around the camp. Another 40 bodies were gathered between two huts, where they had been doused in fuel and set on fire. Of the 80 neatly arranged sunken barracks around 12 (situated along the edge of the perimeter fence) had been razed to the ground. Bizarrely, at one end of the camp, piled high on the edge of a makeshift parade ground, were hundreds, maybe even thousands, of filthy overcoats.

The camp commandant was 55-year-old Hauptmann der Wehrmacht Johann Eichelsdorfer. A father of three, Eichelsdorfer lived and worked just outside the wire in the SS quarters, pampered by a small staff of female servants, who were all Jewish. Before taking over KZ-IV in January 1945, Eichelsdorfer had previously worked in other Kauferings and another camp at Augsberg. By April there were 2,900 inmates at Hurlag, overseen by 33 guards including two senior NCOs, SS-Oberscharführer Riedel (in charge of catering), and SS-Hauptscharführer Vetter. The overall commander of the camps around Landsberg was SS-Sturmbannführer Förschner, whose immediate superior was Dachau commandant SS-Obersturmbannführer Weiter.

The chief medical officer for all ten camps was Dr Max Blanke, who lived near KZ-IV in Hurlag village with his wife Agathe. It would appear that 36-year-old Blanke did very little, if nothing, to ease the suffering of the people at Camp 4. Despite its being an infirmary, daily work *kommandos* (labor details) were still sent out to bury those who had died and bring back food and firewood. Although each hut had its own stove, wood was strictly rationed, even during the bitterly cold winter. Of the 600 Czechoslovakian Jews who found themselves at Hurlag during this time, only a handful made it out alive.

On April 25, with Seventh Army fast approaching, the order was given by SS-Obersturmbannführer Weiter to evacuate the Kaufering prisoners to Dachau. Those unable to walk from KZ-IV were sent to the railway sidings opposite the camp, where dozens of open boxcars were waiting. Although only a short distance away, the process was painfully slow for the decrepit typhus-ridden prisoners. To speed things up, Eichelsdorfer cut an exit through the barbed-wire perimeter fence. In the meantime, Dr Blanke set about procuring all available horse-drawn transport, while Eichelsdorfer and his guards destroyed as much evidence as they possibly could.

During the night dozens collapsed en route to the train. In the morning bodies littered the sidings, as those still living shuffled toward the waiting boxcars. Dr Blanke went home to Hurlag after the train departed for Dachau. That afternoon he poisoned his wife Agathe before committing suicide. Many senior camp staff, like Reidel and Vetter, simply disappeared and were never seen or heard from again. Captured a few days later, Johann Eichelsdorfer was brought back to KZ-IV by the Americans to face the world's media and final justice.

Tragically, shortly after leaving the station, the packed train was attacked by a squadron of P-47s, killing a number of prisoners. Ironically, the pilots had targeted the open carriages thinking they were full of German troops. Before reaching Dachau, the train was attacked again and more innocent people killed. If that was not bad enough, because of the intense overcrowding at Dachau, 7,000 prisoners (including those from Landsberg) were then forced to march southeast toward Tegernsee. Many were shot during the journey or died from hunger and exhaustion before the guards eventually fled, leaving any survivors to be picked up by the advancing Allies.

Man's inhumanity

By now the 506th PIR had reached a temporary holding area west of Landsberg. On April 28, selected personnel from Regt HQ and

E companies were sent to KZ-I to assist the 12th Armored with the humanitarian clean-up operation. Situated northwest of Landsberg, close to the underground factories Weingut and Diana II, the semi-abandoned site was made up of around 60 wooden huts. Camp commandant SS-Sturmbannführer Otto Förschner and his staff were nowhere to be found. Förschner had been running the camp for the last three months and, like Eichelsdörfer, tormented without pity his prisoners who were predominantly women from Hungary and Lithuania. Around 100 slave workers had been left behind suffering from typhoid and the latter stages of malnutrition.

Now working for the 506th public relations section, T/4 Dave Phillips describes his memories of that day:

> The wooden barracks were all built into the ground except for the roofs. In the hut I entered there must have been around 20 people lying in their own excrement on two wide shelves that ran the length of the building bisected by a narrow central walkway.
>
> On his back in the aisle lay a naked, emaciated male whose skin was quivering with a barely perceptible shiver. My presence produced no reaction as I tried to explain to the people that they were now free. A few looked at me but the rest simply continued to stare at the ceiling, which was just a few inches from their faces. Two youngsters who seemed in a slightly better physical condition managed a smile and started to talk. The teenagers had been members of the Dutch Underground, captured shortly before our invasion of the Netherlands, so I asked them about the naked man on the floor. It seemed that when a person was close to death all clothing would be removed and recycled before the individual was rolled into the aisle for collection [to KZ-IV].

After leaving the hut, Phillips stopped another inmate and recalls: "Like the others he was terribly emaciated with a horribly blackened mouth. While we were talking through an interpreter, I noticed what appeared to be a set of goal posts behind him just like you'd see on an American football field and inquired, 'What the hell are they for?' 'Sometimes,' the guy told me, 'if a women prisoner happened to give birth, the SS guards would suspend the baby from those posts and charge on horseback, impaling the infant with their cavalry swords.' The man then went on to say that many of the female inmates were often sexually abused and beaten by the guards!"

When the 506th arrived, the gates were open and some prisoners who were able to walk had already made their way into Landsberg looking for food. Members of Regimental HQ were detailed to go after the starving inmates and bring them back to the camp. Col Sink contacted a nearby graves registration unit, who in turn got hold of SHAEF HQ for additional emergency care. "Before outside help arrived we did everything in our power to make the survivors comfortable," recalls Ed Shames. "Most, like me, readily gave up our own food but all that did was send the poor wretches convulsing in agony to the floor. When the International Red Cross eventually arrived they immediately told us to stop feeding the people because their digestive systems were not able to cope with our army rations!"

Without further delay the medics set up a high-protein feeding program that primarily contained an easy-to-digest nutritional mixture of raw eggs, milk, and sugar. "If we'd have caught the individuals responsible for this hellish place, then I think we would have executed each and every one of those bastards without pity," continues Ed. One of the Dutch survivors, whom Dave Phillips had spoken to earlier, befriended Piet Luitens and volunteered for the regimental IPW team.

Earlier that morning 4th ID began a push from Beuerbach in the north. But it would be a further two days before Munich surrendered. Simultaneously Combat Command A (116th Cavalry Regt) and Combat Command B (92nd and 101st cavalry regiments) crossed the recently repaired railway bridge at Kaufering and headed toward the Lech. When Combat Command B reached the river they changed course to take on the 17.SS-Panzergrenadier-Division, who were defending a new stop line further east near Lake Ammersee.

Meanwhile elements of H/506 moved up to invest the southern edge of Landsberg. Capt "Skunk" Walker's men were temporarily attached to L Co, 411th IR whose XO, Bill Prosser, recalls: "Around 700 Hungarian troops had just surrendered on the eastern side of the city. However, 100 German soldiers across the Lech in the southern district still wanted to fight. L Co had been given the job of mopping them up and bringing in the Hungarians."

Defending the shallow valley overlooking the river was a German 20mm antiaircraft gun. After the two-man crew was neutralized, L Co continued through sparse woodland until reaching the large hydroelectric dam at the foot of the hill. The newly commissioned concrete barrier spanned the Lech along the regional border with Gau Swabia. Luckily for L Co, Staustufe 15 (as the dam was officially known) had not been demolished due to the enormous collateral flood damage it would have caused to Landsberg, less than 1 mile away to the north.

The GIs found a subterranean passageway through the dam, enabling them to cross the river. Once on the western bank, L Co turned north in single file and almost immediately came under fire from the high ground to their right. At this point L Co were forced to split into five groups, and as they were observing strict radio silence, command and control became a problem. The company consolidated along the edge of the river and waited for mobile artillery support to arrive before finally moving into Landsberg.

Things were much quieter for Capt Walker, Bob Stroud, and their men who were following on behind. Stroud had only just returned to 1 Ptn from hospital after being wounded at Bastogne. Hank DiCarlo and Pvt John Kelly went ahead and scouted a route past the knocked-out antiaircraft gun down to Staustufe 15.

Opening the eastern access door to the dam, they could clearly hear the turbines humming away in the background. DiCarlo reflects: "Upon closer investigation we followed a set of steps and quickly found our way into the deserted tunnel. I nudged Kelly, who was a 6ft 2in

Texan, and motioned him forward: 'After you, Cowboy.'" DiCarlo and Kelly climbed the hill on the other side and halted at the top to take stock. Over to Hank's right was Landsberg. Beyond the main B17 highway in front of them, the two men could see a forest and several columns of dense black smoke rising into the sky. As DiCarlo surveyed the landscape he noticed a crowd of *Volkssturm* (Home Guard) militia handing over their weapons and armbands to the 411th IR.

3rd Bn followed the 411th IR into Landsberg by truck, passing KZ-I, while H Co made their way through Staustufe 15 and headed toward the edge of the woods. Ralph Bennett and Hank DiCarlo took their respective assault teams and moved forward to investigate the smoke. Advancing through the trees, the men began to choke on the stench of burning gasoline. Although they did not know it at the time they were about to enter KZ-VII – one of the last Kaufering camps to be liberated. Reaching the main entrance, Bennett and DiCarlo saw a number of smoldering huts and buildings. Except for one or two piles of burned corpses, KZ-VII appeared empty. Ralph took his men across the camp to investigate two huts that were still intact, while Hank approached a nearby pile of charred bodies: "I distinctly remember turning to Jimmy Igoe and saying, 'What the hell would they burn logs for?' It was then that we realized they weren't logs but human beings. One man still appeared to be alive but was in a terrible state. As I stood considering what to do next, Jimmy came over and put the poor guy out of his misery."

The remaining huts had both been doused in gasoline. "I broke open the first door and found people inside," recalls Ralph. "The other one seemed so overcrowded that some individuals looked to me like they had died standing up. We asked the people to come out, and when they realized we were friendly everyone wept. We didn't know what to say. They couldn't speak; it was overwhelming and I hope to God that some of them made it. I never want to see anything like that again because it changed me and the other boys forever." It was rumored that before they surrendered a small number of *Volkssturm* had entered KZ-VII and killed two SS men who had remained behind to destroy the camp. About a dozen SS guards were brought back to KZ-VII after being captured hiding in the local area. "My machine gunner, Jack Grace, took these men aside and directed them to dig a pit," recalls Hank DiCarlo. "When the trench was big enough, Grace directed them to stand in front while he mounted his machine gun on a tripod. Realizing what was about to happen, the SS men began begging for their lives." Jack was just about to adamantly close the top cover on a belt of ammunition when Lt Ed Buss (who had recently been posted in from the States) came over and chewed him out. DiCarlo adds, "I truly believe that if the lieutenant hadn't arrived when he did then those SOBs would have ended up at the bottom of the pit underneath the emaciated corpses of their victims."

Shortly after KZ-VII was "liberated," 1st and 3rd battalions, along with Regimental HQ, Service Co, C/326, and A Battery, 81st AA Bn moved into Landsberg. 2nd Bn remained at Buchloe, 7 miles away to the east, while 321st GFA were sent to Holzhausen 3 miles west of Landsberg. The 12th Armored Division took control of the Kaufering camps and did an amazing job sanitizing and saving the surviving inmates from further harm.

Even though Harley Dingman was acting sergeant major, his previous rank insignia remained in place. "Generally, when it came to selecting a billet for Col Patch and Battalion HQ, I'd choose a larger property owned by an elderly couple. We did our best not to disrupt families with children. Normally we would order, '*Um 11 Uhr sind Sie raus*' – 'be out by 11am.'" Clearly this was not the case for Harold Stedman and his 60mm mortar squad: "Five of us arrived at our billet and the family just stood and stared like we were from a different planet. There was a zither in the corner and I tried to tell them that I liked the kind of music it made. At this point the mother anxiously motioned to her daughter to play it for me. The girl turned out to be a very competent musician and the sensitive sounds she produced brought a welcome change from all the madness." Piet Luitens and his team commandeered an expensive automobile from a local family.

"The couple were so outraged that they went to see Col Sink and complained. Can you believe that? Of course the colonel told them to take a hike and threw them out into the street."

"Once things settled down, the local population were instructed to bring any weapons they had to the center of town," recalls Lou Vecchi. "They brought in everything you could imagine, from antique shotguns to hunting rifles. A Sherman from 12th Armored then drove over the entire collection, crushing it to pieces. We figured most of those people who lived around the camp must have known what was going on. Some local factories paid peppercorn wages to the SS, who then supplied them with slave labor, so don't tell me they didn't know. These people were as much a part of the war effort as the German Army, but when death and destruction became a possibility most towns like Landsberg quickly displayed the white flag of surrender."

Upon orders from division, 1st and 3rd battalions rounded up as many of the townspeople as possible and escorted them to KZ-IV and a couple of the other camps so that they could witness for themselves the results of the atrocities committed by their fellow countrymen.

Jim Martin recalls: "Although later on we visited in small groups like bizarre tourists we were somewhat unaware of the potential health risks." Again, the men were warned not to feed or hand over food, but Jim Martin and his friends decided to ignore the order. "When we went in through the back gates I stupidly handed out some K rations, which was soon stopped by the authorities. The sight of this particular camp and the stench that permeated into our clothes was hideous." Capt Cann, Ira Morehart, and Bob Izumi were speechless as they watched one ex-prisoner stoop to rip the gold teeth from a corpse before nonchalantly moving on to the next body.

Lenny "Sam" Goodgal had only just returned to I Co after recovering from trench foot:

> Thankfully, I never got to see any of the concentration camps, as the battalion had me manning a machine-gun position on the outskirts

of town with Pfc Ed Austin. Nearby we spotted three emaciated inmates in tattered striped clothing walking toward us. These three men turned out to be Russian and we gave them some of our bread and boiled up some D-Bars in a canteen to make it easier to eat. One of them was shaking uncontrollably and Ed gave him his overcoat. "Are you out of your mind … you'll get charged for that – leave it to the Red Cross," I scolded. "I've gotta do it Sam," he replied, "I mean the guy is in poor shape and needs something now, not tomorrow!" A short while later an MP came along and took the Russians away, but it was only after they'd gone that I wished I'd done the same thing as Austin. Not long afterwards we picked up another inmate called Maurice who spoke five different languages and became a tremendous asset to I Co. He stayed with us until the end of the war and eventually became one of our cooks in Austria.

The terror and despair of Dachau

On May 2, the regiment moved east toward Munich (which had surrendered two days earlier) to Starnberg, situated on the northern end of Lake Starnberg. The 321st GFA transported about 80 Kaufering camp survivors to a German military hospital near Munich, as Ray Nagell recalls: "Many of the wards were requisitioned and the walking wounded ordered to make room for the emaciated prisoners. One German soldier with his arm in a sling refused to budge but quickly changed his mind when one of our guys pointed his pistol at him."

The 506th were given the job of helping process thousands of German soldiers who had surrendered around Munich. Many were just sitting around waiting for someone to come along, like these men witnessed by Piet Luiten and the IPW team as they drove along the river Isar: "We were riding in a German staff car and came across about 50 soldiers sitting by the roadside. As soon as they saw the vehicle they all started waving. When I got out they immediately called, '*Wir ergeben uns*' – 'We surrender' – and started holding white sheets above their heads. As we were so close to the main highway, I told them to shift their butts and hand themselves over to next passing convoy."

Before the regiment moved to Miesbach, Col Sink summoned Ed Shames to discuss the possibility of sending a small team to Dachau (liberated on April 28). Ed was asked by Sink to provide him with a personal assessment of the camp that was believed to be a central hub for over 140 subsidiary facilities, including Landsberg. Sink handed Shames a file containing a few pieces of paper plus an aerial photograph and gave him two days to complete the task. Ed went back to his platoon, now billeted in a nearby barn, and carefully studied the picture and his maps before formulating a plan of action. "I selected Carl Fenstermacker (who had recently returned after a spell with the Pathfinders) as my driver/translator and left Roy Gates and Paul Rogers in charge, before heading off at dawn the following morning."

Located about 10 miles northwest of Munich, Dachau was the first camp of its kind to be opened and operated by the Nazi regime for political prisoners, regular criminals, homosexuals, Jehovah's Witnesses, and Gypsies. Developed from a former World War I munitions factory, the "correctional facility" at Dachau was dramatically enlarged by the SS in 1937 using the plentiful supply of prison labor. Thirty-two enormous single-storey huts were built in two neat rows either side of a central roadway. Every block encompassed a set of self-contained barracks, each designed to hold 208 prisoners. The industrial area and railway sidings adjacent to the new camp were converted into a vast training center for the SS. At the same time, SS leader Heinrich Himmler began recruiting personnel to staff hundreds of new labor camps based on the blueprint modeled by his "super facility" at Dachau.

The Jourhaus Gate, where the SS administration also had their offices, was the main entrance to Dachau. Access was via a small bridge across the Würm canal, which ran down one side of the camp. Although Dachau was not a death camp like Auschwitz it still possessed a gas chamber and small crematorium that was enlarged in 1942.

Dachau was a labor camp where the prisoners were used in local German industry. Those who could no longer work were originally sent by rail to the Hartheim Center near Linz where they were murdered by lethal injection. However, toward the end of 1944 the SS began to use a rifle range and gallows located inside the crematorium compound to kill those deemed unable to continue working. Dr Fritz Hintermayor headed a small medical team that included Dr Klaus Schilling and Dr Bruno Fialkowski. These two physicians were responsible for thousands of malaria experiments conducted on over 1,200 priests who had been imprisoned due to their opposition to the regime. Dr Hans Eisele was in charge of Dachau's surgical department and during the course of the war carried out countless cruel experiments on hundreds of innocent men, women, and children. By the end of April 1945, conditions rapidly deteriorated as more and more prisoners arrived from other camps like Landsberg.

On the morning of April 28, 3/157 from the 45th ID reached the outer perimeter of the SS complex more or less at the same time as the 42nd ID. Ironically, ten of the guards had already fled, plus commandant SS-Obersturmbannführer Weiter and the medical staff. At the time the garrison contained around 560 SS troops, who were either recuperating from wounds in the base hospital or attending courses at the training school.

At 1100hrs, after a brief gun battle (in which 30 SS soldiers were killed), junior SS officer Heinrich Wicker surrendered to BrigGen Henning Linden, outside a secondary entrance that led into the camp from the SS compound. As the scale and purpose of Dachau became apparent, elements of I/157 led by their XO, 1st Lt Jack Bushyhead, headed into the SS area where almost immediately they gunned down 122 enemy soldiers who were mostly from the Waffen-SS. Around 40 of the guards who had donned civilian clothing were also caught and beaten to death with shovels by some of the inmates. Over the next 3 hours several hundred more SS troops were killed by I Co, while the 42nd ID cleared the area up to the Jourhaus Gate.

Four days later, as Ed Shames and Carl Fenstermacker were driving toward Dachau, they noticed the same disgusting smell that had permeated around Landsberg, but far worse. The weather was getting warmer as Fenstermacker turned off the main road alongside the railway tracks originally designed to support the nearby munitions factories. Among the open carriages parked in the sidings were 30 abandoned boxcars from KZ-IV at Kaufering and Buchenwald. With double doors wide open, each carriage contained around 20 corpses rotting in the morning sun. Several large piles of clothing lay nearby, left behind by the inmates who were marched to Tegernsee.

As the two paratroopers stood motionless surveying the scene they concluded that this must have been the very last train to arrive. Wiping away the tears, Ed and Carl got back in their jeep and drove through the industrial area, past the Kommandantur's HQ, toward a neatly planted row of tall poplar trees either side of the main entrance. Crossing over the bridge outside Dachau's Jourhaus Gate, the vehicle was stopped at a US checkpoint before being given permission to enter. Ed stole a glance at Carl as they continued ahead through the low archway that opened onto an enormous parade square or *Appellplatz* (which had previously been the site of countless executions).

The first thing Ed noticed was the three-storey, 60ft high guard tower on the other side of the square. The place was ridiculously overcrowded, with over 30,000 people, many simply wandering around devoid of all human reason. The men were overwhelmed by the scale compared with what they had previously seen at Landsberg. Being Jewish, it was unbelievably hard for Ed to absorb.

Many of the prisoners were dressed in filthy blue and white-striped jackets and trousers with blue skullcaps. However, others, still wearing civilian clothes, had large white crosses painted on their backs because the camp quartermaster had run out of prison clothing several weeks before the liberation.

Over on Ed's right were the main support buildings belonging to the SS, containing kitchen, laundry, showers, and workshops as well as a prewar underground cell system. The large U-shaped structure spanned the entire width of the camp and had the following message emblazoned in gigantic white letters across its roof: "THERE IS ONE PATH TO FREEDOM. ITS MILESTONES ARE OBEDIENCE, HONESTY, CLEANLINESS, SOBRIETY, HARD WORK, DISCIPLINE, SACRIFICE, TRUTHFULNESS & LOVE OF THE FATHERLAND."

To their left, Shames and Fenstermacker could see the two rows of wooden barracks partly obscured by smoke emanating from thousands of small cooking fires. Putting the jeep in second gear, the two men slowly drove through the crowds along the central roadway to the far side of the camp where the gas chamber was located. The sizable building was officially known as "*Brausebad*" or "Shower bath." German records state that these were very rarely used, as the SS preferred to work their prisoners to death – hence the need for an on-site crematorium to dispose of the corpses. The piles of naked bodies that were still waiting to be cleared away made Ed feel sick. Carl kept asking, "*Entschuldigung bitte, spricht hier jemand Deutsch* [excuse me, does anyone here speak German]?"

"As we were moving around I noticed one particular lady whose behavior was different from the rest," recalls Ed. He continues:

> Like many others she was just skin and bone but seemed to be making a terrible, penetrating, primeval wailing sound. Eventually we came across a guy who seemed much stronger than the other inmates who could talk to us in German. The man was from a small village in western Poland, called Zary, near Zagan (close to the German border) where his parents had run a bakery. He went on to say that his family had all been murdered and he'd survived because of his baking skills, which had been deemed useful to the Germans here in Dachau.
>
> During our conversation with the baker we inquired about the woman who was still shrieking in the background. "Oh her, well, yes, she's a kind of 'show piece' – a trophy for the Germans," he

replied. "What on earth do you mean by trophy?" "About two years ago she arrived here with her six-year-old daughter. A couple of the guards tried to separate them at the station but she put up quite a struggle before they eventually prized the child away. One of the guards threw the kid to the ground and stamped her to death until the intestines ran from her mouth." Carl and I were almost speechless and just couldn't understand how afterwards the mother could become a "trophy." The baker soon put us right. "Don't you people get it? They used her as an example to others as to what might happen if discipline and obedience weren't observed." Carl was becoming an emotional wreck as he translated all of this crazy stuff to me and the morning just went on and on like that. Totally unbelievable.

The full death toll at Dachau will never be fully known but it is estimated to be somewhere around 28,000 people. In the words of Ed, "The stench and horror of that place will stay with me for as long as I live, and I'd like to tell you more but it's now buried so deep inside me that it can never come out."

Eventually some justice was done. Johann Eichelsdorfer was tried and summarily executed on May 29, 1946 at Landsberg Prison (which became US War Criminals Prison No. 1), along with 22 other war criminals responsible for Dachau and other satellite camps.

14

"The roaring silence"

Berchtesgaden, Austria, and France – May 4–November 30, 1945

While looking around Miesbach for a suitable billet, Harley Dingman came across a large property with a grand piano. An accomplished pianist, Harley sat down and began playing a haunting romantic melody by German composer Robert Schumann. "As my fingers moved over the keys I magically lost all sense of the surroundings. Bizarrely, a small audience of older people began to gather behind me. As the last note tapered away I turned around and smiled as the crowd dispersed without uttering a single word."

"If we found a nice place to stay I simply evicted the owners," recalls Ed Shames. "Often when entering a village I'd go straight to the Burgermeister with a demand that all weapons be brought in for disposal. Anyone found to be hiding anything after the amnesty would be severely dealt with. It was amazing what would turn up alongside the regular rifles and pistols, such as the most beautiful antique hunting rifles and swords. Of course we helped ourselves to many of these items before handing the rest over to the authorities. My particular interest was the 9mm Luger but each one I acquired had to be in pristine condition."

Col Sink and the regimental combat team were still in Miesbach when alerted for the move toward Obersalzberg and the Austrian border. The authorities had informed Gen Taylor that they were expecting the Waffen-SS to make a last stand around Hitler's Alpine resort at Berchtesgaden.

Commander of Heeresgruppe Süd (German Army Group South, which became known as Heeresgruppe Ostmark) Generaloberst Lothar Rendulic wanted to fight on to the end but Feldmarschall Albert Kesselring, who had taken over from Gerd von Runstedt as Commander-in-Chief West on March 9, denied the request. Earlier on April 20, Bavarian-born Kesselring was at his HQ in Motzenhofen near Munich when the order came to defend Obersalzberg, and Heeresgruppen C and G immediately began withdrawing to bolster the "Alpine fortress."

Favored by Hitler and his Reich chancellery, Berchtesgaden was a beautiful place centered in the middle of three jagged massifs. At 6,017ft, Kehlstein Mountain overlooked Berchtesgaden from the east, while the much lower features of Baderlehenkopf and Kälberstein protected the western approaches. The fast-flowing river Ache courses through the eastern edge of town before dividing into the Ramsauer and Königssee valleys.

Dominated by the awe-inspiring twin peaks of Watzmann Mountain (8,901ft), the nearby spa resort of Königssee nestles alongside a huge lake whose crystal clear waters are among the deepest in Germany. Set in the center of the lake, next door to the church of Sankt Bartholmä, was a hunting lodge owned by Hitler, who often sailed on Lake Königssee while his girlfriend Eva Braun sunbathed naked on the shore.

The writing was on the wall when the Allies easily overran what should have been the most "heavily defended" parts of southern Bavaria. After transferring his HQ to Alm, Kesselring, with permission from Grossadmiral Karl Dönitz (appointed by Hitler as his successor), sent a notice of possible surrender to SHAEF HQ. Despite his obvious foresight, 60-year-old Kesselring was no politician and struggled to organize public security with the regional *Gauleiters* (branch leaders personally selected by the Führer). At a conference in Königssee, those *Gauleiters* who bothered to attend refused to accept the situation and naively demanded that the German Army continue to fight "guerrilla style" so that the Nazi Party could maintain some sort of civil order. Propaganda Minister Joseph Goebbels called these guerrilla fighters "Werewolves," who in the event never really materialized as most of the German troops now flooding into the Alps simply wanted to surrender and receive a hot meal.

As overall commander, Kesselring insisted that there would be no "Fight to the Death." To avoid looting, he ordered the *Gauleiters* to hand over any surplus food and clothing to the civilian population. When General der Panzertruppen Hans Röttiger's Heeresgruppe C surrendered on May 2, the Alps were thrown wide open. Two days later negotiations were scheduled to begin at Salzburg. Kesselring sent the commander of 1.Armee, General Hermann Foertsch, and a small delegation to conduct the talks that really amounted to a series of unworkable demands. During this period Feldmarschall Kesselring made his first personal approach to Eisenhower, who declined any dialogue that did not involve the total surrender of all German forces.

Two weeks earlier, northeast of Berlin, 52-year-old Reichsmarschall Hermann Göring had abandoned his beautiful château, "Karinhall," in the Schorfheide Forest. On specific instructions from Göring, Karinhall, along with its recently completed museum wing, was then completely demolished by the Luftwaffe.

Before leaving Karinhall, Göring sent a long telegram to Hitler, who was furious when he read: "In view of your decision to remain in the fortress of Berlin, do you agree that I take over at once the total leadership of the Reich, with full freedom of action at home and abroad as your deputy in accordance with your previous decree? If no reply is received by 10 o'clock tonight, I shall take it for granted that you have lost your freedom of action and will act for the best interests of our country and our people."

Hitler accused Göring of "high treason" and ordered his immediate arrest. After being betrayed by Himmler, Hitler was showing absolutely no mercy to those he felt were deserting him. Even Eva Braun's brother-in-law, Hermann Fegelein (Himmler's Berlin representative), did not escape the firing squad. Unaware of Hitler's less than positive reaction, along with hundreds of other leading Nazis, Göring headed south via Pilsen to Berchtesgaden. Accompanying the Reichsmarschall were his second wife Emmy, seven-year-old daughter Edda, nanny Christa Gormans, personal adjutant Oberst Bernd von Brauchitsch, and a small protection force.

The southern rim of the Bavarian Alps with its front extending toward Switzerland had been heavily fortified during 1943 but never completely finished. The area was garrisoned by SS security forces and mechanized infantry who were under jurisdiction of *Gauleiter* Franz Hofer at Innsbruck.

Upon reaching the Alpine fortress, Göring and his staff were taken into custody by the SS based at Obersalzberg, which had just been bombed by the Royal Air Force. Many buildings were damaged during the raid, including the Berghof (Hitler's house), Göring's holiday home, and the SS caserne. Luckily for Göring, because of the bomb damage the SS were forced to move them further south into Austria. The Reichsmarschall's good fortune continued when he was rescued en route by a small contingent of loyal troops belonging to the Luftwaffe. On April 30, when news of Hitler's suicide reached Bavaria, Göring once again tried to take control of what was left of the Third Reich and sought to negotiate with Gen Eisenhower and his immediate subordinate Gen Jacob Devers (CO of the US 6th Army Group).

An die allen Kameraden – Berchtesgaden, May 4–10, 1945

The road from Munich was one of the first autobahns built by the Nazis when they came to power. The motorway also connected Berlin and Nuremberg to Salzburg and Linz in Austria. On the morning of May 4, 1945, Harley Dingman and the 506th PIR were traveling east on the highway toward Siegsdorf behind the US 3rd ID. Civilian wood-burning steam vehicles and an assortment of jeeps and trucks made up the ragtag convoy. DUKWs were also available in case the regiment came upon any serious water obstacles. Dingman recalls: "We were driving a heavily armored, 16-cylinder Mercedes touring car that used more oil than fuel! Everyone was issued with 'strip maps' – a simple planner showing salient features along the route. As we all knew where we were going the journey turned into a bit of a free-for-all! Driving down the autobahn I recall passing a number of dense wooded areas that had been carved out to create dozens of individual makeshift hangars for the Luftwaffe. Even the concrete hard standings that led out onto the road had been painted green. The natural canopy was left in place, leaving a cleared area underneath for the planes." Reaching Siegsdorf the battle group ran into the back of a massive traffic jam, causing Col Patch to send troops from G and I companies southeast along a secondary road.

Attached to the 3rd ID was French Division Blindée, commanded by Philip Leclerc de Hauteclocque. Easily recognizable by its distinctive "Cross of Lorraine" insignia, a detachment designated Combat Command V was already in front of the 3rd Bn advance party, leaving a trail of havoc behind it. Ironically, Sgt Manny Barrios and his squad decanted from their comfortable DUKW into several smaller vehicles before heading off toward Inzell, along with a squad of engineers carrying collapsible boats.

Twenty-five miles from Berchtesgaden, around 1030hrs, they came upon the rear elements of the French armored force at the river Rote Traun where the bridge had been recently demolished. As the 2nd French Armored Division had no bridging equipment, their tanks were stranded, although some had already made it across before the bridge was blown. "To be honest, I wasn't happy about the detail to begin with, but what can you do?" recalls Barrios. "After reporting our location and situation via radio to battalion we were told to sit tight and await further instructions." It is somewhat unclear what happened next but it seems likely that a squad from 3 Ptn G Co was sent back to scout an alternative route in from the west. Using a liberated fire engine, Sgt William Bowen was in charge of the G Co team, who included privates Macrae Barnson (who had sweet-talked his way out of jail for his actions at Bastogne), Harry Barker, and Bob Izumi.

Back at Inzell, Sgt Barrios was listening to the French soldiers engaging enemy forces somewhere across the river when the order came for them to advance and form a defensive perimeter on the opposite bank. "I had to calm the lads down who were moaning that we were all gonna get killed! Once we'd paddled over, I set up our arcs and waited. That night, not long after my watch began, I heard French voices and hollered out the password ['Double Good' – 'Tonight']. Suddenly a single shot rang out, followed by fleeing footsteps. My guys came rushing over and we went to investigate and found a German soldier lying on the ground with his brains blown out. Go figure that one!"

Early the following morning (May 5), the main body arrived. "It took a while for the engineers to move up the line, and ironically the heavy bridging equipment they were using overbalanced and toppled into the river," recalls Harley Dingman. At that point Sink decided it would be quicker to use the DUKWs and ordered 3rd Bn to prepare for the crossing. "Everyone was feeling apprehensive at this stage because the French had encountered small pockets of fanatical Hitler Youth who didn't want to surrender," continues Dingman. Because of the increasing delays Col Sink established a temporary CP and sent his XO, Robert Strayer (Charlie Chase was still working at Division), with 1st and 2nd battalions back to the autobahn with the intention of reaching Berchtesgaden via Bad Reichenhall – a huge detour of over 50 miles.

Dingman and his team, plus elements of Co HQ and B Battery 321st GFA, also went along with them. Tanks and trucks from both divisions were now clogging every arterial road. 2nd Bn had not been on the autobahn long before they encountered 3rd ID, who had been held up for several hours at another sabotaged bridge. "During this phase we seemed to be under constant sniper fire," recalls Ray Nagell from B Battery.

Earlier the previous afternoon (May 4) a few miles northwest of Berchtesgaden, Karl Jakob, Obersalzberg's *Landrat*, or District Commissioner, had been brokering a "peaceful" surrender at Winkl with elements of 3rd ID, who had been traveling south from Bischofswiesen. Before leaving Berchtesgaden, Jakob and his staff burned many files and distributed a leaflet urging all locals to stay calm and place white flags outside their homes.

Accompanied by district attorney Dr Müller, Jakob's vehicle was stopped by a Sherman tank that happened to contain Col John Heintges (CO 7th IR) who, contrary to his original mission of capturing Salzburg, ordered Jakob and Müller to return with him to Berchtesgaden. Thus 7th IR became the first Allied unit to enter the town. Heintges came in from the north and drove straight to Schlossplatz (the main square) and parked opposite the unusual Gothic twin spires of Sankt Peter und Johannes der Täufer – the abbey of St Peter and St John the Baptist.

Here, in the shadow of the abbey and the World War I memorial, Col Heintges began negotiations for the full and unconditional surrender of the "Alpine" prize. East of the river Ache at Obersalzberg, before Heintges arrived, the SS set fire to what remained of the Berghof.

Situated 1½ miles east of Berchtesgaden, the area of Obersalzberg was the nucleus of Hitler's mountain hideaway. On the left of the steep road leading to Hitler's home was the Gutshof – built as the blueprint for all future German farms. Close by were the beautiful properties belonging to Göring and several Cabinet ministers (known as *Reichleiters*), including Martin Bormann – all of which had been badly damaged during the earlier RAF raid.

By early evening, the recon group led by Sgt Bowen in his firetruck had crossed into Austria and were now heading northeast from Lofer back toward the Ramsauer valley. Ascending the steep, single-track road, the convoy was forced to stop at Stockklaus, where the bridge over the river Klausbach had been destroyed. Capt Cann ordered Bowen by radio to take advantage of the situation, establish a checkpoint, and settle in for the night.

Late the following day a message came through: "Effective immediately all troops will stand fast on present positions. German Army Group G in this sector has surrendered. No firing on Germans unless fired upon. Notify French units in the vicinity. Full details to be broadcast, will be issued by SHAEF."

Despite the good news, Bowen continued with his duties and posted guards as per Cann's instructions. While Bowen was sweeping the area with Barnson and Barker they bumped into a nervous German sentry who luckily did not open fire. The enemy soldier marched the three men at bayonet point to a nearby farmhouse full of SS troops, including several senior officers. Looking around, Bowen reasoned this was more than a company or battalion CP. It took a while but Barnson, who spoke a little German, managed to convince the soldiers that a ceasefire had been declared and there was no need for any further violence. Amazingly, the Germans agreed that Barnson could speak to their commander but Bowen and Barker would have to stay behind as "collateral."

A few minutes later, Barnson was standing in front of Generalleutnant Theodor Tolsdorff, the commanding officer of the 82.Armeekorps. Highly decorated and still only 35 years old, Tolsdorff had previously been in charge of 340.Volksgrenadier-Division, who fought against the 506th during the later stages of the Battle of the Bulge. The korps were a newly assembled "assault force" attached to Heeresgruppe G, under overall command of General der Infanterie Friedrich Schulz. Tolsdorff had around 1,200 men at his disposal collected from various divisions. After an hour or so of discussion, Tolsdorff was more than happy to surrender but only to someone of equal rank. Bowen remained behind, while Barker and Barnson went back to the checkpoint and called Derwood Cann, who immediately sent their platoon commander, 1st Lt Perrin Walker, down to take control.

To expedite things, Walker procured a horse from a local farm and headed across the mountain to Stockklaus while official arrangements were being made to take Tolsdorff's surrender.

"Early the following morning (May 6) I was forced to fire a warning shot into the air when a man approached our position on horseback," recalls Bob Izumi. "It was only when the guy came closer that I realized it was 1st Lt Walker! When Capt Cann found out what I'd done, he thought it was hilarious and congratulated me for sticking to his orders."

Walker met with Tolsdorff and informed him that Capt Doughty would be along as soon as possible with an interpreter from the divisional IPW team to take him back to Berchtesgaden for a meeting with Col Sink. At the time (1030hrs), Sink and the regimental combat team (with E Co as spearhead) had only just arrived in Berchtesgaden behind 3rd ID from Bad Reichenhall. Col Sink quickly established his CP at the Hotel Geiger where a squad from 1 Ptn F Co were allocated as perimeter guard. The 60mm mortar squad were assigned to secure a tunnel situated less than half a mile northeast of the railway station. Hidden inside the 250-yard-long passageway was the train containing part of Hermann Göring's art collection sent on ahead before he left Karinhall in April. 1 Ptn leader Ben Stapelfeld was also instructed by Sink to post squads at a nearby ammunition dump and set up a POW enclosure in a building overlooking the neck of the Ramsauer valley.

Harley Dingman and his team, who had been traveling with the main body, drove around looking for a suitable place for the battalion CP. This part of Berchtesgaden seemed deserted as Dingman reached a street called Nonntal. Here he found a four-storey hotel that seemed perfect for Col Patch's needs, but there was just one small problem – the enormous red swastika banner hanging above the entrance.

"I told the boys they could have the flag if they could get it down," Dingman recalls. "After much effort and much to my surprise, the men presented it to me as a token of their appreciation. Tears rolled down my face as the guys started to thank me for everything I'd done for them – especially Chester Molawa, who still couldn't believe that after all this time he was now a technical corporal!"

Inside the building (which no longer exists) on the ground floor was what appeared to be a locked strong room. Thinking there might be loot inside, Dingman asked Molawa if he could pick the lock. "Yep, sir, of course, but I don't want you guys watching while I do it." Harley and the boys left Chester to get on with opening the incredibly large mechanism. A minute or so later the door was open, revealing hundreds of bottles of the finest French Cognac, Champagne, and wine. Despite being a non-drinker, Dingman turned to his men and laughed, "Well that oughta get the party started fellas!"

Earlier that morning 1st Squad from F Co was sent to Obersalzberg to guard the properties belonging to Reichsmarschall Göring and his chief liaison officer, General der Flieger Karl Bodenschatz. Badly burned during the failed assassination attempt against Hitler, Bodenschatz had been arrested the previous day while recuperating in the military hospital at Bad Reichenhall. While Ben Stapelfeld's men were clearing Bodenschatz' HQ they came across the body of General der Flieger Gustave Kastner-Kirdorf. The 64-year-old senior Luftwaffe staff officer had shot himself in the head before the French arrived.

No turning back – the Ramsauer valley

The day before, on May 5, after successfully crossing the river at Inzell, H Co, who had been designated as Battalion Assault Group, drove ahead in their DUKWs to clear the way along the Ramsauer valley.

The area was surrounded on both sides by tall, densely forested mountains, covered by a carpet of snow on the upper slopes and summits. Along the route, patrols were sent out to clear re-entrants and isolated buildings, as Hank DiCarlo recalls: "I was carrying a BAR when we noticed someone furtively sneaking into a house about 70 yards away, and despite calling for him to come out we received no reply. Bracing the heavy gun on a wall I fired a short burst through the windows, and about 20 German soldiers appeared with hands raised. Those Krauts were damned lucky that it was us and not the French who took their surrender."

Further up the road, Hank and Sgt Luther Myers were ordered to take their respective squads and investigate several houses that formed the tiny settlement of Weisbach, as Hank remembers: "After leaving the road we fired a few token shots at the buildings and several German soldiers emerged under a white bed sheet of truce." While herding the prisoners back toward the company, the men came under artillery fire from the slopes above. DiCarlo recalls:

> Pfc Claude Rankin and Wilber Johnson were in front of me as we double-timed behind the Germans. Another shell came screaming in over our heads and exploded close to Rankin, who carried on running for a few steps before falling to the floor. Incredibly, a large piece of shrapnel had ripped through Claude's upper body. I could see right through Rankin's torso to the German soldier in front who also went sprawling to the ground dead. I still cannot believe something as senseless as this actually happened! Especially when we learned shortly afterwards [1750hrs] that Army Group G had surrendered and there was now a ceasefire in place! Tragically, at the time Claude had family problems back home and was waiting for compassionate leave.

The shelling also killed Pvt Nick Kozoroski and seriously wounded Pvt Bob Dunning (both from HQ Co), who had to be carried back down the road for emergency treatment to his stomach. Rankin and Kozoroski were to be the last combat casualties suffered by the 506th PIR in World War II.

The German artillery was quickly located and identified as a pair of 88mm antiaircraft guns. B Battery, from 321st GFA, who had been attached to the battalion, fired a barrage of phosphorous rounds at the 88s. Several four-man patrols from H Co were then sent up the hill to flank and neutralize the guns from behind. It transpired that the "men" crewing the 88s were in fact boy soldiers from the Hitler Youth, as Ralph Bennett recalls: "They were easily disarmed when our guys overran their positions, forcing the kids to give up. I saw a few of them afterwards, when they had reverted from 'deadly killers' back to being children." Members of G Co, including Jim Martin, were also part of the hunter force and arrived on scene about 10 minutes after the guns had been captured.

"Later, while continuing toward Berchtesgaden," recalls Ralph, "we stopped one young fellow about 12 years old to find out what he was doing. The boy had been one of the Hitler Youth kids up on the hill and after being processed and given a pass by one of the other groups had then been told to go home. All he could tell us was that he was going to see his mom. Sgt Bob Hoffman [who was later assigned to Regimental HQ as an interpreter] asked where his mother lived. The teenager named a town nearly 200 miles away! A little astonished by the kid's response, Hoffman replied, 'How on earth do you think you are gonna get there?' The young German arrogantly blurted out, 'I don't know, but I'll walk every damn step of the way if I have to!' With that, I swung around shouting 'Raus' and planted my boot firmly up the kid's arse to help him on his way!"

After the 88s were silenced, the battalion was held up by another blown bridge 4 miles further along the road at Unterjettenberg. Jim Martin remembers seeing three Shermans that had been abandoned by the French after becoming stuck while trying to ford the boulder-strewn river further downstream. At this point the men de-trucked, scrambled across the rubble, and continued on foot.

Advancing uphill, 3/506 passed the beautiful 15th-century church of St-Sebastian at Ramsau. From here the road crosses back and forth over the river Ache as the awesome valley ascends toward the railway station on the southwestern edge of Berchtesgaden. With 2 Ptn G Co on point the troopers walked the last 6 miles, arriving late in the evening of May 5. "There were only a few civilians in town when we finally got there," recalls Ralph Bennett. "However, we could clearly see the damage caused by the French, who had driven their Shermans through the front walls of several buildings."

By then the French had moved across the Ache and were looting Obersalzberg. Execution squads brought a number of SS and regular soldiers down to the river before cutting their throats and throwing the bodies into the clear blue mountain water. Most of the dead were eventually recovered and buried in a communal grave at the town's cemetery.

"The 101st turned a blind eye to most of this," recalls Jim Martin, "but things really started to get out of hand when we heard that one of the French soldiers had raped a ten-year-old girl. Col Sink wasn't going to stand for this and, as I understand it, issued an ultimatum to the French commander that if his forces did not leave Obersalzberg immediately, then the 506th would commence combat operations against them … and thank goodness they listened."

The battalion was divided up and billeted in various buildings around the resort. "I was based at the Berchtesgadener Hof Hotel [on the southwestern edge of town along Haniel Strasse] where everything was immaculate, even the pure white bed sheets," recalls Bennett. "The boys took virtually every piece of expensive china and silverware from the beautifully appointed wood-paneled dining area."

The hotel was well known for the view across the mountains from its magnificent rear terrace and over the years had seen an impressive array of guests, including the Duke and Duchess of Windsor (who visited on October 27, 1937), Neville Chamberlain, and David Lloyd George, as well as many leading figures in the German government and military. Even Eva Braun had lived here with Hitler's younger sister, Paula Wolff, while the Berghof was being refurbished.

"I don't recall seeing any enemy soldiers or civilians; the place seemed totally deserted," remembers Lou Vecchi. "A number of our guys from the outfit, including my platoon, were shown to the Berchtesgadener Hof. As platoon sergeant it was my job to designate the rooms to the men. The room I was sharing with Sgt Bob Martin must have once belonged to a German officer because we found a beautiful pair of leather boots that fitted me perfectly, so I kept them as a souvenir."

"The residents of a plush two-storey apartment block in the main street were evicted and 2 Ptn moved in," recalls Jim Martin. "Painted either end of the building's outside walls were the most beautiful murals depicting local scenery. We were living three or four guys to each apartment, and the previous owners of my quarters had left behind dozens of glass photographic plates showing local Nazi buildings such as the SS barracks at Obersalzberg."

First lieutenants Lewis Sutfin (HQ Co 81mm) and Clark Heggeness (H Co) rejoined the battalion in late April 1945. Clark recalls: "After the 506th occupied Berchtesgaden, sovereignty and control transferred to us. Immediately afterwards a curfew was enforced, schools were closed, and all public amenities such as post, bus, and rail services stopped, along with daily newspapers."

Bob Harwick, who had recently returned to active duty with the 501st PIR, wrote the following letter to his wife Eileen and daughter Bobbie on notepaper previously belonging to Adolf Hitler: "This morning at one minute past midnight the War [in Europe] came to an end. I send you all my love and hope with all my heart to be with you once again. With Victory I am suddenly very tired, very conscious of missing friends and very anxious to be home."

On May 7, 1945, the German Army surrendered and the first VE Day of sorts was quietly celebrated. Officially, at 0230hrs, representing Karl Dönitz, Generaloberst Alfred Jodl (chief of operations of the High Command of the German armed forces) surrendered to Gen Eisenhower at his temporary HQ in a small schoolhouse at Reims.

"To think that I had a very good chance of getting home alive was almost more than I could believe," recalls Harold Stedman. "When we heard the announcement, I climbed the nearby hill by myself and cried for an hour until my stomach hurt and the tears ran dry."

After some intense negotiations Generalleutnant Tolsdorff and a small party of senior officers from 82.Armeekorps arrived at Hotel Geiger to formally sign a surrender deal with Col Sink. The next day Sink received this short note from Maxwell Taylor: "A German colonel has arrived at the HQ of 36th Infantry Division from Hermann Göring. The colonel has a letter that he is taking to generals Devers and Eisenhower. He states that both Göring and Kesselring are present with a small staff just north of Bruck – go get them." Patrols were sent and roadblocks established but Sink was too late as BrigGen Robert Stack (deputy commander of 36th ID) was already one step ahead.

Hermann Göring had gone to ground in Austria and sent his adjutant, Bernd von Brauchitsch, to discuss possible surrender terms with elements of the 36th ID who escorted him to the SS Cavalry Center at Schloss Fischhorn (Fischhorn Castle) in Bruck. After several frantic telephone calls, Von Brauchitsch was able to locate Göring and his convoy, who were waiting along the roadside at a small village close to Bruck.

Göring, his family, and around 75 personnel (including the Luftwaffe soldiers who had previously rescued them) surrendered at this location to BrigGen Stack on May 7. A reconnaissance company from 636th TD Bn was then sent ahead to Fischhorn, and around 2330hrs the first dozen or so vehicles led by Stack arrived at the castle. Göring was riding in a large Mercedes containing his wife, daughter, Von Brauchitsch, and nanny Christa Gormans – who were all allocated rooms on the second floor and given a hearty meal.

Bizarrely, the Luftwaffe troops who had rescued Göring were placed on guard duty around the building alongside the GIs from the 636th and a small contingent of SS cavalrymen who were already stationed there. Also residing at the castle was the ex-commander of the 37.SS-Freiwilligen-Kavallerie-Division (Volunteer Cavalry Division) Lützow, SS-Standartenführer Waldemar Fegelein (whose brother Hermann had been executed by Hitler on April 28), and Reich chancellery chief Philipp Bouhler (who happened to be "No. 12" on the Allies' "Most Wanted List") along with his wife Helene. The following day Gen Stack sent Göring, Von Brauchitsch, General Franz Ritter von Epp (Governor of Bavaria), Fegelein, and his adjutant to 42nd ID HQ at Kitzbühel before they were flown to Seventh Army HQ in Augsburg.

Back at Berchtesgaden, teams were sent out to look for any facilities that might contain weapons and ammunition. Hank DiCarlo remembers finding plenty of equipment but no "Werewolves." "One trick we learned was to spray any suspicious areas with water, because this often showed if the ground had been disturbed. The civilian population made a quantum leap, as many former military men and government officials tried to pass themselves off as innocent bystanders."

S/Sgt George Allen was one of the first counterintelligence specialists from regiment to start work in the area. He recalls:

> Myself and Eric Albrecht found three substantial archives containing reports of Hitler's High Command meetings and many other important pieces of information. Eric and I were quickly involved in the arrest of two senior members of the Forced Labor Organization, Dr Robert Ley and Fritz Sauckel. Others we apprehended included Hitler's sister Paula Wolff, who gave her address as Alpenwirtschaft Vorderorand, Gemeinde Königsee, Kreis Berchtesgaden, and Hitler's former butler, Albert Kannenberg.
>
> We also picked up SS-Obersturmbannführer Erich Kempka, who had served as Hitler's chauffer since 1934 and provided us with some previously unknown details about Hitler's death. Amidst all this my ex-boss, M/Sgt Charles Wahler, happened to bump into me in the street. Wahler always called me "Sport" or "Chief" because he couldn't pronounce the soft "G" in George and went on to say in his heavy Austrian accent, "Chief, you chust got yourself five points."

At the core of the US Army Demobilization Plan was the point system. Points were awarded for the number of years and months spent overseas, medals, commendations, campaign battle stars, and other factors such as Purple Hearts, Presidential Unit Citation, and even number of children. The magic figure for being sent home was 85 points. "At that moment," continues Allen, "I didn't fully comprehend what Wahler was talking about. He then explained that our IPW detachment had been awarded a Bronze Star, to be given to the person who most deserved it. They all agreed it should be me because of what I'd done for the German prisoners back in Bastogne! This award meant that potentially I now had 90 points and could be home before Christmas, which was unbelievable."

Due to constantly changing attachments the regiment struggled to get its correct ration allotments from either Seventh or Third armies. Consequently, Harley Dingman was involved in several hunting parties scouring the surrounding high ground for animals such as goats and sheep. "We even had beaters to flush out wild birds and groups catching fish."

"Officially we hunted and ate anything that would keep our troops fed except for larger animals like cows," Dingman continues. "It was brought to my attention that cattle were being killed, but as most of the men didn't know how to process the carcasses properly they started getting sick. We liberated a duplicating machine from the district commissioner's office and I ran off a bulletin sheet with instructions on how to butcher and cure bovine meat before consumption – with the proviso that the killing of cows was still strictly against regimental policy and anyone caught would face a heavy penalty." Bob Izumi recalls, "We were so hungry that I shot a cow and Sgt Bob Parks butchered it for the guys to cook and eat. Nobody told Captain Cann who was most upset when he was forced to pay for the missing animal."

Pfc Ray Skully returned to G Co around this time after being wounded in Holland and was put on light duties in the mess hall. "The guys liberated dozens of bottles of Cognac from Göring's cellar and stored them under my bed. The window to my room on the ground floor was always open, giving the boys easy access to the booze which was then decanted into Marmite containers so the officers wouldn't find it!" It was rumored that Göring's cellar contained over 10,000 bottles of vintage wine and spirits, although only a fraction was pilfered before F Co placed the store under permanent guard.

2 Ptn G Co patrolled Kälberstein and Lockstein mountains, looking for any sign of "Werewolf" activity but there was none. "We just hiked around enjoying ourselves and the wonderful scenery," recalls Jim Martin. "Later Captain Cann told me off for shooting some German

girls in the behind with a .177 air rifle from the upstairs window of our apartment. The girls had been fraternizing and cheering small groups of German soldiers coming in to surrender."

"We spent less than a week at Berchtesgaden, and during that time security was pretty slack (no reveille or formations), and as long as we told our platoon sergeant where we were going you could do pretty much what you liked," Martin continues. "There was a lot of looting, and vehicle theft began to get out of hand. When guys started getting injured in road traffic accidents the division started to clamp down. There was a scheme set up to vet some of the DPs (displaced persons), mainly women, as domestic staff for our officers who often shared the same house." The refugees had to wear black armbands about 4in wide with the letters "DP" stenciled in white. "We began to see posters pinned up by some women DPs looking for a man who could provide food and shelter in exchange for work and sometimes other more personal services. It wasn't unheard of for some German men to have five women living with them. I recall seeing one guy in particular sitting in a cart being drawn by a number of women, just like they were pack mules."

Checkpoint "KESSELRING"

Ed Shames and the regimental patrols platoon had been amongst those tasked to find Göring along the Austrian border. "We had been sent south by Maj Clarence Hester to establish roadblocks around Saalfelden. There were several incidents when drivers refused to stop, forcing us to open fire, killing the occupants. I was given photographs of wanted Nazis, both military and governmental officials, which made it easier for us to identify anyone trying to flee from the country."

Sgt Rod Strohl stopped a small convoy heading north and was astonished to discover it contained Feldmarschall Kesselring. He recalls: "At that point in time, to my knowledge, Kesselring and his entourage were the only command who still hadn't officially capitulated."

Previously, leaving his chief of staff at Alm, Kesselring had decided to transfer himself, along with a reduced HQ, to a train (that had belonged to Heinrich Himmler) now standing empty in a siding at Saalfelden station. From here Kesselring appointed staff member Generaloberst der Waffen-SS Paul Hausser (ex-commander of Heeresgruppe G) to oversee the efficient surrender of all SS troops in the area.

What happened between the Feldmarschall arriving at the train and his small convoy running into 3 Ptn is unclear. However, Ed Shames picks up the story from his perspective:

> At that moment I was at one of our other vehicle checkpoints (VCPs) with Roy Gates when the call came in for me to get over to Strohl's VCP. When I arrived there were three vehicles – two sedans and a saloon in which Kesselring had been traveling. All told there were about 16 people who made up the Feldmarschall's immediate staff. For what it was worth, Kesselring was a very big fish for us to catch. When I approached, he smiled and confirmed in very good English exactly who he was. Before I arrived there had been a brief argument with Strohl after he demanded the Feldmarschall's sidearm. "Popeye" Wynn was also jumping around wanting to shoot everyone, so we had to calm him down first.
>
> Kesselring turned to me for help. I wasn't going to comply and politely requested that he please remove his pistol, which he refused. Drawing my .45 I pointed it at his head, which seemed to do the trick. Begrudgingly he slid the petite holster from his belt and handed it over. I was surprised to find that the pistol was an unusual 7.82mm semiauto with wooden grips that had been made under license in Czechoslovakia. Placing Strohl in charge, I sent them all back to Berchtesgaden and the rest is history.

The Feldmarschall was taken to Sink's CP at Hotel Geiger before Gen Taylor collected and took him to the Berchtesgadner Hof Hotel. Climbing the steps to the main entrance, Taylor snapped back a salute at the two soldiers guarding the door (both from 1/506), while Kesselring raised his ornate baton in semi-acknowledgment. The Feldmarschall's entourage were then given the best rooms in the house and allocated a chaperone, Lt Brown, a German speaker from Division.

Spoils of war

The 101st handed out several pamphlets to the troops, such as "A short guide to the Bavarian Alps." Despite being told that certain areas of Obersalzberg were out of bounds, many decided no matter what restrictions were in place they could not and would not let the opportunity to visit the Berghof or the Kehlsteinhaus slip through their fingers.

After crossing the bridge over the Ache, there were two granite pillars displaying a banner which read, "*Führer, wir danken dir*" ("Führer, we thank you"). The road from here was called Kehlstein Strasse and was the gateway to Obersalzberg and the northern face of Kehlstein Mountain. The drive up to Obersalzberg was comparatively short but nevertheless convoluted as the road climbed steeply to the ruins of the Berghof and Hotel Züm Turken (previously occupied by the security men from the Reichssicherheitsdienst), passing what remained of Hitler's enormous greenhouse and the shattered SS barracks before turning off toward the famous Kehlsteinhaus or, as it became known by US forces, "The Eagle's Nest."

Designed originally as a private tea and function room for Hitler, the Eagle's Nest was engineered into the tip of Kehlstein Mountain. The views across Berchtesgaden from the Kehlsteinhaus northwest to Baderlehenkopf and Kälberstein were world famous, as was the incredible southern vista down the valley toward Königsee and the Watzmann Massif.

Carved into the mountain directly below the Eagle's Nest was an impressive stone archway. Beyond the bronze entrance doors was a long tunnel leading to a circular domed waiting room where a brass-lined elevator (powered by a U-Boat engine) climbed vertically 407ft to the nest. The complex (staffed by SS troops) consisted of three levels, all serviced by the elevator. Inside the facility were maps, books, pictures, all manner of antique furniture, and a beautifully appointed kitchen.

Ralph Bennett and his best friend Pfc Spencer Phillips were among the first members of 3rd Bn to ride the "golden elevator" up to the Kehlstein house where almost everything worth having had already been stolen by the French. Ralph recounts his experience:

> Spencer and I decided to walk back to the tunnel entrance via the zigzag footpath situated just to the left of the Eagle's Nest. On the way down we came across a dining set all marked with an eagle sitting on a swastika between the initials "A – H." I picked up the solid silver service and was on my way back to Göring's house when we were stopped by a major in a command car who asked, "What have you got there, sergeant?" I told him it was a souvenir but he snapped back, "Nope, that's loot; you know the rules – hand it over!" As Spence and I were sheepishly walking away another officer, a colonel, approached the major and did exactly the same thing. RHIP: Rank Has Its Privileges. No doubt about it.
>
> By way of consolation we came across a Mercedes open touring car that had been pushed down the side of the hill by the French and I assigned some of my people to guard it. The next day, I asked one of the tank recovery guys to retrieve the vehicle. We got it running and drove the Merc around for three or four days changing roadblock guards, etc. until I was ordered to hand it in because apparently the car belonged to Göring… I don't think we'd have got that one home in an envelope even if we tried!

Before leaving for Saalfelden, Ed Shames managed to pick up a bottle of Martell Cognac marked with the Führer's initials: "It was the only thing I took from the Eagle's Nest. We eventually opened the bottle about 16 years later to celebrate my son Steven's Bar Mitzvah. We did, however, liberate a lovely Mercedes touring car from Hitler's garage at the Berghof. The windows were bulletproof and we all took a few potshots with several different caliber weapons but nothing we had could penetrate the glass." The following day guards were placed at the tunnel entrance to the Eagle's Nest with only field grade officers above the rank of major permitted to pass.

Everyone else had to traverse the steep winding path on foot to the top of the mountain. Manny Barrios walked up and took a 144-page book, consisting mainly of photographs, from the library, while Len Goodgal and his buddy Eddie Austin helped themselves to a couple of ceramic dishes complete with lids that didn't actually fit.

The book Manny found was called *Wirvom Alpenkorps* and contained eight signatures underneath this dedication: "*Horrido! Zur Erinnerung – An Die – Allen Kameraden – Im Kriege Marz 1941,*" which translates to "Horrido! For Remembrance – To the – Old Comrades – At War March 1941." "With the exception of the book, I never really went around stealing and never let my squad do it either," recalls Manny. "However, they could purchase items if they were for sale. Most Germans at that time were desperate for money and would sell their sister if the price seemed right."

Located on the slopes below the mountain, Haus Göring was still standing, despite being seriously damaged by the RAF. The three-storey property was situated in the most picturesque part of Obersalzberg below the Berghof. Originally built as a small hunting lodge, the property was a gift in 1933 from the Nazi Party to Göring – who over the next eight years developed it into a large palatial home complete with its own outdoor swimming pool. When 3 Ptn I Co took over guarding the house from F Co, it was obvious that just about everyone who was anyone had been there before.

"'Dopey,' the I Co runner, had previously modified a small tool that could be inserted into almost any lock," recalls Harold Stedman. "I took the 'skeleton key' and made my way upstairs to the master bedroom where I 'forced' one of the dressing tables." Reaching to the back of the drawer, Stedman discovered six silver commemorative coins, all minted in 1913 to commemorate the 300th anniversary of the Romanov Dynasty. The beautifully made tokens depicted the first tsar, Mikhail Fjodorovits, and the last Russian emperor, Nicholas II. Also in the same drawer was a small glass jar containing around 20 uncut diamonds and five rubies.

Shortly after being promoted to first lieutenant, Fred Bahlau was appointed to 1/506 as supply officer. "Although the Berghof had been badly damaged it amazed me that Hitler's fancy toilet and seat was still intact! There was a big feature window that had been completely blown out by the bombing. Just to the right of the main building were the offices belonging to the Führer's personal bodyguard – Leibstandarte SS Adolf Hitler. The Leibstandarte occupied several floors, the first being a food store, second a kitchen area, and the third was stocked with hundreds if not thousands of bottles of wine."

Directly behind the Berghof was the entrance to a 2-mile-long underground tunnel system that not only acted as an emergency HQ for Hitler and his immediate entourage but also connected with Army HQ to the southwest of Obersalzberg. Heavily fortified with machine-gun ports, the main tunnel accessed the bunker system below Zum Türken and the SS barracks before coursing deep under the road to Martin Bormann's private bunker and house in the northeast. The tunnels contained art treasures and other precious objects, and Bahlau's team were tasked with locating and guarding the many entrances. More stolen treasure was discovered in a bunker beneath the Luftwaffe HQ and rest center (today the Hotel Hubertus) along the road running south to Königssee.

Bahlau's men were waiting for an international delegation to arrive, led by Capt Harry Anderson, who had been given the job of cataloging the works of art that had been stored within the tunnels, especially the separate system belonging to Göring himself. "Of course we had a good look around," recalls Fred, "and found a 16th-century classical portrait from Italy lying on the ground with the nose cut out. The people from the commission were not pleased by the damage, but despite a detailed search we failed to locate the missing appendage!"

On May 10, the regiment handed over control to a new governing body and moved with a recon troop from 813th TD Bn to Austria. Once again the idea was to enforce the terms of surrender and help establish a temporary form of military government. Before leaving, 1st Lt Denver Albrecht was re-assigned to G Co and took over 1 Ptn assisted by new boy 2nd Lt Charles "Chaz" Schaefer. After Sink moved out, Gen Taylor relocated his Divisional HQ from Bad Reichenhall to the Berchtesgadener Hof Hotel. As Bob Sink departed for Zell am See he officially handed Albert Kesselring over to Divisonal HQ where he became Taylor's "houseguest." Kesselring and his aide were allowed to move "freely," albeit accompanied by the 101st counterintelligence section. Over the next few days Kesselring was interviewed by the world press and gave several conferences at the hotel and the train in Saalfelden. On May 15, he was taken via Augsberg to a special camp at Mondorf, near Luxembourg, where reluctantly he was forced to hand over his medals and prized Feldmarschall's baton.

SS-Obergruppenführer und General der Waffen-SS Gottlob Berger was also held at the Berchtesgadener Hof. Forty-nine-year-old Berger was Heinrich Himmler's assistant and instrumental in the creation of the SS. Berger was arrested by troops from Seventh Army on May 6, while trying to escape along with 2,000 soldiers and civilians, who included the head of the Reich's chancellery, Dr Hans Lammers, and Himmler's wife Marga and their teenage daughter. Nicknamed "the Almighty Gottlob," Berger was responsible for the forced marches imposed on Allied POWs, which included many 3rd Bn members detailed earlier.

Booty and boxing

Col Sink earmarked the spacious and undamaged property previously belonging to Göring's liaison officer, General der Flieger Karl Bodenschatz, as a training center for the newly re-formed regimental boxing team.

At the time the regimental team, coached by 1st Lt John Kelly from D Co, consisted of Jesus Fernandez, Harry Smith, Moose Analoff, Ken Moore, Macrae Barnson, Charley Hogan, Tony Torries, Bill Bitnoff, Andy Sfrisi, Richie Shinn, and Harold Stedman. Harold recalls:

> The place had been turned over and things scattered everywhere but the furniture was still in place. Most of the cabinet and dresser drawers were locked and Lieutenant Kelly strictly forbade us from opening them. Native American Indian Charley Hogan (from the Blackfoot tribe) was first upstairs and almost immediately a chest of drawers came crashing down outside. "What in God's name are you doing?" I shouted and rushed up the staircase only to find him dragging a bed toward the nearest window. "Jesus Charley – it's a bed, for Christ's sake … you know the kind we haven't slept on for about three months. Put the damn thing back and shut the heck up!"
>
> Later I came across a book of gold coins, several large tankards (all made from solid gold), plus a beautiful hunting rifle and pistol.

The boxing team were kept here in relative isolation, training 10 hours a day and fighting every Friday night at Zell am See where they never lost a match against the 82nd Airborne or the 10th and 11th armored divisions.

Just down the hill from Bodenschatz' HQ was a small artificial lake that ran into the river Lackmühelbach where Harold and the boys fished for trout. As the Berghof was just around the corner, Charley Hogan, Harold, and a few of the others decided to visit, as Harold recalls: "There was nothing really left but Charley managed to take a nice picture of me sitting in a chair overlooking the Alps from Hitler's picture window. We also discovered the tunnel underneath our billet and had just begun to explore when division posted guards and sealed it off but that is another story. A couple of weeks later we left our mountain training camp for Zell am See. Because my contraband weighed so much, before we departed I dug a hole nearby and buried some of the larger items, like the silver tankards and several jewel-encrusted plates. The only thing I took with me were the Russian coins and precious stones, which I put into a sock and secreted down the small of my back."*

The heroes of Purple Heart Lane, Austria, May 11–August 2, 1945

The division sent their resident art expert, Harry Anderson, to interview Frau Emmy Göring who was still in residence at Schloss Fischhorn with her daughter and nanny Christa Gormans. Harry was on the trail of a missing painting by 17th-century Dutch artist Johannes Vermeer called *The Woman Taken in Adultery*.

Although Frau Göring denied any knowledge, surprisingly she handed over six other paintings that had not been on Anderson's radar. As he was leaving, Gormans called Anderson to her room and presented him with the missing Vermeer, saying that it had been a personal gift from Mr Göring. Ironically *The Woman Taken in Adultery* turned out to be a forgery. A few days later, on May 12, Emmy and her daughter were transported to Saalfelden before being sent by train to Berlin, where she was given a 12-month jail sentence. While Emmy was in prison, Göring himself escaped justice by committing suicide in his cell at Nuremberg on October 15, 1946.

Shortly after Frau Göring was sent to Berlin, Fred Bahlau arrived at Fischhorn. At the time the *Schloss* was still cluttered with a variety of art treasures looted by Fegelein and his SS colleagues from Poland and Holland. By coincidence, Fred was billeted in the same suite that had been previously occupied by the Görings. "On opening one of the drawers in the bedroom, I found seven letters from Hermann to Emmy and kept them as souvenirs." While Fred was at Fischhorn around 200 silver, .900-grade fine hammered cups were discovered,

* While serving in Germany with the US Army, Harold Stedman's son Tom returned to Obersalzberg in the early 1980s with a map drawn by his father, only to find that a large parking lot had subsequently been built over the site.

originally designed and produced in Innsbruck, possibly as gifts from Göring although more likely by Fegelein for loyal party members.

After being tasked by Col Chase (who was now also billeted at the castle), Bahlau commissioned a silversmith in Saalbach to customize around 40 of the vessels by adding a pair of silver jump wings before individually engraving the name and campaigns of every surviving officer (including those with battlefield commissions) who had taken part in combat operations with the 506th PIR beginning with Normandy. Each chalice cost 210 marks (then equivalent to $21.00) and was deducted from the recipient's mess bill.

The 321st GFA were separated from the 506th and sent north to the beautiful, ancient baroque city of Salzburg, birthplace of classical composer Mozart. On May 15, Ray Nagell won a "golden ticket" home, recalling: "It was like a dream come true and I knew that was it; I would probably never be coming back. Shortly after leaving Salzburg I was at the back of a convoy filled with other lottery winners when the lead vehicle struck a civilian truck on a mountain road and tumbled over the edge, killing everyone on board. For those of us who witnessed the accident it was a tragedy beyond comprehension."

Being platoon sergeant, Lou Vecchi had already decided to stay on, when Bob Martin won his "golden ticket" back to the States. "I appointed one of the replacements called Miller as 1 Ptn guide. Should've gone for Hank but I knew he wanted to go home. Miller was a real handful and had a great line of bull but when it came to women, he was in a league of his own."

The paratroopers from the 506th were sent to Austria in support of the Third and Seventh armies mission. "Each battalion was allocated a specific sector," recalls Manny Barrios, "which was then subdivided by company. Roadblocks were a key factor to controlling and monitoring all German military and civilian traffic." The VCPs were required to record the license registration, type and make of vehicle, time stopped, and number of occupants, along with direction of travel. Over the occupation period, the 506th apprehended around 50 people wanted for war crimes. "Other than that the German troops either marched in or arrived at our locations by word of mouth. Our job was simple – disarm and direct them to the discharge centers where they could be processed and sent home. My squad rotated with two other teams, one week on, two weeks off."

Initially the regiment was given control of the Southern Area of Operations and deployed along two glorious steep-sided Alpine river valleys located either side of the Kitzbüheler Alps, covering a total patrol footprint of some 430 square miles. North of the Kitzbüheler was the Glemm valley, with its rugged terrain divided by the river Saalach, along which are the villages of Hinterglemm and Saalbach. Crossing south over craggy snow-capped peaks, the mountains drop sharply into the more densely populated Pinzgau region and the Salzach valley. At the mouth of these two valleys is Lake Zeller See and the spa town of Zell am See, where the 13th-century Schloss Fischhorn guards the southern end of the lake at Bruck. The 506th was deployed at Zell am See, Bruck, Kaprun, Uttendorf, Stuhlfelden, Saalfelden, Saalbach, and further east at Lend.

After a short period at Saalfelden, leaving G and I companies in situ, Col Patch moved his CP to Zell am See (where six German military hospitals were also located). Patch established 3rd Bn HQ in the gorgeous five-star Grand Hotel close to Regimental HQ and Col Sink who had his CP at Hotel Zell. The Grand had access to a private "Regimental Beach and Recreation Center" overlooking the lake, complete with rowing boats and a bar selling subsidized local beers. Other facilities included a movie theater offering two films per day and a weekly USO stage show.

Saalbach – home of the free

Being so isolated, H Co organized and maintained its own training regime. Clark Heggeness even posted a radioman overlooking the valley road to warn of any unexpected snap inspections or visitors. 1 Ptn H Co was billeted in a spacious ski lodge at the southern end of Saalbach.

"The second floor was turned over for our accommodation and I had my own room with a proper duvet," recalls Lou Vecchi. "2 and 3 platoons were split between the surrounding hotels and private homes. We had a club area on the ground floor that served as our breakfast, lunch, and recreational room. The buffet-style meals all came from ten-man (10 in 1) ration packs." Hank DiCarlo adds, "The lodge was run by a man in his 30s who purported to be the owner. His wife was a lovely redhead and heavily pregnant, who claimed that her husband had been operating the business throughout the war. We could tell by the way he moved that he'd been a soldier but as they were looking after us so well we never said any more about it."

"For the most part we did our own thing," continues Vecchi. "Some of the guys enjoyed a spot of fishing in a fantastic little trout stream that ran directly behind the lodge."

The men soon began using the ski lift to Kohlmaiskopf to go sightseeing up in the Bayerischer Saalforst mountain region northeast of Saalbach. Vecchi found a pair of skis and tried them out on the lower slopes but could not get the hang of them, although it might have helped if he'd had a proper pair of ski boots!

"Any deer we came across was killed and butchered and the meat distributed evenly with the locals, as food still seemed scarce for all of us," recalls Lou. "It was funny; we weren't allowed to fraternize with the Austrians but we could with DPs." At that time there were around 5,000 DPs living in the area, mainly in the camps set up at Fischhorn or Kaprun (where 2/506 were based). During the latter part of May, a number of DPs, mostly women, had taken up residence in the surrounding towns and villages. "To get over any fraternization issues," continues Lou, "some of our guys would get a handful of armbands from the supply sergeant and have the Austrian girls wear them so that they could date! Before Bob Martin went home we used to visit two girls who lived by themselves and grew their own fruit and vegetables. We would buy blueberries and share them in their kitchen with lashings of fresh cream but that really was as far as it went."

Located on the edge of the "French zone," Saalbach boasts an unusual Catholic church, Heilige Nikolaus und Bartholomäus, situated close to the main square and instantly recognizable by its clock tower topped by an unusual onion-shaped dome. "The officers lived at the northern end of town, beyond our Company Headquarters and we only ever saw them at formations and evening meals," recalls Vecchi. "One day Ralph Bennett was duty NCO and invited me into the CP to have the pick of a bunch of German Luger pistols that had just been handed in. Normally the officers would get first choice on anything like this." Alex Andros, who was now H Co XO recalls: "Guys like Ralph Bennett were so lucky to get through without as much as a scratch. I worked it out that each man who'd served in 3 Ptn from the start and survived had been wounded at least twice."

Mopping up

Most evenings H Co paraded on the grassy area at the top of town before falling out for dinner, which was served in an adjacent building. "For the most part it was my job to collect the hot meals every night before curfew from Bruck, which was about 10 miles away by road," recalls Lou Vecchi. "I had a German driver who always became frustrated if ever we got stuck behind a farm cart because the road wasn't wide enough in most places to overtake. All the SS men picked up in our area were taken to Bruck before being discharged. Most of the battalion rotated through this place at one time or another to guard the road system. The only people who were allowed in or out were either residents or American occupying forces. There was a big five-storey hotel [Gasthof Lukashansl] where the SS officers were kept while waiting to be transported by train to Munich." The hotel, which has over 80 rooms, was built in 1908 and stands at the foot of the Grossglockner, one of the highest mountains in Austria. Vecchi continues his account:

> Sometimes when my guys were on perimeter guard we would watch the two German Wehrmacht lieutenants who were in charge of the

paperwork. I remember one particular day they got very agitated with this SS officer who wasn't doing what he was told.

Most of these SS guys had a woman in tow and behaved like they were on some sort of summer vacation, but in this instance it was way after curfew. A lot of them were sitting out on the hotel balconies with their girlfriends, enjoying the evening sun, but some like the guy in question just wouldn't adhere to curfew. I started getting pissed off with the overall attitude of the people on the balcony, who were jeering, and shouted back at them to move inside. When they wouldn't listen, I instructed one of my guys to fire a shot into the doorway leading from the nearest balcony, which really put the fear of Christ up them. I mean, we'd not long been fighting these damn people, and to see them sitting around on their loungers really made my blood boil.

Despite being ordered to surrender by Generaloberst der Waffen-SS Paul Hausser, many SS men absconded, only to be hunted down over the coming weeks under the automatic arrest policy. Patrols were sent northwest from Saalbach up the valley into the mountains to look for any suspicious people or activities. There are over a dozen peaks above Saalbach, the highest being Speilberghorn at around 6,000ft above sea level.

"The renegade SS troopers were hiding in the mountains by day and coming down into the valleys at night to plunder their own people for food," recalls Hank DiCarlo. He continues:

We received a tip concerning the location of one of these bands and Bob Stroud took my squad for the operation. Climbing up through the low cloud base we could see a large two-storey building with a herd of goats grazing outside. No one was anxious to cross the open area leading to the house. We really didn't know if there were enemy soldiers in there or not, so we reconnoitered around and discovered a spring about 35 yards down-slope, out of sight from the farm. Lt Stroud was not in favor of an assault and neither were we, but he figured whoever was in there would need fresh water sooner or later. Around 1700hrs we heard someone approaching from the house. Sure enough, it was an SS man carrying two buckets. As the guy bent over to fill one of the pails, Pvt Frank Parker stepped out and slapped him across the back of the head with the butt of his rifle. Still somewhat dazed, the soldier was defiant and uncooperative when we suggested he return and inform his comrades that they were surrounded – but soon changed his mind when I placed the point of my bayonet at his throat. About 10 minutes later, he came out of the house, hands in the air, accompanied by 22 others. The farmer who owned the property was overjoyed to be rid of his unwelcome guests and tried to give us several enormous wheels of cheese. We thanked him profusely but ever so politely declined!

Initially it would seem that elements of 2 and 3 platoons from G Co along with 2 Ptn H Co were sent to Uttendorf in the Pinzgau valley (6 miles west of Zell am See) to guard a newly constructed enclosure. Overlooking the "facility," high above Uttendorf, was a large hydroelectric power plant in the Stubach valley. The water drained from a natural Alpine reservoir through a 3-mile-long pipe (5ft in diameter) to supply power to a nearby underground factory.

"The factory had previously been producing tracks for tanks," recalls Jim Martin. "Here literally thousands of German troops marched down from the mountains to surrender. Capt Cann requested that any people we dealt with were to be treated respectfully. The Germans who came marching in behind their officers and senior NCOs were ordered to stack their weapons according to type before we searched them. After the men had been moved to their specific holding areas, I decided to take a closer look at a huge pile of pistols. Guarding the weapons was one of our GIs and a German sergeant who, for a packet of cigarettes each, were quite happy to trade me a Luger and P38. I had no idea that every gun had already been accounted for, and the next day Capt Cann searched our accommodation for the missing pistols but they were too well hidden for him to ever find."

A few weeks later another camp was established at Kaprun in order to continue maintenance and development work of a nearby hydroelectric project. The prisoners consisted mainly of troops whose hometowns were now in the Russian occupied zone. Many German soldiers were used to restore communication and power lines. Engineer and other units rebuilt roads and bridges while prisoner labor was utilized to repair German Army vehicles that were then used by the military government. To facilitate better cohesion, the Germans were organized into two separate commands. Generalleutnant Hermann Ochsner was responsible for the south and General der Kavallerie Siegfried Westphal, the north.

Each Airborne rifle company was given complete control of its own specific *Landkreis*, or area. Shortly after settling in, all vehicles that had been liberated over the last few weeks were recalled due to a fuel shortage experienced by Third Army. Most companies were allowed to keep one vehicle, but many individuals just destroyed what they had rather than letting them go to a higher authority.

Ed Shames, who was now based at a doctor's house in Saalfelden, recalls: "Roy Gates and I weren't going to let anyone else have the pleasure of our 'company car,' so with Roy's help, which I always jokingly said was his only contribution to the war effort, we pushed our 'Berghof Merc' over the edge of the Grossglockner Alpine road south of Bruck and told Sink that it had all been a terrible accident."

"As a gesture of goodwill, the Russians who were occupying another nearby sector sent us four crates, each containing 100 bottles of vodka," recalls Harley Dingman. He continues:

> One crate was offered to each company, but as H Co were now miles away they simply forgot to collect, not that they really cared. Therefore, Capt Walker's allocation was quite literally absorbed by HQ Co. The vodka was very strong and almost instantly we began to have problems with drunkenness. It got so bad that Andy Anderson

> had to alternate the duty roster between "dry" and "wet" days – at least this way only 50 percent of the company was under the influence at any one time! Even then we still had issues. Chester Molawa came into my office and shakily proclaimed he was having difficulty making Maj Anderson's bed! "You idiot, what are you talking about?" Slurring his words, Molawa responded, "I'm sorry, sir, but I just can't seem to get his sheets flattened out." When we got to Andy's room, I had to laugh because he was still comatose in bed after a heavy drinking session the night before!

The division began to construct rifle ranges and introduce a regular training program, which consisted of preliminary marksmanship and practice firing of all squad weapons, PT, marches, orientation, reviews, and close order drill. In the afternoons athletics were stressed with regular inter-company competitions, including basketball and baseball, while most anxiously waited to hear if they had accrued sufficient points in order to go home.

"My platoon was sent to Zell am See for two weeks' R 'n R," recalls Manny Barrios. "We were billeted at an inn next to the Grand Hotel, where the dining area was open 24/7." Here, in the Grand's main restaurant, the regimental orchestra would perform at company parties. A local string quartet played classical music on a regular basis at meal times for officers and senior NCOs. "As I was a non-drinker," continues Barrios:

> I spent a lot of my free time in the local coffee shops with Pfc Lawrence Lane, who was from southern California. Because he was much older and had a long, thin face and nose, we called him "Granny," but he hated the nickname. One time, while walking to the Grand, we started to get peckish and joined what we thought was a chow line but when we got to the door a fat madam was collecting money. At that point we made our excuses and hastily walked away! One evening Granny and I took a rowing boat out on the lake for a midnight cruise. Afterwards,

> walking through the lobby of the hotel, we found Andy Anderson on a couch in a stupor and carried him back to his room and put him to bed.

Shortly afterwards Manny and the guys rotated back to their "day jobs" at the foot of the mountains near Stuhlfelden, as Manny recounts:

> I was in charge of a large warehouse building. My squad was given the job of processing the German soldiers who'd recently surrendered. The main reception room had a number of large tables labeled "pistols," "rifles," "automatic weapons," "knives and bayonets," etc. We had local Austrian women at each table noting the guns that by then had all been made safe and cleared. There were also two Wehrmacht officers working with me who briefed the German troops on what to expect before they handed their weapons over. The ladies meticulously recorded each item, which would then be stored in a specific section out back for collection. All personal effects were also listed before being returned along with a carbon copy of the original. Any live ammunition was picked up by truck and taken away for disposal. Before leaving Austria, I managed to send six German rifles home by regular mail … can you believe that! On my last rotation, the two German officers presented me with a beautiful Luger and a Walther P38 (which was later stolen during my voyage home).

On June 5, the survivors of Normandy, 135 men, held a special party in honor of Col Wolverton in Berchtesgaden at the Eagle's Nest. Around this time many senior NCOs like Oscar Saxvik from G Co were encouraged to apply for Officer Candidate School (OCS). Oscar, who had been hospitalized for three months after Bastogne, was accepted and graduated from OCS before being posted to Germany, where he remained on occupation duty until May 1946.

After spending one month in transit from the United Kingdom, S/Sgt Bob Webb returned to HQ Co on June 21, whereupon he was allocated a 15-man room at a hotel in Saalfelden. At the time, Battalion

HQ and HQ Co had temporarily relocated back to Saalfelden from Zell am See to take over the local Discharge Center.

Capt Harrell assigned Webb to the Discharge Center in Saalfelden. There was also another center located a few miles further north closer to Zell at Maishofen. Both centers were situated close to main railway stations from where most of the German troops were transported out of Austria eastwards through the Pillersee valley. "I was working with a blonde Lithuanian girl who spoke the most perfect English I've ever heard. My job was, from 8am to 7pm, typing up the personal statements and information supplied by the German prisoners coming through our doors."

In total, over a three-month period, nearly 50,000 German troops were discharged through the centers at Saalfelden and Maishofen. "The rhetoric from most of these people made me sick," continues Webb:

> They all seemed to have despised Hitler, didn't want to fight, and had never shot at anyone, anytime or anywhere. To be honest, I actually preferred the Waffen-SS guys, who before giving the Nazi salute often told us to our face that they hated our guts. At least they stuck to their principles and you had to admire them for that! I had Sundays off and after my first week back at work, Leroy Vickers, myself, and two other Texan guys who also happened to be from Leroy's hometown, Silsbee, took a jeep to Obersalzberg. By then everything had gone and the only thing I could find worth keeping was a sheet of Hitler's personal notepaper and a light switch hanging off a wall in the Berghof!

Three weeks later Webb was summoned to Regimental HQ.

> I was asked to chaperone German Colonel Friedrich Laibach, who was to be working for the American military government. I was given permission to book a double room at a downtown hotel, which was to be our billet for the next month.

> During the day we were both based in the same building and after work we'd walk back to the hotel. I got to know 55-year-old Laibach well over the next few weeks and learned that he'd been an internationally respected professor of science before and also during the war. We played chess and engaged in deep discussions about politics, the war, and National Socialism, which, in part, he believed did many positive things for Germany! Captain Harrell suggested I should just shoot the son of a bitch if he persisted with this sort of rhetoric but I still kinda liked him all the same.

By the end of July the center at Maishofen was shut down and Saalfelden placed under control of the divisional artillery.

On June 22, the boxers from the 506th were pitched against the more than capable artillery team. The tournament took place in the personnel building at Zell and each bout was over three 2-minute rounds. Andy Anderson was one of the judges. Despite hard-hitting light heavyweight Pvt Macrae Barnson being beaten senseless, Sgt Harold Stedman, Sgt Andy Sfrisi, Pvt Ken Moore, and Pvt Richie Shinn hammered the opposition in their various weight categories to win five to three.

Earlier Gen Taylor had addressed the regiment and said, "We have reached another critical point in our lives and in the life of the division. It is time to face the prospect of future action in the Pacific. This commitment is only probable – not possible." Taylor then went on to say that the 101st would be going home on January 1, 1946, and that everyone would be entitled to a one-month furlough before being re-formed in North Carolina as "general reserve."

> So the future for most of you low point men at this stage is unknown. I cannot see why a top-notch division like this should be allowed to remain in the States but that is entirely up to General MacArthur. Back home this division tops the hearts of the nation and the eagle patch is recognized everywhere. The American civilians haven't relaxed their efforts because of VE Day and everyone is anxious to see Japan crushed.

> Those of you with 85 points or more will be leaving soon for America and I will see you later to say goodbye. I am sure that the men from the 506th would earn the same fine reputation on the shores of Japan that you made on the shores of Normandy and the battlefields of Belgium.

Postponed due to bad weather, the regiment held a special Fourth of July event on July 5. The celebration commenced with a battalion-strength parade through Zell am See followed by a talk from Col Sink and the military governor. The highlight was a free-fall display and a static line parachute drop into the Zeller See by members of Regimental HQ. Aquatic sports were also held, with swimming competitions and boat races, while beer and ice cream was served at the regimental beach. The amazing day came to a close at 2100hrs with a display of confiscated German fireworks over the lake.

During the party at Zell, Hank DiCarlo saw medic Andy Sosnak, who had provided immediate first aid to him in Normandy. "Over a few beers we discussed that first day at the road bridge in great detail and it was clear to me even then that Andy was suffering with some form of PTSD. About 20 years later, I was heartbroken to learn that Andy committed suicide after being diagnosed with cancer."

Sometime around the middle of July, Hank and Sgt Allen Westphal (D Co) were sent to Munich to write and edit a history of the regiment from July 20, 1942 to July 4, 1945. The team, led by Lt Van Horn from Service Co, also included cartoonists Pvt Mike Marquez and Pvt Irving Fitzig. "Throughout May, June, and July the regiment was encouraged to submit anecdotal reports for possible inclusion in the book," recalls Hank. "Allen and I sifted through hundreds of pieces of paper and selected those we thought were most memorable. Apart from our own personal experiences, much of the content had to be based on what we were told had occurred. That being said, the book has my DNA stamped all over it, with little references here and there to 'Airborne Hank' and H Co." The finished product was beautifully printed with fully illustrated maps and photographs and was entitled *The Currahee Scrapbook*. When the job was complete Hank and Allen returned to their respective units and, bizarrely, never saw or spoke to each other again.

Jim Martin recalls his platoon's return to Saalfelden:

> Things began to change… Again we occupied private dwellings, but discipline started to tighten with regular morning parades and inspections. However, there was an upside. One weekend about half a dozen of us visited a nearby German ordnance depot and took as many explosives, flares, and small-arms ammunition as we could carry into the foothills for a party. Before we departed we had our photographs taken with the vast array of shells and mortars. We spent the day firing thousands of rounds, blowing up trees and anything else we could find with *Panzerfausts* and plastic explosive. Capt Cann heard some of the explosions and saw smoke drifting over the valley. Thinking it was some form of enemy activity, Cann sent out a patrol to find out what was going on.
>
> Later that month, our food supplies began to dry up and at one point it became so bad that some like me in G Co were on the point of malnutrition. It didn't take long for us to find out that certain senior members of the QM Department, who were responsible for our rations, were in fact hauling them over the Alps from Innsbruck through the Brenner Pass down into Italy to sell for immense profit on the Black Market!
>
> At the time Capt Cann was trying his best to resolve the situation but when things got worse I decided to go sick. My weight was always on or around 134lb, but when the doctors weighed me I was horrified to see that I was down to 109lb. The medics just couldn't believe that we'd been denied our regular rations and immediately began an inquiry to find out why this had happened. I was admitted to hospital and placed on a seven-day high-protein diet along with some of the other urgent cases. Not long afterwards a colonel from the QM Corps and several senior enlisted men were brought up on corruption charges and sent to prison.

Like many others, Bob Webb was relieved when his second Purple Heart came through, lifting his ASR score to 87 points. "Everyone was wandering around shaking hands and calling each other 'Mister.' No damn South Pacific for us. Now I could get a decent sun tan, go home, get married, and not have to go through all this crap again."

On June 28, around 400 men with a minimum of 85 points were alerted for transfer to the 501st PIR, which was to be the first regiment scheduled for deactivation. At the same time the 501st re-assigned 655 of its low-point troops back to the 506th. Shortly afterwards, the regiment began to decrease its area of operations by about 50 percent and stepped up its training on a variety of individual weapon skills. All units fired preliminary and record courses with their personal weapons. "HQ Co spent two mornings on the ranges, starting at 4am," recalls Bob Webb. "I scored 182 out of 200 with the M1 and qualified as 'expert,' which was no surprise as God knows I'd had enough practice over the last 12 months!"

Before leaving Austria, Col Sink gave the "Old Boys" a moving and heartfelt speech, as Hank DiCarlo recalls: "While we were all gathered in the sunshine he told us of his pride in the 506th and thanked us for what we'd done for our country over the last two years before wishing us goodbye and good luck."

Since June 1944, the division had spent an astonishing 214 days in combat. During that time over 2,000 soldiers had been killed and over 8,000 wounded or missing in action. In total the division was awarded two Congressional Medals of Honor, 47 Distinguished Service Crosses, 516 Silver Stars, and 6,977 Bronze Stars.

France, August 4–November 28, 1945

The regiment received orders on July 31 for a move to Auxerre in the Burgundy region of France. Over the next two days the unit moved out by road and rail and by August 4 was established in the crumbling French garrisons of Joigny and Sens. Meanwhile, most of the high-point enlisted men had been transferred to the 501st and sent further east to a large three-storey barracks at Nancy.

Clark Heggeness and Fred Bahlau were shipped home on the SS *Mariposa* out of Marseille, heading for Boston. Fred was no fool and had three solid wooden containers built to covertly hold all the souvenir handguns collected by 1st Bn. "Every pistol was oiled and individually tagged with the person's name and company. I had a beautiful collection of mint-condition Lugers and P38s. These were the last items to go into the third box before they were all sealed with steel strapping. When we got back to the States, I discovered that one of the boxes had been tampered with at the dockside in France. It was even worse when I found out that it was only my pistols that had been taken. Luckily, I had enough sense to store four more in my footlocker so at least I had something to bring home other than just Frau Göring's letters."

After reaching Nancy, Bob Webb recalls, "We didn't do a damn thing except sit around waiting for our education courses to begin. We were only allowed to take two subjects. I chose 'Arithmetic' plus 'Book-keeping and Accounting' so my time here, although limited, wasn't totally wasted. One of the guys in my room had a radio so we were able to keep up to speed on current events and listen to a bit of music."

Much to Hank DiCarlo's surprise a note arrived informing him that he was to be awarded the Silver Star:

> I didn't really know what I'd done to deserve it, but what the heck. To relieve the boredom, I volunteered for Chute Patrol and was paired up with a regular army MP called Joe Bellante. We patrolled a lot around the local brothels. The most famous was called "Number Nine" and owned by a middle-aged Italian couple, Maria and Arturo Sargento, nicknamed "Mama and Papa." The place was off limits to enlisted men on weekends when it was strictly officers only. I was amused but also confused. Did this mean Uncle Sam was a pimp? Because we both spoke Italian, the Sargentos took an instant shine to the pair of us. Bellante couldn't believe it when they offered us access to all their

> amenities, including food, laundry, and a place to sleep. I didn't want to go home with a sexually transmitted disease so politely refused. But it took me another 15 minutes to convince Joe to do the same. I wasn't popular but I think ultimately it was a smart move.

Shortly after the second atomic bomb was dropped on Nagasaki, the high-point men were transported south by train to a transit camp near Marseille. While his colleagues were heading down the Rhone valley, S/Sgt Ralph Bennett was on his way to England to marry the very special and lovely Miss June Earl, whom he had met prior to Normandy when the 506th was based in Ramsbury.

The wedding took place on August 15, 1945 (the day Japan officially surrendered) at Saint Mary's Parish Church, Church Street, in Slough. As Ralph recalls, "Spencer 'SO' Phillips was supposed to be my Best Man and left France ahead of me, carrying all the wonderful wedding presents I'd purchased in Paris. Spencer presented the gifts to June as if they were from him before disappearing on a seven-day bender and didn't even bother to turn up for the wedding!" June adds, "Due to SO's absence I had to ask one of our neighbors, Arthur Marsdon, to step in. Because it was VJ Day, we all had to sit and listen to a long sermon about the end of the war. The wedding cake looked stunning, but as it was made with powdered eggs the whole thing went off and was inedible!" Although Ralph returned home in November it would be another year of waiting before he and June were reunited in the States.

"At Marseille, the newly built wooden huts seemed reasonably comfortable considering the amount of men who were passing through the port," recalls Jim Martin, who was part of a 50-man group from G Co sent to the 501st. "My group was attached to a motley crew of regular infantry and paraded with them every morning for two weeks until it was my time to go home."

While waiting, Jim met up with his old platoon buddy Sgt Guerdon Walthall, who had since fully recovered from the wounds he had received six months earlier on "Hell Night." "Every morning at formation, we were checked for VD as the army wouldn't let anyone return to the US with a sexually transmitted disease. Walthall was tearing his hair out because he was being treated for an STD and asked me to cover for him at next roll call. I did this for a couple of days until he successfully smuggled himself onto another troopship! Despite the ban on cameras, I always carried an Argus A2 35mm and took photos wherever and whenever possible. During my time at Marseille, I had five rolls of combat film stolen before being able to get them processed. I never knew who took them or where they went but I know that there were many images of Bastogne that would now be regarded as historically important."

While waiting for a ship, Manny Barrios was put in charge of a large post exchange (PX). "They gave me my own private bunk and issued me with a sidearm. It wasn't all work because I still found time to see the Bob Hope USO show before handing over to another NCO and packing my bags for home."

Around September 1, 1945, Manny Barrios, Hank DiCarlo, Teddy Dziepak, Jim Martin, Bob Webb, and dozens of other "high-pointers" from 3rd Bn and the 506th, sailed for America on the troopship SS *Manhattan* and arrived at Camp Shanks, Orangeburg, New York – ironically the exact same place from where the regiment had departed in September 1943.

Shortly after arriving, the men boarded a number of different trains that carried them back to the military camps from where they had originally enlisted. Jim Martin recalls:

> The woman at Fort Indiantown Gap, Pennsylvania, who processed my paperwork, wrote in the "Organization" box at the top, "513th Parachute Infantry." I know this was the unit we were all re-assigned for discharge but personally that wasn't good enough for me. There was no mention of the 506th or the 101st, and when I asked her to change the Unit ID, she tutted loudly and refused. However, I insisted and reluctantly she typed out a new discharge form with "506th Parachute Infantry Regiment" at the top. It may seem a little crazy now but then

> it meant a heck of a lot to me! Two weeks later, I met Donna Verveka, from Newton, Iowa, who was building aircraft in Dayton at Wright Field. We soon started dating and I quickly realized that she was the one. We were married on March 10, 1946 and are still together today (2014).

Bob Webb was honorably discharged on September 22, at Fort Sam Houston, Texas, where he had started out three years earlier. Clark Heggeness was sent to Camp Miles Standish in Massachusetts. "From here they gave me a rail ticket to Camp McCoy, Wisconsin, where I was officially discharged and eventually returned home to my wife in North Dakota." Teddy Dziepak was sent to Fort Dix, New Jersey, for demobilization.

Before going home every soldier was asked to declare any injuries, as Ted recalls: "The military authorities made it totally clear that if we had any medical issues connected to our service then it could possibly delay discharge. Despite having had emersion foot and some shrapnel in my arm, when asked, I said everything was fine. The following year after arthritis began to set in, I visited the VA (Veterans Affairs) hospital in East Orange, New Jersey, who turned me away because I hadn't declared any combat-related injuries on my discharge papers!"

Hank DiCarlo was also demobbed at Fort Dix. "Within two years I was missing the army so much that I re-enlisted into the 82nd Airborne. But when my Dad got sick and died of bowel cancer in 1950, I finally decided to hang up my boots to take care of my mom."

Joigny – the last paycheck

The 101st Airborne Division was now in Supreme Headquarters Reserve and 3rd Bn posted to Joigny. The camps at Joigny, Sens, and Auxerre (Divisional HQ) were situated along the banks of the river Sens and had seen better days.

After two weeks of easy living, Harold Stedman was granted seven days' leave to Switzerland, "where I had crowns put in to replace my missing teeth … all for the princely sum of $35.00! After returning to base, Andy Anderson told me that I would be fighting middleweight for the 506th on August 25, at the ETO Championships. This was a bit of a surprise because I thought they were going to send me home. Anyhow, this was by far the biggest and most important boxing event that I'd ever competed in … and after almost three weeks off, I'd put on around 13lb and just wasn't prepared mentally or physically for the task." Macrae Barnson was also selected for the team as a light heavyweight. Despite his bravery throughout three campaigns, as a persistent AWOL offender Barnson still only had an ASR score of 70. "The competition was spread over three nights," recalls Harold. "Although I was boxing in a heavier class, I won my first two fights. But by the last evening, after knocking James Wagoner (327th GIR) out in the third round, I lost in the final. I was devastated at being beaten by Wagoner and really felt that I'd let Richie Shinn (who won the welterweight championship), the team, and the regiment down. A few days later I got into a fight with a senior NCO who was picking on a young replacement in the chow line. The situation got a little out of hand and I broke the guy's nose and jaw plus a couple of ribs. Disciplinary action followed and I was busted back to private, but luckily Andy Anderson kindly stepped in and saved me from going to jail."

After Japan formerly surrendered the whole dynamic changed and the prospect of the 101st Airborne seeing any further action quickly became a distant memory. "I wasn't guilty about the atomic bombs being dropped on Japan, as the thought of the Pacific was just too horrendous to contemplate," recalls Harley Dingman. Shortly afterwards, Maxwell Taylor handed over command of the division to BrigGen William Gilmore. Taylor returned to the USA, whereupon he became superintendent of the West Point Military Academy, while his faithful assistant, Gerald Higgins, took command of the Parachute School at Fort Benning. William Gilmore stayed in charge for just over a month until being replaced on September 25 by BrigGen Gerald St Clair Mickle. During September, the division announced that every parachute-trained individual had to make one last clean fatigue jump (without equipment) to qualify for "Para Pay." During the next four weeks over 5,000 descents were carried out. "On September 21, it was my turn to jump," recalls Lou Vecchi. "I was earning around $160.00 a month (most of which I sent home to my mother) and needed to stay in date. Many said they weren't prepared to participate because of the risks but they were transferred shortly afterwards to serve out their remaining days in regular infantry outfits. We jumped in company groups onto a grass DZ because it wasn't actually big enough to take a full battalion insertion. I was happy to take part, the weather conditions were fantastic, and it became my 21st and last jump."

"It was all very casual," recalls Harley Dingman. "There were even local vendors selling refreshments and cotton candy [candyfloss]! A delegation from the House of Representatives were sent over to observe the jumping and assess the future of the division. Soon afterwards the powers that be decided to shut down the 101st in favor of the 82nd, but to be honest none of us really gave a damn just as long as we got to go home."

Bob Dunning returned to what now remained of HQ Co after being wounded in the stomach en route to Berchtesgaden. "Jack Manley and I immediately went AWOL and toured around Europe for a while like we were on holiday." When Bob and Jack decided to come back, 1st Lt Chaz Schaefer (who had recently been posted in from G Co) informed them that they would both be on the next shipment home. "We went AWOL again, and when we returned the lieutenant threatened to tie us both to a tree to make sure we didn't disappear again."

Although many of the original players, like Joe Madona and Albert Gray, were now dead, the "Champagne Bowl" football game between the 506th and the 502nd, which had been interrupted by the Battle of the Bulge, was finally rescheduled. This time, as a mark of respect, two matches were played and both regiments declared winners.

By the middle of October the remaining troops began transferring to the 82nd Airborne Division. Bob Izumi was among the first to be re-assigned along with 21 other enlisted men from G Co and sent to Germany, where the 82nd had become the main occupying force in Berlin.

The 508th PIR were selected to act as security for SHAEF HQ now based in the IG Farben HQ at Frankfurt. On June 10, the 508th arrived and requisitioned apartments and houses in the suburb of Heddernheim. Izumi was sent to 2nd Bn, whose "Occupation Mission" was to patrol the towns of Oberusel, Bad Homburg, and Königstein. "I was assigned to F Co in Bad Homburg," recalls Izumi. "Before leaving Europe, we stood guard during a visit from Eisenhower and several other dignitaries, such as Patton and Gen Joseph T. McNarney, CO Mediterranean Theater of Operations."

Back in the USA, two vehicles that had once been part of the fleet belonging to Adolf Hitler and Hermann Göring went on tour as part of the US Treasury Department's effort to raise money for a victory loan. Seven men, including two officers from the 506th, were sent home to take part in the tour, including S/Sgt Charlie Maggio from 3 Ptn G Co and S/Sgt "Red" Falvey from 2/506, who had been wounded on January 13, in the woods above Foy.

Despite now having the correct number of points, Harley Dingman was held back and ordered to organize the formal Honor Company for a big parade on November 7, to mark the end of the 506th PIR. "Of course I had no idea how this should be carried out nor did anyone else, but Andy Anderson handed me a manual 4in thick and told me to get on with it. The training and rehearsals took about two weeks but everything went smoothly on the day and I must say the drill and the men looked amazing."

The divisional G3, Col Harry Kinnard, wrote the last bulletin issued by the 101st Airborne, then commanded by BrigGen Stuart Cutler. "To those of you left to read this – do not dwell on the disintegration of our great Unit, but rather be proud that you are of the 'Old Guard' of the greatest Division ever to fight for our Country. Carry with you the memory of its greatness wherever you may go, being always assured of respect when you say, 'I served with the 101st.'"

"Before Ralph Bennett went back to the UK, he offered me his place at Officer Candidate School but I wasn't interested," recalls Lou Vecchi, "I just wanted to get home." By early October, Lou was transferred along with several thousand others to the 291st IR in Germany. "When I finally reached Marseille, they ordered me to sew on the 75th ID's blue and red rectangular badge on top of my eagle patch. A week or so later we boarded a Liberty Ship bound for the USA and ten days later docked at Newport News, Norfolk, Virginia."

When the 506th was officially deactivated on November 30, 1945, Harley Dingman and the remainder of the regiment were sent to Orleans and then Marseille before boarding the fast cruise liner SS *America*. "I was given a private state-room for the trip and placed in charge of the men as a kind of acting adjutant." Even before boarding, Ray Skully had lost all his money shooting craps. "When we set sail I borrowed $15 from a friend and within the day had won $3,700. I gave $3K to Capt Cann to look after, and took the remaining cash to the upper deck, where all the big games were held, and promptly lost the lot."

"We arrived in Boston on December 18, 1945, the same place I'd left from to come to Europe," recalls Harley. "They sent me back to Camp Miles Standish in Taunton, Massachusetts, where much to my annoyance I was given the job of temporary admin NCO."

"Its funny we were all given recommendations for what sort of jobs that would best suit us on the strength of what we had achieved in the service. I imagined with my college background it would be something like teaching, but the army came up with blacksmith! After a week at Miles Standish I simply typed my own name on the discharge list and left! I got home on December 18, just in time for Christmas. That night, as I trudged through the snow with my heavy barracks bag, my folks were waiting for me on the bridge into Carthage. It was only then that I could truly believe my war was over."

Epilogue

On Wednesday June 5, 1946, around 50 survivors from 3/506, including Ed Shames and Ida Aframe, who was now his wife, Jim and Donna Martin, Fred and Dorothy Bahlau, Ray Calandrella, George Rosie, Dud Hefner, Oscar Saxvik, and Johnny Gibson, traveled to Missouri to gather as per LtCol Robert Wolverton's last wishes at the Muehlebach Hotel in Kansas City. For various reasons, many – such as Harold Stedman, Bobbie Rommel, Bill Galbraith, Don Zahn, Don Ross, Bob Webb, Harley Dingman, Hank DiCarlo, Lou Vecchi, Ralph Bennett, and Barney Ryan – were unable to attend, while others, such as Joe Doughty, Andy Anderson, and Jim Morton, had their own informal gathering on the east coast.

On the eve of D-Day, Wolverton had designated the Midwest's most prestigious hotel during his "one year from today" speech, in which he discussed the possibility – if things went well – that everyone would be home by June 1945. Bob's wife Kathleen (known as Tachie) along with Helen Briggs arranged the reunion to honor her husband and the 200 men from 3rd Bn who had lost their lives since that fateful night.

Now working for Gulf Oil in Pittsburgh, Bob Harwick left his wife Eileen at home in Chadds Ford with their daughter Bobbie. Briggsy had last seen her lover on an ambulance train in Paris and was now engaged to Roy Ramsey – although rightly or wrongly she had chosen not to invite her new man to the event. Mr and Mrs Kangas were also in attendance, remembering their son Bob who died defending Foy. People came by bus, train, plane, and automobile from all corners of the States. Only recently released from hospital, Johnny Gibson drove from Tucson with his girlfriend Pearle in a 1936 black Ford sedan. "The car cost me $400 and I wasn't sure we'd make it. Unfortunately

Pearle was with TWA at the time and had to work in their local office and therefore could only be around for the evenings."

Situated downtown, the ten-storey hotel dominated the corner of 12th and Baltimore between the Orpheum and Gayety theaters. The first reunion of its kind centered on the Muehlebach's beautiful ballroom with its polished wooden floor, enormous mirrors, 25ft-high ceiling and ornate art deco moldings.

A memorial service was held in a local Presbyterian chapel, where Kay Wolverton read aloud her husband's pre-D-Day prayer:

> God Almighty! In a few short hours we will be in battle with the enemy. We do not join battle afraid. We do not ask favors or indulgence but ask that, if you will, use us as your instrument for the right and an aid in returning peace to the world. We do not know or seek what our fate will be. We only ask this, that if die we must, that we die as men would die, without complaining, without pleading and safe in the feeling that we have done our best for what we believed was right. Oh Lord! Protect our loved ones and be near us in the fire ahead, and with us now as we each pray to you.

The prayer was followed by an alphabetical roll call of the dead while a bugler played a haunting version of "The Last Post." Several, including Gibson, were already tearful but then began to weep uncontrollably when Tachie read out the list of names beginning with Pvt Philip D. Abbey.

Phil's death occurred at sunrise on June 6, 1944 and was witnessed by Rosie and Gibson, who desperately tried to render first aid as their friend's life slipped away. With the deactivation of 506th PIR many began to wonder if the sacrifice of their kin had been worthwhile. For others it would take 50 years to accept the time spent in Europe as being a positive experience, but time was and still is a great healer.

Some of the men stayed in touch after the reunion, while others simply got on with their postwar lives, raised families, and never saw or spoke to each other again. Andy Anderson went into the cotton biproducts business before marrying Tachie Wolverton on July 19, 1947. The last-minute simple ceremony coincided with a business trip to Atlanta, and with the exception of Andy's brother Bunk, nobody else was invited. It would seem that the couple just wanted to put the past behind them and look toward the future. Shortly after tying the knot Anderson adopted Bob Wolverton's son Loch as his own. Strangely, they shared the same birthday – August 24. Although Andy struggled with alcohol addiction for many years, he and Kay raised three children: Kathleen (also nicknamed Tachie), Fred III, and Ann. Although Andy was a caring father to all of his kids he only ever talked about the funny things that happened during the war. Like Bob Harwick, Andy died long before his time after returning from a pilgrimage to Normandy in 1985 … he had hoped for many more. David Phillips was a gifted poet and wrote these simple words that perhaps make a fitting end to this incredible story about a special group of individuals:

Though dead, we are not heroes yet, nor can be,
till the living, by their lives that are the tools,
carve us the epitaphs of wise men,
and give us not the epitaph of fools.

Bibliography

Listed below are works that I have consulted during my research. To their authors I offer my sincere thanks.

Books and Papers

Baumgardner, Randy, *101st Airborne Division – Screaming Eagles* (Turner Publishing, 2nd Edition, 2001)

DiCarlo, Hank and Westphal, Alan, *Currahee Scrapbook* (506 PIR, 1945)

Forty, George, *Patton's Third Army at War* (Ian Allan Printing Ltd, 1978)

Hannah, Harold W., *A Military Interlude* (self-published, 1999)

Höjris, René, *Anthony "NUTS!" McAuliffe* (Roger Publishing House, 2004)

Kesselring, Albert, *The Memoirs of Field-Marshal Kesselring* (William Kimber, 1974)

Koskimaki, George E., *The Battered Bastards of Bastogne* (Casemate reprint, 2011)

Levitt, Sgt Saul, "The Siege of Bastogne," *Yank Magazine* (1945)

McAuliffe, Kenneth J. Jr, *NUTS! The Life of Anthony C. McAuliffe* (self-published, 2011)

Mehosky, Ivan Paul, *The Story of a Soldier* (Rutledge Books, Inc., 2001)

Rapport, Leonard and Northwood, Arthur Jr, *Rendezvous with Destiny* (Infantry Journal Press, 1948)

Terrify and Destroy: The Story of the 10th Armored Division (The Stars & Stripes, Paris, 1944/45)

Saga of the All American (reprinted by The Battery Press, 82nd Airborne Division Association, 1946)

Webb, Robert, *Freedom Found* (self-published, 2000)

Reports and Personal Letters

326th Airborne Medical Co AA Reports, c/o John Klein

Bastogne Recollections H/506, October 1991 (tape recording), c/o Pat McCann

G Co Morning Reports 1942 to 1945, c/o Tim Moore

Headquarters 506th PIR "After Action Reports" (17 December 1944–August 1945)

"He Beat the Odds," World War II memoir of Donald Clifton Ross, c/o Sharon Bunker

Interview notes from War Crimes Investigation Team, October 1945, c/o Gerhard Roletscheck

Personal memoir and notes of Joe Beyrle, c/o Joe Beyrle II

Personal letter of Dobbins, NARA, c/o John Klein

Personal letters of Robert Harwick, c/o Bob Smoldt

Personal letters of Clark Heggeness, c/o John Klein

Personal letter of Harry Krig, c/o Bob Izumi

Personal letter of Carwood Lipton, c/o Reg Jans

Personal letters of David Morgan, c/o Neil Morgan

Personal letters of James Morton, c/o Fred Bahlau

Personal letter of Bill Prosser, c/o Gerhard Roletscheck

Personal letters of Helen B. Ramsey, c/o Bill Wedeking

Transcript of George Rosie interview, c/o Joe Muccia

Personal letters of Jay Stone, c/o Reg Jans

Personal letters of Bob Webb, c/o Bob Webb, Jr

Tape recordings of interviews with Robert Webb (1980s), c/o Bob Webb, Jr

US Army Military History Institute, George E. Koskimaki Collection: personal letters and documents, including 101st Divisional AA Reports (December 1944), 101st Airborne Signal Co, 321st GFA Bn, Troop Carrier & Glider Information, George Allen, Albert Ballinger, Al Cappelli, Keith Carpenter, Bill Chivvis, Marty Clark, Stan Clever, William Desobry, Roger Dominique, Wilbur Fishel, Bob Flory, Lonnie Gavrock, Richard Gleason, Len Goodgal, Guy Jackson, John Kilgore, Frank Kneller, Robert Hayes, Sam Hefner, Robert Higgins, Ewell Martin, Owen Miller, Ed Peterson, David Phillips, John "Jack" Prior, Barney Ryan, Victor Sauerheber, Lester Smith, Ben Stapelfeld, Stan Stasica, Chuck Richards, Allen Westphal, Shrable Williams, and Vinnie Utz.

Glossary

AP	armor piercing
ASR	Army Service Record
AWOL	absent without leave
BAR	Browning Automatic Rifle
BC	battlefield commission
Bn	Battalion
Co	Company
CO	Commanding Officer
CP	command post
DP	displaced person
DZ	drop zone
FAC	forward air controller
FO	forward observer
GFA	Glider Field Artillery
GIR	Glider Infantry Regiment
HE	high explosive
ID	Infantry Division
IR	Infantry Regiment
IPW	interrogation of prisoner of war
LOD	line of defense
LZ	landing zone
MG	machine gun
MLR	main line of resistance
MP	Military Police
OC	Officer Commanding
OP	observation post
Ptn	Platoon
PIR	Parachute Infantry Regiment
SD	Sicherheitsdienst (Security Service)
SHAEF	Supreme Headquarters Allied Expeditionary Force
SPG	self-propelled gun
TCG	Troop Carrier Group
TD	tank destroyer
USO	United Services Organization
VCP	vehicle checkpoint
XO	executive officer
ZI	Zone of the Interior

Index

References to maps are shown in **bold**

About the author

Ian Gardner served for five years in Support Company, 10th Battalion, The Parachute Regiment as a medic before leaving the Territorial Army in 1993 due to injury. Always enthusiastic about military history, several years after leaving 10 Para Ian became interested in World War II US Paratroopers. After a visit to Normandy in 2000 he decided to focus on the 101st Airborne Division, and in particular the Third Battalion of the 506th Parachute Infantry Regiment, which led to the critically acclaimed *Tonight We Die As Men*, co-written with Roger Day, and *Deliver Us From Darkness*. This, his third historical work, concludes their story.